Blenheim
Strike

This book is dedicated to the memory of the
18 Squadron Blenheim crew of Flight Sergeants Ian Bullivant,
Jock Gallery and Bob Hind.
For me, the saga of the Blenheim started with this crew.

Blenheim
Strike

The history of the Bristol Blenheim in RAF service
between 1935 and 1942,
incorporating a case-study on operations & losses
over the Netherlands.

by

Drs. Theo Boiten

Air Research Publications

First published 1995 by
Air Research Publications
PO Box 223, Walton-on-Thames,
Surrey, KT12 3YQ
England

Typeset in Great Britain by
A.C.E. Services,
Radlett, Herts, WD7 8LU

Printed in Great Britain by
Antony Rowe Ltd
Chippenham
Wiltshire

ISBN 1-871187-31-1

CONTENTS

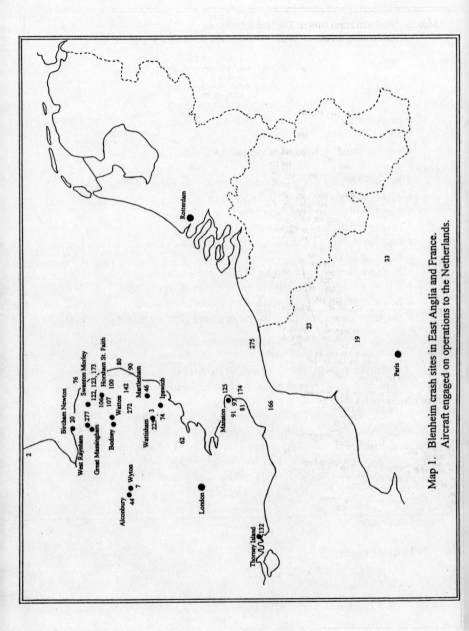

Map 1. Blenheim crash sites in East Anglia and France.
Aircraft engaged on operations to the Netherlands.

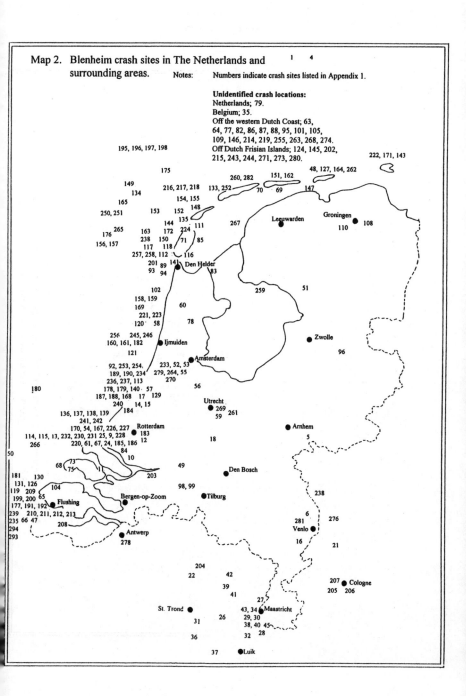

Map 2. Blenheim crash sites in The Netherlands and surrounding areas.

Notes: Numbers indicate crash sites listed in Appendix 1.

Unidentified crash locations:
Netherlands; 79.
Belgium; 35.
Off the western Dutch Coast; 63, 64, 77, 82, 86, 87, 88, 95, 101, 105, 109, 146, 214, 219, 255, 263, 268, 274.
Off Dutch Frisian Islands; 124, 145, 202, 215, 243, 244, 271, 273, 280.

Foreword

by

Air Marshal Sir Ivor Broom, KCB, CBE, DSO, DFC **, AFC.

Drs. Boiten explains in this book how he developed, as a schoolboy, an all consuming interest in the operations of the Blenheim bomber over the Netherlands in the early years of World War 2. Many years of detailed research into every sortie have culminated in this book and I must say that I have never read such a meticulous examination of the operations of any single aircraft in the Royal Air Force.

The Blenheim was the only aircraft in Bomber Command capable of carrying out daylight raids in 1940/41 after the fall of France and Drs. Boiten considers that they took on many unrealistic tasks against overwhelming odds. He particularly highlights the low level attacks on shipping off the Dutch coast in the summer of 1941 and questions whether the results justified such horrendous losses. He has contacted innumerable aircrew who survived and their personal accounts of raids in which they participated provide a very personal touch to the book. Their reports however, reveal high morale despite the losses as all were conscious that the Royal Air Force provided the only means of carrying the war to the enemy at a time when all of Europe was under the heel of the Nazi dictatorship. He mentions the great effect of those raids on Dutch morale when they saw the RAF roundels on low flying aircraft. I will never forget the ecstatic reaction by the Dutch people as we hedge-hopped across Holland in the raid described in Chapter 7 of the book. Their waving brought home to me, and many other aircrew, what the war was all about and that they, and Europe as a whole, would not be liberated until the Nazi regime had been defeated.

The role of the Blenheim in the early days of World War 2 is sometimes forgotten and it is good that a Dutchman should highlight the operational tasks it carried out against great odds.

Ivor Broom.

Origins and acknowledgements.

My interest in the Blenheim was first aroused when my parents bought a holiday cottage near the village of Anjum in the north of Friesland in 1977. Being a boy with a strong interest in aviation history, I soon discovered that in the cemetery of the local Protestant church, a British Flight Sergeant pilot rested. His name was Ian Arthur Bullivant, killed in action on 9th June 1941. As no-one in Anjum could tell me anything about this airman, I decided to try and find out how he died and what his background was. Some years of research followed and I found out that Ian Bullivant served as a pilot with 18 Squadron during 1940 and 1941 and was shot down and killed on his very first daylight shipping attack. After publishing a newspaper article on the events of the 9th June 1941, I decided to further explore the Blenheim campaigns in the early war years, as very little had been published on this subject before. After graduating from University in 1992 I decided to devote a book to the Blenheim campaigns in the early war years, with a focus on the operations and losses over the Netherlands. I have chosen this approach as a large part of the Blenheim operations went to the Netherlands, where the Germans had built up a strong defence, and where, as a consequence, losses were severe. By this method not only the development of the various Blenheim campaigns are dealt with, but by using the 'oral history' method it also clearly illustrates these raids from the airmen's point of view. What really sparked off a deep-felt and lasting affection for the Blenheim and her crews were my years-long correspondence and interviews with dozens of surviving Blenheim air and groundcrews. The gripping tales of their experiences in those far-off days convinced me that their largely unsung story should be recorded and preserved for posterity. It is also fortunate indeed that a Blenheim has been restored to flying condition by Graham Warner and his team at Duxford. Millions of aviation enthusiasts now have the opportunity to see the aircraft in action on many air displays all over Europe.

At the start of WWII the RAF had more Blenheims in service than any other type of aircraft. It was the main bomber in her inventory, and it was to serve in each of the RAF Commands. Although within a few months of operations it became crystal clear that the Blenheim was no match for the German *Flak* defences and Messerschmitt fighters, there was no alternative but to keep the aircraft in service until it could be replaced by modern medium bombers and long-range fighter-bombers. The Blenheim crews were thrown into the breach time and again, suffering dreadful losses. The story of the operational employment of the Bristol Blenheim in the early war years is a tale of great sacrifices when pressing home the attacks in the face of daunting odds. Still, the brave Blenheim crews kept up the offensive, mainly by day but also by night. Many new strategic and tactical concepts were tested in the harsh reality of modern air warfare for the first time. Many lessons were learnt the hard way when the dirty work was done by the 'Blenheim Boys', who were employed in just about every conceivable operational role by the RAF. The Blenheim crews were the first to be employed in radar-controlled night fighting, pioneered in the night bombing offensive, paved the way for the later successes of the Beaufighter anti-shipping and intruder campaigns, the 2nd Tactical Air Force offensive, the Mosquito night intruder campaign and photographic reconnaissance.

Apart from a thorough strategic and tactical analysis of the various campaigns in which the Blenheim was employed, the personal accounts from Blenheim air and groundcrew provide the main background to this narrative. I have chosen this approach as this should enable the reader to reach a better understanding of this early period of the war. In past decades, the Bristol Blenheim has often been referred to as the 'Forgotten Bomber' by those who survived operations in the aircraft.

I hope that this book may put the record straight and contribute towards giving the Blenheim and her crews a well-earned place of honour in the history of the RAF and in the memory of the nation.

The following men and women, Blenheim air and groundcrews and next of kin and relatives of those 'Blenheim Boys' that didn't make it back or of those who have passed away since the war, have supported me tremendously. Without their help this book could not have been written. Between brackets are the Blenheim units in which they or their relatives served. I have omitted ranks and decorations which would otherwise overwhelm these pages:

Don Anderson (29 Sqn); Rodney Armstrong (21 Sqn); Arthur Asker (226 Sqn); Arthur T.R. Aslett (235 Sqn); Eric Aspinall (139 Sqn); Eric Atkins (139 & 114 Sqns); Douglas Attenborough (82 Sqn); Charles Bardswell (Watton Intell); Jack Bartley (21 Sqn); Denis Boissier (82 Sqn); Bill Bradshaw (21 & 18 Sqns); Geoff Brazier (235 Sqn); Bill Bridget (101 Sqn); Bill Bromley (40 Sqn); Jim Brooker (40 Sqn); Ron Brooks (248 Sqn); Ivor Broom (107 Sqn); Doug Brown (107 & 110 Sqns); Frederick 'Doc' Buckler (21 Sqn & Watton M.O.); Bill Burberry (114 & 13 Sqns); Graham Burrell (114 Sqn); Nancy Bury (114 Sqn); Richard Butt (139 Sqn); Dorothy Caban (18 & 139 Sqns); Philip Camp (XV Sqn); Tony Carlisle (88 Sqn); Douglas Chapman (226 Sqn); Geoffrey Chapman (18 Sqn); Ken Collins (82 Sqn); Bob Coles (139 Sqn); Douglas Cooper (110 & 21 Sqns); Bill Corfield (21 Sqn); Noel Corry (25 Sqn); Dick Couchman (59 Sqn); Keith Cudlipp (105 Sqn); Peter Cundy (53 Sqn); Leslie Davies (21 & 88 Sqns); Les Deadfield (18 Sqn); John Douch (18 Sqn); 'Red' Eames (XV Sqn); Sam Elworthy (82 Sqn & 2 Group H.Q.); Paddy Embry (109 Sqn); Lawrence Ewals (21, 40 & 107 Sqn); Ralph Fastnedge (139 Sqn); Len Fearnley (107 Sqn); Philip Felton (21 Sqn); Mick Ford (110 Sqn); Ken Gamble (59 Sqn); Bill Garrard (Special Duty Flight); Geoff Garside (59 Sqn); Hugh George (XV Sqn); Bill Gray (226 Sqn); Charlie Guesford (110 Sqn); Ken Hallam (XV Sqn); Frank Harbord (18 & 105 Sqn); Gilbert Haworth (44 Sqn); Steve Hebron (235 Sqn); Mike Henry (110 & 107 Sqns); Wilf Hepworth (139 Sqn); John Holmes (40 & 101 Sqns); Harry G. Huckins (21 & 18 Sqns); Arthur Hughes (18 Sqn); Len Hunt (59 Sqn); Bob Iredale (114 Sqn); Jim King (139 Sqn); Aubrey Lancaster (235 Sqn); Jim Langston (21 Sqn); Molly Lewey (226 Sqn); John Low (82 Sqn); "Chiefy" Lucas (21 Sqn); Kenneth R. Lusty (25 Sqn); Tom Mann (21 Sqn); Dick Maydwell (53 Sqn); Alec McCurdy (59 & 18 Sqn); Don McFarlane (82 Sqn);

Douglas McKenzie (82 Sqn); Frank Metcalfe (82 Sqn); J.W. 'Dinty' Moore (18 Sqn); R.I. Mowatt (248 Sqn); Rodney Steele (235 Sqn & No.1 P.R.U.); Dick Muspratt (53 Sqn); Edmund Nelson (139 Sqn); Charles Oakley (XV Sqn); Terence O'Brien (53 Sqn); Bill O'Connell (226 Sqn); George Parr (18 Sqn); George Parry (110 & 107 Sqns); Vic Parsons (235 Sqn); G.J. Cristopher Paul (90 Sqn); Roger Peacock (40 Sqn); A.F. Peirce (604 Sqn); Ted Pennill (21 Sqn); Janet Pieters (18 Sqn); Doug Pole (235 Sqn); Charles Pollard (18 Sqn); Hayden Porter (21 Sqn); Paddy Quirke (107 Sqn); Roy Ralston (107 Sqn); Eric Ramsey (114 Sqn); J.B. Robertson (101, 21 & 82 Sqns); Walter Robinson (82 Sqn); Geoff Rowland (105 Sqn); Peter Russell (53 Sqn); 'Rusty' Russell (21 Sqn); Peter Sarll (21 Sqn); Peter Saunders (226 Sqn); Norman Savill (235 Sqn); Monty Scotney (18 Sqn); Bill Service (53 Sqn); Denis Shanahan (114 Sqn); Vera Sherring (18 Sqn); George Shinnie (139 Sqn); Ted Sismore (110 Sqn); Peter Smith (59 Sqn); Les Spong (139 Sqn); Terence Staples (114 Sqn); Pat Stapleton (614 Sqn); Jo Stevenson (40 Sqn); John Thompson (500 Sqn); Tommy Thompson (18 Sqn); John Townsend (114 Sqn); Albert Turner (139 Sqn); Don Turner (248 Sqn); Tony Valle-Jones (114 Sqn); Hugh Wakefield (235 Sqn); Peter Ward (21 & 139 Sqns); Ian Webster (114 Sqn); Roy H. Welch (XV Sqn); Adrian White (139 Sqn); John Whitehead (82 & 110 Sqns); Ken Whittle (139 Sqn); George Williams (53 Sqn); Lady Patricia Williams (Watton C.O. & 2 Group H.Q.); Bob Willis (114 Sqn); Ken Wolstenholme (107 Sqn); John Wray (53 Sqn); Ronny Wright (248 Sqn).

The following *Luftwaffe* and *Kriegsmarine* veterans and next of kin have kindly helped me in my research:

Hilde Bendert (*JG 27*); Hans-Ekkehard Bob (*JG 54*); Alois Dierkes (*Jägerkreis Nord*); Wolfgang Falck (*ZG 76*); Adolf Galland (*JG 26*); Justus Hollmann (20th. *Vp.Fl.*); Otto Keller (Captain *Flak*-ship *H811*); Heinz Lange (*JG 21* and *JG 54*); Theodor Lindemann (*JG 26*); Friedrich Mundt (20th. *Vp.Fl.*); Hanns Veit von Obernitz (*JG 54*).

I wish to thank the many people and organisations whose help in the past years has been instrumental in the completion of this book:

Kim Abbott; Air Crew Association; Air Gunners' Association; *Air Mail*; XV, 57, 88, 107 & 110, 139, 248, 600 and 604 Squadron Associations; Jaap Bakker; BBC Television; Bart Beckers; Pieter Bergman; Victor F. Bingham; Andrew Bird; Lucien Bogers; Bomber Command Association; Michael J.F. Bowyer; Dick Breedijk; British Embassy (The Hague); Wybe Buising; Bundesarchiv (Koblenz); Nigel Buswell; Albert Butterworth; Caterpillar Club; Peter Celis; Bill Chorley; Commonwealth War Graves Commission; Coen Cornelissen; Ted Daines; Dirk Decuypere; Douwe Drijver; Johan Edelhausen; Gerard Faux; Fly Past magazine; Michael Gardener (152 Sqn); Les & Jeanne Gibbs; Goldfish Club; Chris H. Goss; Peter Grimm; Wyb Jan Groendijk; David Gunby; Peter B. Gunn; Vic Hand; Max Hastings; Marcel Hogenhuis; Wout van den Hout; Gilbert F.Howard; K.M. Hunter; Imperial War Museum; Ab A. Jansen; Richard Johnson (152 Sqn); Arie de Jong; Kriegie Call magazine; Paul Lincoln/RAF Watton Museum; Erwin van Loo; John van der Maas; Jock Manson; Wim de Meester; Paul Michel; Municipal archives of Den Helder, Maastricht, Oostdongeradeel; National Defense H.Q. of Canada; Aad Neeven; C.J. Olsthoorn; Hans Onderwater; S.W. Pope; Public Record Office; Ron Putz; RAF 2 Group Officer's Association; RAF EX-P.O.W. Association; RAF Museum; RAF Personnel Management Centre; RCAF magazine; *SAGA* magazine; Johan Schuurman; Stuart Scott; *Sectie Luchtmachthistorie van de Koninklijke Luchtmacht*; *Service Historique de l'Armee de l'Air*; Eric Shipley; Spitfire Society; The Sunday Express; Jan J. van der Veer; Max Vansichen; Walter Veugen; Hille van Dieren; Hans van Soest; Colin Waugh; Frank Weber; Eric Webster; 'Cactus' Waldrop; Hans Wijers; Gerrit Zijlstra.

My special thanks go out to Betty and Hugh George of the Blenheim Society, who supported my research in any way they could; to Hans de Haan with his profound knowledge of RAF losses during WWII and to Rob de Visser who has been a mine of information on *Luftwaffe* operations over the Netherlands during 1940-42. Bill O'Connell, Jim Moore and Victor Bingham kindly proof-read the manuscript, for which I am much indebted. A word of gratitude also goes out to my father Harry Boiten, who supported me financially when a successful

13

completion of this book was endangered due to lack of funds. Finally, my gratitude to my girlfriend Margryt, for her patience and support throughout the more difficult periods experienced during the writing of this book.

If any readers can offer additional data, stories and photographs they will be most gratefully received as aids to my continuing research into the fascinating history of the Blenheim and her crews.

Drs. Theo Boiten
Oosterkade
9E 2 9711 RS Groningen
The Netherlands.
March 1995.

Chapter One

Development and the Phoney War

The development of the Bristol Blenheim and Operations
during the Phoney War, September 1939-April 1940.

During the twenties and thirties, the backbone of the RAF was an offensive bomber force rather than a defensive fighter force. Through the driving spirit of the Chief of Air Staff, Sir Hugh Trenchard, the RAF relied on the strategic concept of the self-contained, self-defending daylight bomber formation to find and destroy any target in the enemy hinterland. 'The bomber always gets through' was the core of the thinking of the day. The bomber would rule the skies and would even, or so it was thought, be able to bomb the enemy into submission by breaking the morale of its working force.

By 1933, the Air Staff sought for modern monoplane replacements of its ageing biplane bombers to keep pace with developments abroad. Specifications for modern light, medium and heavy bombers were issued to the British aviation industry. These resulted, a few years later, in the development of the Battle, Hampden, Whitley and Wellington bombers. The fifth standard bomber with which Bomber Command would enter the war in 1939, the Blenheim, however, was the result of a private venture of the Bristol Aeroplane Company. In 1933, the Bristol Company proposed a twin-engined, low-wing, cabin monoplane to carry six passengers and a crew of two. The project caught the attention of Lord Rothermere, proprietor of the *Daily Mail*, who was looking for a fast British executive aircraft as counterpart to the new generation of American Douglas and Lockheed transport monoplanes. He was so impressed by the promising design that he decided to finance the building of an adapted version of the aircraft. Thus the Bristol Type 142 was born. Powered by two 640 hp Bristol Mercury VI engines, a top speed of 250 mph was expected, which would make it a sensationally fast aircraft for those days!

On her maiden flight on 12th April 1935, Type 142 indeed met these high expectations. This in turn attracted serious interest from the Air Ministry - which Lord Rothermere had always had in the back of his mind. He therefore soon abandoned his resolution to keep the aircraft for his own use. Generously, he presented Type 142 to the nation and christened it *Britain First*. Bristol proposed to convert the aircraft into a three crew mid-wing bomber. During airworthiness trials at Martlesham Heath, Type 142 reached a speed of 285 mph at a maximum loaded weight and a top speed of 307 mph - a true sensation! The bomber of the future was some 50 mph faster than the Gloster Gladiator, which had just been ordered as the RAF's new front-line fighter. That this fighter was a more or less outdated stop-gap biplane was ignored by the publicity people. A first contract for 150 Mk.Is of the aircraft was ordered off the drawing board in August 1935 and the type was named the Blenheim. The name originated from the small Bavarian village of Blenheim where, during the War of the Spanish Succession, the Grand Alliance led by John Churchill had defeated the French in 1704. Bristol now modified Type 142 to bomber configuration with the wings raised to a mid-fuselage position to cater for a bomb-bay beneath the mainspars. The bomb aimer's position was fitted in the nose to the right of the pilot and a mid-upper turret was installed on top of the fuselage. The turret was equipped with a single Vickers gas operated .303 machine gun fed from circular pans each containing one hundred rounds of ammunition. The Air Ministry was satisfied with the developments and planned to use the aircraft as an interim medium bomber while better aircraft types were being developed and tested.

As the production of the Blenheim I commenced, the RAF was fundamentally being reorganised. Since 1925, the RAF had been centrally controlled in the 'Air Defence of Great Britain' (ADGB). The increasing specialisation within the various Royal Air Force units and the rapid growth of the RAF due to the Expansion Schemes made the existing command structure impracticable. Therefore, on 13th July 1936, ADGB was subdivided into four functional Commands: Fighter, Bomber, Coastal and Training Command. The first Group formed in

Bomber Command was 2 Group, which was now equipped with the new Bristol Blenheim. 114 Squadron was the first unit to receive the aircraft in March 1937. Forced by the threat of the rapidly re-arming Nazi Germany, the RAF Expansion Programme was stepped up. As a result, new orders were placed for the Blenheim I and, by July 1936, the Air Ministry had placed orders for no less than 1,450 of the aircraft.

Squadron Leader G.J. Christopher Paul took over command of 90 Squadron at Bicester in January 1938 as the the second RAF unit to be equipped with the new type. Squadron Leader Paul recalls the introduction of the short nosed Blenheim in RAF service:

"Apart from Avro Ansons few RAF pilots at that time had flown monoplanes. Retractable undercarriages, variable pitch propellers and flaps were all new to those of us hitherto accustomed to the lines of Harts and Hinds, Nimrods and Furys and Gladiators and Gauntlets.

"In the Blenheim Mk.I the pair of two-pitch propellers were set to 'FINE' for take off and initial climb out; 'COARSE' for all subsequent flying until final approach to land when they were reset to 'FINE'. The other new controls were located low down on the right-hand side of the pilots seat. They comprised three push/pull handles which controlled a hydraulic system which could operate flaps and undercarriage, or be switched to provide power for the gun turret. The system did not permit operation of all three things simultaneously.

"We had no dual aircraft. Conversion to type started with thorough cockpit drill culminating in proving ability to find and operate all controls blindfolded. Next came flying as passenger with an experienced pilot, followed by solo practice until proficient.

"Single engine handling was reasonable if understood. Inability to feather the propeller of a dead engine created excessive drag on the side of the dead engine. One manoeuvre to be avoided was a single engined overshoot from low down with undercarriage down.

"We all grew to like the short nosed Blenheim. It could run away from nearly all the current fighters; once new controls were mastered they gave a much extended range of performance, whilst the comfort and exceptional view from its greenhouse cockpit made it easy to handle and enjoyable to fly by day or by night. On sunny days I often topped my flying hat, with a straw hat.

"To sum up, the short nosed early Blenheims took a little knowing; but once mastered proved an exciting and delightful aeroplane, which we all liked and enjoyed."

Corporal Gilbert Haworth, observer with 44 Squadron, converted onto the Blenheim Mk.I bomber at Waddington in April 1938. He gives a fine impression of the qualities and vices of the

new aircraft:

"There was a great deal to be learned about the high-speed and high-flying Blenheim Bomber and they had only been located at Waddington for about four months at the most. I soon found out that there had never been a real course of study, so nobody had 'done the course'.

"Within two or three days I was given my first exciting flight; the sensation of sitting in a cabin aircraft free from the merciless blast of cold air slipstream was delightfully novel, so was the very firm push I could feel in my back as we rapidly accelerated along the ground under the influence of two powerful engines. The forward field of vision from the Air Observer's seat was unobstructed by any structural parts and this facility made a welcome change from the old biplane and it all helped to contribute to an exhilarating impression of colossal speed.

"However I had something of a shock awaiting me when the time for landing arrived and the pilot shut the throttles and the noise of the engines died away. To maintain speed for this high-speed monoplane he was obliged to point the nose well downwards so that we appeared to be almost diving at the ground. This was a most unwelcome change from the older types of aircraft. It was now that the excellent forward view gave me the alarming impression of very hard ground rapidly looming up in front of my nose. He pulled back on the control column with what seemed to be an almighty heave and not a second to spare, surprising me with a beautiful smooth landing. I began to breathe freely once more.

"Most of the personnel were very young indeed and, in any case, the older pilots were at home only with good old fashioned open cockpit single engined machines, which were as different as chalk from cheese. It had always been difficult for old dogs to learn new tricks and many of the so-called highly qualified and experienced men were decidedly at sea when handling a speedy aircraft that had two motors, bothersome retractable wheels, landing flaps and adjustable airscrews, all factors that exacted stern retribution if mishandled. Moreover there were some regrettably unsatisfactory design faults that were cruel traps for unwary innocents, things that were never tolerated in more enlightened years. No really thorough instruction was given and a pilot might often be seen furtively consulting a handbook before climbing aboard.

"The scene was well and truly set to provide a fair number of *ARDUA*, the accident rate was positively high, incidents of varying degrees of gravity were frequent, the sight of a Blenheim resting ignominiously on its belly with wheels collapsed being particularly familiar. All the ground crew staff developed an unprecedented degree of wariness whenever they were obliged to walk under aeroplane wings."

With production of the Mk.I in full swing, Bristol improved the aircraft with more powerful Mercury XV engines. Also, extra fuel tanks for longer range were installed in the outer wings. Since the navigator's position in the nose of the Mk.I proved to be too cramped, an extended nose was designed. After further development, the typical asymmetrical nose was built for the Mk.IV, which both satisfied the pilot's view and improved the navigator's 'office'. The long-nosed Mk.IV went into production in the summer of 1938. With the short-nosed Mk.I bombers largely being replaced by Mk.IVs in the home-based squadrons, some 150 aircraft were converted to Blenheim fighters by July 1939 and a specially designed four-gun pack was installed under the belly of the aircraft for this purpose.

Flying Officer John Wray served with 53 Squadron in Army Co-operation Command between 1937 and 1939. He tells of the conversion of his squadron on the Blenheim Mk.IV:

"At the end of 1938 it was announced that Nos. 53 and 59 Squadrons were to re-equip to the Blenheim IV, more commonly known at the time as the long-nosed Blenheim. No. 53 Squadron were, in fact, the first squadron in the RAF to get this aircraft.

"Five pilots, of which I was one, were selected to go to Bicester and be converted onto the short-nose Blenheim by the resident squadron. After conversion we were to return and convert the rest of the squadron pilots when our new long-nose Blenheims arrived. None of us had flown a twin engined aircraft before, nor had we experienced retractable undercarriages, wing flaps or two-speed airscrews. Moreover, this aeroplane was considerably faster than anything any of us had flown before. The whole technique of taking off and landing was very different and of course there were many features in the instrumentation and controls that were new.

"However, we were all experienced pilots and we soon became acclimatised to all these new things and, after about two hours dual instruction, we all went solo. Mind you, things were going to be quite testing when we got back to our squadron because for quite a while we didn't have an aircraft with dual control. This meant teaching the other pilots without any means of taking over control should something go wrong.

"At that time the aircraft was quite a revelation. After all, *Britain First*, Rothermere's aircraft from which the Blenheim was developed, was reputed to be one of the fastest aircraft in the world and one felt this immediately with the Blenheim. We had far greater range, speed, height, no wind blowing you about and heat if you need it. Moreover, one could communicate with one's crew more easily."

Whereas the Blenheim on her introduction in 1936 was much faster than any aircraft then in service, fighter development had overtaken the aircraft a mere three years later. During mock fights with Hurricanes and Spitfires the painful fact emerged that the Blenheim had not the speed, manoeuvreability nor the armament to successfully make a stand in daylight against the new generation of German Messerschmitt fighters - the Bf109 and Bf110. C-in-C Bomber Command, Air Chief Marshal Ludlow-Hewitt even prophesied to the Air Ministry on the eve of war that he anticipated his force of Blenheim medium bombers would be destroyed in just three and a half weeks when ordered to undertake an all-out daylight offensive against Germany. He only gave his force of 'heavies' seven and a half weeks. Indeed, the alternative of night raids was considered but, due to Trenchard's daylight policy 'The bomber will alway get through', there was hardly any night flying training. Therefore, Bomber Command was to attack only definable military targets not situated in the enemy hinterland, the German Navy at sea and was to provide close support to the British Army in France. This course of action would on the one hand avoid the risk of bombs falling on German civilians, which, it was thought, could in turn provoke a mass air assault upon the British people. On the other hand, this would also conserve the bomber force. At the outbreak of war the RAF had 1,089 Blenheims on strength - more than any other type of aircraft. In the UK, more than 100 were converted Mk.If fighters and some 140 Mk.IVs equipped ten bomber squadrons.

In accordance with the policy of conserving the bomber force and avoiding German civilian casualties and thereby escalating the conflict, on the outbreak of war on 3rd September 1939, the British government gave full priority to RAF bombing raids on German Naval units, both in northwest German ports and at sea. Blenheim N6215 of 139 Squadron, flown by Flying Officer Andrew McPherson, was the first RAF aircraft to penetrate German airspace in World War Two. McPherson flew a successful photo-reconnaissance of Wilhelmshaven harbour within hours of the Declaration of War. The Blenheims of 2 Group got their first bloody nose in the first attack on the German Navy, on 4th September. Five Blenheims of 107 and 110 Squadron were shot down during a low level bombing raid on naval shipping in Wilhelmshaven harbour.

The second task of 2 Group was the systematic photographing of Germany - shipping, military transport and *Luftwaffe* airfields were to be closely watched.

After some three weeks of these operations, shipping sweeps were temporarily halted. Emphasis was now laid on Army

Co-operation, the task for which 2 Group was originally created in the mid-thirties. H.Q. Bomber Command decided that the Group's Blenheims and Battles were to strike against German troop concentrations and columns in the event of a German invasion of the west. In this way, the enemy advance could be slowed down in support of the Allied ground forces. Also, 2 Group aircraft would fly reconnaissance missions to supply the army with frontline intelligence. While the light and medium bombers of 2 Group operated over the frontline, the RAF 'heavies', Whitleys, Wellingtons and Hampdens, were to destroy strategic targets in the enemy's hinterland. However, throughout the Phoney War, none of these aircraft were permitted to drop bombs on German soil in case this provoked reprisals from the enemy. The heavies instead were engaged in dropping propaganda leaflets on German towns and cities.

Meanwhile, the British government decided to help their French Allies by sending an Expeditionary Force (BEF) to France on the outbreak of war in September 1939. Supporting the BEF was the Air Component, consisting of eight Hurricane and Lysander squadrons and four Blenheim units. 2 Group's No. 70 Wing, comprising 18, 57, 53 and 59 Squadrons together formed the Blenheim branch of the Air Component. In addition No. 1 Group, made up of ten squadrons of Fairey Battles, was transferred to the Rheims area; this force formed the Advanced Air Striking Force (AASF) of the BEF. 53 and 59 Squadrons were to operate in the Army Co-operation rôle to hold up an advance by German ground forces in the Low Countries and France, whilst 18 and 57 Squadrons took on the task of reconnaissance flights over the front line and into Germany. After only a few weeks of operations over the French/German border, the Battles proved to be too vulnerable in daylight and were then confined to night operations. The task of daylight reconnaissance against the enemy became the sole responsibility of 18 and 57 Squadrons.

In December 1939, the AASF day-bomber force was reinforced by 114 and 139 Squadrons, which replaced XV and 40 Battle Squadrons. The latter were sent back to the U.K. to re-equip with Blenheims in 2 Group. The AASF Blenheim bomber and reconnaissance force in France now comprised 18, 53, 57, 59,

114 and 139 Squadrons. Daylight photo reconnaissance missions were flown by 18, 57 and 114 Squadrons into enemy airspace on a regular basis, suffering several losses. 57 Squadron, for example, lost L9465 on 14th April during a sortie covering the Münster-Hamm-Bielefeld area. The aircraft was intercepted by Bf109s of *I./JG 20* and was shot down in flames near Babberich by *Oberfeldwebel* Arnold Lignitz. Flying Officer Graham-Hogg and his crew were buried with full military honours at Arnhem.

2 Group and Army Co-operation Command were not the only RAF units to be equipped with the Blenheim however. Four squadrons - Nos. 254, 235, 236 and 248, all equipped with Blenheim Mk.IVfs - were transferred from Fighter to Coastal Command in January 1940 for 'trade protection' duties. Fighter Command had six Mk.I fighter Blenheim squadrons on strength in 1940.

Offensive North Sea reconnaissances and flights over enemy territory were regularly flown by 2 Group crews during the Winter of 1939/40. Frequently, Bf109s scrambled from 'dromes in NW Germany and intercepted these aircraft and the lesson was brought home rather painfully to the RAF: Blenheims were no match for the modern daylight fighters of the *Luftwaffe*. No less than five out of 37 reconnaissance Blenheims were shot down by Bf109s between 20th September and 25th November. This alarming situation caused much discussion at group and squadron level on the inadequate armament and speed of the Blenheim. It was realised that the 'wonder-bomber' of only a few years back was outclassed by the Messerschmitts. Therefore, Blenheim reconnaissance sorties over Germany were halted by 25th November 1939. The need for operational improvements of the aircraft led to a number of modifications. Armour protection for the crews and vital systems and self-sealing petrol tanks were installed. Also, a rear-firing gun in a streamlined blister under the observer's position was added to the aircraft. In one or two squadrons, rear-firing 'scare guns' were fitted in the engine nacelles. As a final measure, the blister and top turret were strengthened with two Browning 0.303" machine-guns - but this was only done in the second half of 1940.

When the reconnaissance sorties over Germany were stopped, 2 Group Blenheims still flew shipping searches over the relatively safe North Sea, 87 sorties being flown between 26th December 1939 and 1st February 1940. The only encounter with German fighters took place on 10th January 1940 and was the first clash between Blenheims and Bf110s during the Second World War. In mid-morning, nine Blenheims of 110 Squadron took off from Wattisham in three 'vics' for a North Sea shipping reconnaissance. At roughly the same time, *Hauptmann* Wolfgang Falck led four Bf110s of *2./ZG 76* from Jever airfield near Wilhelmshaven on a westerly course over the North Sea for a routine patrol.

When flying some 200 kilometres north of Terschelling Island, one of the German pilots spotted a handful of specks on the horizon and warned his leader on R/T. Swiftly, the sleek *Zerstörers* curved onto the course of the British intruders. Within seconds, Falck identified the dots as Bristol Blenheims and ordered his Flight to attack. At 11.52 the fighters dropped onto the tails of the Blenheims, which immediately tried to avoid the German attack by diving to sea level in plus 9 boost. It was to no avail - *Schwarmführer* Falck's cannon shells struck home and Blenheim P4859 of 110 Squadron exploded on the surface of the sea. Sergeant John Hanne and his crew were killed and are still missing. Two other Blenheims of 110 Squadron were badly shot up during the running battle - N6203 crashed on return at Manby in Lincolnshire and N6213 was written off at Wattisham and were actually claimed destroyed by *Leutnants* Helmut Fahlbusch and Maximilian Graeff. After expending all their ammunition, the four German fighter pilots broke off the fight and jubilantly flew back to base, all with slight damage. This was the first encounter between Blenheims and Bf110s and another painful lesson was learnt: the Blenheim was no match for this fast and heavily armed twin-engined fighter either. Pilot Officer Douglas Cooper flew one of the Blenheims of 110 Squadron on that fateful day:

"I took part in the first daylight scrap with German fighters during a sweep over the North Sea. Nine Blenheims, led by Squadron Leader Ken Doran, were ordered to carry out a reconnaissance in a search for German Naval shipping. 110 Squadron had carried out the first raid of the war on the German Navy at Wilhelmshaven, which earned Kenneth Doran the first DFC to be awarded. We were flying at between 2,000 - 3,000 feet half way between England and Denmark with no land in sight when we were unexpectedly attacked by four Bf110's.

"At that time the Blenheim, having no under armament, was very vulnerable to attack from below so Doran led the formation of three vics of three aircraft down to sea level. Regrettably one Blenheim flown by Sgt. Hanne was lost in the first attack. A running battle followed during which one enemy aircraft was seen to crash in the sea and two others damaged during the 25 minute engagement. Following this encounter Doran continued with the reconnaissance, which earned him a bar to his DFC."

During the period from 14th February to the end of March 1940, Blenheims of 2 Group completed another 250 North Sea shipping sweeps, which resulted in the loss of only four aircraft and their crews. They all fell victim to German fighters. One of these was N6211 of 110 Squadron, again shot down by *Hauptmann* Falck of *2./ZG 76*, on the 17th February North of the Dutch Frisian Islands. Sergeant Bigg and his crew were reported missing and are commemorated on the Memorial at Runnymede for those members of the RAF and Commonwealth Air Forces who have no known grave.

During these shipping searches, six bombing attacks were carried out against German shipping. The most successful sortie took place on 11th March, when Squadron Leader Miles Delap of 82 Squadron spotted a surfaced German submarine off Borkum. He straddled the boat from low level and soon U-31 sank. Delap's aircraft was damaged by bomb blast while overflying the submarine that nearly resulted in the loss of the Blenheim and its crew.

The German *Wehrmacht* struck with numbing speed on 9th April, not on the Western Front, but in Denmark and Norway. Bomber Command sorties now were mainly directed to these countries in raids on shipping and airfields, in an effort to delay the enemy advance. Yet, it was to little avail. In no time the two Scandinavian countries were overrun by the German aggressor. Hitler was now ensured of a wealth of Scandinavian raw materials, including the vital iron ore for his war industry. Within months, the Germans organized a continuous sea-borne supply of millions of tons of iron ore. Along the coastal shipping lanes of Norway, Denmark, Northern Germany, the Frisian Islands and Holland the ore was shipped south and, in the Northern German and Dutch ports, it was transhipped and further transported to the large steel mills in the Ruhr Valley. Within a year, the Blenheim crews were to be involved in one of their bloodiest and fiercest campaigns of the war, with shipping attacks against these convoys in the coastal shipping lanes between Norway and France. A consequence of Bomber Command's operations over Denmark and Norway during April 1940 was the discontinuation of virtually all daylight operations by Hampden and Wellington bombers. These 'heavies' had proved to be too vulnerable in daylight and therefore from now on concentrated on night raids together with the Whitleys. 2 Group was now the only Group in Bomber Command left to bear the brunt of daylight operations against the enemy.

On the eve of the German invasion of the Low Countries and France in early May 1940, the RAF had the following offensive Blenheim squadrons at its disposal:

2 Group Bomber Command

XV Sqn.	Wyton, England.	Bomber
82 Sqn.	Wattisham, England.	Bomber
107 Sqn.	Wattisham, England.	Bomber
110 Sqn.	Wattisham, England.	Bomber
21 Sqn.	Watton, England.	Bomber
40 Sqn.	Wyton, England.	Bomber
101 Sqn.	West Raynham, England.	Reserve

Army Co-operation Command

18 Sqn.	Meharicourt, France.	Strat. recce.
57 Sqn.	Rosiéres-en-Santerre, France.	Strat. recce.

Advanced Air Striking Force

114 Sqn.	Vraux, France.	Bomber
139 Sqn.	Plivot, France.	Bomber

BEF Air Component

53 Sqn.	Poix, France.	Bomber
59 Sqn.	Poix, France.	Bomber

Coastal Command

235 Sqn.	Bircham Newton, England.	Fighter
254 Sqn.	Bircham Newton, England.	Fighter

Fighter Command

25 Sqn.	North Weald, England.	Fighter
229 Sqn.	Digby, England & France.	Fighter
600 Sqn.	Manston, England.	Fighter
601 Sqn.	Tangmere, England/ Merville, France.	Fighter
604 Sqn.	Northolt, England.	Fighter

2 Group had 96 operational Blenheims at its disposal, plus 62 reserve aircraft. Combined with some 90 Blenheims of the six squadrons of the AASF and Air Component in France and some 100 aircraft of Fighter and Coastal Command Blenheim squadrons, the RAF had a force of around 300 front-line Blenheims ready for offensive operations against the enemy in the event of an invasion of the Low Countries and France. Even though Sir Charles Portal, successor of Ludlow-Hewitt as C-in-C Bomber Command had serious doubts about the employment of the by now clearly outdated Blenheim in daylight raids, the RAF had no alternative but to use the aircraft in this rôle. They were simply by far the most numerous offensive aircraft in the RAF inventory available at that time.

Chapter Two

Five Days in May

Operations during the invasion of the Netherlands
10-14 May 1940.

Before the break of dawn on Friday 10th May 1940, the long-expected German invasion of the Low Countries, code-named *Fall Gelb*, was put into effect. The Dutch people were awakened at around 05.30 hours by the droning formations of German bombers and fighter planes passing overhead. In Phase One of the invasion, the *Wehrmacht* planned to wipe out the Dutch Air Force in one blow by pre-emptive strikes against the main airfields in Western and Middle Holland. The aerodromes at Texel, Den Helder, Bergen, Schiphol, Valkenburg, Ypenburg, Waalhaven, Hilversum, Soesterberg, Eindhoven and Gilze-Rijen were raided in lightning attacks that resulted in almost half of the Dutch Air Force being eliminated.

Shortly after these strikes, over 400 Ju52 transport aircraft lumbered into Dutch airspace. The slow, low-flying aircraft suffered heavy casualties from the accurate Dutch *Flak*, but thousands of paratroopers of the *7th Fliegerdivision* and *22nd Luftlandedivision* were dropped over four air bases in the heart of Holland, Ypenburg, Waalhaven, Valkenburg and Ockenburg. After short but violent battles the four airfields were captured. The Germans then tried to force their way into The Hague to capture the Dutch Government and the Royal Family, but got stuck on the way due to stiff resistance from the Dutch Army.

As soon as the news of the German invasion in the Netherlands reached Great Britain, all 2 Group Blenheim units were put on immediate readiness. In order to assess the situation in Holland, 2 Group HQ dispatched four Blenheims from XV and 40 Squadron from Wyton at 09.00 hours. Their orders were to reconnoitre the German advance in the Netherlands. The two aircraft of XV Squadron successfully completed their sorties, but 40 Squadron was less fortunate. Squadron Leader Paddon in L8833 encountered scores of enemy aircraft immediately after crossing the Dutch coast and had to fight off a Ju88. Although his machine was on fire, Paddon made a perfect landing at base and the crew escaped from the Blenheim before it burnt out. The second Blenheim of 40 Squadron failed to return. Flying Officer Burns and his crew flying L8776 reconnoitred the Hook of Holland-Rotterdam area, where they saw scores of Ju52s dropping parachutes. They then set course for Venlo. While hedge-hopping to avoid enemy fighters, a Ju88 was engaged by Flying Officer Burns, but to no effect. From Venlo, course was set for Hengelo, but soon after, light *Flak* began holing the Blenheim and after a big bang, the starboard engine erupted in flames. Shortly after crossing the River Meuse at very low level, Burns belly-landed the aircraft in a grassy field. The crew scrambled from the burning aircraft, only to be greeted by Frisian cows and enemy troops and they were taken prisoners.

This was the first aircraft to be lost by 2 Group in the 'shooting war'. Also, from France, Blenheim reconnaissance missions were flown over the battle front. Three 18 Squadron Blenheims took off From Meharicourt with orders to find out how far the enemy had advanced in the Maastricht area. Two never made it back to base; L1405 and L8860. Only Pilot Officer Smith and his crew in L9185 managed to return by dodging intense light *Flak* and repeated attacks from a Bf110 over Limburg Province.

By 11.00, sufficient information had been obtained on the situation in Holland to plan a series of attacks on Dutch airfields now in enemy hands. Blenheim fighters of 600 Squadron were to bear the brunt of this battle. Six crews of 'B' Flight were briefed to attack Waalhaven airfield, just to the South of Rotterdam. Ju52 transports were busy flying in supplies and troops at Waalhaven and, with support from the air by 600 Squadron, the Dutch would now launch a counter attack on the airfield. Led by Squadron Leader Jimmy Wells, the fighter Blenheims swept in from low level and shot up the airfield. Much confusion was caused among the German paratroops on the airfield and at least one Ju52 transport was shot down in flames in the middle of the 'drome. However, after the first strafing pass on Waalhaven, the six British attackers were bounced by a dozen Bf110 *Zerstörer* long-range fighters of *3./ZG 1*. The Germans were led by *Oberleutnant* Streib, who was to gain fame as a leading night fighter pilot in the later war years. A fierce dog-fight started, but it was very much a one-sided affair, as the lightly-armed and vulnerable Blenheims were no match for the fast and cannon-armed German fighters. Within minutes, five out of six Blenheims were shot out of the sky. Only Blenheim 'O', flown by Pilot Officer Norman Hayes and his air gunner Corporal J. Holmes, was able to return to Manston in his badly holed aircraft. Norman Hayes tells us of the disastrous 10 May operation:

"The squadron was standing by the whole morning and we had just been sent off for a quick bite of lunch in the mess. I think this must have been at about twelve o'clock midday. We were just about to get out of our cars to go into the mess when we were told to get back to dispersal immediately. We were briefed by the Sector Commander, who was Wing Commander Price. His opening words to us were - I remember them very clearly - 'You chaps have a tough job'. He then told us that information had come through that German troops had landed in Rotterdam and had taken over Waalhaven aerodrome there. Our brief was to fly there, engage enemy aircraft over the airfield and if we could see no aircraft, we were to beat up the airfield and shoot up the German aircraft we would see there.

"When we took off - it was a lovely sunny May-day - we flew over the North Sea in two vics of three. Jimmy Wells, the CO, led us to the area. There were fires burning and we flew at about 5000 feet. My gunner and I kept our eyes open but there were no aeroplanes in the sky at all. Jimmy put us into echelon to the right and led us down to attack the airfield. I was flying number two to Jimmy. I followed him down. I do not know what target he selected at the airfield, but I selected a Junkers 52 and shot that up. As I was climbing away I saw a large group of Messerschmitt 110s diving down on our tail. I turned as hard as I could towards these aircraft and I was able to evade them. I looked around to find a target to shoot up, when I saw a '110 attacking a Blenheim. I got on his tail and tried to shoot him down. In the meantime I had a '110 on my tail. It hit me several times.

"What happened after that is very confusing as the fighting was very confusing. It was difficult to see any aeroplanes at all. I decided that the situation was so hopeless that our only hope was to get away. My aeroplane was quite badly hit. What really worried us was that the fuselage was full of petrol. My starboard petrol tank had been hit. In fact we found an incendiary bullet in the tank, which I still have. We should have been in flames, but the aeroplane never caught fire.

"We slowly got back to Manston. I think it was Wing Commander Price who met me when I got out of my aircraft. I said, 'Who is back?'. He said, 'You are the first.' I said, 'Well in that case there won't be any of the others back.'"

A few hours after the disastrous 600 Squadron action over Waalhaven, 2 Group mounted two bombing raids on Dutch airfields. First airborne was XV Squadron, whose nine Blenheims made low-level runs over Waalhaven and hit sixteen Ju52s in mid-afternoon. Several aircraft were damaged by ground fire, but all returned to base safely. Then it was 40 Squadron's turn, four sections of three aircraft bombing Ypenburg by 17.00 hours. A hangar was left in flames, the airfield was cratered and scores of enemy aircraft were damaged. The third and fourth vics encountered a large formation of some forty Bf109s and '110s in the target area, where three Blenheims were shot down in flames. The only surviving aircraft of the third vic returned to base crippled and Flight Lieutenant Hugh Smeddle and his crew were rushed off to hospital with serious injuries. Smeddle received an immediate DFC for bringing back his shot-up Blenheim, his observer and WOp/AG both got the DFM. Flying Officer Jo Stevenson flew P4908 to Ypenburg airfield in the last vic of 40 Squadron with Sergeant Usher, observer and Leading Aircraftsman Corney as his WOp/AG:

"40 Squadron sent off two reconnaissance aircraft, one (Flying Officer Burns) was shot down but he survived as a prisoner of war. In the afternoon, two 'A' Flight 'vics' each of three aircraft went off at five minutes intervals followed by Flight Lieutenant Hugh Smeddle plus two aircraft. Then, five minutes later, myself plus two aircraft. My No.2 was Sergeant Robertson, who did not return and No.3 Flying Officer Peter Wakeford. Bomb load was four 250lbs and we had to climb to 1,000 feet to release them.

"It was a glorious sunny afternoon. We headed, at low level, for the Dutch coast and noticed black dots in the sky - our Luftwaffe reception committee. There was R/T silence. I changed to plus 9 boost and we climbed to 1,000 feet over the airfield, which was strewn with gliders and parachutes. Bombs gone, steep left-hand 180 degrees turn and we were 'skating' over a beautiful lawn on the landward side of a magnificent brick building. Ahead, one ack-ack gun towards which two Dutch soldiers, sleeves rolled-up, ran but recognising an ally, stopped short of the gun. The coast flashed below us and I remained at 'nought' feet.

"We experienced no ack-ack as there were too many Me's around. Corney became very busy on his 'pea-shooter'. The round pans held only 100 rounds so he had to change them rapidly. Meantime, he called, on the intercom, for Usher to fire his gun on each change of pan. Usher, lying flat in the nose, had a Browning 'scare gun' (he had a mirror, but it was useless because of vibration). Corney also called to me to bank starboard or port. One

starboard turn I saw the '110 turning in to attack but he could not get below
us and I 'admired' the twin splashes of his cannon fire under the starboard
wing. I saw Wakeford away to port (hurray!) but did not lead my pursuer
towards him. Corney announced: "110 has broken off action'. I believed him
but remained at 'nought' feet until Orfordness, our landfall (and departure
point) was in sight. We had to climb to a specified height to cross the coast,
fire the colours of the day (Very pistol) and switch on the I.F.F. to
discourage our own enthusiastic ack-ack and fighters (aircraft recognition
had not become an art yet).

"Having landed, the 9mm holes were identified but the damaged
starboard wing tip was due to my hitting something. Flight Lieutenant
Smeddle landed before us - he had been shot in the leg, with considerable
loss of blood but, with help had applied a tourniquet. The cockpit was
spattered with blood, so he had done well to bring the aircraft all the way
back to base and not landed at Martlesham Heath on the coast. (Mrs.
Smeddle must have been pleased). At de-briefing our very popular Wing
Commander Cecil Barlow made a remark about our having had a 'dicey do'.

"Flight Lieutenant Smeddle was awarded an immediate D.F.C. and sent
to RAF Hospital, Ely, where we visited him. He later returned to 'B' Flight
as a Squadron Leader to command. I, meantime succeeded Hugh as Deputy
Flight Commander and remained so until leaving '40' in August."

Flying Officer Bill Bromley was the pilot of one of the
Blenheims in the first vic of 40 Squadron to attack Ypenburg
and, after the bombing, he did a little attacking of his own:

"This was our first real attack of the war. I decided to fly over The Hague,
more or less as a tourist after we had broken formation and headed west
independently. When I was nearly over the city, I saw what appeared to be
like sparks from a gridstone coming towards me and accelerating as they
passed around my aircraft. I was then I suppose about 1,000 feet in height.
The penny dropped fairly quickly and I realised I was being shot at by
machine-gun tracer. That irked me a little so I did a diving turn to the
north and headed along the beach to a line of about eight Junkers 52's that
had landed there earlier to disgorge German troops. I would then have been
at 2-300 feet and, being rather excited at having been shot at from The
Hague, opened fire with my one miserable forward-firing gun. As I was
firing, a soldier in grey uniform jumped out from the fourth or fifth aircraft
and started running up the dry sand towards the sand hills. He was unwise
to have moved, as it was most unlikely he would have been hit. I was able to
direct accurate fire at him, as each bullet spurted up sand. He suddenly
spread-eagled and fell on the sand. Afterwards I thought, 'Well, dammit, you
could have killed some poor so-and-so in cold blood'. But it wasn't really in
cold blood, except perhaps on his part. I was in the mood having just been
shot at by small arms over The Hague. I then turned out over the sea and
headed back to base at Wyton."

Due to lack of proper communication, the British did not yet
know that Ypenburg had already been partly recaptured from

the German paratroops when the crews of 40 Squadron started their attack. Successful counter-attacks by Dutch infantry troops ensured the re-possession by the Dutch of three aerodromes by the end of 10th May -Ypenburg, Valkenburg and Ockenburg. The German invasion plan of rapidly conquering Western Holland on the first day of the *Blitzkrieg* campaign had failed. Only Waalhaven firmly remained in German hands.

The three Blenheims lost over Ypenburg brought 40 Squadron's total losses on the first day of the 'shooting war' to five aircraft and four crews lost, with Hugh Smeddle and crew in hospital. Sergeant Roger Peacock served with 40 Squadron as WOp/AG (he was shot down and taken POW on 25/26th July 1940 near Jever) and endeavours to give an impression of life with 40 Squadron in the Summer of 1940:

"We were, as I see clearly at so great a remove, only children playing at war. When the war started I was nineteen years old, the product of a working-class family, well-educated (thanks to a scholarship) but well used to privation and insecurity. The RAF gave me security: a bed, three meals a day, an assured roof over my head, a framework by which to live - rules to keep and rights to protect me; most WOp/AGs came from a similar background. Many of them, far too many of them, were dead before reaching the age of twenty - many, not long after an eighteenth birthday. Each day was taken as it came. We did not think about a future: indeed, most of us accepted that for us there could be no future. We did not talk about this: it was a probability that was best left unmentioned. We lived twenty-four to a room and on many days during early 1940 there were empty beds at night.

"During the actual fighting of May and June Blenheims were used mainly in a tactical rôle: tank columns, supply dumps, bridges, aerodromes and such. Our kites were, at best, obsolescent and immensely helpless against Bf109s and Bf110s. German *Flak* was intense and deadly: it was not unknown for a whole squadron to be sent out and for only one, or even none, to return. On 40 Squadron we had three Commanding Officers; one arrived in the early evening one day, to replace a man known to be dead, put his name on the dawn battle order, went out at 3.30 a.m. and did not return - he had not even unpacked.

"Such losses had an effect on us, of course. We cultivated a certain grim humour: many of our witticisms spoke of the Grim Reaper, nor did we allow ourselves to mourn - at least, not openly. We were, and certainly I was, totally egotistic in such matters; we took cognisance of only what directly affected us and lay down to sleep of a night conscious only that we had survived one more day. It was a time of lunacy. Human lives were squandered without valid purpose and to little effect. We plebs did not query all this: our betters must - we felt - know what they were doing. Clearly, however, they didn't. 'History passes verdicts on wars. The people, however, must never so much as suspect that mistakes have been made. Otherwise it loses faith in the cause and it is the people, of course, who must die for it.' Guess who wrote that? Dr. Goebbels (Tagebücher 23.12.'40)!

"Finally: though it may seem strange, we loved our Blenheims. Those of us who had enjoyed them in peacetime retained our loyalty even when our losses were insupportably high."

Late in the afternoon of 10th May the German invaders endured one more Blenheim raid. Masses of Ju52 transport aircraft had landed on Scheveningen beach during the day. These were the targets for twelve Blenheims of 110 Squadron, escorted by six Blenheim Mk.1fs of 604 Squadron 'B' Flight in the early evening. 110 Squadron had already lost two Blenheims during an attack on the Albert Canal bridges just west of Maastricht a few hours previously - now the squadron left Wattisham for their second raid of the day. One of the flyers to get his 'fire baptism' in this raid was Leading Aircraftsman Arthur Pierce. He manned the turret in Sergeant MacDonald's fighter Blenheim of 604 Squadron:

"I was a member of 604 County of Middlesex Squadron - flying short-nosed fighter Blenheims - to which I was posted on the outbreak of hostilities. This squadron was used as fighter cover for twelve Blenheims carrying bombs, who were stationed at Wattisham. We were based at Kenley and, on May 10th 1940, we flew over to Wattisham, landed and topped up with fuel - there was only six of our squadron - and finally got airborne.

"We were led by the bombers to a beach at Scheveningen where a number of German troop-carrying Ju52's had landed. The bombers were to destroy the aircraft but, having failed to do this, they departed and our Flight Commander decided to shoot them up. We each dived to attack with our four forward firing .303 Browning guns carried in a pan under the fuselage belly and with the power operated gun turret amidships. After several such attacks many of the Ju52's were on fire. We had done a lot of patrol work over the Channel protecting shipping going to Dunkirk etc., but this was the real thing! I was terribly excited and not the least bit scared. There was a certain amount of light AA fire and my plane was hit, but one aircraft was lost - we believe by the pilot failing to pull out of his dive. This is known as 'target fascination'. Luckily the crew were unhurt and they both walked to The Hague and eventually got back to England. Our aircraft was hit by light *Flak* and when we landed back at Wattisham the pilot discovered that his brakes would not work as the pressure pipes had been hit. Fortunately the field was large enough for the pilot to bring the aircraft to a halt. We flew back to Kenley in another aircraft, which had been flown by a Flight Commander. The trip from Wattisham to Holland had lasted 2.45 hours."

After crashing in the dunes of Wassenaar, Pilot Officer Ian Joll and his gunner Jim Pickford set fire to their Blenheim by dipping Joll's tie into the fuel tank and using it as a fuse. The two men then walked to The Hague. From there, they were shipped back to England on 13th May. As a result of the Blenheim raids by XV, 40, 110, 600 and 604 Squadrons on Waalhaven, Ypenburg and Scheveningen beach, dozens of Ju52s were either destroyed or heavily damaged. This was a major contribution to the destruction of no less than 224 Ju-52s on 10th May over the Netherlands. For example, *K.G.z.b.v. 9* lost 42 out of 55 Ju52s that headed for Ypenburg and Ockenburg. The flat lands around The Hague were literally strewn with wrecks of these transport aircraft. Although this was a severe blood-letting for the Nazi para-transport force, the Germans had so many reserves of these aircraft that only four months later a little under 1,500 Ju52s stood by for the invasion of Great Britain.

In the early hours of 11th May 1940, it was clear to the British that the German advance into Belgium had to be halted, or at least delayed, by bombing attacks on the vital road bridges in the Maastricht area and on German troop columns on the Maastricht-Tongres road. It was clear that the enemy had advanced far into Holland on the first day of the invasion and Maastricht was deemed to be the bottle-neck for the south and southwest-bound enemy troops. In fact, the *4th Panzer Division* and six infantry Divisions of the Sixth German Army had rolled up the Dutch defences east of Maastricht in no time on the 10th, while paratroops had successfully overwhelmed the Belgian fort Eben Emael just west of the city. The paratroops had also succeeded in capturing intact two road bridges over the Albert Canal just West of Maastricht. Moreover, strong enemy mechanised columns were reported on the morning of the 11th to be moving from Aachen through Maastricht and towards Tongres. Thus, a critical situation arose for the Allied defences in Eastern Belgium....

Eventually, two England-based Blenheim squadrons were briefed to deal with this situation. Eleven aircraft of 110 Squadron left Wattisham at 14.50 and bombed the road and railway bridges at Maastricht. As expected, the *Flak* barrage was fearsome and L9175 and N6208 were lost. Three men died, one was taken PoW and two were injured. No results of their

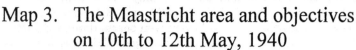

Map 3.   The Maastricht area and objectives on 10th to 12th May, 1940

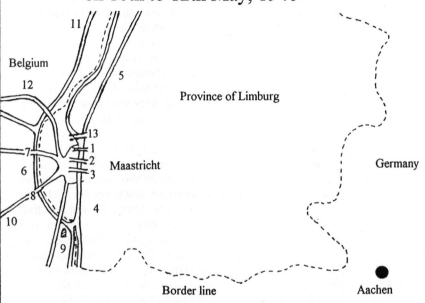

1:      Railroad bridge, codename AM9
2:      Road bridge, Wilhelmina bridge, codename AM9
3:      Servaas bridge, codename AM9
4:      River Meuse
5:      Juliana Canal
6:      Albert Canal
7:      Vendwezelt bridge
8:      Vroenhoven bridge
9:      Fort Eben Emael
10:    Maastricht-Tongres road, codename AM6
11:    Zuid-Willemsvaart
12:    Railway line
13:    German pontoon bridges (two)

attack were observed by the crews of 110 Squadron as they sped for home. Indeed, the targets were not hit, but a few houses were damaged near the bridges.

21 Squadron had been at readiness since 04.30 hours and eventually eleven aircraft took off from Watton at 15.10 to strike at the German columns pouring out of Maastricht and into Belgium. 18-year old Aircraftsman 1 Jack Bartley served as a WOp/AG in Sergeant Outhwaite's crew of 21 Squadron in 1940 and relates this operation:

"During the advance of the German army into the Low Countries, signalling the end of the 'phoney war' in May 1940, 21 Squadron, in which I was serving at RAF Watton, was called upon to carry out a low level daylight bombing and strafing attack on enemy mechanized columns on the road from Maastricht to Tongres, in an attempt to stem the *Panzers* progress.

"We took off at mid-afternoon on May 11th, overflying Holland and Belgium at around 15,000 feet, through sporadic anti-aircraft fire from 'friendly' gunners, whose aircraft recognition left much to be desired, eventually spotting the long line of vehicles that were to be the target. Diving down to attack, the bombs were released from a few hundred feet and pandemonium broke out as the troops scattered for shelter amid bomb bursts and machine-gun fire. I saw a dogfight going on in the distance between biplanes. Climbing away from the target with my turret gun assembly elevated and firing the remaining rounds of ammunition, a sudden loud and sharp metallic bang sounded through the aircraft as we were hit, possibly with return fire or more probably from shrapnel from the preceding attacking Blenheim's bombs. Our aircraft then led the formation back at zero feet all the way.

"Being subsequently fully occupied in scanning the sky for sight of enemy fighters, it was some time before I could spare time to look for signs of damage. When I did, I discovered the gaping hole in the platform of my turret, which framed a view of the landscape below. Inspecting the roof there was no corresponding hole and I assumed that the missile had exited through the open sector of the cupola, which allowed for gun barrel traverse and elevation and concluded that I had been very fortunate to be unscathed.

"After landing at Watton the airframe mechanics busied themselves with the job of patching up the damage whilst we went to debriefing. Late that evening I was to be found in the NAAFI with a group of WOp/AGs, drowning the sorrow of the loss of one of our number who was found to be dead in his turret on our return from the sortie. Paddy Charlton was killed by the only bullet that hit the machine and pierced his lung. Our sojourn was interrupted by a tired and thirsty mechanic who laid an object on the table in front of me. It was a jagged and twisted piece of shrapnel about 3/4" cube. 'That was fused into the sponge rubber of your turret seat', he announced. As my sphincter nerve gave an involuntary shudder he proceeded to draw further pieces of metal from his pocket, just recognisable as pieces of a medium size screwdriver. 'This', he said, 'was lying between the turret platform and the fuselage'. In taking the full force of the shrapnel, leaving it with only sufficient momentum to fuse itself into the sorbo rubber of my turret seat there is no doubt that the screwdriver, accidentally dropped into an inaccessible and hidden space, had certainly been responsible for my continued ability to adopt a sitting, or possibly any other, posture."

Although only one aircraft of 21 Squadron escaped unscathed from the 11th May attack west of Maastricht, all Blenheims returned safely at Watton and the raid was considered to be a success. Bartley's crew were to be shot down only two days later, during the disastrous bombing attacks in the Sedan area, when 40 out of 71 RAF bombers failed to return. Jack and his crew were fortunate in escaping from their wrecked Blenheim in the Belgian Ardennes and later rejoined their squadron at Watton.

The third day of the shooting war started with a Blenheim operation to give cover for the evacuation of Queen Wilhelmina, at the Hook of Holland. At 05.00 hours on the morning of the 12th May, three fighter Blenheims of 235 Squadron left Bircham Newton to rendezvous with a French-based fighter escort over the Hook. However, for unclear reasons the Hurricanes failed to arrive and the Blenheims started their patrols by 06.00 under a brilliantly clear sky - it would be another lovely spring day. A few thousand feet under the circling Blenheims, a reception committee of 200 Royal Marines were then disembarked from two destroyers at the Hook and these awaited the arrival of the Dutch Queen.

After patrolling over the Hook for about an hour, suddenly a gaggle of Bf110's arrived on the scene and a wild dog fight started. Pilot Officer Savill in L9189 claimed one of the German fighters shot down but then five Bf109s of *II./JG 27* that were on a free-lance patrol over the Waalhaven-Rotterdam area, rushed at the British aircraft and started head-on attacks. It was a hopeless situation for the 235 Squadron crews. Flying Officer Peacock shot down another fighter, a Bf109 that was seen to crash between the Hook and The Hague, but then the three Blenheims were overpowered. 'Pissey' Peacock's crew watched Blenheim L9324 'P' of Pilot Officer Smith swerve off with the starboard engine on fire. Only moments later it crashed in the Nieuwlandse Polder near the Hook, next to two

Ju52's that had landed there on the morning of the 10th May. There were no survivors. Then Pilot Officer Savill's aircraft was riddled, killing his observer and gunner. Norman Savill was very lucky to escape death by baling out of the burning aircraft at very low altitude. Only seconds after pulling the ripcord he landed near Oostvoorne and was immediately taken prisoner by Dutch soldiers. The Dutchmen were convinced Norman was German and made preparations to shoot him. Although he was in a bad state and covered with burns, Savill managed to convince the soldiers that he was a genuinely British pilot. He was then transported to Vlaardingen hospital, where he spent the next nine months recovering from his burns. Then it was four years in PoW camp *Stalag Luft III*.

At 09.10, Flying Officer Peacock landed his damaged aircraft at Bircham Newton, the sole survivor of the original vic of three. The Dutch Royal family eventually left Holland from Ijmuiden harbour late in the evening of the 12th. Queen Wilhelmina departed in a Royal Navy destroyer from the Hook on the 13th, followed, shortly afterwards, by the Dutch government. 235 Squadron flew further patrols over the Flushing area during the 12th May. Flying Officer Bain, Pilot Officer Randall and Sergeant Tubbs encountered seventeen Ju88s and He111s over Flushing harbour on one of these patrols, but neither side suffered casualties in the ensuing fight.

After the second day of the invasion of the Low Countries, it was clear to the British forces that the weight of the AASF and 2 Group operations had to be focused on the destruction of the Maastricht bridges. The primary targets for the coming raids were these two road bridges in the centre of Maastricht and a railway bridge in the north of the city, code-named AM9. The secondary target would be the Maastricht-Tongres road, code-named AM6. It was argued that eliminating the strategic transit points at Maastricht was the only way to slow down the advancing enemy troops, which appeared as to be rushing towards Brussels. On the 11th and in the night of 11/12th May, the 6th German Army had fortified its positions around Maastricht and two road bridges over the Albert Canal just west of the city had been captured intact.

However, defending Dutch troops had blown up the Eastern entrances of all three bridges over the Meuse River at Maastricht on the night of 9/10th May when the local Dutch Army Commander was certain the Germans were to invade the province of Limburg within a few hours. This successfully delayed the advance of the tanks of the 6th Army into Belgium when German troops arrived in Maastricht on the morning of the 10th. In order to get their Panzers across the Meuse, the Germans swiftly constructed two pontoon bridges a few miles north of the destroyed bridges in the outskirts of Maastricht. The confusion of the day and failing communication had prevented this becoming known to the RAF in England or to the AASF in France. The Allies were still convinced that the old bridges over the Meuse at Maastricht were intact and had to be destroyed at all costs. When planning air strikes against these bridges, the British supreme command failed to consult the Dutch Chief of Staff on the strategic situation at Maastricht. And so the scene was set for a tragedy.

Before break of dawn on 12th May, 139 Squadron took off from Plivot aerodrome to attack the advancing German troops west of Maastricht. Eight aircraft set course to the north with an early morning sun glistening on the wings and perspex of the cockpits and gun turrets. A ninth Blenheim, of Pilot Officer 'Lemmy' Menzies and crew, was late taking off and was never able to overtake the formation. This probably saved the crew's life. In the confusion of the day, the promised French fighter escort did not appear and Wing Commander Dickens AFC decided to press on without fighter protection. On arrival over the Belgian-Dutch frontier just west of Maastricht, the crews were warmly received by a barrage of *Flak*. Then a swarm of Messerschmitts of *I./JG 1* and *I./JG 27* bounced the scattered formation. The Blenheims were literally slaughtered; seven out of eight aircraft were mortally hit by the Bf109s. One of the pilots, *Staffelkapitän* of *2./JG 1 Oberleutnant* Walter Adolph, shot down three Blenheims in quick succession. N6216, flown by 'A' Flight Commander, Squadron Leader Scott, appeared to receive a direct hit on the bomb load, which resulted in the explosion of his aircraft and also caused one of his wingmen to cartwheel down minus one wing. Wing Commander Dickens'

Blenheim was the only one to escape destruction and hedge-hopped back to base with his gunner very badly wounded in the chest. Sergeant Payne, his observer, crawled back into the turret and applied first aid to the gunner. He then manned the gun and drove off the attacking Messerschmitts. On landing, Dickens' aircraft turned out to be so badly shot up that it never flew again. When 'Lemmy' Menzies arrived over target, the fight was in full progress. He sneaked in between this and Maastricht and successfully bombed the target. Although three Bf109s broke off to chase him, Menzies made for the deck in plus nine boost and succeeded in out-distancing the fighters.

Wing Commander Dickens was awarded the DFC and his observer a much deserved DFM.

With virtually the whole 139 Squadron wiped out and 114 Squadron destroyed on the ground at Vraux airfield on 11th May, the AASF medium bomber force was more or less eliminated as an effective force. Indeed, only one raid had been carried out by them: the raid on Maastricht by 139 Squadron.

Four of the downed aircrew of 139 Squadron escaped captivity after force-landing on German-held territory and walked into Plivot aerodrome a few days later to rejoin their squadron. Two other men were taken PoW. Fifteen men however were dead, amongst whom was Flying Officer Andrew McPherson DFC, the first RAF pilot to successfully penetrate enemy airspace on 3rd September 1939. A very dark day for 139 Squadron and a grim outlook for the Blenheim crews who were soon to attempt a second attack the Maastricht bridges.

At 08.10 another formation left England to attack the bridges over the Meuse river, twelve crews of 107 Squadron and twelve of XV Squadron, led by the indomitable Wing Commander Basil Embry, CO of 107 Squadron. The aircraft formated over Wattisham and 24 Blenheims headed east, the two squadrons briefed to attack the bridges individually. The North Sea was soon crossed and 70 minutes after take off XV Squadron reached the target in the Meuse valley, with 107 Squadron arriving a few minutes later. Despite a very heavy *Flak* barrage, through which the aircraft had to fly for over five minutes, the gallant British crews pressed on and some 60 bombs were dropped in the target area at around 09.20 hours. Alas, the

intensity of the *Flak* hosing up threw the Blenheim crews off
their aim and the bridges were not hit. A number of houses near
one of the road bridges were demolished. Twenty-two Dutch and
Belgian civilians were killed and 35 injured. Also, seven Belgian
prisoners of war and five German soldiers lost their lives when
the facade of one of the houses collapsed on top of them.

All 24 Blenheims were damaged by light *Flak* on the run-up
and soon an aircraft plunged from the sky. Then another one
spiralled down in flames, followed by five more. Now that the
two compact formations were scattered by the deadly accurate
Flak, this was the moment the German fighters milling
overhead had been waiting for. Again, Bf109s of *I./JG 1* and
I./JG 27 pounced on the damaged bombers. Despite the
Hurricane escort from No.1 Squadron, which tried to hold off
the enemy, another three Blenheims were shot down in a
running battle over Belgium. Young fighter pilot *Leutnant* Erbo
Graf von Kageneck of *I./JG 1* was the victor over two of these
Blenheims. When approaching the Belgian coast, the bombers
were at last left to themselves and the eight surviving
Blenheims of 107 Squadron and six of XV Squadron limped back
to their bases. On landing at Wyton, only two aircraft of XV
Squadron were still serviceable; all the others were heavily
damaged. Out of 36 aircrews of XV Squadron who left on the
raid, half were missing. A number of other men came back
wounded in their badly shot-up aircraft. Basil Embry, the leader
of the second raid on Maastricht, recounts this attack in his
autobiography:

"On Sunday, 12th May, we were ordered to attack two bridges at
Maastricht. The formation was to be at Wing strength and 107 Squadron
was detailed to be the leading unit. Before taking off we were told of the
importance attached by General Georges, the French Commander-in-Chief
of the entire North-Eastern Front, to stopping the enemy's thrust through
Maastricht, thought to be his main axis of advance and the most dangerous
threat to the Allies. We were warned that enemy fighters were very active
over the area and that Maastricht and its approaches were heavily defended
by anti-aircraft artillery. Finally, we were instructed to press home our
attack and do our utmost to bomb as accurately as possible in view of the
seriousness of the situation.

"After careful study of the map, the topographical features of the
surrounding country and the forecast of the cloud conditions, Whiting
(Embry's observer, T.B.) and I discussed in detail the tactics we would use.

Realising that the bridges were small targets to hit, we decided that we must make a steady approach for the last ten miles, with as few turns as possible. This was particularly important in view of the size of the formation. You cannot make sudden big changes of direction with a formation of twenty-four aircraft and carry out accurate bombing. We also decided to approach parallel to the alignment of the bridges because this would give us a more direct line on the target and a better chance of hitting our objective and the approach roads.

"Bombing height also had to be decided. Whiting was an excellent bomb aimer, but each bridge was no more than thirty feet in width and, to have any real chance of success, we decided we must bomb from 4,000 feet. We realised this was a suicidal height from the point of view of light anti-aircraft fire, but we thought the importance of the task justified the risks involved.

"The squadrons were divided into two sub-formations of six aircraft each, flying in 'box' formation and the leading navigator in each was to aim the bombs of his sub-formation. In this way four navigators were taking separate aim, which increased the chances of hitting the target whilst retaining the advantages of dropping the bombs in formation and obtaining an effective pattern of bomb bursts over the area.

"The two squadrons made rendezvous over Wattisham at 9 o'clock and set course for Maastricht at a height of 4,000 feet. We had an uneventful flight to within five miles of the target area, except for some ineffective shooting by our own guns at Ostend, but we were becoming accustomed to being shot at by both sides! We now turned on to our final approach and after flying for two or three minutes on our bombing run a tornado of fire met us from the ground. One could hear the continuous crash of bursting shells all about us and see the tracer coming at us from every direction. So intense was the enemy's fire that the whole earth seemed to be erupting. The sky was filled with hundreds of black puffs intermingled with the flash of bursting shells and the criss-cross pathways of the tracer. Every few seconds my aircraft shook as it was struck by flying splinters and I wondered if anything could live in this inferno. I turned my head to see how the others in my formation were faring and as I did so two aircraft burst into flames and went crashing down like meteors. Three more were to follow almost immediately.

"Whiting's voice, perfectly calm and unruffled, was saying, 'Left, hold it - steady' and at last, 'Bombs gone'. As we turned away I noticed German fighters above us and to one side, waiting to pounce on us as soon as we were clear of the anti-aircraft defences. Obviously they hoped that the fire from their guns would break up our formation and leave single aeroplanes for them to hack down at will. Realising their intentions, I ordered the squadron to close up and prepare for combat. We did not have long to wait before the enemy attacked and our air-gunners returned their fire. I could not see what was happening but Lang (Embry's WOp/AG, T.B.) reported that two of the enemy broke away, smoke pouring from them and, though we did not confirm that they had been destroyed, we took comfort from the hope that we had helped to level the score.

"As we withdrew, I counted seven aircraft burning on the ground, but that was not to prove our total loss that day because, of those that remained of the original twenty-four, two crash-landed and were damaged beyond repair and all the remaining aircraft of 107 Squadron were battle scarred in a greater or lesser degree. The two that crash-landed had lucky escapes. The first was piloted by Rotherham, who had been my adjutant shortly before and was now flying in my formation. He had to break away on the return flight home, hit in both engines. The last I saw of him that day was spiralling down with a German fighter on his tail shooting at him. He was lucky, because the German turned away thinking he had shot him down and Rotherham was able to crash-land without hurting himself or his crew. As he stepped out of the wreckage, he found himself face to face with the King of the Belgians, who arranged for him and his crew to be looked after and later repatriated to England. Tubby Clayton, the pilot of the second aeroplane to crash-land, was also fortunate. His aircraft had been badly damaged over the target and it was astonishing that it did not disintegrate in the air, but, showing great determination, he flew it back to Wattisham, where he landed with the undercarriage retracted. The nose was smashed in and his navigator, Innes-Jones, was lying seriously wounded on the floor of the cockpit. I remember vividly the scene at Wattisham on our return, with Sergeant Barrett, an ex-policeman from London, trying to cut through the nose with an axe to get at Innes-Jones, who appeared to be bleeding to death. Happily his life was saved and after the war he returned to his native New Zealand.

"Photographs taken during the bombing showed that one of the bridges had already been damaged and we learned that this had been done by a Battle squadron based in France. Our bombs although not actually hitting the bridges, fell on houses alongside and effectively blocked the approaches. It is difficult to assess the operational effect of this attack, but it seems clear from later events that it did not delay the enemy's advance through Maastricht very seriously, which is depressing when the cost in life and aircraft is considered."

It seems that a number of crews saw, on arrival over Maastricht, that the original targets had already been destroyed and aimed for the pontoon bridges instead. Pilot Officer 'Red' Eames, pilot with XV Squadron recounts:

"I saw the town bridges had been breached but there were two pontoon bridges in place, slightly to the north. We attacked in loose formation from about 5,000 feet and I aimed at the pontoon bridges in turn. When pulling out of the dive, my aircraft was hit by accurate light *Flak*. No results were observed and we left the area at ground level, alongside the Albert Canal. I rejoined the section leader (Squadron Leader Lawrence) and returned to base."

Red Eames doesn't mention that he was hit over the target by a shell that exploded between his seat and rudder bar, which resulted in serious injury to one of his legs. On landing at Wyton he was rushed off to hospital.

Indeed, when the photographs taken during the raid by XV and 107 Squadron were developed, it was at last discovered that both the road bridges and the railway bridge across the Meuse had already been demolished before the raid took place. The photographs also clearly showed German armoured columns pouring over the river on the two newly-built pontoon bridges in the northern outskirts of Maastricht. This discovery was made too late for the Blenheim crews that had braved the *Flak* and fighters over the city. The morning of the 12th May was only a few hours old, yet 139, 107 and XV Squadrons had already lost 17 out of 35 aircraft that had departed for the Maastricht bridges and Maastricht-Tongres road. Two more Blenheims were written off. 19 valuable bombers lost, 36 men dead, 9 PoWs and a few more wounded. This was an unbearably high price to pay for two failed raids.

During the 12th May, Battle squadrons of the AASF, supported by the Blenheims of 82 and 21 Squadrons, mounted several raids on bridges and staging-areas near Hasselt, Tongres and Sedan. French and Belgian aircraft also tried to disrupt the enemy advance in this area but failed in their efforts due to the overwhelmingly superior German defences. At least another 23 Allied bombers and fighter aircraft were shot down. It had been a long and gruelling day for the aircrews, but there was even more suffering to come.

With the big air battles in progress over Maastricht, eastern Belgium and France, a very special event took place off the Hook of Holland. During 1939 and early 1940, several Blenheim fighter units were equipped with the new AI (Airborne Interception) radar. 25 and 604 Squadrons, the Fighter Interception Unit and the Special Duty Flight undertook the difficult task of trying to intercept enemy aircraft at night and in bad weather with the new top secret equipment. Often, this was done in co-operation with long-range radar stations on the British coast. The Special Duty Flight from Martlesham Heath for example, had been engaged for some time in experimental radar flights in association with the radar station at Bawdsey, situated on the coast near Orfordness. On 11th May, 1940, a fighter Blenheim of the Flight was sent over to the Dutch coast for the first time to intercept an enemy aircraft. The aircraft failed to make contact on this sortie, however. In the late morning of 12th May a second attempt was made. Blenheim Mk.IVf P4834 took off from Martlesham Heath for a radar directed AI sortie over the North Sea and this time the Blenheim was successfully directed to an enemy aircraft by Bawdsey R.D.F. Some 30 miles off the Hook of Holland an He111 - possibly of *KG 27* - was then picked up by P4834's top secret radar, manned by Aircraftsman 1 A.W.Newton. Pilot Flight Lieutenant Christopher D.S. Smith DFC intercepted the German bomber at 14,000 feet and forced it down in flames off the Hook at 10.45. The first successful A.I. interception in history was a fact. However, Flight Lieutenant Smith had overlooked the cupola underneath the Heinkel and the German gunner got off a few rounds at the attacker before crashing into the sea. As a result, Smith was wounded in the chest and arm and P4834 returned to base in flames. The aircraft burned out on the airfield and the successful pilot was taken to Torquay hospital for medical treatment. He eventually returned to the Flight on 9th July to assume command of 'A' Flight. Sadly, Squadron Leader Smith DFC was killed in action whilst serving with 79 Squadron on 22nd December 1941, flying a Hurricane IIB. He has no known grave.

Early in the Battle of Britain, on the night of 23rd July 1940, Flying Officer Ashfield of the FIU was the first man in history to shoot down an enemy aircraft with the use of AI at night, a Dornier Do 17Z of *2./KG 3* that crashed in the Channel south of Brighton. In the years to come, airborne radar was to revolutionise air warfare at night and in bad weather completely. Sergeant Kenneth Lusty served as an air gunner with 25 Squadron during 1939-40. The squadron, equipped with fighter Blenheims I and IV, was the first RAF unit that became involved in AI radar trials in 1939. Kenneth tells us of the introduction of AI radar in Blenheims:

"I thought the Blenheim was really great. I never crashed in a Blenheim and although it was very cold I was happy. When we got AI it all seemed a bit unreal. In fact we didn't think much of it - it often let us down and the poor 'erks' who first worked the AI were usually A.C.2's who did all sorts of rotten jobs when not flying. We felt they had a raw deal as they did not even have the privileges of the Sergeants Mess. In a 'scramble' we sometimes took off without them. As time went by we began to respect them and were glad when they were 'made up' to Sergeants and really became Aircrew. The radar sets broke down frequently and I consider the training was not as good as it might have been.

"AI improved a lot and the Mk.IV was, I thought, quite good. We had lots of practice when doing standing patrols at night and I suppose it was quite something to get on the tail of another aircraft in a dark night.

"The introduction of AI therefore was not very successful in the early days - poor training, unreliable sets and pilots found it difficult to trust the operators at times. Like all good ideas, it got better - a lot better."

On the fourth day of the German invasion, 13th May, the weather had broken. Low clouds, rain and bad visibility prevented accurate raids against the enemy front-line troops. Because of this, and in an effort to conserve the remaining bomber force, 2 Group and the AASF did not operate and rested during the day to lick their wounds and await the next German move. This was to come at Sedan in northeastern France, where the Germans had massed five *Panzer* Divisions for the assault on the Meuse bridges in this area.

235 Squadron, together with Blenheims of 248 and 254 Squadrons, defied the weather and again operated off the Dutch coast. Allied warships were covered by four crews that engaged five Bf110s and four Ju88s. Sergeant Tubbs claimed a Bf110 shot down, but Flight Lieutenant Morewood's aircraft was badly shot up in the dogfight. Eight other crews of 235 Squadron covered the evacuation of Dutch non-combatants at The Hague and carried out offensive patrols off the Dutch coast. Heavy anti-aircraft fire was encountered, but all aircraft returned safely to base. One day later, nine crews of 235 Squadron patrolled the The Hague area and covered a landing of British Marines at the Hook of Holland, without loss.

In the late morning of the 14th, six crews of 82 Squadron attempted to block the road east of Breda and cut the railway leading to Tilburg. This was to support the French Seventh Army's attempt to delay the enemy advance in Belgium. Heavy *Flak* upset their aim and the attack was unsuccessful. The main target for the AASF's crews on 14th May were the Meuse crossing points at Sedan, where the Germans had already set up a bridgehead. It was imperative to destroy these bridges to at least delay the German advance for a few precious hours.

During the afternoon, successive waves of Blenheims and Battles attacked bridges and troop concentrations in this area, but the price they paid for their daring was horrible; 40 out of 71 bombers failed to return. The French Armee de l'Air threw in most of its remaining bombers, but they too were badly mauled by fighters and *Flak*.

With the rapid advance of the victorious *Wehrmacht*, the main targets of the AASF and 2 Group shifted to the south at the end of 14th May. Moreover, the Dutch armed forces laid down their arms on this day, after only five days of war. The heart of Rotterdam had been brutally bombed out in mid-afternoon on the 14th by He111s of *KG 54*. There was no choice for the Dutch Commander-in-Chief but to give in. The Dutch government had already fled to England early on the 14th to carry on with the battle from London.

Over Dutch territory, few RAF sorties were flown in the following weeks. In the six weeks between the invasion of Holland and the fall of France, the RAF Blenheim crews fought like tigers. Day in, day out, enemy troops, armoured columns, bridges and other front-line targets were raided and the coastal areas patrolled. The price was very high. More than 200 Blenheims were lost and the majority of the crews that had gone into battle on 10th May were dead, missing or reported PoW by the end of June. The AASF and 2 Group reported 167 aircrew killed in action. Almost all these men were pre-war, well-trained regulars and the losses were felt deeply at squadron and group level. Sir Charles Portal's anxious thoughts on the deployment of the Blenheim on the eve of the German invasion in May had sadly come true. On the 16th May, Group Captain Hugh Pughe-Lloyd, Senior Air Staff Officer (SASO) in 2 Group, commented in his private diary on the insupportably high losses:

"Bulletins mention 69 Battles and Blenheims from France as having gone out to attack advancing German columns. We lost 35. On the 12th May we also sent out 69; 35 failed to return. This goes to prove that the aeroplane is not a battlefield weapon and should be used a long way back. Against that is the fact that we haven't a bomber which can penetrate the enemy defences in daylight... we have no day bomber in our armoury."

On 19th May he added:

"There is precious little left in this Group. The cream has gone; lost, squandered."

Chapter Three
Holding the Line

*Offensive Blenheim operations during the Battle of
Britain, June till September 1940.*

With the fall of France, Great Britain was on her own and an
invasion of Britain was expected in the near future. Still, by the
end of June, Hitler still had doubts about the necessity of an
invasion of Great Britain. With her back to the wall, the British
government would now surely give in and sue for peace with
victorious Nazi Germany - or so Hitler thought. Still, on 16th
July the Führer issued his *Guideline for the Conduct of War
Nr.16*. This directive exposed for the first time the procedures
for an invasion of England, under the code-name *Seelöwe* ('Sea
Lion'). This landing, between Brighton and Folkestone, would
consist of a combined operation of paratroopers and ground
forces to be brought in by modified barges. The German Navy
and *Luftwaffe* were to safeguard the invasion forces. For the
time being however, it was crystal clear that no invasion was
possible without air superiority over southeast England. It was
intended that the Luftwaffe was to ensure this superiority over
RAF Fighter Command. Hitler even hoped that absolute
Luftwaffe air superiority over southern England would lead to
Britain suing for peace, which would remove the necessity of a
landing altogether. This, in turn, would enable the *Führer* to
turn his full attention to the East, where Russia threatened to
take control over the Rumanian oil fields, so vital for Germany.

In the meantime, the German Navy gathered as many barges
as possible in the harbours of Northern France, Belgium and
the Netherlands. In all, some 2,400 vessels were swiftly
converted into invasion barges. Most of these had a loading
capacity of 500-800 tons. In Holland, barges were ferried to
Flushing and Rotterdam from the end of June. From the port of
Rotterdam, the 17th and 35th Infantry Divisions were to be
shipped for disembarking on the coast just South of Folkestone.
In all, by the end of August a fleet of 3,000 vessels was ready to

sail for the invasion from the coastal harbours of the Low Countries and northern France.

It was of crucial importance to Great Britain to destroy this Armada. If there were no barges, there could be no invasion. While Fighter Command went into battle with her much stronger adversary over England, the RAF bombers incessantly pounded the concentrations of invasion ships during the summer of 1940. At night, the Hampdens, Wellingtons, Whitleys and even the obsolete Fairey Battles attacked the enemy ports - while the 2 Group Blenheims, both by day and night, carried on the offensive. Bomber Command Wellingtons bore the brunt of the attacks on Rotterdam and Flushing harbour; Blenheims of 2 Group did attack the barges in these ports but only with limited success. Coastal Command also played a crucial part in the Battle of Britain. Her Ansons, Hudsons and Blenheims flew daily anti-invasion patrols along the enemy coasts to keep a close eye on German shipping movement.

Before exploring further the Blenheim anti-invasion effort during the Battle of Britain, attention should be paid to another type of operation that was devised in these months. On 5th June, Bomber Command H.Q. sent a new directive to 2 Group. From this day, the Blenheim crews had to carry out cloud cover 'hit-and-run' attacks by day, both in the Occupied countries and in Germany. With this tactic, the RAF aimed to force the enemy to deploy Bf109s for defensive purposes, thus spreading the fighter force and preventing it from being used offensively as escort fighters over Great Britain. Thus, 2 Group's Blenheims were to be used in a tactical role of 'bait' for the German fighters - which would prove to be a rather hazardous business. In order to give the Blenheims some protection on these operations, the directive emphasized that these raids should only be executed when sufficient cloud cover (7/10th) was available over enemy territory. The result, by nature of these operations, was a high percentage of early returns.

The brilliant summer weather in 1940 prevented a real start to be made of the cloud cover offensive until the autumn of the year. Therefore, the Blenheim crews would, for the time being, concentrate mainly on surprise attacks on coastal targets. The adventures of 82 Squadron, which officially opened the offensive on 21st June, are illustrative of the low efficiency of the cloud cover raids during the Battle of Britain. Of the ten crews despatched to Bremen's oil refinery, only three pressed on due to lack of cloud cover over enemy territory. Two of these bombed targets of opportunity, Haamstede and Schiphol airfields. Only one dare-devil crew reached Bremen and bombed the primary target.

When the Blenheims pressed on with little or no clouds to hide in and then ran into German fighters, losses were usually heavy. No.235 Fighter Blenheim Squadron was to experience this painfully on Thursday 27th June 1940. Pilot Officer Hugh Wakefield served as an observer with 235 Squadron from April to November 1940 and tells of this particular operation:

"We were to undertake a visual and photographic recce of the Amsterdam and Zuider Zee area to try to establish the presence and strength of German naval units, this to include Texel and the islands off the German and Dutch coasts in the vicinity. We were informed that the British Army were very interested in this operation and requested any information as to the movement and disposition of German Army units in the area we were ordered to survey. However, no information was offered as to how we could provide reliable data. Finally, Bomber Command asked us to undertake a square-search for a bomber aircraft believed to have ditched the previous evening off Ijmuiden. In the Operations Room at Bircham Newton our CO Squadron Leader Nobby Clarke recommended sending one aircraft in the belief that a lone aircraft was less likely to create a response from the German air force. He was overruled by Group who stated that the information required was so important that six aircraft should ensure a positive outcome to this sortie. And so the scene was set!

"We were airborne in N3542 at 12.55 with six Mark IVf long-nosed Blenheims, four Brownings under the mainframe and the odd Browning fitted to the wings. This was done under something, which in those distant days was called Squadron Mods (modifications) which meant that if you wanted additional guns fitted in the wings, an additional gun in the rear turret, or indeed - and I had one for a short spell - a gun fitted to the nose of the observer's cabin, you had but to ask the Flight Sergeant Engineer who would install with little thought as to whether or not we could take off with the additional load.

"Flight Lieutenant Andy Fletcher led the first flight of three Blenheims with my pilot Flying Officer (Pissey) Peacock leading the second flight of three on the port side. We approached the Dutch coast flying at about 5,000 feet. There was no cloud at all over the sea but there was cumulus over land, which appeared to be about 9/10ths. This however was an illusion as the cloud was at 5,000 feet and when we crossed the coast at Noordwijk aan Zee it turned out to be about 2/10th fractured cumulus with a lot of clear blue sky in between.

"We crossed the coast heading for Amsterdam, flew over Schiphol, which was cluttered with German aircraft, some of which appeared to be taking off to attack our sortie. What is totally clear to me is perhaps the most stunning, glorious and frightening moment of my life when (and I may have the count wrong and, perhaps, this was understandable in the circumstances) some 18 Bf109's shot out of the glorious but little cloud there was, in a head on attack straight at us. It looked a stupendous sight and it lasted for 2-3 minutes before we found ourselves as a broken formation milling around the sky with Bf109's as our dancing partners.

"Before getting back to the narrative I should point out that the Bf109 was capable of 360 mph, the Blenheim Mark IV 280 mph but with four Brownings under the belly this top speed dropped to around 255 mph although a booster called Plus 9 would give additional speed but only for a short while before the engines were damaged. But, and this is important, a Blenheim could easily turn inside a 109 if we knew precisely when to do it. To this end, we had devised a system as a result of an encounter with a Bf110. When we were under attack I moved back from the navigator's position, opened the cockpit behind the pilot, stuck my head out looking rearward and signalled my pilot with my thumb exactly when and in which direction to turn.

"We were first attacked by a '109 somewhere south of Schiphol from the upper rear port side. He closed to around 400 yards, I signalled pilot hard left, the '109 overshot, we turned hard right and got in a burst as he went away, the result of which we could not ascertain. We were then attacked by a '109 coming in from above and to the right with somewhat similar results. We may have hit one or both aircraft but this I rather doubt."

We now leave Pilot Officer Hugh Wakefield and Sergeant Aubrey Lancaster the observer in Pilot Officer John Cronan's crew takes up the story when they were attacked by the Bf109's. These, in fact, were fighters of *I./JG 76* and *I./JG 21*, scrambled from Soesterberg airfield to intercept the 235 Squadron formation:

"From the outset this trip had a no return feeling. However the trip across the North Sea was uneventful and we finally crossed the Dutch coast just North of the Maas and Scheldt estuaries when we turned North towards Amsterdam. We continued on this course for a few minutes when suddenly we were beset with German fighters - Messerschmitts and all hell was let loose. We were the subject of a burst of machine-gun fire, which ripped through the length of the aircraft, killing the gunner and hitting the pilot in the shoulder. I got a slight crease on my left leg but I was OK.

"The pilot slumped over the stick and I leaned over to try and help him out of his seat so that I could take over (I had learned to fly for just such an occasion). However my efforts to move him brought him round and he sat back to try and fly the aircraft but as soon as he moved the stick he realised that the controls had been shot away. He yelled at me to get out (note we were told that we should never go out of the top hatch of a Blenheim because you would almost certainly be hit by the tail and that the escape should be from the forward downward hatch in the nose). I went immediately to the hatch and pulled the opening mechanism but apart from showing daylight round the edges refused to budge. I banged it, jumped on it, cursed it but it remained closed. I remember (by this time we were about 2000 feet) heading for a herd of cattle and thinking what a mess there would be when we hit.

"Although this takes a long time to tell they are mainly thoughts that flashed through my mind in seconds. Realising that there was no future in the forward hatch I turned to the main top hatch, noticing as I turned that the gunner's body was riddled with bullets. The pilot must have seen what was happening to me and got out through the top hatch so that I could get out by standing on his seat. This I set out to do but suddenly remembered about the tail coming along. I deliberated for a second or so to see if there was any way in which I could get on to the wing and drop off that way.

"There was no escape that way and whilst I was thinking there was a sudden jerk and a bang and I was both out of the aircraft and also knocked unconscious. This probably lasted only a second or so but when I came to I was tumbling head over heels. I went to pull the rip-cord but my parachute wasn't there and when I looked around me there it was floating about above my head - unopened, but still attached to my shoulders. I pulled it down towards me and pulled the rip-cord and watched the canopy open up and thought what a big thing it was. I then looked down at the ground and hit the ground almost immediately.

"I picked myself up and made my way to a small cottage farm where an old farmer and his wife were looking fearfully round the door. They asked me inside and told them, using English and German, that I was English but had great difficulty in making them understand me. I had not been there more than a few minutes when a Dutch Doctor and nurse appeared and they bandaged my leg and arm. A few minutes later a Dutch policeman appeared who told me that he was forced to take me prisoner. We then proceeded, in the Doctor's car (an old Renault with a wash-board radiator) to where my pilot lay. He had done what was usually expected and hit the tail with the side of his face, which was a horrible mess. Whilst I was stood there wondering what would happen to me a German motorcycle and sidecar roared up and a *Leutnant* told me that I was his prisoner and would I ride on the pillion or in the side-car - I opted for the side-car.

"I was taken from there to a house-boat on a canal just outside Schiphol Airport entrance where the Jerries seemed to have established an HQ. After listening to some lengthy discussions as to what they should do with me it was discovered that *Luftwaffe* PoWs were received at Frankfurt am Main and, as it happened, there was a *Major* in the area who was going there. He offered to take me and we roared off through Holland to Arnhem and the German border where an *autobahn* started. We travelled overnight through the Ruhr and got to Frankfurt by about 9am the next morning. It eventually transpired that of the six Blenheims in the raid, four were shot down and I was the sole survivor."

Pilot Officer Hugh Wakefield now brings his story of the disastrous 27th June operation to an end:

"At the end of the engagement with the Bf109's we found ourselves alone in about 5/10ths cloud well to the South of Schiphol. We talked and decided that it would be unwise to return the way we entered and so we flew South to Amsterdam, photographed the harbour with no signs of German naval units - flew along the inner coast of the Zuider Zee and passed Hoorn to Texel. We then sighted a Heinkel 115 floatplane proceeding from Texel in the direction of Den Helder at about 2,000 feet. They fired off a 4-star recognition cartridge (presumably thinking we were German). We replied with a 2-star signal, closed, and emptied our remaining ammunition into this aircraft, which appeared to drop towards the sea. But whether it was actually shot down is a matter of some conjecture. We then attempted to photograph the harbour at Den Helder but were fired on by German naval units, so we at once set course for home.

"During these various engagements we lost through G-force most of the pilot's canopy and the side and front perspex windows, so we returned in a somewhat draughty condition to base at Bircham Newton.

"The aircrew losses in my squadron at that time were very heavy and, because we were posted away in November 1940 to form new squadrons or to train new aircrews, we never really knew what happened to our missing aircrew. Were they killed or were they PoW.? There was a strange story of a pilot Pilot Officer Wales who flew with us that day and was shot down on 27th June. It was reported that he died on 30th June 1940 flying an Allied aircraft (Dutch or French) when he was attempting to return to England. How true this is I do not know."

Alas, Hugh Wakefield's story about Pilot Officer Wales is not true. Together with his observer and gunner, he died in Blenheim N3543 on 27th June 1940. This aircraft, shot down at 15.30 hours by *Leutnant* Schypek of *2./JG 76*, crashed between Oegstgeest and Leiden. The three men were laid to rest at the cemetery of the Green Church at Oegstgeest. Apart from Aubrey Lancaster, of the men in the other three downed aircraft of 235 Squadron, no one survived. Seven of the crews are buried in the Netherlands at The Hague, Nijmegen, Amsterdam and Bergen-op-Zoom. 235 suffered a severe blow, as the crews of the four fighter Blenheims shot down represented virtually all that was left of the original squadron.

Pilot Officer Steve Hebron served as an observer with 235 Squadron in 1940 and early 1941. He was one of the lucky few to survive the disaster on 27th June 1940 and gives his opinion of the Blenheim as a fighter aircraft:

"I spent the year March 1940/March 1941 in reconnaissance flights over the North Sea and along the Frisian Islands, Heligoland Bight and the west coast of Denmark and the main problem was that our Blenheims were much too slow. They had the range to cover the coasts of Denmark and Norway but were easy meat for the Bf109, being more than 100 m.p.h. slower, whereas Spitfires and Hurricanes, which could take on the Bf109 did not have the range. The Spitfire and Hurricane were of course much faster but in these days their range was very short and there was no alternative to the fighter Blenheim for daylight reconnaissance as it had the range, but was no match for the Bf109. Looking back, after more than fifty years, the Blenheim seems to have been pretty inadequate for the work it was called on to do. The Fighter version was accurately described in the official RAF history as a 'makeshift' fighter.

"On 27th June 1940, Group insisted that six Blenheims should be used. The theory was that six Blenheims in formation could defend themselves and see off any opposition, including Bf109s. It was a complete fallacy. It is true that the Blenheim had a power turret, but it only held one .303 Vickers 'K' gun with ammunition pans of 100 rounds, whereas the Bf109 was at least 100 m.p.h. faster and could pick and choose its method of attack. It is difficult to understand the insistence that the mission should be attempted by a formation, rather than by a single aircraft, as the theory that bombers in formation could defend themselves against much faster fighters had already been disproved (The 18th December 1939 Wellington disaster, T.B.). Still, theories can be persistent and, on July 13th, 235 was once more ordered to carry out a daylight recce with six Blenheims, this time of the Elbe and Weser, again looking for invasion barges. This time, we did not see any barges or fighters."

Sergeant Rodney Steele, WOp/AG with 235 Squadron during the Battle of Britain, reflects on the fighter Blenheim:

"We were flying the latest type of aircraft - there was nothing better to our knowledge anyway and we liked what we had. As a fighter it was a bit heavy and not very manoeuvreable compared with a Spit' or a Hurricane. However, we liked it and felt fairly safe! I thoroughly enjoyed flying in the Blenheim as we never had any failures, but it was never any match with Jerry - hence the big losses. I was just lucky!"

As a typical day's operation for the RAF Blenheims in the Summer of 1940, we now look closely at 18th July 1940. A Blenheim of 82 Squadron attacked twenty barges West of Pernis/Rotterdam, but no results were observed. Another 82 Squadron Blenheim flew an armed recce to the Zuiderzee area, with only a few ships observed.

Coastal Command Blenheims of 53 and 235 Squadrons were also active off the Dutch coast on 18th July. A 53 Squadron crew bombed Flushing harbour but no results were observed. Pilot

Officer Hugh Wakefield, observer in Flying Officer Peacock's crew with 235 Squadron, tells us of his squadron's operations on this day:

"235 Squadron had had a busy day escorting RN Destroyers laying mines off the Dutch and German coasts. We returned around 14.30. Later that day we were ordered to fighter escort six Hudson bombers in a night attack on German Naval Units at Emden. The escort comprised three Fighter Blenheims of 235 Squadron. We set off at 22.07, it was the first time the squadron had taken part in a night operation. As I remember it, and I have a very clear recollection of this particular sortie, there was little cloud and a partial moon. With 300 miles to target we carried four 250lb. bombs. We were about at 8/10,000 feet, the Hudsons below and ahead of us were clear over the North Sea but disappeared over the region of Texel. We continued on track for Emden. This was my first night sortie over Germany and I was interested in the scale of the thunder and lightning until I realised that we were being subject to heavy but not very accurate anti-aircraft fire. We dropped our four 250lbs on Emden (I wonder?) and set course for home.

"You will appreciate that in those days navigation at night was not as precise as it later became, 300 miles or so later we were either over 1: The Thames, 2: Ipswich or indeed even the Wash. Flight Lieutenant Fletcher in command of the leading flight of three Blenheims had more petrol left than we did and suggested that if we were short of petrol we should land at Fakenham in Norfolk. This airfield proved to be a dummy to collect German bombs and we eventually landed at an airfield near Bircham Newton with almost empty tanks."

Of all the Blenheim sorties on 18th July 1940, one aircraft of 53 Squadron failed to return. Blenheim IV R3661 took off from Detling for an armed reconnaissance of Flushing harbour, but was intercepted and shot down by a Bf109 of *6./JG 54* into the mouth of the River Scheldt. Flying Officer Joe Mahony and crew were killed in the crash. The pilot and observer are still missing and are commemorated on the Runnymede panels 6 and 16. The body of Sergeant Exton, the WOp/AG, washed ashore and was buried at Adagem in Belgium. Flying Officer Mahony and crew was the first operational loss from 53 Squadron in the Dutch coast area. Together with 59 Squadron, this Blenheim unit of Army Co-operation Command was transferred to Coastal Command in early July 1940 for the vitally important anti-invasion reconnaissance sorties off the Low Countries and France. The squadrons' crews were kept busy surveying and photographing the build-up of the German invasion barges fleet at Flushing, Hook of Holland and Rotterdam harbours each day. They also carried out shipping and harbour attacks when the opportunity arose. Flight Lieutenant Dick Maydwell served as a pilot with 53 Squadron in this period and he recounts the operational activities of the squadron in the Summer of 1940:

"No. 53 Squadron took part in the battle for France during May and June 1940 and was employed on long distance Army Co-operation tasks. The aircrew were well trained in map reading at low level and reported the position and movements of enemy armoured and infantry formations. Also taking oblique air photographs, whenever possible. However, after the evacuation from France and, with the imminent threat of invasion, No. 53 Squadron was transferred to Coastal Command and was active in bombing the Channel ports in order to disrupt the build-up of large numbers of ships and barges. Army Officers in our squadron, who were skilled in tank recognition, now had to turn their attention to ship recognition. Personally, I did not find this difficult, because in 1933, I served aboard a tramp steamer, which sailed to Aalborg in Denmark with coal, and then went on to St. Petersburg in Russia to load pit-props for Hull. I could therefore estimate the tonnage and type of various ships at a glance.

"In July 1940, our squadron was stationed at R.A.F. Detling, which was a grass airfield near Maidstone. My second operational flight from Detling in a Blenheim was a night raid on 20th July against the Vlaardingen oil refinery in Rotterdam. Six Blenheims took off in the evening and planned to be over-the river leading up to Rotterdam at nautical twilight (which is twenty minutes later than last light on the ground). Our aircraft were in open formation at 4,000 feet and dived down on the huge refinery, which was clearly visible. I crossed it at 100 feet and dropped my bombs. It was a very exciting experience. Some heavy bursts of accurate light AA came very close to my starboard wing as I turned across the river and headed for home. The shells were so close to my aircraft that I could hear them crack as they passed. I was now flying at fifty feet in the moonlight following the river and managed to escape without damage. Our raid certainly set fire to two of the large storage tanks. Later, photo-recce revealed that with so few aircraft in the attack, we had not done much damage to such a vast complex. However, at least we had hit the target and all our aircraft returned safely.

"On 23rd, 24th and 31st July, I flew sorties to Ijmuiden and Amsterdam. Visibility for bombing was fairly good, because of the reflection of moonlight from the water in the canal leading to Amsterdam. Our navigation aids on the return flights to Detling were very primitive. The black-out was very effective. One aircraft hit a balloon cable over Dover, but managed to land at Manston. Another aircraft got lost and landed in the marshes in the Thames Estuary and the crew were killed.

"Our losses in aircraft were not bad. I estimate one aircraft in thirty sorties, but of course, over the next couple of months, they added up and we lost a lot of friends. The quality of aircrew in the squadron was very high, particularly the replacement pilots, most of whom were University students. Their loss so early in the war was very sad. When I was finally posted from the squadron to an OTU in December 1940, I was in actual fact the last survivor of the 21 pilots that went to France in September 1939. The others were killed, PoW or sick.

"During July and August 1940, the squadron flew a large number of low level daylight cross-over patrols fairly close to the Dutch coast to ensure that enemy forces could be located and attacked in the North Sea. Later in August, September and October, Hook of Holland-Ostend (*HOOKOS*) patrols were carried out every night to keep a track of enemy convoys steaming along the Dutch and Belgian coasts."

During these cross-over and *HOOKOS* patrols in the critical period of the Battle of Britain and while attacking targets along the Dutch coast, 53 Squadron lost a considerable number of aircraft and crews. In all, 10 Blenheims were lost and 21 crew members were killed. One of the 53 Squadron pilots that failed to return was the squadron C.O., Wing Commander 'Sphinx' Edwards. On the night of 31 August, T1940:D was shot down in flames while bombing the oil refinery at Pernis/Rotterdam. Edwards and Sergeants Benjamin and Beesley were killed instantly when their Blenheim crashed in the target area. Flight Lieutenant Dick Maydwell recounts this loss:

"Our courageous, efficient and much admired Commanding Officer, Wing Commander Edwards, was shot down and killed in a low level raid on Vlaardingen Oil Refinery. War is such a sad human struggle, so often the best pilots and aircrew 'get the chop'".

Sergeant Bill Service, a Canadian observer with 53 Squadron, also gives us an impression of his CO:

"On July 31st Wing Commander Edwards was my pilot on a strike at Emden. It was supposed to be in formation, but a little over half-way there we ran into an unexpected frontal system and had to break formation and go it alone. The Wing Commander had had a previous crash that culminated with a steel plate in his jaw. He always pressed home his attack at a low level and would scare the wits out of you wondering when he would level off, so the poor joker in the nose could line up and drop the bombs. I was with him again on August 22nd on a midnight raid on the German fighter aerodrome at St. Omer. It was another hair-raising trip. In September he was hit attacking the oil tanks at Rotterdam. He was seen to be pressing home the attack as usual when he got a direct hit and went straight in. I never met a man as dedicated as he was."

Bill Service now tells us of his experiences in the Summer and Fall of 1940. After having seen quite some action during the Battle of France in May and June, his crew was sent back to England. His crew was then heavily involved in anti-invasion patrols and shipping and coastal target attacks from July till

October 1940, as Bill's account clearly illustrates:

"My pilot was Pilot Officer Stanley Collins and the WOp/AG was Leading Aircraftsman, later Sergeant, Arthur Cowling. I was a Sergeant at that time. On July 3rd the squadron moved to Detling near Maidstone in Kent. The squadron returned to operational duties under Coastal Command. Uppermost on everyone's mind was Dunkirk, the Battle of Britain and the forthcoming invasion. On July 7th we did our first North Sea patrol, as far as Texel island. It was coded as (SA9). We tried to keep an aircraft on patrol whatever the weather, as the threat of invasion was very real. We did about eight of these patrols. No bombs were carried on these trips as we were to carry out a full patrol of the coastline.

"We did our last patrol on September 9th. I guess the invasion threat had eased somewhat, so we concentrated on bombing the coastal ports, barges and shipping. We dropped our first bombs on July 13th at Zeebrugge. It was nice to be able to retaliate after all the recces and patrols we had done. Also, shortly after the squadron arrived at Detling, four Ju88's carpet-bombed the airfield. Sergeant Cowling and I were caught in the centre of the landing strip and a few prayers were said as we hastily pulled off our helmets from the gas mask bag and tried to disappear into the grass field. I don't know of anything worse than laying there watching the bombs falling and then the first distant explosions at the far end of the field. In a matter of seconds the bombs burst up to us, over us, and then receded down the field. We both felt things hitting us, but we escaped unscathed. They were simply clods of mud and tufts of sod grass. Arthur was lucky as one small bomb crater was about fifteen feet away. There was some satisfaction to hear that three Ju88's had been shot down on their way home. It would seem they loved to catch the English at their 4 o'clock tea time break, which was where we were going.

"July 20th there was a dusk raid on the oil tank farm at Rotterdam. The oil tanks were well defended with heavy AA and *Flak*, but there was a good fire going when we left. July 23rd was a dusk raid on the docks and barges at Amsterdam. It was well defended with AA batteries. On July 26th we carried a mix of bombs and mines to the Rotterdam area. The bombs were dropped on a heavy accumulation of barges and the mines (12-pounders I think) were dropped in one of the canals. It was a cloudy night and map reading the area was difficult. I ended up over the sea, and it took a while to get re-orientated due to all the water, islands and canals we were flying over. However we did find our drop area and completed the mission. Pilot Officer Ritchie was the pilot on that trip as Pilot Officer Collins was sick. July 31 Wing Commander Edwards was the pilot on a strike at Emden. I was with Wing Commander Edwards again on August 22nd on a midnight raid on the German fighter aerodrome at St. Omer. The evening of August 12th the targets were the docks and barges at Den Helder and we had a good fire going when we left. On August 13th there was a very bad raid on Detling with *Stuka* dive bombers and an escort of '109s. Between the two squadrons we lost about twenty aircraft on the ground. However none of the Stukas got back to France. They told me that 'Lord Haw-Haw' in his news that night said that 'Detling ground crew run like scared rabbits'. It was more like the aircrew from what I remember of my antics. August 25th we did a night raid in the Ostend area. September 5th was a night reconnaissance around Dunkirk, Calais and Boulogne, but there were no concentrations of shipping or barges. September 7th a night strike on Boulogne docks.

"On September 8th we did a night strike on shipping off the Hook of Holland and set one ship on fire about four miles off Ostend. September 9th a daylight attack on about forty ships off Ostend. September 11th we attacked enemy shipping at Zeebrugge and Ostend. On October 1st we did a night patrol of the Ijmuiden and Ostend areas. Oct 6 a daylight attack on Le Touquet aerodrome. October 7th a night raid on docks and barges at Rotterdam. There was heavy *Flak* and AA. October 9th another daylight raid on Le Touquet aerodrome. October 10th a night raid on docks and shipping at Den Helder. Moderate *Flak* and AA. October 13th a night raid on Flushing but clouds forced us to bomb the alternate target - Zeebrugge. October 14th a night patrol off Ijmuiden and Ostend. All quiet this night. October 21st a night strike on Boulogne docks and shipping and a close shave with a balloon. October 24th we did a daylight raid on Ijmuiden and the Hook of Holland. We spotted two hospital ships and seven MVs off the Hook. We had permission to attack the hospital ships, as they were not being used according to the rules of the Geneva Convention. However we did not. October 25th we did a night raid on Antwerp. There was some light and heavy *Flak*.

"The Oct 25th raid was operation No.44 for me. At that time no one knew how many trips you had to do to complete a tour. The next morning Pilot Officer Collins met us and said there is a decision to be made. We have finished our tour and can go back to Andover as a Screen Crew. Or we can do ten more trips and we would each receive medals. We went to the nearby town of Maidstone that night and, over dinner at the hotel and a few beers, individually decided our future. I was tired and was sure this war would last at least as long as World War I. So I opted for a rest as Screen Crew. Collins agreed and said he would go back to Andover. Cowling decided to do ten more trips, which would entitle him to receive a DFM.

"Unfortunately a few weeks after Collins and I had returned to Andover, word came through that Cowling was missing in action. He was on the third of his ten extra operational trips. A sad day for me, as he was a great friend to have. Pilot Officer Collins was a very steady and reliable pilot when on operations. He came down with lung TB and spent some time at a Sanatorium near Torquay. He passed away some time in 1941. During my first tour of operations, many crews and a good many friends failed to return, but my thoughts and feelings during that period were always positive. Somehow I felt that we would always make it back. I think a top-notch crew alongside you helps to build up the morale.

"The bombing raids we carried out on the docks, barges, oil tanks and aerodromes, I can only guess at the damage we did. We seldom heard about the results of our forays, although the operations officer debriefed us thoroughly after each strike. I can remember a rumour that the Germans had heavily increased the defence with AA guns at the oil storage tanks at Rotterdam, after they had emptied the oil tanks. When we attacked they would light fires to make it look like we had made some direct hits. I never did find out if there was any truth to it."

In addition to the anti-invasion patrols that the Blenheim crews flew during the Summer of 1940, another type of operation gained importance. These were daylight cloud cover raids against *Luftwaffe* aerodromes in the Low Countries and France, which the Germans now started using for their bombing raids against Great Britain. In order to counter this threat, Blenheims of 2 Group started a bombing campaign against these targets by mid-June. Schiphol airfield was the first target on the 19th, when six aircraft of 110 Squadron out of a force of eighteen Blenheims pressed on despite brilliant sunshine and a complete lack of cloud cover. The crews successfully bombed the dispersals of the aerodrome south of Amsterdam and suffered no losses. Despite this promising start of the campaign, the statistics for June indicate a high percentage of early returns on daylight cloud cover raids. Sufficient cloud cover was seldom present in the persistent fine summer weather. Of 82 sorties only 22 resulted in bombing attacks and five Blenheims were lost in the process over Holland. Also, whenever the primary target for a Blenheim crew was situated in Germany but cloud cover was not sufficient to press-on, *Luftwaffe* airfields in the Low Countries were raided as secondary targets. Schiphol airfield was a popular target for the Blenheim crews, being situated near the Dutch coast and always a tempting target for a hit-and-run attack. On 19th July, Group Captain. Hugh Pughe-Lloyd, SASO at 2 Group, commented in his private diary on the disappointing cloud cover Blenheim offensive:

"The weather is most disappointing, it is clear by day with a sort of 6 to 8-tenths covering and that is a deathtrap when we rely on cloud cover. One got through to the Ruhr today - fourteen failed to do so. The same every day -the same with aerodromes. The crews become so bored with it that they take chances - a sort of determined hardening of the will to do it today sort of feeling. That is how we lose them and we have to be so careful in insisting on cloud cover."

One Blenheim pilot who experienced the frustrations of aborted cloud cover operations was Sergeant Les Spong, pilot with 139 Squadron. His log book entries during the Summer and Autumn of 1940 are typical: no less than seven out of thirteen daylight sorties aborted due to lack of cloud cover, with another two aborted due to bad visibility or storms. In order to bring down the high number of abortive cloud cover sorties, each 2 Group station was ordered to dispatch a Blenheim early in the morning for a weather recce off the enemy coast. This indeed helped raising the effectiveness of the cloud cover offensive as Sergeant George 'Jock' Shinnie, WOp/AG in 139 Squadron, recalls:

> "Although I found single aircraft bombing sorties, whether low level or using cloud cover extremely exhilarating, often frightening, I must admit that my greatest satisfaction came as wireless operator during the long weather and shipping recces. Good early morning weather reports were of paramount importance to the success or otherwise of 2 Groups overall operations for the day in question. On a typical early morning sortie prescribed areas were probed overland by single aircraft using cloud cover or low level techniques. After retreating rapidly the weather reports were passed to base using a simple code. The process was repeated as each area was penetrated. To me it was most rewarding in as much that I proved it was possible to send reports over a long range at fairly low altitudes provided the operator calibrated his transmitter meticulously prior to each flight."

A typical day in the Blenheim cloud cover offensive in the summer of 1940 was the 29th July 1940. Twelve Blenheims of 82 Squadron were sent off to the oil refineries at Hamburg, with airfields in the Netherlands as secondary targets. Of this force, only five crews carried out bombing attacks, with three of these raiding targets in Holland. Two crews bombed barges in the canal of Groningen but scored no hits. The third crew, Flight Lieutenant Bill Keighley and crew in R3619, decided not to press on to the primary target due to lack of cloud cover and bombed Leeuwarden airfield instead. However, two Bf109s of *II./JG 27* scrambled from Leeuwarden and intercepted the raider over the Frisian coast. Before reaching the safety of a cloud-bank, the Blenheim was riddled by cannon fire of *Leutnant* Herbert Kargel's Messerschmitt, which killed the gunner. Keighley had no alternative but to crash-land his Blenheim in a cornfield at Texel Island and the two survivors were taken PoW. The second Blenheim of 82 Squadron that took off from Watton for Hamburg was R3821 of Pilot Officer Donald Wellings and crew. Observer was Sergeant Don McFarlane:

> "We took off at 09.50, target was the oil storage tanks at the Hamburg docks. We planned this operation with some trepidation, thinking it a

near-suicidal mission by single aircraft in daylight during the glorious summer weather conditions of that year. We set course for the middle of the Zuider Zee, aiming for Hannover as a feint, intending to alter course at the Wannsee to roughly northeast, thence turning to follow the course of the River Elbe into Hamburg. We now know that the Germans had primitive radar, but the Gods must have been with us and, over the North Sea, climbing to stay above thickening cloud and driving rain, we crossed the Zuider Zee in a severe electrical storm.

"However, the outcome was that after leaving the East coast of the Zuider Zee, the weather cleared miraculously. We dived and found ourselves crossing Holland at 5,000 feet in a clear blue sky, dotted only with small cotton-wool puffs of summer cumulus cloud. From being extremely anxious and tense at the outset of the flight, I now found myself very calm, probably relieved at not having been struck by lightning in the fierce storm. I was even looking around with detached interest at the surrounding countryside, even having plenty of time to make out a reconnaissance report of a long train carrying tanks and other no-doubt military items towards the west.

"We followed our plan to the letter and eventually made a shallow dive-bombing attack on the oil storage tanks. As soon as the bombs were released, the anti-aircraft guns opened up and, with their usual accuracy, were closing rapidly on our tail. Our dive took us over the German fighter aerodrome at Stade, which we flew across at 1,000 feet and could see fighters taxiing to their take-off point. But we were in full flight and went on to cross the coast between Cuxhaven and Wilhelmshaven and thence out to sea.

"Our troubles were not over yet, as the air gunner pointed out three dots on our starboard quarter, which turned to follow us and became closer, being identified as Bf109's. We increased our speed to a maximum of about 275mph and dropped to sea level. After a few minutes the fighters peeled off and flew east: we could only think that they had been on patrol and were short of fuel. Flying close to the Frisians we sped on and then flew northwest over the sea to Watton and home, returning at 15.05. On our way into the target we had set the camera running and the resultant line-overlap, when developed and printed, showed a liner, either the *Bremen* or *Europa*, in Hamburg docks, with steam up. We heard later that a squadron of Hampdens were sent out that night to pay her some attention."

From 3rd July 2 Group's campaign against the *Luftwaffe* airfields in Occupied Territories was intensified. This immediately resulted in mounting losses; no less than 31 Blenheims were lost in July. Of these aircraft, 12 came down on Dutch territory. In order to counter these heavy losses somewhat, night intruder attacks were commenced from mid-July.

After the capitulation of Holland in May, the aerodromes at Leeuwarden, Gilze Rijen, Schiphol, Twenthe and dozens of other airfields were expanded very rapidly. Squadrons of He111 and Ju88 bombers operated daily against Great Britain from these bases. One of these airfields that was of great strategic importance for the Germans was Leeuwarden aerodrome. Within a few months, the small airstrip just north of the city was expanded into one of the largest airfields in western Europe. During the summer of 1940, over 7,500 Frisian workers laboured for the Germans and a modern airfield was knocked up. To strengthen the runways, the Germans laid rubble from the bombed-out inner city of Rotterdam. While all this work was in progress, 2 Group Blenheims regularly attacked the *Flieger-horst* and, during one of these surprise raids, on 30th July, seven Frisian workers were killed by shrapnel.

Let us now study a few typical dates on which Blenheims of 2 Group flew out to strike aerodromes in the German-Occupied countries beginning with 2nd August 1940. 36 Blenheims were dispatched by 2 Group to attack *Luftwaffe* bases in Holland, Belgium, France and Germany. In Holland, airfields at Soester-berg, Haamstede, Leeuwarden, Schiphol, Texel, Flushing and Waalhaven were on the target list. Of the 36 Blenheims, 24 carried out successful attacks and 10 returned early, mainly due to lack of cloud cover. Nine bombers attacked the airfields at Soesterberg, Schiphol, Haamstede, Waalhaven and Leeuwarden. Three Dutch civilians were killed by bomb blast near Hilversum. Also, a vessel, a railway track and a bridge in the Netherlands were attacked by three crews as targets of opportunity.

As usual, German fighters rose to intercept and six Blenheims were engaged over the Netherlands. One of these aircraft, L9422 of 18 Squadron was shot down by a Bf109 of *II./JG 54* flown by *Leutnant* Malischewski after a successful attack on Haamstede airfield, killing Sergeant John Davies and his crew. The second aircraft lost on this day was L8780 of 110 Squadron, which was damaged by *Flak* during an early morning attack on Soesterberg airfield, injuring the pilot Sergeant Hards. The aircraft crashed on return at Wattisham.

Sergeant George Parr served as an observer with 18 Squadron and 2nd August 1940 was the day of his crew's first operational sortie. George's story vividly illustrates the primi-tive nature of the early-war daylight bombing operations by

Blenheims of 2 Group, when Britain with her back against the wall was fighting the German aggressor:

"The squadron had suffered severe losses in France and the survivors were assembled at Gatwick to re-form with new recruits like us. We were divided according to aircrew category, - pilots, air observers and wireless operator/air gunners, always referred to as WOp/AG's. The senior observer was Sergeant Joe Strong, only pilots being commissioned in those days. We each gave Joe details of our experience and were graded accordingly. I had amassed a total of 50 hours flying as navigator/bomb aimer, including one and a half hours night familiarisation before the war in an Anson aircraft. On the strength of this I was declared qualified for operational flying by day and night, which demonstrates how desperate was the situation. Invasion threatened, and more offensive air action was considered essential, even at the cost of dispensing with the usual Operations Training Course.

"Some time in July we moved up to our operational base at West Raynham in Norfolk, which we shared with 101 Squadron. I was crewed with Flying Officer A.J.Douch, a 'veteran' of 38 hours flying experience on Blenheims. Flying Officer Douch was a calm and sensible officer who had learned to fly at University. In the coming months we were to have good cause to be grateful for John Douch's level-headedness. The third member of the crew, the WOP/AG, was Sergeant Reg Bassett, a cheerful character who must have been the original model of the London Cockney. His small stature was a distinct advantage in the cramped conditions of the gun turret. Before we set out on our first operational mission he, like me, had never seen a Blenheim. Neither had he had any gunnery training.

"On the 1st August we were briefed for our first operation, which was to be on the airfield at Brussels/Evére. As for all the operations that followed we had few explicit instructions. We were given the target, a weather briefing, the appropriate radio frequencies and call-signs and that's about all. Our route, flying height and method of attack were left to us. The only limitation imposed was that if by day the cloud cover fell below eight-tenths we were to abandon the mission. Naturally this left a fair degree of interpretation and initiative to the aircraft captain.

"I prepared my flight plan with the pilot's approval and marked up my chart with great care, and was escorted to the aircraft by the squadron commander himself. The first problem on meeting a Blenheim was to discover how to get into it. The Wing Commander showed me the covered foot-holes in the side of the fuselage and I clambered up on the wing walkway, where he handed me up my parachute and navigation bags and the 'colours of the day', - two colour cartridges to be fired from a Very pistol if we were to come under actual or threatened attack by friendly forces. I lowered the baggage and myself through the hatch onto the seat by the pilot, which was my position for take-off and landing.

"When John Douch and Reggie Bassett had taken their places and the pre-flight checks had been made, the roar of the Mercury engines being run up felt comforting and a few minutes later we were airborne and climbing. I had hardly taken my place in the navigator's office in the transparent nose of the aircraft before Bassett announced on the intercom. that we were recalled to base because of adverse weather conditions. The anti-climax left us with mixed feelings, first of relief, then of disappointment at having failed to complete our first mission.

"We did not have long to wait for another chance. The next day our target was the airfield at Wenzendorff, southeast of Hamburg, at the limit of our range. I planned a route well north of the Dutch and German coasts to avoid detection and then down the Elbe, which would lead us to our target. This was a patently stupid thing to do, since we would have to fly right through the Hamburg defences and the anti-aircraft artillery all along the river. But my first aim was to find the target and to identify and bomb it accurately. We soon learned that these objectives could be achieved with a greater regard for survival.

"All went well at first. We were flying in solid cloud at medium height and after a while I asked the pilot to drop down below cloud for a moment to check our position on a light-ship I had marked on the chart. To my delight, although I did not show it so as to persuade the others of my infallibility, there was the light-ship immediately below us. Some time later the cloud thinned and soon we were flying in bright sunlight and feeling very naked. We saw a seaplane to the south but decided not to go after it while we still had bombs on board and, as we approached Hamburg with not a cloud in sight, the captain wisely decided to turn about and make for the secondary target, which was Leeuwarden airfield in the Netherlands.

"At this stage we committed another indiscretion. Our route passed quite close to Heligoland, so we spent a few minutes circling the island at fairly low level while I took a series of photographs with the Leica hand-held camera issued to us for such purposes. I don't suppose that the pictures would have been of much use, being taken through perspex. We thought that the island was heavily defended, which is why we took the pictures, but the inhabitants must have been asleep or at the cinema, because nobody interfered with us, and we quietly continued on our way towards Leeuwarden.

"I plotted a new track and course and soon we found the sanctuary of the cloud again. Shortly before our estimated time of arrival at the target we dropped below cloud to check our position and make a run in to the airfield. I have a very vivid memory of people in the town of Leeuwarden waving to us enthusiastically, including the driver of a horse-drawn vehicle, whom I took to be the milkman. If any proof were needed that we were fighting on the right side, this was it. However, being unable to wave back, we continued with the job in hand, again, I must say, with more enthusiasm than efficiency.

"From 1,000 feet it was easy to identify a large number of Bf109's distributed about the airfield. I selected the largest group and we turned away to come in on a bombing run at about 800 feet. Not surprisingly several fighters were now taking off with the intention of doing us harm, and indeed the gunner spoke up from the back to announce that there were three Messerschmitts behind us and asked if he should shoot them down. At this Douch showed a remarkable if unjustified sang froid by asking Bassett to keep quiet while we were trying to bomb. Fortunately we were practically at the point of release and the enemy aircraft were not on attack heading. By the time they were we had completed our business and gone. I let go the stick of four 250 pounders, the pilot put on full power and, over Texel, the cloud hid us once more. Fortunately we had attacked on a westerly heading and we escaped without a scratch. As for the results, as always our bombs were fitted with an eleven second explosion delay for our own safety, so that from low level we were not able to see the point of impact. But at 800 feet it was difficult to miss and I am confident that we must have caused some significant damage and perhaps reduced to a small extent the German capacity in the battle for air superiority that was taking place over southern England. At least we were not so naive as to go back to take a look."

Indeed, three Bf109Es of *5./JG 27* were scrambled from Leeuwarden to intercept and shoot down the British intruder, but this was not to be. Sergeant Bassett had a lot of beginners' luck; he shot down the German formation leader! *Hauptmann* Albrecht von Ankum-Frank, Commander of the 5th Flight was mortally hit by .303 bullets and crashed just north of the airfield at Jelsum village.

Only a few days earlier, on 28th July, the WOp/AG of Wing Commander Lart (CO 82 Squadron) shot down a Bf109E of *II./JG 27* near Franeker. On 1st August Leeuwarden was the target for two Blenheims of 101 Squadron. This proved to be a highly successful raid - although the crews didn't observe the results; three Bf109Es of *5./JG 27* were destroyed on the ground. This German fighter unit had been withdrawn from the front-line on 13th July to recuperate from her severe losses in the Battle of Britain. The short 'rest' at Leeuwarden airfield became a memorable and sour one due to the Blenheim attacks on 28th July, 1st and 2nd August. On 5th August the *Staffel* flew back to Normandy and into battle and again the unit was to suffer heavy losses over Southern England. Leeuwarden airfield was now taken over by the He111 bombers of *KG 26*, the 'Lions Wing', which soon started bombing raids on Great Britain.

A few days later, on the 7th August, a Blenheim crew of 82 Squadron scored a chance hit on Haamstede airfield. Although this day has gone down in history as one of the many failed cloud cover raids of the summer of 1940 - only 2 out of 29 despatched Blenheims reached and bombed their targets -

research has revealed that the Germans suffered quite a blow from an 82 Squadron crew. In late afternoon, twelve Blenheims of the squadron took off from Watton to try out a new tactic - high level formation bombing of an enemy aerodrome. The target was Haamstede airfield. The weather however was so atrocious that one by one the crews turned back to base - except one. R3821, flown by Pilot Officer Donald Wellings, Observer Sergeant Don McFarlane and WOp/AG Sergeant Peter Eames, reached Haamstede and Don McFarlane dropped a stick of bombs over the airfield through a gap in the low clouds. What the crew failed to observe, due to the cloud and pouring rain, was that the stick of bombs exploded exactly in the middle of a row of Bf109s that were waiting to take off with their engines ticking over. Two fighters were completely destroyed and four more heavily damaged. Five German airmen were killed and seventeen injured. The *4 Staffel,* of *JG 54* had had a break from operations at Haamstede for a few weeks and was now ready to fly back to France to re-commence operations in the Battle of Britain. The 82 Squadron attack effectively prevented this and *4./JG 54* was withdrawn for one month from the Battle to recover from the unexpected blow.

This new tactic, high level daylight formation bombing of enemy airfields, was tried again on the 13th August, but this time the outcome was a complete disaster. Twelve Blenheims of 82 Squadron set out to bomb Aalborg airfield in northern Denmark; eleven reached the target but all were shot down.

During the 8th August, 2 Group dispatched thirteen Blenheims to the Continent, all from 18 Squadron. Nine were forced to return due to lack of cloud cover, only two carried out bombing attacks on Valkenburg and Schiphol aerodromes. L9472 failed to return; it was shot down into the North Sea by *Flak* off the Dutch coast. Another crew in R3663 had a narrow escape over Leeuwarden airfield, as pilot Pilot Officer Arthur Hughes entered in his diary that evening:

"Today I nearly killed all three of us. I could not get to Handorf, so attacked Leeuwarden instead. Joe Strong's ETA was wrong, perhaps due to a wind change, and we arrived five minutes earlier than expected, with the result that we flew past before we saw it. So we made a wide sweep around the town and came back. Inevitably there would be the only really low cloud and drizzle in the area over the target, so that I was quite blind with a smeared windscreen and had little idea where the aerodrome was.

"The Jerries were in no such dilemma and tracer began zipping smartly past. I threw the engines into plus 9 boost and up went the nose taking us immediately into the cloud and, before I could grasp the message of the instruments and take corrective action, we were doing a stall turn right over the centre of the airfield, a perfect target as we dived out of the cloud. As we came out, the rudder controls went dead and the old Blenheim pulled out of the dive and went into a steep climb, which I could only correct by putting my knees up against the control column. We had no time to release our bombs and had a most tiring and uncomfortable journey home: knees are not designed for use on the control column and any attempt to remove them resulted immediately in a climb. Examination after we landed showed that the shell that hit our tail not only severed the rudder controls and the elevator trim tab controls, both of which had been obvious to me, but had also cut through most of the strands on the elevator controls. If they had given way, we would have made a nice big hole in the middle of the aerodrome.

"Poor old Hutchison (WOp/AG, T.B.) had a great fright, for I was so busy fighting for control and Strong was so aghast at my efforts, that neither of us answered his urgent enquiries and when we went into that headlong dive, he thought we were out of action and gave himself up for lost. So three men's lives hung by a thread..."

During August 1940, it became perfectly clear that the Blenheim was unsuited for further daylight raids against the enemy. The aircraft simply was too vulnerable in daylight. Therefore, new operational roles had to be devised for 2 Group - at night. Group Captain Hugh Pughe-Lloyd, SASO at 2 Group described the situation as follows:

"...we have no rôle by day except cloud cover and the occasional very high single attack... The idea for night use is to be a nuisance to the enemy bombers coming home. To bomb his aerodromes particularly when brilliantly lighted for the return journey - to shoot them down at night around the flare path. To drop delay action bombs and to harass the flare path parties with the odd bomb at intervals."

This exactly outlined the night intruder rôle in which the Blenheim was to be used, but it would take more than a year before 2 Group was completely taken off daylight operations to take on this night intruder role. For the time being, single night bombing attacks on German aerodromes were carried out by 2 Group Blenheims in increasing numbers during August and September 1940.

On 16/17th August 1940, 150 Blenheims, Hampdens, Wellingtons and Whitleys went to the Ruhr and Frankfurt, to the distant targets of Jena, Leuna and Augsburg and to airfields in

Holland. 118 aircraft reported bombing successfully and seven bombers, four Whitleys, two Hampdens and one Wellington, were lost.

One Blenheim was dispatched to De Kooy airfield near Den Helder. This was an aircraft of 18 Squadron and for its crew it was to be their operational 'blooding'. Sergeant Jim 'Dinty' Moore, the WOp/AG of this Blenheim crew vividly remembers his posting to 18 Squadron and his first trip. His story is typical for the young 'sprog' crews that joined 2 Group during the Battle of Britain:

"On the 12th August, the day the *Luftwaffe* launched their 'Eagle' Attack, which was to be the prelude to the invasion, two new crews arrived at RAF West Raynham, having been posted to 18 Squadron, which had reformed after her mauling in the Battle for France. One of these crews were Sergeants Roger Speedy, the pilot, Bob Weston, the observer and myself the WOp/AG. The three of us had met, after completing our training, on our arrival at RAF Upwood, one of the two Operational Training Units set up in April of that year to prepare crews for posting to the operational squadrons of No. 2 Group.

"We had all arrived at Upwood on the 14th June with little idea of what was in store for us and no idea of the appalling losses being suffered by the Blenheim squadrons we were destined to join. We WOp/AGs initially, kept together as a group which, in view of the fact the pilots and observers held the rank of Sergeant or Pilot Officer, was not too surprising. Remember, we WOp/AGs were still Aircraftsmen 2nd Class. However, our arrival had coincided with the decision by the Air Ministry to give all aircrew, who were not commissioned, the rank of Sergeant which, on our first pay day, came as much of a surprise to the staff, as it did to ourselves. Contrary to what may have appertained elsewhere, the selection of who would fly with who, was decided by the staff, to whom I shall be forever indebted as Roger and Bob were ideal colleagues. The purpose of the Course was to weld us together as a unit, each improving on our own particular skills and getting to know the Blenheim in which we were to risk our lives. By the time our posting came along, we were as ready as we would ever be for operational flying, or so we thought.

"On the 16th August, four days after our arrival at West Raynham, on looking at the Battle Order for the day, Roger, Bob and I found our names at the top of a list of six crews. I don't know about the others, but my own reactions were a strange mixture of excitement and apprehension. Night operations were a new experience, not only for us, but also for the experienced members of the squadron who, up till then, had only operated in daylight. All our operational training had been to prepare us for day 'ops', in fact we had only flown three hours and fifty minutes at night at Upwood.

"On attending the briefing we were informed that our target was the *Luftwaffe* airfield at De Kooy in Holland though, apart from the time of take off, the route to and from the target was left to the individual crew. The 'Met' Officer gave us details of the expected weather for the night and we were also advised as to the places to avoid where the anti-aircraft defences were most dangerous.

"The time seemed to drag before we collected our parachutes, then suitably clothed in flying suit, flying boots, 'Mae West' (in case we came down in the sea) and parachute harness we staggered out to our Blenheim ('L-for-Leather'). Roger, like most pilots, sat on his parachute, which was secured to his body for, once we were airborne, he could no longer leave his seat, having no automatic pilot, or as in larger aircraft, no co-pilot, no matter how long we were in the air. Bob combined the duties of navigator, bomb aimer and air gunner, the latter duty being to fire a gun fixed underneath his compartment, firing to the rear, to cover a blind spot under the tail, sighting on any target through a mirror. He sat in a seat beside Roger for take-off, before moving into the nose of the aircraft to carry out his varied duties. I was separated from them by the bomb bay, with a narrow gap through which I might just have been able to crawl, but in touch with them on the inter-com. My position was in the hydraulically operated turret, which was hardly designed for comfort separated from the radio by the central pillar. In order to operate the turret there was a set of controls resembling the handlebars of a motor-cycle, twisting the grip backwards elevated the gun and depressed the seat, twisting it forward and the reverse applied. By turning the grip to the left or to the right rotated the turret to the left or to the right, whichever was desired. There was only one gun, a Vickers Gas Operated .303, which you fed with tensioned pans, each containing 100 rounds of ammunition. Spare pans were stored at the side of the turret. The radio was located on a shelf aft of the turret, which was difficult to operate, needing both hands, for communication with base had to be in morse. Verbal communication could only be carried out with other aircraft in formation or on the intercom between members of the crew. We were to find we needed accurate radio bearings during our 'night ops' to help in finding our way home and thankfully we always managed to get through.

"So it was in such an aircraft at 9 pm that evening we fledglings took off, flying over the Norfolk countryside in daylight, wondering what was ahead of us. On course for the target, we climbed steadily as we crossed the sea and the daylight faded, although it became a clear moonlight night. I heard Bob say he could see the coast ahead and turning around I could see the coast of Holland as if I was looking down on a large map. We did not seem to be welcome visitors for, as we crossed the coast at a height of about 10,000 feet, we were greeted by the beams of searchlights probing the sky and bursts of *Flak* which, thankfully, were not too close. We flew on towards De Kooy where, as we approached I could hear Bob directing Roger on the bombing run, 'Steady - steady - left - steady' and so on until I heard him say those welcome words 'Bombs gone' and I felt 'L-for-Leather' lift as we were relieved of the weight of the bombs. Those minutes on a bombing run, when there is no question of taking evasive action are, as I was to learn, the most uncomfortable period of any operation for, flying straight and level, we were at our most vulnerable.

"It was now time to turn our thoughts to our return to West Raynham and I heard Bob give Roger a course for home and felt the aircraft turning away from the target. It was at this point, much to my surprise, I saw a single-engined fighter, silhouetted in the moonlight, behind and slightly above us. It was the accepted policy to avoid combat with enemy fighters if at all possible so, resisting the natural temptation to open fire, which would have given our position away, I gave Roger directions to take evasive action and we soon lost him. This brief encounter brought home to me very forcibly the necessity to remain constantly on the alert. On the return journey I did battle with the radio obtaining, to my pleasure and surprise, the necessary bearings for us to steer, from the radio operators sitting comfortably in their ground stations in East Anglia.

"Finally, after our inaugural operation, which had lasted three and three-quarter hours, we saw our runway, illuminated by kerosene lamps, waiting for us and Roger brought us in to land. We felt well satisfied with ourselves, particularly when we found the others on the Battle Order had not taken off, though we did not appreciate how lucky we had been and how much more difficult our operational life would become. By the end of the year we were to fly a total of 28 further operations over North-Western Europe including attacks on the Channel Ports, enemy airfields and targets in Germany."

The final date to be studied in the story of the Blenheim attacks on *Luftwaffe* airfields in the Netherlands in the summer of 1940, is the night of 26/27th August 1940. On this night, eighteen Blenheims of XV, 18, 40 and 110 Squadrons left their bases in East Anglia to attack airfields in the Occupied Countries. Four crews of XV and 18 Squadrons were briefed to bomb airfields in the Netherlands at Flushing, De Kooy, Haamstede and Texel. At De Kooy and Texel, hits were claimed on the targets and a large explosion at Texel causing seven fires was reported by Flight Lieutenant George of XV Squadron. 21-year old Hugh George recalls this memorable trip:

"In my logbook I had recorded that the attack took place on the night of 23/24th August 1940, the target being De Kooy aerodrome, but later researches have led me to believe that this date is wrong. I have since checked the squadron records and found that they show that the attack took place on the night of 26/27th August. We were operating under great pressure at the time and it often happened that one didn't get round to filling in one's logbook until days or even weeks after the event.

"My aircraft was Blenheim T1859 and my crew Sergeant Moffatt (observer) and Sergeant O'Donnell (WOp/AG). The attack was to be a high level one. I well remember that as I did my run up to the target at about 20,000 feet. I was met with what I have noted in my logbook as 'exceptional light anti-aircraft fire' (tracer shells and machine-gun fire, with star shells and parachute flares). There was also a great many searchlights, which very rapidly 'coned' me and which I was unable to shake off.

"The effect of all this was to make it impossible for me to do a 'straight and level' bombing run, which was necessary for accurate high level bombing and, after three attempts, I decided to adopt a different form of attack. I had concluded that the searchlights (most of which were concentrated in a circle) were being controlled by sound predictors and therefore I cut my engines and carried out a steep dive attack aiming at the centre of the circle. Sure enough they were unable to follow me and I was able to release my bombs at 600 feet and get away at low level over the North Sea. As we cleared the target area there was a tremendous explosion followed by multi-coloured fires.

"I had been milling about for some time in the target area, alerting all the defences in the process, which served to indicate very clearly what was the most sensitive area, and that was what I bombed. I must say that the ensuing spectacular explosions and fires took us all rather by surprise - so much so in fact that having pulled out of the dive very low I completely forgot to open the throttles again and we very nearly finished up at the bottom of the sea. Fortunately a rapid approaching white-topped wave brought me to my senses just in time. How stupid can you get? I have often wondered what it was that was responsible for the multi-coloured explosions and I had assumed that I hit a bomb dump."

Unfortunately, no German records remain that could ascertain the cause of the large explosions resulting from Hugh George's crew's attack.

In September 1940 the decisive air battles in the Battle of Britain were fought out over Great Britain between the Luftwaffe and RAF Fighter Command. The invasion of the country was expected at any time - in fact, on 16th August, Hitler had determined the date for the execution of 'Seelöwe' as the 15th of September. On 10th September, he decided to fix the 24th till 27th of the month for the landing. In anticipation of the invasion the RAF fought the enemy with every available means. Each and every night, the Blenheims of 2 Group and Coastal Command raided the coastal harbours in northwestern France and the Low Countries where a fleet of thousands of invasion barges were set to sail, especially in the ports of Ostend and Dunkirk. While the Hurricanes and Spitfires inflicted severe losses on the *Luftwaffe* over Great Britain, the Blenheims and other bombers of Bomber and Coastal Commands sent some 12% of the invasion vessels to the bottom. For example, 214 out of the assembled fleet of 1,918 converted Rhine barges were destroyed during the Battle and the Blenheims of Coastal Command kept a close eye on the enemy shipping traffic. These two factors, together with the inclement weather that had held up preparations, contributed decisively to Hitler's decision to postpone the invasion. Goering's bomber and fighter crews had not succeeded in gaining air superiority over the Channel and southern England and the invasion fleet was constantly pounded by the RAF bombers. In the event of putting out to sea, a weak German Navy could in all probability not protect the invasion fleet sufficiently from carnage by the Royal Navy. Under these circumstances an attempted invasion of Great Britain would be a perilous undertaking. The failure of the all-out *Luftwaffe* attack on 15th September made Hitler decide to postpone the invasion for the time being; on the 19th the *Oberkommando der Wehrmacht* ordered to stop the assembly of the forces and disperse the transports lying in the embarkation ports.

The Blenheim crews of 53 Squadron for example noticed the effects of this decision almost immediately. On 20th September a crew had still counted some 650 river craft, mainly Rhine barges, in the ports of Flushing, Hook of Holland and Rotterdam during a shipping reconnaissance: from early October this large number slowly but steadily declined as their sorties clearly showed. On 12th October, the Führer ordered to break off the preparations of *Seelöwe* and to put off the operation to the spring of 1941. However, by early 1941, Hitler turned his attention East towards Russia and all serious plans of an invasion of Great Britain were shelved.

The fate of Great Britain and of the Free Western World had trembled in the balance during the summer of 1940, but the RAF had turned it in Britain's favour. 2 Group and the Coastal Command Blenheim squadrons had paid a high price for their crucial contribution to the outcome of the Battle of Britain. In July, the Group lost 31 aircraft during attacks on the invasion barges, airfields and on sorties to Germany. In August, 28 Blenheims were reported missing and during September a further 19 aircraft failed to return with 6 more written off in England. Whereas 2 Group had her greatest front-line strength during the summer of 1940 with 180 Blenheims and crews available for duty, 78 Blenheims lost in a three-months period meant a serious blood-letting for the Group. Of these losses, 25 Blenheims were shot down on operations over the Netherlands. Coastal Command lost a further 8 Blenheims in the Dutch coast area during the Battle of Britain.

Chapter Four

Clouds and Darkness

*Cloud cover and night bombing operations,
Autumn/Winter 1940/41.*

In early October 1940, it became clear that the *Wehrmacht* was not going to invade Great Britain that year. As a result, Bomber Command resumed its strategic bombing offensive of German targets. The 2 Group offensive against the invasion fleet was halted in favour of intensifying the night offensive against *Luftwaffe* bomber airfields, in an effort to stem the *Luftwaffe* night *Blitz* against London. For example, 2 Group sent out 35 Blenheims to enemy airfields to prevent the bombers taking off to raid Coventry on the evening of 14th November. A wide variety of other operations were also flown by the Blenheim crews during the autumn and winter of 1940/41. These included night raids on German targets, coastal target attacks, reconnaissance missions, roving commissions by experienced crews and strikes against coastal shipping. When these sorties were flown in daylight, cloud cover was effectively used, but the majority of these raids took place under cover of darkness. Sergeant Terry Staples, a pilot with 114 Squadron in 1940, tells more about the 2 Group operations in the autumn of 1940 and of one memorable attack on Den Helder harbour:

"In the latter part of 1940, after the threat of invasion had receded, the Blenheims of 2 Group were used to maintain a daylight strike capacity to keep the enemy occupied and for night intruder operations. This was a period of retrenchment and building up our forces after heavy setbacks and in daylight we operated for the most part singly and were briefed only to cross the enemy occupied coast when there was an element of cloud cover for protection. We were only allowed to attack shipping or, over land, strictly military targets in the occupied territories such as airfields.

"My only attack on shipping in the Dutch coastal area was on 6th October 1940, a Sunday afternoon. We had been briefed that some shipping had been reported in the vicinity of Den Helder and I was sent as a single aircraft to find and if possible to attack it. We found nothing at sea, but saw a ship in a dock which my navigator identified as Den Helder. There was plenty of cloud cover and the cloud was quite low. I entered the cloud and did a timed circuit in order to bring myself into position for the attack. This worked out well and the ship was directly ahead of us broadside on as we emerged from the cloud. We made the attack at low level (50 feet) with the four 250lb bombs with which we were armed. They were fitted, as was usual, with an eleven-second delay fuse to enable them to be dropped from such a low level. My gunner in the rear turret thought, from the explosion he saw, that we had hit the target. As we passed over the ship after dropping our bombs, I saw a civilian at the dockside, just beyond the ship, fishing. This left a lasting impression on me and the deepest regret that he may have been a Dutchman and an innocent casualty of that Sunday afternoon."

When autumn turned into winter, two types of Blenheim operations evolved. Night raids against targets in Germany, as part of the strategic bombing offensive was the first one. The second type of operations were attacks against *Luftwaffe* airfields in the Occupied Countries. These operations were intended to disrupt the take-off and landing of enemy bombers, in order to bring some relief to the British cities that were suffering badly from the night Blitz. It was a trimmed-down 2 Group that undertook these operations: XV, 40 and 218 Squadrons were incorporated into 3 Group in November and were now busy converting onto Wellington bombers.

These night raids in Blenheims were often 'dicey do's', as becomes clear from the following stories of a few crews who flew on these missions. Sergeant George Parr is the first to recount his memories of these operations. He was the observer in Flying Officer Douch's crew of 18 Squadron and, together with his pilot, recalls an operation to Hamm in the Ruhr Valley that took place on the night of 16/17th November 1940. Parr and Douch remember one of the biggest enemies of Bomber Command in the 'pioneering' years 1939-1942; bad weather:

"On 24th October we made our first visit to Germany by night. The target was Soest, east of the Ruhr. In November we attacked Antwerp on the 5th, then a series of targets in the Ruhr and Hamburg, mostly power stations and railway marshalling yards. One incident stands out in my memory. The target was the marshalling yards at Hamm. The weather was foul, with cloud base too low for low level navigation so we climbed through cloud in severe icing conditions to over 20,000 feet. We had oxygen, but there was of course no heating. Heavy clothing, including up to three pairs of gloves made accurate chart work difficult, particularly as every exhalation of breath produced a small shower of snow. My idea was to intercept the railway line south of Hamm and follow it in to the target. The descent through cloud was violently bumpy and ice built up rapidly. It began to look as if the local cloud base was going to be too low for safety, but we eventually broke through with very little to spare."

Flying Officer John Douch takes up the story:

"It was pitch dark below cloud and raining. I could see nothing outside the cockpit, but Parr claimed to have picked up a railway line and thought we could drop our bombs on a bridge. Parr was instructing me accordingly when Bassett (WOp/AG, T.B.) said 'We are icing up, there is half an inch of ice everywhere.' After a short interval he said 'There is an inch of ice now,' and then 'It is now an inch and a half.'"

Sergeant Parr continues:

"It was some time before I saw the railway line and then not before we were practically over it. I called for a right-hand turn and continued to call right as the pilot put the aircraft in a very steep turn under the conditions. Suddenly there was a severe jolt as the aircraft flipped over onto its back. The captain shouted that he had lost control, which was very obvious. We were uncomfortably close to the ground. It was not a recommended manoeuvre to spin a Blenheim at any time, but with a bombed-up aircraft, heavily iced, at under 2,000 feet at night, it was positively dangerous. We were violently thrown around in our straps and I thought we should have already hit the ground before I was able to reach the bomb release and get rid of 1000 lbs. of high explosive and iron. A second or two later Douch managed by some miracle to level the aircraft and start to climb away.

"His problems were not yet over. As we re-entered cloud and started the long climb, now at a very slow rate because of the weight of ice and loss of lift resulting from wing aerodynamic inefficiency, the pilot's instruments became unreadable as our breath condensed onto the glass. I sat beside him continually wiping the main instruments. Meanwhile lumps of ice kept flying off the propellors and crashing against the sides of the fuselage. Eventually we came out over cloud. I was never so glad to see the moon. That I did so meant that I was able to celebrate my 21st birthday a week later. I have to say that we came nearer to disaster on that occasion than ever we did as a result of enemy action."

Another Blenheim veteran of 1940/41, Sergeant Harry Huckins, was an observer with 21 Squadron and was one of the lucky few aircrew to survive the Battle of France. In late 1940, 21 Squadron was employed on night raids to Germany. Sergeant Huckins recounts a raid to Cologne on 26/27th November 1940:

"It was November 26th when we were sent out at night to try and hit Cologne in Blenheim YH-R 3900. Our route was Watton-Den Helder-Cologne and return via Orfordness. We chose the route because there was a moon up that night and we hoped to map-read to our turning points. We had no nav' aids except to get bearings (QDM's) by morse key. It was an uneventful raid to begin with. We found our turning point over the Dutch coast as it could be clearly seen and we took a direct course over Holland to Cologne. We could not make out anything at all after leaving the Dutch coast and there was an eerie time period where we saw no lights or anything, not a peep out of ack-ack. We had to drop our bombs 'on ETA' rather than return home with them. No results were observed. The Rhine river could not be seen.

"After setting course on our D/R position over Cologne we did not see anything coming out and we were lucky to see Orfordness on the Suffolk coast. It seemed this raid was going to be 'duck soup'. All that was left to do was to get to the red flashing 'chance light' near Bodney, our Watton satellite.

"Unfortunately, Britain was rapidly becoming fogged in and we could not make out our flarepath. Gunner/WOp Bill Bradshaw literally saved our lives by getting QDM's on four separate runs from the chance light and just luckily the fog broke for a few seconds and we were the last aircraft to get back. Others did not make it."

Indeed, Blenheim R3914 of 21 Squadron crashed into a hill near Middleton in Durham county on return from Cologne, killing Sergeant Collinge and crew.

Pilot Officer Charles Sherring was a WOp/AG who joined 18 Squadron at RAF Great Massingham in December 1940. His pilot was Sergeant Hawkins, with Jacky Crouch as their observer. Hawkins had done four trips when Charles joined his crew. Crouch was a pre-war regular who had survived the Battle of France and had completed nineteen trips. Pilot Officer Sherring vividly describes a number of operations he flew to northwestern German targets and the Ruhr in the winter of 1940/41, that give us a clear impression of these early strategic night bombing operations:

"We took off on 1st January 1941 at 19.30 in the evening and the target was Bremen docks. The night was very dark and when we got to the Zuyder Zee, Crouch couldn't make up his mind where he was and we went round and round the coast with about three guns firing at us steadily. Actually Holland was under flood and, what with that and tide being in or out or something different to his maps, it was understandable his getting a bit confused.

"Crouch was swearing at Hawkins for not steering the exact courses he gave him and the long journey overland seemed interminable. There were quite a lot of lights on the ground, aerodromes, dummies etc. and then far ahead we could see a dull red glow in the sky. It was Bremen burning and visible then at 80 or 90 miles distance. As we approached, the opposition got much stiffer, and about twenty miles from the target, there was a dummy Bremen lit up with fires, with imitations of sticks of bombs bursting. For the first time I saw bright coloured tracer coming up at us - red and green - and as it left the ground it looked like a sort of toy train running along and seemed to float up at you. Just as we started our bombing run they put up a box barrage which was about thirty or forty yards to port but we saw an aircraft go down in flames from the middle of it.

"Down below was an amazing sight; the docks were clearly visible and there was a huge fire over half a mile long by nearly half a mile wide; all the centre was a dull red glow, dark red and the edges were bright. Close to this was another very large fire, though nothing like as big. Crouch wanted to put his bombs between these two fires, which he seemed to do, though it was difficult to tell with the smoke and *Flak*. Just after we had bombed, a shell went off right underneath our aircraft and blew in the camera hatch, which is immediately forward of my turret. The cold became agonising, though I had electrically heated clothing. The leads on my gloves were burning my hands while my feet were really painful and I was afraid of my face getting frozen. The wireless set froze up stiff and was u/s for a long period.

"It seemed an eternity getting back to the Dutch coast, I began to wish something would knock us down, so that I could get out. The Bremen fires showed clearly from 100 miles away coming back. At last we got clear of the Zuyder Zee and came down pretty low - the relief of getting warm again was wonderful. I unfroze the wireless set quickly by holding my heated gloves against the reaction and volume controls and got a couple of good bearings for home. The observer's instruments read -39 degrees centigrade and were at their limit and he was at the warm end of the aircraft. We finally landed at Massingham at five past one.

"January 4th and operation No.4; the target was Hamburg. The crew was Hawkins, Crouch on positively his last trip, and me. The weather was clear over England but after crossing the Zuyder Zee clouds started piling up until we could only occasionally see the ground. We could tell Bremen as we passed it fairly near from the huge amount of searchlights and *Flak*. When we got to Hamburg there was 10/10ths cloud and, though Crouch said by the searchlights and *Flak* and his ETA we were over the town, he wouldn't drop his bombs unless he could see something to aim at. So we went to Bremerhaven - again identified by the *Flak* - then down to Emden, which he couldn't pick up either; by now Hawkins and I were both saying for heaven's sake drop the bombs and go home. He then went to Rotterdam to try the docks and, when that was a failure, he dropped his bombs safe in the sea and we all came home. I got my first homing bearing from the Dutch coast and I thought that was terrific. Everyone else dropped their bombs on Germany, bombing through cloud wherever they thought was about right. This was the last time Jacky Crouch flew with us and he went on rest to West Feugh as a Bombing Leader.

"So Hawkins and I looked for new blood. Bobby Sharp (18 Sqn. CO, T.B.) found Flying Officer Buskell's old observer, one Butler by name, and put him with us for a bit. Buskell won a DFC when flying with him and came off after about twenty trips. Our first target was Gelsenkirchen, the oil refinery and synthetic oil plant. We were given a lecture on how the whole show worked and then, on January 9th, we took off at 18.05 for the target. It was a lovely night and we crossed the Dutch coast OK and, after a time and a very peaceful journey, Butler said, 'Well, here we are, now I'll just make certain of the exact target'. So we started circling; over to our right was a pretty fair lot of searchlights and some *Flak*, but where we were there was not so much, though there were four or five guns that fired at us spasmodically and without stopping for long for the next 50 minutes, while Butler looked for Gelsenkirchen.

"Finally he gave it up and we set course back; on the way we passed Essen with a lot of *Flak* coming up and he tried a bombing run, but as there was some cloud he abandoned that and we came back to the docks at Flushing, where, to give him his due, he dropped a picture stick right along the very edge of the inside dock, and we got quite a lot of *Flak* coming up at us all the time. It was very clear coming home again and we landed at 22.20. Butler recounted his experiences in the crew briefing room and really, I have never heard such a line-shoot in my life.

"Op. No. 6 was on January 12th, an intruder op. on the aerodrome at Chartres and operation No. 7 was on January 15th and we were briefed for Wilhelmshaven, with take-off at 20.45. It was a fine night with a big moon. Bucker, once Hugh Maxwell's observer, a scruffy type but a pre-war regular, had just returned to the squadron from a sick leave (which he was always a bit prone to) and we took him as our observer. It was clear leaving England, and calm and quiet going over the sea. We sighted Texel Beacon and turned north, counting up Islands, and watching the *Flak* going up at the other bombers, which were running along the coast. As there was snow on the ground all over Germany and it was pretty cold, we were flying along at about 7,000 feet for the extra warmth. Just as we got to the top of the Islands and near Heligoland, a *Flak*-ship or heavily armed boat of sorts nearly shot us down, as we had been taking no evasive action and were just watching for fighters.

"The fires of Wilhelmshaven were very clearly visible from a long way off. To dodge this *Flak* from the boats, we turned out to sea, and climbed high as we circled round, and finally headed back for land at 15,000 feet to 16,000 feet, our highest yet. The land looked flat and sandy down below, with a few small belts of wood. Ahead was a huge blaze, and we had 20 or 30 miles to go across this flat strip to reach the town, which began to look like half a moon below, showing dark against the moonlit water.

"The defences seemed to have collapsed, as searchlights were waving about aimlessly, and though guns were heard firing hard, nothing came anywhere near us. It was the only time I have been over Germany when the defences seemed to have been quite swamped. Down below the fires were so big that you could clearly make out streets and buildings, and it looked as if a good quarter of the whole town was actually on fire. We dropped our small load in the middle, and turned for home, out to sea and back the way we had come. A night fighter picked us up, and followed for some time, but without ever making an attack, though we were ready. As we got down to Texel Beacon, we could still see the red glow from Wilhelmshaven, 140 miles away. It was a good trip home with small clouds casting shadows on the sea, looking like small unknown islands and we came in to land at 01.10.

"The following day it stated that *Admiral* Raeder (C-in-C German Navy, T.B.) himself went down to Wilhelmshaven and gave the population a pep talk. It was the biggest raid up to then attempted by Bomber Command, and must have been the most successful, as the town appeared on the small side and very compact, and the damage must have been terrific. Our raid was in retaliation for Plymouth."

Another Blenheim veteran of the 1940 days is Sergeant Les Spong. He flew a tour of operations as a pilot with 139 Squadron between August 1940 and April 1941 from Horsham St. Faith near Norwich. He relates more of the primitive nature of night flying and its more lighthearted side-effects, in the early war years. One must remember that the pre-war RAF bomber strategy was based on daylight raids, so night operations were a new feature to the RAF in 1940:

"Night flying then was of course vastly different from now, with all the navigation aids and the whole of the country lit up like a vast Christmas tree. Then for navigation we had only the compass assisted by the direction indicator and dead reckoning and at the beginning of the war the grass airfield was laid out specially on each occasion with paraffin flares - hence of course the name flarepath. I remember, when learning the technique, being rather surprised that it was possible to make a fair landing with such a minimum of reference points in the all-pervading blackness. Such a flarepath was of course an obvious target for enemy aircraft and the flares were soon superseded by glim lamps which could only be seen from limited angles and a limited distance. The new flarepath could be quickly doused if there were hostiles in the vicinity. To enable us to locate the airfield a beacon was stationed a few miles away, in a different position and flashing a different code each night: we had to fly over the beacon and then set the course which we had been given for the occasion.

"Night bombing was not a favourite form of operation. Although one knew there were probably many others engaged on the same task, it was a lonely business and the time both outward and homeward dragged. The pyrotechnics of the *Flak* were somehow more heartstopping than the daylight puffs of smoke and when caught in the glare of searchlights one felt much more exposed and vulnerable than when over enemy territory in daylight. All this was only made more difficult to withstand mentally by the numbing cold.

"In the unheated Blenheim cockpit at 20,000 feet at night in winter the temperature could reach -20 centigrade and the cold penetrated despite all our precautions. Of course we had the silk aircrew underwear, with the fur-lined flying suits on top of all our normal wear, aided by 'Everhot' bags. These were like small hot-water bottles filled with some kind of crystals. One poured water in, screwed back the stopper, and then shook vigorously for five or ten minutes as the bag slowly warmed up. Once it reached a certain critical temperature the process continued without further shaking. A couple of these bags installed in strategic positions within ones clothing did a good deal to maintain morale; and in the locker room before an operation one could see the fighting men wandering around with rapt looks shaking their bags. Unfortunately the bags were temperamental things: sometimes if the preparation had not been sufficient thorough or I suppose if the bag was defective the initial heat would be lost as soon as one was in the air, while on other occasions the bag could go on getting hotter until one could regret placing it too close to the skin and a mid-air re-adjustment would be necessary.

"Of course the cold encouraged the working of the urinary system and, although one always took the opportunity of seeking the shelter of the aircraft's tail before take-off for a last-minute leak, one usually on these cold occasions needed to pass water again before the end of a four and a half hours trip. There was a tube placed conveniently close to the pilot's seat for this purpose but I personally found that, with all the layers of clothing with which I was encumbered and the shrinking effect of the cold on one's tender part, it was impossible for me, using one hand only, both to make the part in question see the light of day and to hold the relief tube in position: and I could not relinquish the control column entirely for the necessary lenght of time. On these occasions I had to ask Mac (Sergeant MacKinnon, observer, T.B.), while I held the tube in position with my one free hand, to perform the more delicate part of the operation. While we were thus preoccupied Jim (Sergeant Granville, WOp/AG, T.B.) was enjoined to keep a specially sharp lookout for enemy aircraft.

"The night operations did have one heartening effect, in that they were rarely aborted and we could thus feel we were playing an effective part in the war after the frustrations of cloud-cover work (too many abortive sorties during the Summer and Autumn of 1940, T.B.)."

Raids on targets along the enemy coastline were also carried out by the Blenheim crews during the winter of 1940/41. The crews regularly paid a visit to coastal towns on the Dutch coast, like Flushing, Hook of Holland, Rotterdam, Ijmuiden and Den Helder. An example of these operations is the raid against Rotterdam by nine Blenheims of 139 Squadron on the night of 21/22nd December. All crews bombed the oil tanks in the harbour area and many fires were started, but it was a well-defended target as Sergeant George 'Jock' Shinnie experienced. He flew on this trip as WOp/AG in Blenheim L9413 of 139 Squadron:

"Having been solely involved in daylight operations we were very surprised to be suddenly given the task of bombing oil tanks at Rotterdam, at night, on 21st December 1940. Nine aircraft of the squadron were involved, operating at medium heights, 10 to 12,000 feet. It was a new experience for me on two counts. My last night flying (training) flight was in early August 1940 and this was to be my first night operation. We were very conscious that the Blenheim in its day operational colours was not exactly suitable for night operations. Furthermore, the navigator positioned in the nose of the aircraft, surrounded by perspex, could only use his navigation table light for very short periods.

"I shall never forget the sudden shock of being illuminated by searchlights and almost simultaneously being subjected to very heavy accurate Ack Ack. Our bombs went and taking steep evasive action, and losing height rapidly, we cleared the town but then experienced considerable light Ack Ack until we crossed the coast. We thought our aircraft had been hit but everything seemed to be in order as we flew home. To our dismay when we were overhead base, and preparing to land, the port undercarriage refused to lower, despite repeated attempts. Since the Blenheim normally accepted a belly landing reasonably well my pilot attempted to raise the starboard undercarriage leg but to no avail.

"My pilot, Sergeant Farmer, did an excellent job keeping the port wing aloft as long as he could until we swung viciously but came to no harm. Regrettably, I forgot in the prevailing circumstances, to disconnect the IFF destruct detonator prior to landing with the result that as we slewed around it blew itself up!"

L9413 was repaired at Horsham St. Faith. On the 21/22nd December 1940 raid, no serious damage was done to the oil tanks. Only on one occasion, on 14/15th March 1941, this target was hit hard by 2 Group. Eight Whitleys and five Blenheims of 18, 82 and 101 Squadrons successfully bombed the oil tanks at Pernis/Rotterdam, destroying a 10,000 ton tank including 3,000 tons of oil. Also, sixteen smaller tanks were hit and 75% of their contents were lost to the Germans. No aircraft were lost; a truly outstanding raid.

The crews of 2 Group were involved in a number of night bombing raids during January and February of 1941, as part of the strategic force of Bomber Command. However, in early March the Blenheim crews got a new operational rôle. Forced by the severe losses among the British cargo ships in the Atlantic, Bomber Command was now more and more employed in bombing raids against German ports instead of strategic targets further inland. 2 Group aircraft were better suited to these operations, as with the small range of the Blenheims these coastal targets were well within their reach.

One of the first raids against enemy ports was on the night of 28th February/1st March 1941. Early in the evening of the 28th, seven Blenheims of 139 Squadron carried out dusk raids against the harbours of Flushing, Den Helder and Lorient. Later in the evening, 116 Blenheims, Hampdens, Wellingtons and Whitleys left their bases in East Anglia to attack the battleship *Tirpitz* in

Wilhelmshaven. Although 75 crews on debriefing claimed to have dropped their bombs in the target area, there are no German reports that confirm these claims. Of the 139 Squadron force, two aircraft were lost on return at base due to a collision. Of the Wilhelmshaven force, one aircraft was lost. This was Blenheim T1895 of 105 Squadron; on the way back to England, the aircraft was intercepted over Groningen by a Bf110 night fighter flown by *Oberfeldwebel* Paul Gildner of *4./NJG 1* and was shot down in flames. Sergeant John Heape was fortunate to escape from the aircraft after a mid-air explosion but his observer and WOp/AG were killed.

Sergeant Ken Whittle was one of the crew members of 139 Squadron who was briefed in the early evening of 28th February 1941 to bomb Flushing harbour. He was the WOp/AG in Sergeant Tom McPhee's crew and vividly recalls this trip half a century later:

"The one thing a 'Blenheim Boy' of 2 Group Bomber Command could not complain of was repetition in reference to the types of operations flown. Day, night, solo, formation, high, medium and low levels and cloud cover in daylight. The briefing today was to prove variety was indeed the spice of life. Present 'the mad Major', Squadron Leader Hill and crew of 'B' Flight, plus a second 'B' Flight crew and one 'A' Flight crew. They were briefed and sent off first, timing the take off to arrive over their target at dusk, yet to operate as individual aircraft. A plum of a target, a submarine crew's rest hotel on the Normandy coast at Quisberom in the Brest area. The target was to be truly plastered through light indifferent *Flak*, and crews and aircraft returned safely.

"The four remaining crews envious, and hoping they too would attack another such target. This was not to be, Flight Lieutenant Hughie Edwards and crew (the VC to be) with Sergeant Bennett and crew of 'A' Flight to attack a target at dusk in the Den Helder area. With trepidation Sergeant McPhee and crew of 'A' Flight and Sergeant Vivian of 'B' Flight awaited their target and drew the short straw: Flushing dock area, a heavily defended dangerous target in daylight indeed, even using 7/10ths cloud cover! What were the implications of an untried dusk attack, at a height neither low nor medium level? There was no voice of experience to offer any advice and McPhee and crew were alarmed and apprehensive. How much light was there left at dusk, when airborne over the target? The briefed method of attack disturbing, McPhee and crew to attack first whilst Vivian patrolled out of the *Flak* ranges then to attack after McPhee had bombed and escaped. Thus, the element of surprise would be lost attacking as one in close formation, why thought the two crews? Our's was not to reason why! Other ideas however born from operational experiences, and the desire to survive. McPhee and crew in R3907 on their 25th operation (ten flown in

R3907), took off at 17.55 to circuit the Horsham St. Faith airfield, awaiting Vivian to formate on R3907. Vivian, wheels up headed straight for the coast not relying on providence or the briefing, McPhee and crew in alarm watching his fast disappearing wing formation keeping lights. It was a case of the 'Devil take the hindmost'. McPhee and crew, attacking roles obviously reversed. Sergeant Vivian had no intention of waiting for his briefed leader, or of being caught up with.

"There was no doubt Vivian had arrived over the dock area, all hell let loose over Flushing, a fearsome soul destroying sight, amplified in the half light of dusk. It had to be faced, the element of surprise attack 'down the drain', defences alerted and practiced now. A crew discussion in strained nervous voices took place at 4,000 feet thick cloud cover, so often our protector and saviour. A foolish decision in the heat of the moment to stay just below the protective cloud was decided. The *Flak* had quietened down as Vivian bombed and we presumed had made his escape seawards. The restless searchlights still probed the skies, reflecting off the 4,000 feet cloud base. In no time the Blenheim was coned in the searchlights, pinned like a moth against the cloud base curtain like background, the crew blinded. The deadly accurate *Flak* opened up, no other aircraft present to share the fearsome barrage, the target R3907!

"Drastic evasive action had to be taken if R3907 and the crew were to survive. Mac responded, down went the Blenheim's nose on full power in a diving turn. This helped to evade the heavy deadly black shell bursts, the searchlights were not fooled however, holding R3907 in a cone of daylight. The speed of the dive brought the Blenheim into the range of the very concentrated and deadly, medium and light ack ack units against low flying intruders. Tracer and incendiary cannon shells and bullets coned the Blenheim fuselage and wings, a terrifying experience, at any time, this was unbelievable. The Blenheim was now into a very steep straight dive as I realised the normal conversation up front had ceased, to a deadly awful silence. I feared the worst, appalled, Mac and Geoff had been hit, R3907 was in a death dive, no way at this angle of dive could I climb forward to the cockpit. I wanted to call them on the intercom but the awful thoughts, fear had robbed me completely of my vocal chords. Twisting my head and body to look down the low angled fuselage and ahead, I noted the tide was out, mud banks clearly visible, growing larger by the second. Sick at heart I collapsed in my turret, the anticipation of the awful sudden end bathed my face and hands in a cold sweat of fear, despite the freezing cold. I prayed to my much forsaken 'God', he answered me. A sudden loud unexpected shout from Mac up front, 'Searchlight port beam, get it Ken!' I had little chance of doing that as a first reaction, I was still busy dying 'the thousand deaths' spoken about, I was no hero. Now my mind responded and took over, oddly I managed to shoot out two searchlights, or discourage them?

"I have no recollection when and if the bombs were released, Geoff Atkins did his required job in silence, nor did I care. Mac called again, this time I managed a high pitched 'castrated' vocal reply, berating him and Geoff for the period of awful frightening silence. Had it really been only seconds?

They understood the strain I had suffered, very apologetic and a firm promise it would not happen again, those fast approaching mud banks live in my memory! The holocaust had faded from view, R3907 was still performing well if damaged, crew no injuries, only a bruised pride. Shattered nerves started to calm down, we were over the sea, in control and heading home. Yet the travail of this awful night was not over for three of the crews of 139 Squadron!

"I was very relieved to busy my mind and shut off those horrible memories of a short while ago over Flushing, busying myself on WT duties. The safety of night darkness enfolded and protected the speeding homeward bound Blenheim. Head down in the turret unsighted against intruders over the 'German Ocean' (*Luftwaffe* supremacy), I contacted base. Always a great thrill in the loneliness of the sky, to exchange morse signals with the ground operators of the home station. Identification of a friendly bomber completed and a navigational check aid, magnetic course to steer given, keep mind and hands busy.

"Listening out, I could hear returning Blenheims of 139 Squadron in contact with base. Nearing Horsham St. Faith, Sergeant Bennett's operator pipped me at the post requesting landing permission, this after Sergeant Vivian had landed. Sergeant Bennett was given that permission. I contacted base and was told R3907 to carry out a circuit and wait for further intructions. Sergeant Bennett's wing formation keeping lights, red and green clearly visible on final approach, suddenly a red cartridge flare was fired, a signal do not land. Following this, sudden explosion of fire broke out towards the end of the grassed runway, with horror McP'hee and crew knew it had to be Bennett's aircraft.

"We were told the next day the sad sequences of events. Hughie Edwards on landing with a damaged undercart, blocked the runway, the runway was changed. Vivian landed alright, at the end of the grassed runway his Blenheim bogged down. (It could have been R3907, McP'hee and crew!). Bennett's Blenheim, *Flak*-damaged, could not go round again, landing safely to unfortunately over run and collide at speed with the bogged down Blenheim and crew. On impact both Blenheims caught fire, the ground crews were superb, the injured crews evacuated safely. Bennett was hospitalised, rejoining the squadron in April 1941, he would not survive the month, missing on Ops Ijmuiden steel works 7 April 1941. His navigator Sergeant Severn fractured his skull and died before dawn. Vivian and his navigator Sergeant Mills were badly injured, not to return to 139 Squadron. The WOp/AGs slight injuries, to fight again.

"What of Sergeant McPhee and crew, depressed, battle weary, and sick at heart, a bird's eye view of the traumatic tragedy below, the nights travail had not ended yet. Base instructed R3907 to divert to Swanton Morley a new station recently opened, depressed and weary Mac turned onto the course given to him by Geoff Atkins. I did not have the station's WT frequency, contact would be made over the airfield by RT. The crew relieved to leave the circuit and the funeral pyre below, and to land R3907 and stand on 'terra firma'.

"Swanton Morley had been alerted to our coming, the flare path a welcome sight below and an end to this awful night in sight. RT contact established and permission to land given, soon with relief wheels and flaps responded on final approach, then sudden darkness below? Mac cursed having to go round again, not comforting completing a circuit over a blacked out airfield below, somewhere. Suddenly the flarepath lighting restored, a second finals approach, a repeat performance black out at the critical point! A third attempt, the same action and results, the crew's tired bodies and minds, now at breaking point. On the fourth attempt in finals Mac screamed out over the RT 'For Christ's sake let us in', we were allowed to land, landing lights stayed on.

"There was a natural tiredness in this final approach and landing, human endurance pushed to the limit. At 21.55 the wheels contacted the grassed field, the weight of the aircraft on the wheels and undercart. *Flak* damaged, the port oleo leg collapsed, the port wing dug into the ground, breaking off at the engine, half wing and engine parted company with the aircraft. The awful expensive sound of rupturing tortured metal was heard. Mac's now calm voice, 'OK chaps I have got her' (whatever that meant?). He as relieved as Geoff and I to be on terra firma and bodily in one piece.

"Bumping and boring in the turret I was past caring, I had reached a nervous saturation point. The Blenheim had slewed around, to finish in a shuddering dusty stop. A tinkling metallic sound was heard as the starboard engine cooled down, galvanising tired limbs and minds into action into evacuating the stricken Blenheim.

"Mac and Geoff lit up the inevitable operational 'fag', both relishing a deep long satisfying draw, the fag half gone in the tension relieving satisfaction. I standing watching this ecstacy, not knowing if I should laugh or cry, or what to do with my nervous arms and hands. I a non-smoker to resist again so many tension filled landings, and temptations to smoke. A very agitated duty pilot arrived, very relieved to see the battered and buckled remains of R3907 had slewed clear of the landing area. Also relieved to find the crew sound in wind and limb, self supporting? Apparently the Blenheim squadron at Swanton Morley were to take off on a night 'op'. We were told the flare path had been extinguished as an aircraft intruder was in the area. Lady luck stayed with us to the bitter end, in circuit we had the red/green wing tip formation lights on, and an intruder up there, somewhere!

The crew were transported to St. Faith to learn the sad ending of Bennett's and Vivian's burnt out Blenheims and injured crews. Two Blenheims out of the seven written off, not really a credit day, February 28th 1941.

Chapter Five

Ships and Fringe Targets: Phase One

The Blenheim anti-shipping and fringe targets campaign March to 7th July 1941.

On 6th March 1941, a new directive was issued by the Prime Minister to Bomber Command giving the war at sea absolute priority. Churchill felt he was forced to issue this directive, as Hitler had initiated a maritime blockade of Great Britain a few days previously. With *U-boats*, warships and long-range maritime aircraft, the *Führer* emphatically declared on 24th February that he would force Albion to her knees within sixty days. This was a very real threat to Britain's sea life-lines of food supplies and her connection with the United States. Losses to British and Allied merchant shipping rapidly rose to an alarming height and the Royal Navy could not cope alone. Therefore, seventeen RAF squadrons were released for maritime attack duties.

Among these units were four squadrons from 2 Group. The Blenheims of 18, 21, 107 and 139 Squadrons were to halt enemy convoys by day; ships carrying Swedish iron-ore and other essential war supplies from the Baltic ports to Rotterdam and other Dutch harbours. It was estimated that some 3,000,000 tons of Swedish iron ore reached the port of Rotterdam each year, for unloading into barges for onward transmission to the Ruhr steel mills. Other cargoes that reached Rotterdam included fertilisers, paper, pyrites and copper ore, grain and timber, totalling some 850,000 tons. Returning ships mainly carried coal and coke to Sweden. On average, eight to ten convoys sailed along the Dutch coast to Rotterdam each month, while another eight to ten convoys steamed northwards towards Scandinavia. The convoys usually comprised of six to twelve merchant ships, escorted by up to eight *Vorpostenboote* or *Flak*-ships. Destruction of these convoys by the RAF was to take place mainly off the Dutch coast and Frisian Islands. The heavy bomber squadrons on the other hand were to concentrate on raiding enemy ports, notably Brest. In the following months, other 2 Group units, 82, 88, 110, 114 and 226 Squadrons, complemented the Blenheim force in the anti-shipping campaign. During 1940 and early 1941, the North Sea shipping lanes had been the almost exclusive hunting grounds of Coastal Command. 22 Squadron's Beauforts had been quite successful in their torpedo-bombing attacks on enemy merchant shipping. This was to change dramatically now as 2 Group more or less took over the brunt of the anti-shipping campaign.

On the basis of German shipping movements in January and February 1941, the coast from Ushant to Denmark was divided into six so-called *Beats* - *Beat A* to *Beat F*. The *Beats* started thirty miles from the enemy coast and each was some 100 miles wide. When arriving at the starting line of the *Beat*, the Blenheims were to fly down to zero feet to get under the German radar, split up in pairs and fly directly to the coast at intervals of some twenty miles. On reaching the coast (some three miles off shore) the crews were to turn and sweep the shipping lane for some twenty miles or five minutes. If no ships were seen, they then returned to base. Any shipping encountered on the *Beats* was to be sunk. This was to be done at any cost, as Air Vice-Marshal Stevenson, AOC of 2 Group, impressed upon his crews. Sergeant Wilf Hepworth, observer with 139 Squadron clearly remembers:

"The AVM gave the whole Group a written pep-talk which was circulated to the squadrons and finished with the prophetic statement that he didn't care if he lost 80% of his crews and aircraft as long as we got results. I can still mentally see the school board and easel on which it was pinned in the 139 Sqn. crew room".

In support of 2 Group, Coastal Command general reconnaissance (GR) aircraft patrolled off the enemy coastlines to monitor any shipping movement. Also, Blenheims, Hudsons and Spitfires of No.1 PRU from RAF Benson supplied information on German naval movements by their daily photo-reconnaissance sorties.

Flight Sergeant Arthur Asker and Sergeant Bill O'Connell, observer and pilot with 226 Squadron in 1941/42, combine their accounts to give us a vivid description of the convoy attack tactics by the Blenheims of 2 Group in 1941. Asker starts off their narrative:

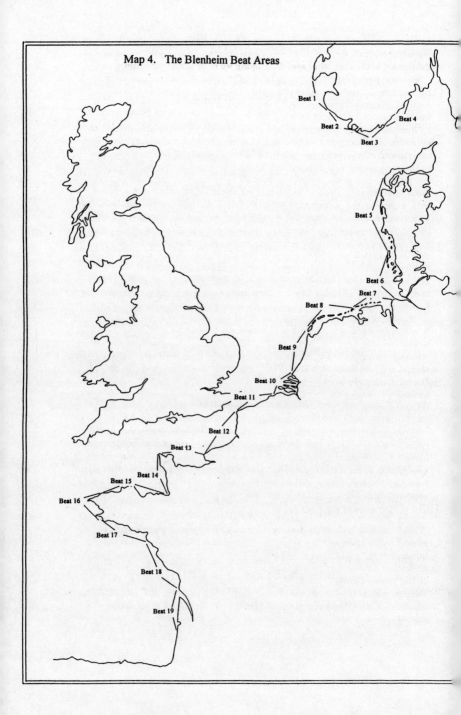

Map 4.   The Blenheim Beat Areas

"For us, in 1941, the day would start at 3 am if we were on stand-by. Then we would wait in the crew-room waiting for the telephone from Ops. to ring. We might wait all day before being ordered off, which was a bit wearing on the nerves, wondering what sort of shipping we might come up against.

"For our purposes, the shipping lanes off the coast of Europe were given *Beat* letters or numbers according their area. Thus, there was no need for detailed navigation briefing, just 'Sea-sweep *Beat B*' for example, and off we would go to the designated area.

"Approach to the target area was usually made from below mast-height to avoid detection by enemy radar, but not so low as to leave a wake caused by slip-stream, which would be visible to fighters searching above. Navigation to the target area was elementary, relying on accurate course-steering by the pilot, and continual checking of drift by the navigator. Final position could sometimes be checked by comparing the coastal outline and contours, with a copy of the appropriate page of marine navigational manuals with which the navigators were issued. These gave coastal views from mast-height, for the use of ships' captains in coastal waters.

"If one passed any fishing boats on the run-in, it was fairly certain that they had radioed in and reported our coming. It was therefore unfortunate for them that they had to be suppressed before they could get a message off. The 'squealers' could usually be identified by their tell-tale aerial arrays and these were given treatment by the front and rear guns. From then on it was time to don 'tin-hats', as steel helmets gave some feeling of protection.

"If visibility was poor, one could be on top of a convoy without notice, and it would be necessary to turn and attack on the way out. The formation would have to try and turn, staying reasonably tight together without colliding with each other. Cross-over turns required a great deal of skill at nought feet, especially when also 'jinking' and carrying out evasive action. During violent evasive action, the navigator was usually to be found pushing himself off the perspex roof of his little 'office', or picking himself off the floor, according to the 'G' forces being applied. The gunner in the rear turret also fared similarly, being whipped up and down like the tail of a dog.

"If the visibility was good, and a convoy was sighted, the navigator would retire from his 'office' and sit alongside the pilot where he could strap himself in and monitor the pilot's actions in case he was hit. In our crew's case it was usual for the pilot and navigator to press their bomb-releases together on the pilot's command, in case one or the other became incapacitated at the crucial moment of release.

Bill O'Connell now takes over the story:

"These convoys, with a scattering of tenders, would comprise of up to fifty coastal freighters, each one armed and being of a tonnage from a couple of hundred tons to as big as 8,000 tons. Many of them looked quite decrepit. Almost all convoys had two heavily armed *Flak*-ships stationed on the flank of the convoy. These *Flak*-ships certainly were deadly opposition, but the German fighters, which often accompanied convoys along the coast, were deadlier for the reason that they could easily catch up with a Blenheim, and they would stick with their attack until they had shot it down. The gunners in the Blenheim were, at best, able to offer what amounted to little more than token resistance. Given the choice between a *Flak*-ship and a section of three Bf109's, I would take the *Flak*-ship every time because the gunners on the *Flak*-ship would have a 'go' at me for only about fifteen seconds, and only about ten of those seconds would be really critical for me. After their fifteen-seconds performance, the show would be over. On the other hand, the Bf109's could stay with me for as long as it took them to finish me off.

"The *Flak*-ships were adapted from the normal coastal cargo ships and were believed to carry some cargo. A round gun turret on one or both ends of a ship readily identified it as a *Flak*-ship. Each turret had an 88 mm gun. They also mounted batteries of 20 mm cannon and light machine guns. The *Flak*-ships were really not too difficult to spot because, apart from the turret or turrets on them, they were almost always ships in the 2,500-ton range. A direct attack on a *Flak*-ship was to be avoided at just about any cost because of its deadly fire-power. So getting in to attack, and getting out fast was of great importance to us."

Arthur Asker further comments on the *Flak* defences of the convoys:

"A high degree of concentration was required when facing a target which was pouring streams of *Flak* at you; one of their objects was to put you off your aim. On one occasion the heavier weapons from a *Flak*-ship seemed to be deliberately firing into the water in front of us, throwing up columns of water to fly through. In amongst all this excitement it was important to avoid collision with the other aircraft in the formation all taking violent evasive action."

Bill O'Connell again picks up the account:

"In addition to their own powerful defences and the many German land defence positions they passed and whose defences they came under, these convoys often had an escort of German fighter aircraft, and the Blenheims, which ordinarily operated on shipping sweeps beyond the effective range of RAF fighters, were, with no RAF fighters to cover them, vulnerable targets for the German fighters.

"Finally, to deter attacks by low flying aircraft, the convoys often flew barrage balloons from some of the ships tethered by steel cables and flown at a height of two or three hundred feet from various strategic stations in the convoy. The whole convoy would be deployed in an area of perhaps one and a half miles along its route and up to one mile in width. Such were the targets faced by 2 Group aircrew flying Blenheims on a shipping sweep in 1941.

"We never attacked a convoy with more than six aircraft at a time, which tended to split the fire of the *Flak*-ships, and at the same time gave each aircraft a little room to manoeuvre. An attack by more than six aircraft created an unacceptable risk of mid-air collision between our own aircraft. From an attack of this kind, there would, in any case, seldom be more than six suitable and vulnerable ships on or near the flank of any convoy. And the targets had to be on or near the flank of a convoy because the pilots had to have a virtually clear run in for an effective attack on a ship.

"Because the bombs were dropped from very low level, the bombs had eleven-second delayed action fuses to allow the aircraft to clear the area before the bombs exploded to prevent mortal damage to the aircraft. The SAP (semi-armour piercing) bombs had a much sharper nose than the GP (general purpose) bomb for penetration, and a much thicker casing as well, and, because of this thicker casing, it was a smaller bomb and held less high explosive material than a GP bomb of the same weight. But the casing would not break open even at very high velocity on impact with stone, concrete or steel. And, when dropped at 260 mph from a Blenheim, the SAP bomb on impact with the ship would have enough velocity to penetrate the steel plates of the ship's hull and explode inside the vessel where it would do maximum damage. Because of the construction of the SAP bomb and the nature of its purpose, the fuse (an acid mixture) was actuated on impact by a mechanism in the tail of the bomb.

"You had to commit yourself to attacking a particular ship at a range of about one mile. To abort an attack within a mile or so of the convoy was usually a fatal mistake. In attacking a convoy the tactics were always the same. One attacked a ship at an altitude just above the wave tops, and doing evasive action on the run-in to avoid as much *Flak* as possible. The idea was to put a bomb through the side of the ship and into the bowels, and the eleven-second delay in the blast gave the aircraft a chance to get a healthy distance from the ship when the bomb(s) exploded without damage to the aircraft. In order to accomplish this, you headed for the mid-section of the ship, which was your aiming point, bearing in mind that you had to climb about 100 feet or more above the water in order to clear the superstructure and all the rigging and antennae. So you kept your point of release (controlled by a thumb button on the control column) until you were a few hundred feet from the ship, started your climb to clear the top of the rigging, and almost simultaneously released your bombs.

"The practised eye was the only bombsight we used. Mechanical sighting devices had been tried, but they had little success with them. All problems in developing a degree of proficiency in pilot release bombing lay in undershooting and overshooting the target. Somewhere in between was the bull's-eye, and it took a lot of practice in the onrushing perspective of the target at very low level to learn the exact instant at which a bomb should be released to get really close to the bull's-eye. A hit on the bull's-eye was quite rare, but many pilots could come close just about every time.

"Having reached a height to clear the masts and antennae, you stuffed the nose of the aircraft down to get back down to wave-top level again."

Asker comments on this:

"The return to nought feet after going over the top of a ship was something guaranteed to upset one's breakfast."

O'Connell again:

"Immediately on stuffing the nose of the aircraft down, both engines would quit cold, and everything would be quiet, except for the odd crack of the

Flak and the airstream. The reason for this was that the aircraft was in a configuration of negative G's (gravitational forces), and the Bristol Mercury XV engines in the Blenheim had only gravity-fed carburettors.

"This was a critical point as the aircraft decelerated quickly with no power. The pilot would, for all practical purposes, be flying a glider with two windmilling, high drag propellers. It would be very quiet in the cockpit, and only the airstream flowing past the cockpit would be heard. In this configuration you always got the impression that you were drawing an awful lot of attention. That was the point at which many Blenheims were shot down by *Flak*.

"But, the situation lasted only a few seconds (or was it really 45 minutes?). The pilot would ease back on the control column to raise the nose of the aircraft to the sudden accompaniment of the roar of two Bristol Mercury XV engines, which would start just as quickly as they stopped. And all this had happened with the throttle levers fully open. On getting back to wave-top height, you weaved your way through the remaining ships (and every ship had armament of some kind) as best you could until you were clear of the convoy and the gun fire. Meanwhile, the WOp/AG would be pounding away at different targets with his twin machine-guns and the camera/oblique installation would be recording photographs of the area to the rear through which the aircraft had just flown. The WOp/AG, who had been issued a hand held Leica camera for the operation, would take pictures of the convoy with the Leica when he was not returning gun-fire from the various ships. But he probably would not have time to use it or he might even forget that he had it.

"In a few minutes the convoy would be far behind. Any two or more Blenheims would join up for mutual defence against German fighter aircraft, and in a short while most of the surviving aircraft would have joined the formation. At the same time, each crew would be looking the convoy carefully over to try and identify the ship they had attacked. In the perspective now lent by the added distance, this was often possible. Smoke emitting from an identified target would evoke satisfaction in the day's work. The formation would then loosen up to relieve some of the tension on the pilots, and it would be time to relax a bit. Having made certain that there was no odour of petrol in the aircraft, the smokers would light their cigarettes (against the rules, but done anyway). And some would bring out candy bars which many carried with them as immediate emergency rations. Often these were shared.

"Conversation would be at a minimum during the return flight to base. There would be observations and speculations about aircraft and crews that were seen to be shot down or missing from the formation and a few questions and answers, and the matter would then be closed. There would be long periods when the inter-com. would be completely silent on the return flight. Most of the time there would be only the rhythmic throb of the two Mercury XV's to listen to, but their ears would now be so much in harmony with the engines that they would not hear them. Each would be with his own thoughts.

"There would be three tired and sober-minded airmen in each of those
Blenheims following their ordeal, but they would be going home and that
would be all that mattered to them now."

The maritime campaign started on 12th March, when six crews
of 139 Squadron flew shipping sweeps off the Dutch coast. Wing
Commander Kyle and a second crew found and bombed a
trawler and two merchant ships off Ijmuiden, but no results
were observed. All aircraft returned safely before lunchtime. On
virtually each day during the the remaining weeks of March, a
handful of Blenheims flew shipping *Beats* off the enemy coasts.
Usually, ships were encountered and bombed, and losses among
the Blenheims were surprisingly low. Only four Blenheims
failed to return; two of 82 Squadron and two of 21 Squadron, all
shot down by ship's *Flak* off the Dutch coast. None of the twelve
crew members survived their crash; flying at zero feet at high
speed the crews hardly had a chance when their aircraft were
hit and crashed in the cold North Sea.

The 23rd March was a black day for one of the Coastal
Command squadrons involved in the shipping *Beats* off the
Dutch coast. In late afternoon, three fighter Blenheims of 235
Squadron had left Bircham Newton for a *Pirate* patrol. Off the
Hook of Holland, three coasters, one *Flak*-ship and an *E-Boat*
were sighted and attacked with 40lb GP bombs, but no hits
were observed. Immediately after, the Blenheims were bounced
by three Bf109s of *3./JG 1*. Flying Officer Green, the leader in
'N' ordered the formation to close but it was too late for
Sergeant Evans and crew. They were lagging and the Blenheim
was immediately shot down into the sea. Pilot Officer Newman
in 'D' tried to formate behind the leader but was attacked and
shot down with the port engine on fire. All six men in the two
crews are still missing. 'N' was attacked by a third Messerschmitt but succeeded in escaping by taking violent evasive
action. The only survivor made it back to base with the petrol
tanks shot through.

It soon became clear to the Blenheim crews that this new type
of operation brought many new dangers on them. 21 Squadron
for example flew its first shipping *Beat* on 26th March, between
Texel and Ijmuiden. Three crews bombed shipping but Sergeant
Freir's aircraft suffered from collisions with sea gulls while
flying low over the sea. One bird smashed through the front

windscreen and hit Freir in the face. He was forced to turn back to base. One day later, a 139 Squadron crew had a narrow escape off Ijmuiden. Sergeant Bob Coles, observer in 139 Squadron, made the following entry on this in his diary that night:

> "Pilot Officer Sidney Smith's crew sighted a convoy of warships, destroyers, *E-boats, U-boats* etc. Dive bombed destroyer and made another pass using guns. Badly shot up. Observer wounded. A shell entered port window and exited starboard blister panel, shrapnel causing flesh wounds. Wing Commander held Sidney Smith's escapade as an example he wished us to follow. We didn't think machine-gunning a destroyer made much sense! Suicidal in fact."

The 31st March 1941 witnessed a new phase in the daylight anti-shipping campaign. On this day, the first 'fringe' or coastal target operation was flown by 2 Group Blenheims. The fringe attacks were aimed at troops, transport, artillery, *Flak* and searchlight emplacements in the hope that these 'hit and run' raids would cause dispersal of the German *Flak* and fighter defences. The honour of this 'first' fell to 21 Squadron. Led by Squadron Leader 'Attie' Atkinson, eight crews flew towards the Dutch Frisian Islands, hugging the waves of the North Sea. Off Texel, two destroyers were soon spotted and bombed. One was hit and seen to list to port belching a black column of smoke. The defending *Flak* of the ships was murderous and two attacking aircraft were shot down into the sea, R3884 and R3900. Sergeant Adams and Pilot Officer Rogers and their crews were all killed. After the attack the remaining Blenheims turned further East in search of fringe targets. At Ameland and Terschelling Islands worthwhile targets were soon found and attacked. These were gun positions, huts, German troops on parade and a radio station. The six Blenheims then set course for home at zero feet, leaving the enemy in chaos and confusion. It was a successful first fringe attack by the 21 Squadron crews, but losing 25% of the attacking force was a high price to pay for their daring.

A positive result of the Blenheim fringe target raids was their impact on the Dutch people. The spectacle of low level Blenheims that went after the detested Huns in broad daylight was a splendid morale booster for the Dutch people. One example may illustrate this. On 14th April, sixteen Blenheims

...eim If of 604 Squadron near North Weald, 1939. *(604 Sqn. Coll.)*

...heim IV L4843:J of 'A' Flight, 53 Squadron, 1939. *(Dick Maydwell)*

F/O John Wray, pilot 53 Sqn. ACC. Shortly before going to France in 1939. *(John Wray)*

...Falck with some of his aircrews of 2./ZG 76 in the ready room at Jever, December 1939. *(Falck)*

Above: Blenheim IV of 139 Sqn at Plivot, France 1939. *(SH B83 3609)*

Left: F/O George 'Red' Eames and F/O Albert 'Bertie' Oakl pilots with XV Sqn 1939–40. Eames was wounded and Oak killed on 12th May 1940. *(Charles Oakley)*

XV Sqn at Vraux, France in 1939. *Back row:* W/O Nightingale, P/O Hugh George, P/O George Eames, P/O Ronnie Clarke, P/O Tom Bassett, P/O Len Trent, P/O Frankish, two F/S groundcrew *Front row:* P/O Douglass, F/O Jess Oakeshott, F/L Paul Chapman, S/L Lewelyn, W/C Wingate, F Webster, F/O Dawson-Jones, P/O Bent, F/O Albert Oakley, P/O Robinson. *(Betty George)*

139 Sqn, Horsham St. Faith, early 1940. *(left to right)* P/O Menzies, F/O Dundee, F/O Rimmer, F Tedder, P/O Nicholson, F/O Sellers, S/L Tideman, F/L Hughman, W/C Dickens AFC, S/L Hendry, Pepper DFC, F/O Webster, F/O Turnbull, F/L Ault, P/O Plinston, F/O Matthews. *(Eric Aspinall)*

James Wells, CO of 600
, killed in action
.1940. (Hans
erwater)

Sgt John Davis, an observer with 600 Sqn, on the quay at Harwich after being shot down at Rotterdam on 10.5.1940. (Hans Onderwater)

Remains of Blenheim IV L8856 of XV Sqn, crashed at Kruis on 15.5.1940. Note the 40 lb bombs in the foreground. (Wim de Meester)

heim IV of XV Sqn in
mer 1940. (Philip Casey)

L8847, a Blenheim IV of XV Sqn, was shot down at Borgharen/Maastricht on 12.5.1940. (G. Zylstra)

ts of 4./JG 27 on return from oper-
ns in May 1940. Uffz Bendert, pic-
d on left, claimed a Blenheim on
.1940. (Hilde Bendert)

600 Sqn, Manston, spring 1940. (left to right) P/O John Barnes, F/O Hugh Rowe, F/O Tony Vickers (KIA), P/O Roger Moore (KIA 10.5.1940), P/O Mike Anderson (KIA 10.5.1940), P/O Tony Tollemache (KIA), F/L Ralph Hiscox. (Hans Onderwater)

139 Sqn Blenheim R3698 crashed at Horsham St. Faith 9.12.1940 after convoy attack off Den Helder. F/O King and crew safe. *(Eric Aspinall)*

Above: 82 Sqn Blenheim IV at Bodney, 1940. *(Paul Lincoln)*

Right: (left to right) Sgt Peter Eames, P/O Donald Wellings and Sgt Don McFarlane of 82 Sqn in front of R3821:N of 'B' Flight at Bodney, summer 1940. *(Paul Lincoln/McFarlane)*

Above: Captured Blenheim IV in Luftwaffe markings. *(Pieter Bergman)*

Left: (left to right) Sgt Granville Wop/AG, Sgt Spong pilot, and Sgt Mackinnon observer, in front of T1832 of 139 Sqn, late 1940. P/O Phillips was killed in this aircraft over Den Helder, 1.5.1941. The aircraft was lost on 16.6.1941, after having flown 49 sorties. *(Les Spong)*

...t to right: Sgts Ken Whittle, Geoff Atkins and Tom McPhee of 139 Sqn, 1941. *...n Whittle)*

...to right: Oblt Leesmann, Hptm Ewald, Lt Rung and Munz at Texel on return from a sortie on 25.5.1941, *...n* Blenheim V6248 of 18 Sqn was shot down and R3666 badly damaged. *(Karl Munz via Rob de Visser)*

P/O Charles C. Sherring, Wop/AG 18 Sqn, 1941, 'very sprog' in 1940. *(via Mrs Vera Sherring)*

...ostenboot, or Flak-ship that escorted German convoys *...d* from Rotterdam 1941/42. It carried three Flak turrets. *...drich Mundt)*

Flak-ship off Terschelling after attack by Sgt Middleton's 139 Sqn crew, 30.3.1941. *(Bob Coles)*

59 Sqn aircrew, spring 1941. *(left to right)* Buchan, Martin, Lishman, Beveridge, Evans, Badland (KIA 28.4.1941), Norton (PoW 28.4.1941), Fry (sitting, MIA 28.4.1941), Custerson, u/k, u/k, u/k, Mike Sandes. *(Alec McCurdy)*

P/O E. R. Phillips, 139 Sqn KIA 1.5.1941 over Den Helder. *(R. Fastnedge)*

Kriegsmarine sailor S. Richter of H811 rescues P/ONorton of 59 Sqn on 28.4.1941. *(Otto Keller)*

Sgt Bob Coles, observer with Sqn, was captured on 7/8.5.19 *(Bob Coles)*

The rudder of Oblt Paul Stolte's 3./JG1 Bf109E-4. The four victory tabs show 22.3.41 (T2433 of 59 Sqn), 23.3.41 (Z6085 of 235 Sqn), 28.5.41 (V6457 of 82 Sqn), 28.5.41 (not traced). *(H. Schubert via Rob de Visser)*

Typical German convoy sailing along the Dut coast. *(Justus Hollmann)*

Sqn officers, June 1941. Back row: F/O Youalls, F/O Leach, F/O Bryce, F/O Redfern-Smith, F/A
[...]eney, P/O Sammels, P/O Edrich. Front row: F/L Bailey, S/L Clayton, S/L Simmons, W/C Petley,
[...] Murray, F/L Richardson (Adj), F/O Welburn. *(Vera Sherring)*

[...] Heinrich Nöcker of 3./JG 1 returns triumphantly to De Kooy
[...]r destroying Blenheims Z5744 and R3903 of 139 Sqn on
[...]1941. *(R. Kress/Rob de Visser)*

Sgt Bob Hind, Wop/AG 18
Sqn 1940–41. Missing off
Schiermonnikoog on 9.6.41.
(Janet Pieters)

[...]rchill visits West Raynham on 6.6.1941. *(left to right)* G/C
[...]ams, AVM Stevenson, u/k, G/C Bandon, Portal, Prof Lindemann,
[...]ston Churchill, Clement Attlee, AM Sir Richard Peirse.
[...]a Sherring/Peter Gunn)

The grave of F/S Ian Bullivant
at Anjum. *(Theo Boiten)*

59 Sqn Blenheim formation, 3.8.1941. *(via Peter Smith)*

226 Sqn crew. (*left to right*) F/Sgt Asker, F/Sgt Brett and F/Lt Shaw-Kennedy return from a shipping attack, July 1941. *(via Arthur Asker)*

Bill O'Connell, pilot with 226 Sqn, 1941–42. Depicted as S/L DFC late in 1943. *(Bill O'Connell)*

Groundcrew of 18 Sqn with W/C Smythe's 'N' at Horsham St. Faith in August 1941. (*left to right*) Ned, Fred, Les Deadfield. *(Les Deadfield)*

Sgt Moore Wop/AG, P/O Milson pilot and Sgt Millar observer, 18 Sqn crew Blickling Hall, July 1941. *(Jim Moore)*

went on a bombing raid to the power stations of Leiden and Haarlem. These attacks had the full approval of the local Dutchmen, as a German report reflects:

"The anti-German feelings of the people clearly came to the surface as a result of a British air force attack on the city of Haarlem on 14th April (Easter Monday). A large crowd of people in the streets quite openly expressed their jubilant feelings for the attacking Englishmen."

In early April, the 2 Group Blenheim anti-shipping and fringe targets offensive was stepped up which resulted in many dozens of attacks. For instance, we can closely examine the operations of 7th April. No less than 25 Blenheims left their bases in East Anglia and headed at low level for the Dutch and Danish coasts. 139 Squadron supplied the majority of this force: six Blenheims of 'B' Flight went to *Beat 12* off the Danish coast and seven aircraft of 'A' Flight raided the Royal Dutch steel mills at Ijmuiden. Sergeant Bob Coles, observer with 139 Squadron, made the following entry in his private diary on the 7th April operations of his squadron:

"7th April. Denmark *Beat*. Nothing seen, went inland in search of anything interesting. Bob's (Sergeant Bob Hale, WOp/AG, T.B.) guns weren't working properly and couldn't be trusted. A Bf109 flew near and made off without attacking. Flew inland at low level. Not a cloud in the sky and visibility 50 miles. Bob and I ventured the opinion that 30 miles inland was asking for trouble in the circumstances, expecting hordes of fighters to intercept on the way home. Bill was in his stubborn mood so we continued, scored a hit on a railway bridge and missed a small cargo vessel at anchor in Glyn Fjord with the smaller remaining bombs. This caused Bill to throw the aircraft around in frustration and still wouldn't act on my course for base. People waved at us from their doorways as did children at school. We weren't happy with this operation and a row developed on return to base. It was foolhardy.

"'A' Flight's attack on Ijmuiden steel-works. One aircraft was lost to fighters. Four aircraft badly damaged by strong force of fighters with harbour and ships defences. Sergeant Dennis' aircraft caught fire on landing. Observer Sergeant Hill shot in leg dragged away subsequently died. Sergeant Waddington WOp/AG hero of the day attended him all the way back and manhandled him over periscope gunsight. One other aircraft written off with wounded crew. A very bad day for the squadron."

On 18th April 1941, Bob Coles continued the tragic story of the 7th April Ijmuiden operation:

"Sergeant Stan Hill laid to rest with military honours. I was a bearer and would have done anything to avoid meeting his wife, but couldn't. This a stout kid and bore it well. They had been married just a few months. A good number of aircrew attended and an escort of twenty airmen. Sergeant

McPhee was told of his DFM today and was congratulated by all. He was visibly annoyed that his crew who had been on all forty operations were neglected and not mentioned."

Sergeant Les Spong, a veteran pilot with 139 Squadron flew on the Ijmuiden steel works raid of 7th April 1941:

"I would like to tell you about our penultimate operation on 7.4.41 in T1832, which was the aircraft which I flew more than any other while on the squadron.

"For anyone who is not familiar with the operating circumstances of the Blenheim a few words of explanation are necessary to enable one to understand what happened. The pilot had of course no view immediately to the rear apart from a small rear-view mirror and only a limited view to the side and rear through the side windows. If one was flying at really low level one was too busy anyway watching the surface and checking one's course to do anything else, so it was necessary to rely on one's gunner in the turret to keep a sharp lookout and promptly report anything happening at the back which was worth noting.

"On the 6th April we had a fighter affiliation exercise to give us practical experience of evasive tactics under attack from a fighter. The idea was that the gunner would report the fighter's approach in a continuous running commentary and he would give the order 'Turn port - or starboard, turn port, GO' just as the fighter was about to open fire, thus putting the attacker off his aim by turning inside his curve of approach and thus increasing the angle of deflection. To do this required a nice judgment on the part of the gunner, to decide when the fighter was about 200 yards away (considered to be the maximum distance for effective shooting) and keeping up the narrative while manoeuvring his turret and getting in a position to return fire. Sometimes one or other of the Brownings would have a stoppage, requiring the gunner to dismantle the gun and clear the stoppage without interrupting his flow of words. A rate one turn on the part of the Blenheim, done at precisely the right moment, was considered by the theorists sufficient to cause the fighter to miss.

"It had been reported that vital parts for submarines were being manufactured in the steel-works of Ijmuiden, close to Haarlem on the Dutch coast and it was decided that this was a suitable target for the Blenheims. No cloud cover was demanded: we would cross at sea level so as to avoid detection as long as possible whether by the radar then being reported or by other means. On reaching the Dutch coast to one side of the target we would climb to 500 feet, turn to make our bomb run while in line with the coast and after 'bombs gone' dive to sea level again and make for home.

"It was an exciting way of carrying out a bombing raid. At night one was very much on one's own in the blackness with few reference points; with cloud cover one was in cloud a large part of the time again with little to show of one's progress; and at height one seemed to be poised stationary in space as the time slowly passed. With the low level approach one was racing across the sea with an immense sense of speed, then once in the target area all was excitement with little time to worry about the *Flak* and, once on the journey back there was the sea flashing by below one's wings again. In the mess we had a record of the 'Thunder and Lightning Polka' which expressed the feeling admirably, starting with a fast rhythm, then developing into a flashy storm which died away into the fast rhythm again. We played it over and over again.

"All went well with our crossing of the North Sea, the eight aircraft flying not in close formation but individually in the general vicinity of each other. We had only one or two of the others in view at any one time, each flying his own course without reference to the others. Mac's (Sergeant MacKinnon, observer, T.B.) navigation was spot on and we made landfall precisely at the point intended.

"We made our bombing run as briefed, had no problem in identifying the target and with Mac now prone over the bomb sight and giving me the necessary corrections, made an accurate drop. It was with some satisfaction that we were able to drop down again to deck level with the engines now in plus 9 boost and set course for base. All went well for about five minutes until Jim (Sergeant Granville, WOp/AG, T.B.) called up on the intercom 'Enemy fighter 7 o'clock' and started to give me a textbook commentary. Just as we had practiced only the day before came the words 'Turn port, turn port, GO' and I went into a near 90-degree bank in the course of which the compass and the direction indicator spun so that, without being able to see the sun because of the cloudy conditions, I had to make a guess as to the point at which I had turned through 360 degrees and could resume our course.

"Of course, I was doing it all wrong according to the theorists and at one stage I caught a quick glimpse of Sergeant McPhee's aircraft about a half-mile away also on the way out obviously also under attack as he did a careful rate one turn to starboard. As was explained to me after we returned, a fighter could always turn inside a Blenheim and a rate one turn was sufficient to spoil his aim. However, when Jim Granville reported a '109 on our tail I had a quick picture in my mind of what had already happened to so many Blenheims in similar encounters and my reaction was to do my damnedest to throw him off. As a result, as I say, I made my compass and direction indicator temporarily useless and Mac told me later that, having come back from his forward bomb aiming position to sit beside me, he briefly blacked out from the centrifugal force in the tightness of our turn. However, the '109 overshot us and I was able to straighten out in what I guessed to be the general direction of Blighty.

"Only too soon Jim was resuming his commentary with an account of another attack. Once again, on getting Jim's 'GO', I threw the aircraft into a vertical turn, keeping as close to the waves as I dared, in the hope that the Messerschmitt pilot would be forced to break off early for fear of flying into the sea. Once again Mac briefly blacked out, while I can only imagine Jim's efforts to control his turret. Again I straightened out on a vaguely estimated course for home.

"Soon the whole procedure was repeated; and after that it happened again, and again, and again...we lost account of the number of times. We thought that the whole action lasted about a half-hour, but we really had no idea while it was happening. Then, finally, I heard Jim's excited voice saying 'He's breaking away. He's climbing...There's smoke coming from him..He's gone into the cloud.'

"We continued at sea level in plus 9 boost, with about 220 on the ASI for several minutes before we felt confident that the fight was finished. Then I pulled up the nose of the aircraft and soon found the shelter of the cloud where I was able to restore the emergency boost lever to its normal position and fly home in a quieter mood.

"There is a twist to the story which I have never been able to explain. After we had been de-briefed Jim tackled me with 'How did you know when to turn on the fourth attack, Les?' It appeared that Jim had had a stoppage in one of his guns and in his struggle to free the jammed gun he had pulled his intercom plug out of its socket. As the '109 came in again I turned just at the moment before he fired, exactly as needed. But Jim didn't tell me to: he was at that moment incommunicado.

"We undertook one operation only after that one: a sea sweep off The Hague and on the 15th April we were posted to 13 OTU Bicester. There was a mess 'do' there not long after and I had a short talk with Wing Commander Kyle, who was, I think, visiting. He told me that there had been an agent's report from Holland confirming that on the occasion of our escapade, a Bf109 had been shot down. We also heard from the safety of Bicester that low level attacks had continued to be made and casualties had mounted. There was a report that a pilot officer whose name I have forgotten and who joined the squadron not long before we left had been promoted to fill vacancies successively to the ranks of Flying Officer, Flight Lieutenant and Squadron Leader and who had been killed in action shortly after."

In Early April, Germany invaded the Balkans and therefore 2 Group received directive *BC/S.24643/Air* on the 10th of the month to intensify day attacks in order to pin down the enemy fighter force in the west. Therefore, 18 Squadron joined the anti-shipping and fringe target force of 21, 82 and 139 Squadron. The 'sprog' crews were soon in action, as on the 11th, 20 Blenheims of 139 and 18 Squadron flew out to Emden, Heligoland and Rotterdam. Led by four experienced crews of 139, four crews of 18 Squadron had their first experience in the daylight trade on a shipping sweep off Rotterdam. Pilot Officer Charles Sherring, WOp/AG with 18 Squadron, recalls this operation:

"Our first daylight trip was on April 11th, when we went to join 139 at Horsham, who were going to show us how to do daylights. There were two different programmes for the day, and our part was to fly at low level to the

Dutch coast, climb into cloud there, which was supposed to be thick, fly near Rotterdam, then come out of the cloud, and do a low level on a couple of destroyers that were there.

"There was a tremendous delay before we finally took off, and when we reached the Dutch coast, flying behind 139, with eight aircraft in the air at the same time, there was Holland straight in front, and not a cloud in the sky.

"There were quite a lot of small rowing boats fishing just off the shore, and we all zoomed over the top of them, turned north and did a three minute shipping *Beat*. To everyone's real regret, we couldn't find a boat of any sort, as eight aircraft trying to bomb one or two ships would have been a great sight. We were well in sight of land all the time, and as we dare not stay longer for fear of fighters, we turned for home and raced 139 back to base. The other part of the programme, which had gone up north somewhere, did not do so well, and we lost Jones and his crew on his 30th trip" (Pilot Officer Jones and crew were killed when their aircraft was hit by *Flak* and crashed near Sylt Island, T.B.).

The first month of the daylight shipping campaign by 2 Group was considered to have been a success. 355 ships had been sighted off the enemy coasts and 121 had been attacked. Of these, six were claimed to have been sunk, eight more plus a destroyer damaged and 89 slightly damaged. Off the Dutch coast, 49 ships were attacked, but none of these were heavily damaged or sunk. The figures of six ships sunk and nine heavily damaged must be considered as inflated, as these shipping casualties cannot be traced in official German, nor in Allied records. *Grossadmiral* Erich Raeder, C-in-C of the German Navy commented to Hitler on this matter on the 20th April 1941:

"The increasing efforts by the enemy to interfere with our sea transports from and to Norway by aerial attack have so far led to pleasingly small losses off the west coast of Norway, in the North Sea and in the Channel due to the efficiency of our forces of the *Flak* arm, *Flak*-ships and minesweepers!!"

What about the cost in Blenheims and crews during the first month of the maritime campaign? The losses were surprisingly light in March, considering the nature of the operations. In March only four Blenheims failed to return, all shot down off the Dutch coast, three of them off Texel. In the first twelve days of April, losses mounted fast: six Blenheims were lost on anti-shipping sweeps (five on Dutch coast operations) and three more on 7th April on the Ijmuiden steel-works raid. This brings the totals for the first month of the anti-shipping campaign at eleven aircraft lost on anti-shipping sweeps and three more on a coastal target attack. Moreover, Coastal Command's 59 and 235 Squadrons lost three more Blenheims on shipping sweeps off Holland during late March. This proved once again that the Blenheim was a vulnerable aircraft in daylight, and especially on the anti-shipping raids, as was becoming clear by now.

Yet, on the 12th April 1941 a new 2 Group Operations Order extended the line of coastal search areas from Bordeaux to Norway, and these areas were divided into 19 *Beats*. This set the scene for a horrible spring and summer for the 2 Group crews.

Also, in late April, two new developments took place. Firstly, it was decided that 2 Group Blenheims should close the Straits of Dover to enemy shipping during daylight. Therefore, squadron detachments were based on a rotational basis at RAF Manston near Dover. Operations against shipping in the *Operation Channel Stop* campaign soon proved very costly in aircraft and crews, with usually at least 50% losses on any one operation. Most of the Channel Stop operations took place in the Channel, but some reached as far as the mouth of the river Scheldt (*Beat 10*).

In late April, 2 Group was also ordered to send squadron detachments to the 'Island Fortress' of Malta for anti-shipping duties against the south-bound Axis shipping. Although these detachments only lasted for about five weeks on a rotational basis, losses usually approached 100%. Malta-based Blenheim crews, co-operating with Beauforts and Beaufighters, operated against Rommel's supply ships until February 1942. By January 1942, Rommel's *Afrika Korps* only had three days of supplies left. The situation was becoming desperate for the enemy in North Africa. The passage of shipping to North Africa had been largely halted due to the efforts of the Blenheims, Beauforts and Beaufighters from Malta. A successful campaign, but gained at a terrible cost.

During the remaining days of April, 2 Group crews flew their shipping sweeps on virtually every day off the Dutch coast and Frisian Islands, and carried out dozens of shipping attacks. One of these was the 23rd April, a busy day. 31 Blenheims and 6 Hampdens of Bomber Command were dispatched to the shipping lanes off Belgium, Holland, the Frisian Islands and Denmark. The majority of the force went to the Dutch coast: six aircraft of 105 Squadron went to *Beat 10* (SW Dutch coast), five others of 105 to *Beat 9* (Western Dutch coast); eight crews of 139 Squadron to *Beat 8* (Dutch Frisians) and seven aircraft of 18 Squadron to *Beats 9* and *10*. In *Beat 10,* six crews of 105 Squadron came across shipping off Domburg (Zeeland) and a bombing attack was launched. German sources confirm the damaging of the *Anhalt,* a cargo vessel of 5870 tons off Domburg. Also, an escorting minesweeper, the *M1404* was hit, killing eight of the ship's crew and injuring eleven. Before being hit, *M1404* managed to shoot down one of the aircraft of 105 Squadron. V6318 crashed into the sea, killing Sergeant Lister and crew.

While sweeping the Dutch Frisians, three Blenheims of 18 and 139 Squadron raided a radio station on the Island of Terschelling, and two *Flak*-ships were hit off Borkum by 139 Squadron aircraft. One of the Terschelling raiders was R3885 of 139 Squadron. Sergeant 'Jock' Shinnie manned the twin-Brownings in the mid upper turret of this aircraft:

"On 23rd April we were detailed to bomb a wireless station on Terschelling Island. Having been in that area a number of times during weather and shipping sweeps, and come to no great harm, we were not particularly worried about this operation. The weather was good and we approached at wave top level attack. Everything looked so quiet and peaceful. We located and hit part of the target but as we were leaving we ran into intense gunfire. We returned to base safely and then discovered that one of our propellers had been hit many times but only one hole in the fuselage."

Pilot Officer Sherring, WOp/AG with 18 Squadron, headed for the Dutch coast in 'V-for-Vera' on 23 April:

"No. 21 operation was a cloud cover sweep for L and R-boats off the Dutch coast, where a little party of them had been reported. As we headed nearer to Holland, our cloud began to thin out.

"Suddenly we came to a gap, and with us two Bf109s came out of the cloud as well. Hawkins seemed to turn in about two Blenheim lengths, and we got back into a miserable little bit of cloud before they were on us. It was a thin cloud, not more than 200 feet thick anywhere, and one Bf109 went above, the other below, while we weaved up to the top and down to the bottom in long irregular curves, and this seemed to fox them completely. We dropped our bombs (at safe) to give us extra speed, and came home as fast as old 'V-for-Vera' could possibly go. Two of the twelve which went out found and bombed the *E-boats* successfully, and no one else saw anything at all.

We must have been a bit north, as further south was where they found the boats and also much thicker cloud".

Sergeant Bob Coles, observer in Sergeant Bill Middleton's crew of 139 Squadron, went on a sea sweep to Borkum, and this proved to be almost 'curtains' for his crew:

"We were near Borkum when we attacked the first of two *Flak*-ships in a dive and scored a hit. Swiftly turning on the second at sea level we dropped our bombs but received a shell which exploded inside my steel helmet laying on the floor. This took most of the impact but left a hole some two feet across and pieces of shrapnel in our clothing. The side of an accumulator had blown off and the slipstream through the hole vaporised acid which mixed with magnesium smoke from two Very lights which were on fire. Other Very lights brilliantly burnt up and the fire spread to maps and charts. The cockpit was so filled with smoke, fumes and burning that Bill couldn't see out, but controlled the aircraft by leaning close and observing the instrument panel, his eyes streaming from the acid. I threw out burning debris through the hole and gun blister and restored some sort of order.

"As I had no charts I guessed a course for Bill to steer. This brought us eventually to be challenged by a British gunboat, and as we couldn't respond by Verey light or Aldis lamp it opened fire on us. We were in the approaches to the Thames estuary. We dropped the undercarriage and flaps and flew at low level along the coast until we recognised Southwold and so to base. My moustache and eyebrows were burnt off, our leather flying clothing were covered in white magnesium deposit but otherwise we were undamaged."

For his coolness under great danger, Bob Coles was Mentioned in Dispatches, as his firm actions undoubtedly saved his crew's lives.

May 1941 started with a large scale Blenheim operation to the enemy coasts on the 1st. In all, 2 Group dispatched 26 aircraft. Three crews of 105 Squadron went to bomb shipping in Rotterdam harbour (two attacked ships) and three of 105 Squadron to the Scheldt Estuary near Antwerp (again two attacked shipping). Six Blenheims of 139 Squadron led by the new CO, Wing Commander Igor Braye DFC, took off from Horsham St. Faith for a raid on the harbour and power station of Den Helder. All aircraft bombed the primary targets.

Sergeant Wilf Hepworth (observer) and Sergeant Albert Turner (WOp/AG) were in the leading Blenheim of the second vic of three aircraft from 139 Squadron on the Den Helder raid. Skipper of Blenheim V5460 XD:J was Flight Lieutenant Thompson, a Canadian who later in 1941 got a DFC while operating from Malta against Rommel's supply ships in the

Mediterranean. Hepworth and Turner combine to tell the story of the 1st May raid:

"Six Blenheims took off from Horsham St. Faiths at 15.35. We flew in two 'V's of three in open formation at low level. Our new CO was leading the first 'V' and Flight Lieutenant Thompson, our pilot, was leading the second. Both sections were flying between 50 and 100 feet. On reaching a position about 4 miles north of Den Helder we moved nearer the coast with the intention of going in North of the Frisian Islands, reaching Vlieland and then swinging into the Wadden Zee and turning west into the target. Each Blenheim had its own target within the power station complex, with 11 second delay fused bombs to ensure we were clear of the blast when they went off. Things became a little disorganized when instead of turning beyond Vlieland, the Wing Commander's crew turned in at Texel's northern tip. Unfortunately a section of the German Army was practising sea-borne landing manoeuvres there at the time. A pitched battle opened up between them and our air gunners as we swept round towards the targets. All hope of surprise attack had gone by the board.

"We crossed the coast at very low level and made a wide circle inland so that we were on a western course of about 270 when we went in to attack the target. As we approached Den Helder each pilot and his navigator had to identify their own target and line up on it. Although we were in open formation on the approach, once individual targets were selected we broke formation and this created great excitement and apprehension as Blenheims were turning and banking to close up on their respective targets. The air seemed to be full of Blenheims, perilously close, going in all directions. We found our target which was the main power house, bombed on target from 100 feet hitting the power house with two 500 and four 25IC bombs, and headed for home. There was considerable light *Flak* and we air gunners were returning their fire. I remember firing at a heavy machine-gun group on top of a water tower we were flying almost level with and then looking astern, saw our bombs go off".

During the run over target a sudden tragic incident occurred in the Blenheim of Pilot Officer Edgar Phillips, Flying Officer Ralph Fastnedge and Sergeant John Allen, who were on their 43rd operational sortie in T1832. Sergeant Ken Whittle, WOp/AG with 139 Squadron, tells of this fatal accident:

"Pilot Officer Phillips joined about the same time as my crew in October/November 1940. Attacking his target through light *Flak*, one round of ammunition (a bullet) entered the starboard side of the cockpit, crossed over the pilots knees and hit the port side metal work. The bullet then did a ricochet off the hard cockpit metal part, and entered the pilots side.

"Although what was to prove a mortal wound, the pilot held the kite long enough for the navigator and WOp to take control of the aircraft and lift him from the pilots seat. The navigator, although wounded in the leg ('splinters of metal in the right thigh, insignificant, but a nuisance and somewhat bloody', as Ralph Fastnedge recalls, T.B.), flew the aircraft back to St. Faith".

Sergeant Hepworth and Sergeant Turner again pick up their story:

"As we were leaving the target a crowd of men in brown overalls came running out onto a small bridge. I don't think they were armed - I imagined at the time they were workers or possibly forced labourers. Some of the air gunners also opened up on them as they came through. Although it was agreed each Blenheim would make its own way home after the attack, our 'V' of three had decided we should try to form up again and, as it happened, Sergeant pilots King and Baron formed up as we crossed the coast with Flight Lieutenant Thompson leading. The effect of this was that the three air gunners could cover one third of the sky each, port side, starboard side and myself dead astern should we be attacked by fighters. Being close to the sea makes it difficult for fighters to attack, they have to pull out of a dive early to avoid hitting the sea and that leaves them exposed to the air gunners fire, which, from three Blenheims means six .303 machine guns.

"The final irony to this all was, as we were heading out into the North Sea outside Den Helder we crossed over at low level a German convoy turning as though to be making for Bremen, being circled by four Bf110s (almost the first time we had ever seen such a sight all the time some of us had been searching for such a target). As we were coming in from the land they must have thought we were Ju88s, which look a bit like Blenheims, for they did not open fire on us. The three air gunners in our section fired at the shipping as we crossed over and expected attacks from the Me's. I called out over the radio 'Formation Fighters' and King and Baron closed in tight formation as we passed over the ships and dropped down close to the sea.

"In the event we never saw the Me's again, but as I looked back I had a glimpse of two Blenheims, some way away, down near the sea, making their home independently. The last Blenheim turned out to be the one flown by our newly arrived Commanding Officer, who was at about two thousand feet banking and weaving to avoid an attacking Bf109 (of *I./JG 1*, T.B.). As we discovered from the remaining two aircraft from the first vic, the Wing Commander's crew, having overshot their target, made a right-hand turn from Den Helder to make another run. We assume that in doing so he must have more or less run into some of the Me's and must have been shot down. Unfortunately his defensive action was gaining him no ground. Some time ago most crews on low level daylight operations had agreed that the only way to have a chance of not being shot down by fighters, was to fly as low and as fast as possible over the sea in a direct line for home. Fighters in those days had a limited duration in the air and they could only follow so far, as they had to ensure they had enough fuel to get back to base. Consequently, they could make one or two attacks only, before having to break off the action. Regretfully, as we made our way home at high speed, I saw in the increasing distance the Bf109 still attacking the CO's Blenheim, the only one which failed to return to base. We were back at base at 17.55".

We left Flying Officer Fastnedge at the moment on which he took over the controls of the Blenheim from his wounded pilot, and again Ken Whittle recalls:

"When Flying Officer Fastnedge reached base, he did not feel competent to land the Blenheim safely. Phillips had lapsed in and out of consciousness on the trip back. He came round at the airfield, was put back into the pilot's seat, and supported by the nav, he made a good landing, passing out again as the aircraft stopped. Sad to say that he died that night in the hospital at St. Faiths. Flying Officer Fastnedge the nav' was awarded the DFC. 139 Squadron lost a very good experienced pilot that day!"

Flying Officer Ralph Fastnedge brings the story of the 1st May raid to a sad ending:

"With the help of the WOp/AG, Sergeant John Allen, we managed to get back to base. When Pilot Officer Phillips died, John Allen and I were offered the choice of joining a newly trained pilot or having a rest period at separate OTU's. We decided on the latter course. After a period at an O.T.U I was posted to 2 Group HQ in August 1941. Phillips, as I was told there by Stevenson (Air Vice-Marshal Stevenson, AOC 2 Group 1941, T.B.), was recommended for the VC, but that Stevenson's recommendation had been overruled. John Allen, who would have received the DFM was not decorated. Allen (then Warrant Officer) was shot down on the night of 22nd June 1943, flying in a Wellington Mark X, with a crew of five. The target was Mulheim. His grave is in the Reichswald Forest War Cemetery, Cleves, Germany".

Flight Lieutenant Goode of 105 Squadron swept *Beat 10* on 1st May, his orders being: 'Attack the biggest possible ship between the Hook of Holland and Rotterdam'. However, after a sweep without sightings, Goode decided to attack the nearby oil tanks at Rotterdam. A successful low level run to this target was made difficult by accurate light *Flak*; during the run observer Pilot Officer Hogan, who was laying flat on his belly in the nose of the Blenheim, was severely injured when a shell exploded in the perspex nose. However, Hogan dropped the bombs on target and the crippled aircraft set course for England. Only a few minutes later, it was intercepted by no less than five Bf109s. With no cloud cover visible for miles, the fate of the Blenheim was all but sealed. During the next twenty minutes Goode's aircraft was attacked by the German fighters. All crew members were wounded and a propeller was shot off. However, through the excellent flying skills of the pilot, none of the Messer-schmitts could get in a deadly burst and Sergeant Rowland the WOp/AG even damaged one of the attackers! Having expended all their ammunition, the Bf109s turned for the Dutch coast again, and Flight Lieutenant Goode safely crossed the North Sea on one engine. After passing the British coastline, the second engine packed up as well and the Blenheim lost the last remaining prop! Undeterred, Goode managed to crash-land the Blenheim near Cookley in Suffolk and the crew of three survived this ordeal as well.

In recognition of their fighting courage and flying skills, Flight Lieutenant Goode and Pilot Officer Hogan both received a DFC from the hands of the King on 22nd May. Sergeant Rowland got a DFM.

The anti-shipping and coastal raids, with their manifold dangers and narrow margin of survival, demanded much of the Blenheim aircrews. One of them was Squadron Leader Edmund Nelson. He took over command of 139 Squadron in early May 1941:

"I arrived on the squadron at Horsham St. Faith early in May 1941, as a new boy although with the rank of acting Squadron Leader. I had in fact arrived straight from India, where I had spent a four year tour in the RAF. As a result, I was more than horrified to be told by my station commander Group Captain Ian Spencer, that the 139 Squadron CO, Wing Commander Pepper, had been reported missing that morning on a shipping attack and was presumed dead. As a result, he informed me that as a senior officer in the squadron I should be taking over command of 139 Squadron, which a few days later I did.

"I carried out several shipping operations off the Frisian Islands and the Texel, Terschelling and northern Dutch coast areas. In all these cases ships were either damaged or sunk, usually with heavy losses to ourselves. As you will appreciate, with such heavy losses, it was very difficult to get to know one's fellow aircrew, especially as over 80% were Sergeant rank and lived in their own mess. Naturally, one did meet more of one's officer aircrew in the mess, but there again, given the abnormally high losses and extreme stress in the summer of 1941, coupled with the amount of time I personally had to spend on administrative matters, my memories of the detailed personalities of these men are somewhat vague.

"One of my administrative tasks was the difficult task of writing to so many families of lost aircrew, many of whom had only just arrived on the station. There seemed so little time to get to know each other socially and so often, the men who had been at the bar the night before laughing and joking about the terror that was part of our daily lives, were dead or missing in action the following night. So many of them were ordinary young men, who showed extraordinary courage and patriotism in volunteering their services as aircrew".

A number of squadron COs and 2 Group Station Commanders became increasingly worried over the rapidly mounting losses amongst their crews. One of these men was Sam Elworthy, CO of 82 Squadron. He was promoted in mid-May to an appointment as Deputy SASO at 2 Group HQ. The heavy and fruitless Blenheim losses on shipping sweeps off the enemy coasts in the spring of the year had caused terrible grief to Elworthy. He was now determined to persuade Air Vice-Marshal Donald Stevenson, AOC of 2 Group, that his command was being wasted in vain on the anti-shipping operations. Although Elworthy was backed in his criticism by other Staff Officers like Group Captain 'Paddy' Bandon, 'Butch' Stevenson wanted to hear no more of it, and during one of these discussions he reputedly threw an ink-well against the wall, shouting in Elworthy's face, 'Churchill wants it'. Stevenson, a very ambitious man, was determined to make the Blenheim anti-shipping and fringe targets campaign a decisive success, and thus make his mark as an outstanding Group Commander. In a key document *Paper on the ideal day bomber force - spring 1941* Stevenson drafted his ideas on the employment of 2 Group. Among other things, he stated:

"...in regard to the day operations of No. 2 Group we have seen that by spreading our attacks over great distances of the enemy coastline and carrying out cloud flying attacks on deeper objectives the enemy fighter force is being dispersed - forced to undertake standing patrols and therefore to expend greater effort requiring greater fighter strength, and probably drawing reinforcements. This is satisfactory as far as it goes.

"The great importance, however, of intensifying our day operations is obvious particularly since we believe that the strength of the enemy fighter force is restricted by limited production and training facilities. Indeed the intensification of our operations may well force the enemy to bring larger reinforcements to the West, and by weakening the strength of his fighters in the Middle East, bring to rest his thrust towards Asia Minor and in North Africa."

This was a most ambitious goal to aim for, the more as Stevenson well knew that the desired re-equipment of his Group with American Bostons and Mitchells would only be effected by late 1941. The outcome was that the Blenheim squadrons continued to attack the dreaded enemy convoys and coastal targets, with ever mounting losses.

One measure that Stevenson took, to try to keep the losses down to an acceptable level, was the order to fly moonlight anti-shipping sweeps in the second week of May 1941. For example, on the night of 7/8th May 1941, six Blenheims of 139 Squadron made a shipping sweep in the Dutch coast area. One 300 tons ship was attacked and claimed hit off Ijmuiden and a convoy off Terschelling was bombed, but no hits were observed due to heavy *Flak*. Small trawlers were also attacked off the Dutch coast.

One Blenheim was lost during this night's operations, P4860 of 139 Squadron. The wreckage of this Blenheim was recovered off Holwerd by the Dutch Air Force Recovery Team in June 1979. Sergeant Bob 'Smudge' Coles was the observer in this crew. He tells us of his crew's 16th operation, which ended on the mud banks off the Northern Frisian coast:

"Whilst serving with 139 Squadron in early 1941, many of the operations assigned to us seemed stupidly hazardous resulting in losses out of proportion to results. Not that we complained, we were all young - I was twenty-two at the time and even though I was as scared as anyone at times I found the life exhilarating, and fierce, single-aircraft operations appealed in a way that the mass bombing of unseen towns would have been repellent. We lived well and were rather pampered - spoilt, some would say. Life on our squadron was informal, a tremendous camaraderie existed among the aircrews which also embraced ground crews upon whom we depended so much. We all drank together off duty and rank did not matter much.

"When I joined the squadron on 21 February 1941 it was engaged in daylight *Circuses* over the Channel ports. Up to twelve aircraft flew in formation at 17,000 feet to lure up Messerschmitts so that they could be pounced upon by six squadrons of escorting Spitfires waiting high above. Few enemy fighters took the bait and *Flak* damage was not severe. These operations were described as 'a piece of cake' in RAF jargon.

"Then followed daylight raids in formation of six on coastal targets. We were briefed to return promptly to base if cloud cover became less than six tenths. Flying at 50 feet in tight vics encounters with Messerschmitts '109 and '110's were frequent. Opposition was now increasing but we were not drawing enough fighters and so tactics changed again to deeper penetration inland at dusk. Operations then became distinctly hair-raising as we were directed to broad daylight shipping sweeps. We flew low in formation to a point about 50 miles from enemy coasts then fanned out at 2 degrees intervals as single and very lonely aircraft. When two miles from the coast we turned to port and for five minutes attacked anything afloat....from single launches to fully escorted convoys. If nothing was seen we turned inland with a wide choice of targets open to us. We made for home at the critical point of fuel supply, unless another decision was made for us by the enemy.

"Attacks were made from 1,000 feet in a shallow dive, releasing bombs at 100 feet but most crews adopted a 'zero feet' run-up from the moment a ship was sighted. So low in fact, that it was not unusual to splash the tail wheel lightly in the sea. Our successes as a squadron were impressive, but losses grew alarmingly. Occupied coasts swarmed with fighters now and we feared more than any those based upon the Frisian Islands.

"Sergeant Bill Middleton was our crew's pilot. A dour Scot from Aberdeen, slow and deliberate of speech, single-minded, highly skilled and fearless as a pilot. Following a fighter affiliation exercise with two Hurricanes from Coltishall, the pilot of one, fighter ace Wing Commander Stanford Tuck, told us that he had never before had a better run for his money from friend or foe. That was the sort of pilot we had. Sergeant Bob Hale, wireless operator-air gunner, equally good at both. Stocky, good-looking extrovert from Coventry. A widower with young son, his wife had been killed in an air-raid. Sergeant Bob Coles, navigator-bomb aimer. I was always known as 'Smudge' to avoid inter-com confusion. Temperament - somewhere between the other two. We operated very well as a crew, but really had very little in common, spending off-duty time separately with our own friends and interests.

"May 7th, 1941 - A beautiful night, brilliant moonlight, the wind very slight, there was little cloud. What more could a flying crew desire. Our Blenheim left its base at Horsham on the outskirts of Norwich, our orders being, firstly, to bomb any shipping we saw on our patrol, secondly, to continue, if none were seen, into the Elbe mouth and make a low-level attack upon three large ships and numerous troop landing vessels reported to be in the Dutch harbour of Delfzyl. Nothing unusual in the operation except that we had previously been engaged solely on daylight raids, and had decided to take advantage of the bright moon and use daylight tactics which in our case was extremely low-level flying at about fifty feet. The more obvious advantages being, that the enemy couldn't hear our engines until we approached within a hundred yards or so, thus giving a good element of surprise, the bombing was more accurate, the aircraft was a target for *Flak* for only a short time, we were well below the usual altitude of enemy night-fighter patrols and they simply could not effect their favourite under-tail attack on our 'blind spot'! Also, the sea-level speed of the Blenheim was equally as fast as the 1941 Messerschmitt. Anyhow, we liked low flying, so why give any other reasons?

"Airborne, I gave Bill Middleton a course to take us to the Hook of Holland and, once clear of the Norfolk coast, we dropped altitude to 50 feet. Very little unusual occurred until we made our landfall, the harbour lights, except for some worried minutes spent trying to turn petrol cocks which had jammed when changing tanks, and the report from Bob Hale in his turret, of exhaust flames of another aircraft visible at the same height as ourselves on a parallel course. This we guessed to be another of our squadron, but skidded away for safety.

"When about one mile from the coast we turned on to a northeasterly track, chugging along our *Beat* at a steady 180 mph on the clock. Then the excitement started. We were now right on the German night-fighter patrol and Bob's reports of the headlights of fighters often caused us to increase our speed or throttle back to decrease exhaust flame, depending on their bearing to us. Also, strange coloured lights on the coast gave us false alarm. Straining my eyes into the distance for fighters and shipping I suddenly did see faintly a small convoy some distance away on the starboard beam between us and Den Helder. The other two did not discern it, but I was certain so Bill turned onto a reciprocal course. We sighted the target and with half the bombs selected dropped down to 10 feet, put on full boost and steered for the biggest craft. She opened fire with light tracer; I remember reminding Bill to be careful of the ship's radio aerial. The bombs were off, the usual pressure of my spine forcing into the seat and the machine pulled up over the ship's masts. Looking backwards I could see red lights reflecting from the engine nacelles and heard Bob's twin Brownings chattering over the inter-communication. So we had scored a good hit. As I dropped down and got in a few bursts with my own guns I heard Bob yell confirmation of this between long bursts from his guns directed at the *Flak* from the escorting vessels. By now the air had become full of tracer streams, flashes of *Flak* shells and 'flaming onions' which hung around us in strings of green fire balls like necklaces, lighting the cabin like daylight. I must admit that I found myself involuntarily ducking low in my seat. I felt SO important that all this fire was meant for our small aircraft! *Flak* seems to be so harmless by day, but this couldn't be ignored. As usual my steel helmet lay forgotten on the floor. We slid quickly down again to the sea and with slight evasive action flew westwards for a few miles in order to examine our hurts, if any, and to decide in peace, away from the fighter infested island of Texel, what to do with the remaining bombs. Because the convoy had not contained any ships of more than approximately 1,500 tons and was ready to re-welcome us, we decided to leave it and continue our patrol. As we set course once more, we saw signs that another of the squadron had found the ships, for the *Flak* had re-commenced. Someone else was taking a pasting!

"Nothing was seen afloat as far north as Borkum island, so we increased speed and flew low, skirting the beaches of that unwholesome place with its two night fighter 'dromes. Bob shouted the approach of a fighter and Bill flew low to avoid an under-tail attack but no attack came. I could not see a fighter looking back through the starboard blister and Bob did not mention it again. We were about to set course to Delfzyl when I saw on the Dutch mainland an object I thought was a bridge. The moon was now obscured by cloud, so I asked the other two to help me identify the landmark in order to check our exact position. Bill glanced to starboard, meanwhile allowing the aircraft to sink -saw his mistake and pulled the stick back, all within a fraction of a second, but at such a low altitude that it spelt disaster for us, for as he pulled the nose up the tail dropped and hit the water with a startling crash. But she took off again with the engines still running smoothly. For a moment a wave of relief surged through me. 'We've made it!' But my relief was short-lived. The next thing was a terrifying impact, blinding lights, deafening noise, pain. 'So this is it', I thought in that instant. We turned three somersaults and crashed again. I must have lost consciousness at this point then recovered completely under water, feet stuck firmly in deep mud. By thrashing around my feet kicked clear of my flying boots and I swam upwards, finding the water quite shallow. Winded badly, groaning to force air into my lungs, I was feeling ghastly. Then as my head cleared I saw the 'plane blazing furiously some twenty yards away and another figure trying like a drunkard to pull itself upright....it was Bill. We released our parachute harnesses and with hardly a word to each other dragged ourselves around the scattered parts of the burning 'plane as near as the heat allowed shouting loudly for Bob. But there was not a sign of him. I couldn't even decide at which end of the crash the tail should be situated, it was such a tangled mess. Bill shouted to me to get away from the machine because of the danger of the unexploded bombs, nothing could be done to save Bob if he was in that chaos, so with great reluctance we turned away and staggered off. In doing so I kicked against the dinghy floating about unopened in its valise. I grasped the rope and towed it behind me expecting that it might be of use to us. It was well I did so because the water became deeper as we headed for the dim outline of the coast of Holland some two miles distant. We were about fifty yards from the wreck when the incendiaries burned up followed by the explosion of the HEs. From the air 250lb. bombs merely make an insignificant puff of smoke as they explode, I'd always felt somewhat disappointed with them, I've since changed my opinion completely. Loud explosions and the shrapnel flew all around us, hitting the water with sharp hissing sounds, but neither of us was hit. Perhaps it was luck or perhaps 250-pounders weren't so good after all! Our attempts to open the dinghy by its rip-cord failed. Whilst cutting it open with a knife though, we heard someone hailing us. The voice we recognised as Bob's and, turning in the direction of the shout we saw the tail with Bob standing beside it, illuminated by the distant flames. Actually, what had happened was that the kite had broken off at the tail throwing Bob clear, the bomb explosions had brought him back to consciousness, his head supported above water by his Mae West life-jacket.

"Having cut open the dinghy valise and released the gas bottle, the dinghy inflated itself neatly. Bill was in a pretty bad way, bleeding profusely from the head, so I bundled him into the dinghy and yelling encouragement to Bill commenced pushing the dinghy, until out of my depth then swimming and kicking with my feet. Bob, too, was badly battered, delirious and insensible of any of my instructions. I had to cut his harness off and bundle him in also. All this time I had felt reasonably well in spite of many deep cuts and so we started the journey to the coast.

"Sometimes with my feet on the mud and sometimes swimming, we pushed forward. The sea-bed would suddenly disappear and I found myself choking with muddy, salt water. Once I got into the boat myself, nearly swamping it, and tried to paddle along, but when we weren't moving in circles, we were fast on mud banks. I got out again. My feet sank in the mud and I pitched forward onto my knees. This continued for about half an hour,

I guess, I was becoming exhausted, the shore didn't seem to be any nearer and although the water was now only a foot in depth, the mud below it became deeper. Finally, I was unable to get off my knees and Bill, in spite of his weak condition, got out and helped me to my feet. Pulling together, we dragged on, often stopping for rests or to assist each other out of the mud. Bob, all this time, was asking, 'What has happened? Where am I?' and shivering from cold and shock.

"After about forty minutes we finally clambered up the beach, half carrying Bob, to a breakwater covered with slimy, stinking seaweed, over which we rolled him, following ourselves, each needing much assistance. But we still were not out of the mire. The mud was some eighteen inches of sucking unpleasantness and a wide stream still separated us from dry land. We could see the outline of houses on the shore. In desperation I shouted, but heard no answer. It seemed inconceivable that with the crash, bomb explosions and the machine still blazing, no-one could have heard or seen it. We spent more minutes walking parallel to the breakwater, clinging to it for support until that way was barred by water. We re-traced our steps to a point where the stream seemed to be narrowest and, holding hands to form a chain, I waded and then jumped for a bank of seaweed, landing on all fours to find that I didn't sink more than a few inches. The others followed and we started towards the shore over the firm but slippery banks. This mud had been the worst ordeal of all, really terrifying, but what faced us now? I remember Bill saying, 'Well boys, prepare for machine-gun bullets', but that seems a bit silly now, it was long before the days of the 'Terror Bombers' when anything could happen, and did.

"We were met by an officer and half a dozen soldiers armed with 'tommy-guns' which they aimed at us. We raised our hands, they surrounded us, patting us in search for arms, with some displeasure because of our coating of slime, and handed round cigarettes which acted like medicine on us. Two of them assisted Bob, smothering their uniforms in doing so, and as we climbed the sand dunes he was placed on the pillion of a motor-cycle and driven off. We were in decent hands, anyhow and, after a short walk, we met Bob again in the kitchen of a Dutch policeman and we were all pleased to sit down for a while. Bill lost consciousness and I was not far from it. For a time, Bill's German carried us along, then an English speaking officer arrived, our wounds were dressed but we were shivering uncontrollably and there was no fire burning.

"Apparently we had selected a remote district for our misfortune, with no doctors at hand and we received no further treatment there. My watch had stopped at ten minutes past midnight, thus fixing the time of the crash. At 1 am a car fetched us and took us along narrow country roads to the local headquarters of the coastal guards where we were led into the officers' mess (salutes all round and one for the *Führer*), seated before a cheerful fire and given coffee (?) and food. We soon felt much better. Bob took his wet clothes off and fell asleep on a bench. One of the Germans put a leopard skin rug over him - with his wet hair all over his face the whole scene reminded me of a vanquished Tarzan! He woke long enough for a Dutch doctor to dress his wounds and he was off to sleep again. Bill and I were bombarded with questions about England. We told the truth but were mostly disbelieved, particularly about the matter of food. They were firm in the belief that Germany's *U-boats* had reduced us to a diet of spuds only. A quick examination followed, carried out by a *Luftwaffe* intelligence officer. We were also searched, most of our property being taken away.

"It was quiet when at 5 a.m. an ambulance arrived. We were placed on stretchers and transported to a Catholic hospital at Leeuwarden. Our bodies were virtually covered all over with highly coloured bruises and there were lacerations over our faces and bodies, many of them needing sutures."

Before compiling an interim evaluation of the Blenheim anti-shipping campaign, we closely investigate the events of another typical day of the campaign in May. On 25th May 1941, eight aircraft of 139 Squadron were dispatched on an early morning sweep off Ijmuiden (*Beat 9*). Sergeant Ken Whittle was the WOp/AG in the leading Blenheim:

"We took off at 05.10 on a sweep off Ijmuiden, with Sergeant McPhee leading the eight 139 Blenheims. It was my crew's 47th Blenheim operation. The weather was foul with driving rain, visibility very poor. The Blenheims split up and paired off as briefed in the search area, McPhee's partner Blenheim, a Canadian on his second operation, Sergeant Bye and his teenage English navigator and wireless operator/air gunner (Sergeants Bye, Bransby and Thorneycroft, T.B.). Nothing was sighted so McPhee turned V6333 for home. As the Blenheim came about the rain cloud lifted and I thought I saw a ship. Alerting the pilot to turn about, we found a large ship, and astern of this ship, a smaller trawler type vessel. The latter identifying its real purpose, a heavily armed *Flak*-ship, aiming at the two Blenheims a fearsome barrage of light and medium deadly *Flak*, a terrifying sight!

"Having committed ourselves to the attack there was no turning back in spite of *Flak* appearing from other angles, and it was deadly. Closing in fast at wave top height the reason for the extra *Flak* soon became obvious: this was in fact a bloody convoy! Not only were the crew on their third contact against the survival 2 Group odds, a convoy, suicidal! Sergeant Bye broke away as par the briefing, more than one ship, separate target attacks. Blenheim V6333 was flying into a veritable cone of white hot metal. It was over and around the fuselage and wings and it was terrifying. 'God help us', I prayed, covering in my perspex turret, conscious of my unprotected head and shoulders exposed to this deadly barrage. I pitied Mac up front having to fly into the fiery storm, what of Geoff Atkins in the exposed perspex extended Mk.IV nose position, it was horrifying!

"Geoff's confident shout 'bombs gone' was followed by the sudden uplifting surge as the Blenheim climbed up and away, over the ships decks and mastheads. This indicated to me that at least we were still flying with Mac in charge and I could now open my eyes. I had closed my eyes to shut out that fearsome sight and opened them again just in time to witness another! At this time I opened fire with my twin Brownings, raking the ships decks, relieving the tension and able to fight back at last.

"In my view was Sergeant Bye closing in on his target, his Blenheim receiving the full attention of the convoy defences now V6333 was no further danger to the convoy. The end had to come. It was impossible for any crew, experienced or inexperienced, to live throu' such deadly *Flak*. The Blenheim mortally hit flew into the ship, and blew up! Such a promising crew, so young, on their second operation and their first contact!

"Over the intercom I had relayed to Mac and Geoff those awful sickening last few moments of Sergeant Bye and crew. Sick at heart our crew started the lonely flight home, there would be for us another tomorrow. Sleep had not come easily over the past few weeks, this night would it never end, disturbed and restless re-living the days tragic events.

"The next day the Air Ministry claimed one ship sunk and one damaged, four of our Blenheims failed to return! Sgts McPhee and Bye had made the only contacts in 2 Group on the 25th May 1941. What a price to pay!"

Probably due to the bad weather, low cloud and driving rain, the two Blenheims of 139 Squadron had run slightly off course. It was off Texel that Ken Whittle spotted the German ships. It was an unfortunate chance encounter: the German ships were four minesweepers and *Flak*-ships, busy sweeping air-laid mines off Texel when the Blenheims arrived on the scene. *Flak* from *Sperrbrecher 33 Silvia* hit Sergeant Bye's aircraft, identified by the Germans as a Wellington, from a distance of 500 metres. Within seconds, R2791 was transformed into a ball of fire, which shot uncontrollably into the direction of her victor. The British machine cartwheeled into the engine room of the *Silvia,* and both engines of the Blenheim crashed through the ship and came out on the other side. The ship was doomed. Fires on board the *Silvia* were soon out of control and within a few hours the German ship sank. 2 Group HQ claimed the 1,049-ton *Silvia* as a 5,000-ton vessel.

After the tragic 139 Squadron shipping sweep early on 25th May 1941, during which Sergeant Bye and his crew had met such a violent end, three more operations were mounted by 2 Group. One Flight of 18 Squadron went to western Denmark (*Beat 5*), eight crews of 105 Squadron were briefed to sweep *Beat 8* (the Dutch Frisian Islands) and eight aircraft of 18 Squadron went to the seaplane base at Nordeney. In *Beat 8*, six 105 crews attacked a convoy off Ameland, losing one Blenheim which was last seen heading for Ameland. Sergeant Jim Moore, WOp/AG in 18 Squadron, flew in the formation of eight

Blenheims of his squadron to Nordeney in the afternoon of 25th
May, and vividly remembers his 38th Blenheim operation:

"On 25th May, 1941, we were briefed, as part of a formation of eight aircraft
to bomb a seaplane base on the island of Nordeney. The plan was to fly in
three vics of three aircraft at wave top height to a point north of Nordeney
before turning to approach the target from that direction with the intention
of confusing the defenders.

"At 1.55 pm we took off into a cloudless sky heading out over the North
Sea. Our crew flew as No.2 to the formation leader, our highly respected
Squadron Leader Johnny Munro. On the ground he had a slight speech
impediment whereas in the air he was articulate, decisive and a born leader.
We came down to wave top level as soon as we had left the Norfolk coast. It
was a beautiful sunny day with excellent visibility and one couldn't help
wondering what the folk at home would be doing on this Sunday afternoon.

"We knew it was to be a long flight, during which time we were constantly
on the alert, searching for any sign of either ships or enemy aircraft. During
operational flights we were required to keep radio silence, to avoid detection
by the enemy, so, when we changed course to head for Nordeney, we could
only make frantic signals to our leader to indicate I had seen the smoke of a
fairly large convoy on the horizon. On this occasion the seaplane base was
our main priority so, although there was the risk of an alert wireless
operator on the convoy notifying the defenders on Nordeney of our approach,
there was little choice but to carry on. Munro obviously decided to take the
risk that we had not been seen and carried on.

"As the island came into view we found a heavily armed German patrol
boat directly in our path and, as if that wasn't enough, five Messerschmitt
109F fighters patrolling over the island. It is stating the obvious to say 'our
cover had been blown' so our fears of an alert wireless operator reporting
our approach were justified. It was abundantly clear it was time to go home.
Whatever Munro might have decided, whether or not to carry on with the
raid, was decided for him as three aircraft turned inside us and headed west
with the rest of us in hot pursuit. We kept close together for our joint
protection, jettisoning the bombs, giving the engines full boost and keeping
as low as possible.

"The fighters wasted no time in coming into the attack, the sea bubbling
and foaming as bullets and cannon shells churned up the sea around us.
There was no time for fear as we fought back, firing as the fighters came
into range. There was the stench of cordite from my Brownings and then a
perspex panel in my turret blew out so I felt as if I was sitting in a
hurricane. I could see the WOp/AG in the Blenheim next to us, slumped
forward with blood smeared all over the back of his turret. One Blenheim of
our formation, obviously hit, plunged into the sea and disintegrated
although this success didn't satisfy the enemy who still came in to attack.
We must have had some success as one of the fighters broke away with his
undercarriage hanging down, then the others withdrew, probably having
run out of ammunition. I don't know how long the engagement lasted but it

seemed like an eternity. I found out later that I had ten rounds of ammunition left in one gun and none in the other.

"They left us to limp home, every aircraft having been damaged. One Blenheim, piloted by 'Tich' Thorne, who had joined the squadron with me, had been very badly damaged, to such an extent I doubted if he would make it back to base. We were unable to stay with him as we had to limp home with a great deal of damage to both wings and tail. The perspex in the back of my turret had blown out and I had been sitting in a howling gale. Thankfully, the dear old Blenheim could take an enormous amount of punishment and still get you home.

"We landed back at our parent 'drome Horsham St. Faith (now Norwich Airport), after a very eventful Sunday afternoon, from a flight which had lasted four hours, feeling distinctly thankful to be in 'one piece'. We hadn't been on the ground for many minutes when we saw another Blenheim, which was obviously in some trouble, coming in to land. The pilot successfully landed and as it taxied towards us we could see it was so badly damaged it looked like a sieve, it was riddled with bullet and cannon shell holes from end to end. Miraculously it was Tich Thorne and his crew who had not received a scratch despite the enormity of the damage. He was commissioned next month but was to lose his life later in the war.

"We now made enquiries to find out 'who had got the chop' and were told they were Flight Sergeant Keane, Sergeant Jock Duffus and Sergeant Gow. The dead WOp/AG was Sergeant Lloyd who had flown with Pilot Officer's Watson and Aires. This had been a bad day for the squadron, as 'B' Flight had lost another crew that morning in attacking a ship (Sergeant Wood and crew in L8864, crashed off Denmark, T.B.). It is difficult to describe one's feelings after the loss of so many good friends for, whilst we mourned their loss, one couldn't suppress feeling very relieved to have survived. The only way you could carry on and retain your sanity was believing, no matter what, you would be the one to get back."

The results and losses during the first month of the daylight anti-shipping campaign have already been considered. From 13th April till the end of May, 2 Group had claimed 77 ships, totalling 220,000 tons, successfully attacked. 21,000 tons were claimed sunk, with further 18 ships of 41,000 tons probably damaged and 54 (52,000 tons) slightly damaged. These claims are now considered to be grossly inflated.

In all, 2 Group Blenheims flew 958 sorties in these seven weeks, including three *Circus*-type operations, of which 419 sorties went to the Dutch coast area. This leads to the conclusion that over half of the anti-shipping and fringe targets operations took place in the Dutch coast area. During these 419 sorties, 171 attacks were carried out on shipping and coastal targets. Five ships were severely damaged as a result of these attacks, some 16,000 tons. Also, the Blenheim crews managed to sink four ships; two *Flak*-ships off Borkum and Texel, a 1,500-ton freighter off Schiermonnikoog, and a Dutch fishing vessel off Texel, totalling just over 3,000 tons. Although this was a reasonably good score, they clearly show that the official statistics that 2 Group HQ compiled over this period were much overstated. There was a reason for this however.

At the beginning of the anti-shipping campaign, a meeting at Bomber Command HQ was held to discuss anti-shipping tactics and claims. Admiralty ship constructors present at the meeting stated that the fragments from a 250-pound bomb were capable of doing vital damage to a ship by holing her from the inside and also by holing watertight compartments so that the whole ship would flood and sink. It was also considered that a 250-pound SAP bomb would sink any merchant ship under 4,000 tons, except when the hit was very unluckily placed. If a ship of about 4,000 tons was seen to be hit by a 250-pound bomb, the vessel could therefore be claimed as a total loss. This was promulgated to the 2 Group Blenheim crews on the 26th April 1941. The result: grossly inflated statistics on shipping damaged and destroyed were compiled by 2 Group HQ, as shown above. This in turn undoubtedly prolonged the 2 Group anti-shipping campaign longer than it should have. It must also be stressed that these statistics were not the result of returning Blenheim crews 'shooting the line' about their shipping strikes, but were entirely the result of the discussion between Bomber Command, Coastal Command and the Admiralty in April 1941.

And what about the losses among the Blenheim crews? During these seven weeks, 2 Group lost 40 Blenheims on operations; 19 aircraft came down in the Dutch coast area. Another aircraft was written off on return and a few came back badly shot up with dead or wounded crew members. Coastal Command lost an additional 9 Blenheims off Holland. These included a complete formation of four aircraft of 59 Squadron shot down by *Flak*-ships during a convoy attack off the Hook of Holland on 28 April. Of the 84 airmen who were lost in the Dutch coast area, only 5 survived to become prisoners of war.

It has already been seen how night shipping sweeps were flown by 2 Group during the second and third weeks of May.

Seventy sorties were flown to the Dutch coast. The rapidly mounting losses in daylight forced Air Vice-Marshal Stevenson to experiment with night attacks in moonlight conditions. However, these were found to be ineffective as no ships were severely damaged, and no more night shipping strikes were to be flown by 2 Group in the remaining months of the campaign. Coastal Command Blenheims kept the German coastal convoys under pressure at night, but also to little avail. Successfully hitting a ship in broad daylight was no mean feat, let alone at night.

The 2 Group raids to the Netherlands in June and the early part of July 1941 merit a lot of attention. On 4th June, 2 Group HQ mounted a large scale operation with 57 Blenheims swarming out to targets on the continent. 30 of these aircraft went to Dutch airfields at Valkenburg (105 Squadron), Haamstede (107), Bergen (18) and De Kooy (139 Squadron), all taking off at 18.55. Although these figures look promising, it would prove to be a bad day for 2 Group. Except for one crew of 105 Squadron that bombed a railway station at The Hague, none of the aircraft attacked any targets in Holland. On the debit side, 139 Squadron lost two out of six aircraft that headed for De Kooy to Bf109s of *3./JG 1*. Both were shot down into the North Sea West of Bergen aan Zee. Sergeant 'Jock' Shinnie, WOp/AG in V6333 of 139 Squadron, would never forget this day:

"One of my most memorable operations, and my last one on Blenheims, was an op. to De Kooy airfield on 4th June 1941. We were a force of six aircraft, forming two vics of three, flying at wave top level. As we approached the Dutch coast, we assumed one or more small ships, who saw us, notified someone of our presence. As we approached our target we saw one Bf109 ahead of us but he ignored us. We did not locate the target and the operation was abandoned. However, we soon became aware, as we crossed the coast outbound, that we were being pursued by four Bf109s. It became apparent that they had not been airborne long as they had sufficient fuel to attack us at low level for a considerable time. Each of our formations was repeatedly attacked by the '109s operating in pairs.

"We lost one aircraft then a second of one formation and it was apparent that the third aircraft was having problems. There was no movement of the gun turret and the '109s, realising this, started concentrating their attacks on this aircraft. Our formation leader reacted quickly. Our vic of three climbed to 100-150 feet and the aircraft in trouble tucked in underneath us. We suffered no further loss but all our aircraft were damaged and two of the crew of the troubled aircraft were injured and hospitalised. One Bf109 was damaged, having been seen leaving with smoke pouring from his engine."

Indeed, a Bf109 of *2./JG 1* was hit in the engine by a Blenheim air gunner and ditched in the North Sea. The pilot was saved by the German ASR. Of the crews in the two 139 Squadron aircraft, Z5744 and R3903, both credited to *Unteroffizier* Heinrich Nöcker of *3./JG 1*, there were no survivors. Pilot Officer Lees and Pilot Officer Baser and their crews vanished without a trace under the merciless grey waves of the North Sea and are still missing.

Three days later, again two operations were mounted to the Dutch coastal shipping lanes. Eight Blenheims of 107 Squadron took off from Great Massingham for a mid-morning sweep in *Beat 9* (Texel-Ijmuiden). In the early evening, seven crews of 105 and one of 107 Squadron left West Raynham for a shipping sweep in *Beat 8* (off Ameland). Of these sixteen aircraft, four found enemy shipping off Ijmuiden and Ameland. After low level attacks on five ships, the crews claimed hits on three. Two merchant ships were in fact hit, the *Ceylon* and *Konsul Karl Fisser*. Although a few German sailors were killed and injured in the attacks, no vessels were sunk or heavily damaged. The enemy convoys were protected by standing patrols of Bf109s that exacted a heavy toll from the British crews. Three aircraft were shot down into the North Sea and all nine crew members remain missing.

Pilot Officer Bill Edrich, the famous captain of the English cricket team, made his operational debut on this day, Saturday 7th June 1941. He flew one of the 107 Squadron Blenheims to *Beat 9* in search of German shipping:

"Churchill himself, with the Chief of the Air Staff, and accompanied by other members of the Government, visited our parent station at nearby West Raynham on June 6th and we were all assembled there to meet him. Wearing a light gray suit, and carrying an unlighted cigar, he mounted a set of servicing steps and addressed us. He began by reminding us that 43,000 civilians had been killed in air raids on Britain in the previous months, and that his promise that the RAF would retaliate by day and night had not yet been fulfilled. He had come personally, he said, to explain the importance of the special tasks we would be undertaking in the next few weeks, when our operations were likely to have a major impact on the course of the war. He then gave us some unpalatable facts. German intervention in the Middle East was turning the war against us in that theatre. 'Germany must be forced to move her fighters westwards', he told us. We would attack targets in the west which Germany would have to defend, and sometimes to lure the *Luftwaffe* into the air, we would be escorted by large numbers of fighters. Our purpose would be to relieve pressure on other fronts, and to ease the stranglehold on our life-lines. 'I am relying on you', said Churchill.

"This eve-of-battle appeal from the Prime Minister certainly did something for our morale. But sitting in the cockpit of my Blenheim next morning with the engines ticking over, waiting for the signal to go, I dare not analyse my feelings. I had been impatient to make a start, and so I knew had Vic and Ernie (Vic Phipps, observer and Ernie Hope, WOp/AG, T.B.). We had been flying together for three months and we needed something to show for it. But these impulses evaporated as the moment approached, and I was left with the uncomfortable knowledge that I was just another freshman pilot on the threshold of a new experience, setting off into the unknown. Some of the old hands on the squadron had teased us by exaggerating the dangers. Others, partly perhaps to reassure themselves, dismissed 'ops' as a 'piece of cake'. I was apprehensive, and yet in a curious way I was also elated. There was only one way of finding out the truth about what lay out there beyond the Channel and the North Sea, and about oneself. I was about to find out.

"In the little cottage attached to the nursery gardens on the edge of our grass satellite airfield, which was all the squadron boasted as a headquarters, we had learned that a large and heavily defended enemy convoy, on its way from Hamburg to Rotterdam, was moving down the Dutch coast. There were two big ships in the convoy, both carrying important war cargoes, according to our Intelligence, and these would be our primary targets. Nine crews were briefed to attack in three "vics" of three. I was flying No. 3 to the leader, Squadron Leader Peter Simmons. He was at the other end of the scale - on the last trip of his second tour.

"At last Peter Simmons gave the signal and we began to roll forward. Vic Phipps was sitting beside me for take-off, with Ernie Hope behind me in the fuselage. Peter did a circuit of the airfield to give us time to form up, and we headed for the coast at 500 feet, dropping down to 30 feet over the sea. Then our way was barred by a white screen of fleecy cloud, stretching from about 600 feet right down to the water, and I wondered if Simmons would turn back. The density looked likely to break up all but the closest formations, but I guessed that the volatile Simmons would not want his last trip to be abortive, and I tucked in even closer. At the same time I noticed that No.2 in the formation, on Simmons's right, was above and a little behind. He wouldn't last long in a fighter attack. And he would almost certainly lose us in that cloud. I hadn't had time to get to know the pilot of this aircraft, but I had exchanged a few words with the navigator. He and I were due to play cricket for the squadron against the village team that afternoon, Saturday, June 7th, 1941. If we got back all right.

"Peter held his course, climbing almost imperceptibly. We were still below 100 feet. Then we were enmeshed in cotton-wool cloud, flying entirely on instruments. I had no experience of cloud formation flying, it was something one just didn't practice, and I was frightened. Did Peter really mean to press on? I had to trust not only my own altimeter, but Peter's as well, and I was terrified of flying into the sea. I edged in closer than ever, determined not to lose contact. All I could see was a dark smudge in the cloud which was Peter's wing-tip. Several times I nearly gave up. But for twenty minutes I hung on, concentrating more fiercely than ever before in my life. Then quite suddenly the cloud thinned. I could see the whole of Peter's Blenheim from wing-tip to wing-tip, and a moment later we were through the cloud and visibility was about two miles. I followed Peter back to wave-top level, and we flew so low that the surface of the sea was rippled by our slipstream. There was no sign of our No.2. We assumed he had turned back. There was no sign, either, of our other two formations of three, and it looked as though Peter and I would be attacking alone. I knew this would not deter Peter. Two minutes later I heard Vic, who had moved down into the perspex nose after take-off, shout over the intercom. 'There they are!' Strung out in front of me like beads, about two miles distant and slightly to the north, I could see the silhouettes of about a dozen ships. This was it!

"We stayed at low level until we were about a mile off. Then, as Peter zoomed up to 250 feet, I broke formation and did the same, pulling in the full boost lever to give me maximum speed - about 240 knots - for the attack. Two big merchantmen stood out from all the others, one in the centre of the convoy and the other near the rear. I estimated them as between 5,000 and 6,000 tons. Typically, Peter went hurtling after the one in the centre. I went for the one at the rear. But I thought mine looked slightly the larger of the two. A five-starred rocket floated up from one of the ships, challenging our identity. Then the ship's guns opened up. I was bearing down on the rear merchantman in a shallow dive, skidding and jinking to put the gunners off their aim. But the fire was horribly accurate. Then I spotted a *Flak*-ship having a go at us three hundred yards to port. My front gun was fixed and I couldn't bring that to bear. 'Ernie, look after that *Flak*-ship!' I heard the clatter of his guns above the engine noise, and glancing to the left I saw that he was right on target. But we were flying now through a terrific barrage from the ship we were attacking and as the tracer squirted up towards me my instinct was to duck. I experienced an extraordinary feeling of claustrophobia, trapped in the goldfish bowl of the cockpit, feeling that if any of those rising balls of light hit the windscreen my whole world would disappear in some abrupt feat of legerdemain. I pressed on my own gun button, letting the tracer hose all over the ship and after seven or eight seconds of this I felt that if the gunners weren't dead at least they would be taking cover. But all this was subsidiary to my main obsession, to time my run so as to sling my bombs into the hull of the ship. The superstructure was floating up towards me at terrific rate and I shouted to Vic, 'Now!' Vic pulled the contact across the switches and we dropped our four 250lb. bombs almost simultaneously. I held on until I was sure they'd gone. The deck of the merchantman filled my windscreen and I thought we must hit her. For some reason the Blenheim was hanging awkwardly to the left. I pulled back viciously on the stick and at once she responded, and with a prayer of thankfulness I zoomed upwards, just in time to clear the masts.

"'Get down!' My climb had taken us up to 300 feet and Vic, fearing fighters, was shouting at me to get back on the water. I pushed the nose forward hurriedly, weaving as I did so to avoid the *Flak*, still flying northwards. After a minute or so of this I judged we were out of range and I turned to port and set course for home. As we turned we looked back at our ship. She was labouring under a billowing cloud of flames and smoke, an almost exact replica of the ship attacked by Peter, which was listing as well. Vic was jumping up and down in his seat, but I knew that Ernie, back in the turret, was the only one who could have seen the bombs fall, I called him on the intercom but there was no reply. 'Vic, see if Ernie's all right'. Vic's reply silenced my fears. 'He's in the turret and he's moving'.

"According to the book I should have looked for Peter and formated on him again, but we had split up for the actual attack and it might have taken some time. I decided that the curtain of cloud we had passed through on the way out would make an ideal refuge, and soon I was back on instruments at 300 feet. Ernie then left his guns and called me up. 'Did you see the bombs hit?' I asked. 'Yes - two just undershot, but the other two must have hit'. 'You didn't actually see them?' 'There were only two splashes on the water. And you saw the ship'. Just then I glanced at my altimeter and was horrified to see that while talking to Ernie I had allowed my concentration to wander and we were right down to nought feet. I felt sick with fear and self-disgust, and I yanked back the stick and pulled up to 500 feet. 'What the hell's happening?' 'It's OK now. We were bloody close to the water'. In the same instant the engines spluttered and coughed. I couldn't believe it. We still had more than a hundred miles of water ahead of us. But within seconds both engines picked up again. The trouble must have been caused by some momentary hiatus in the petrol feed, through suddenly pushing the nose forward after a steep climb.

"When we landed back at Little Massingham we found that quite a lot of the rudder had been shot away, which explained the way we had hung to the left just after the attack. But the Blenheim would take a lot of punishment, and I was learning to have tremendous faith in the aircraft I was flying, V5529. I was never quite so happy in any other machine. At the interrogation which followed, Peter's crew and mine were able to corroborate our respective claims. For leading this highly successful attack on his last trip, Peter was awarded a bar to his DFC. We learned now of the experience of the other seven crews - or anyway, of five of them. They had run into patches of dense fog and had turned back. Even though they had not been in action, one aircraft was missing from the other two vics. And of our own No.3 nothing more was heard or seen. I re-lived that ghastly moment when I had so nearly flown into the sea through faulty instrument flying, and I wondered if that was what had happened to the missing two. They were as inexperienced at that sort of flying as I was. Their absence threw a damper on the exaltation we felt at our own success. I thought, though, that we had made a positive response to Churchill's appeal.

"Within 10 days of Churchill's visit 107 Squadron was involved in the

Circus type of operations, the combined bomber-fighter sweeps which he had envisaged to force the Germans to disperse their air strength. Compared to the tensions of unescorted low-level flying in close formation over the sea, against shipping and other perimeter targets, which was our normal occupation, *Circuses* were almost fun".

Air Vice-Marshal Stevenson, AOC 2 Group, was very optimistic about his Group's efforts, as he told Air Marshal Sir Richard Pierce on 8th June:

"...yesterday...two hits each by 250-pounders destroyed two ships -one of 6,000 tons and one of 5,000 tons... You will have heard that we had a go at a salvaged ship yesterday alongside a large submerged wreck. A photograph taken at the time shows another useful wreck - quite a good size ship close by with masts and superstructure just showing above the sea. This report coupled with others from further south and round the corner towards Ijmuiden of sunken ships, give one the feeling that at last we are making a grave-yard of German ships similar to the one that we see from the air in the Downs and off Dungeness and also a 'windy corner' that isn't ours."

However, Stevenson's claims for the attacks on 7th June cannot be verified as there is no evidence of any sinkings on this day off the Dutch coast. Two days after Bill Edrich's first operational trip, 2 Group Blenheims again swarmed out on shipping sweeps. Six bombers of 18 and 107 Squadrons went to *Beat 10* (mouth of the River Scheldt) in late afternoon, but no ships were seen and all aircraft returned safely. Another formation of six aircraft of 18 Squadron had left Horsham St. Faith at 15.25 for a sweep in *Beat 8* (off Ameland). How did they fare? One aircraft disappeared without a trace in a fog bank off Texel before reaching the *Beat* area. On entering the fog bank, three other crews aborted the operation and turned back to England. Two crews pressed on regardless and attacked a 1200 tons cargo vessel in a convoy off Terschelling, one Blenheim being damaged by ship's *Flak* and finished off by a Bf109 of *3./JG 52*.

The 9th June 1941 also saw the operational debut of Bomber Command Wellingtons in the daylight anti-shipping campaign. It was to be a rather bad debut. One crew attacked a ship in a convoy of fourteen off The Hague but the four 'Wimpys' of 9 Squadron were intercepted by Bf109s and two were shot down off the Scheldt Estuary. Among the victims was R1758 flown by the squadron CO, Wing Commander Arnold.

This is the story of 18 Squadron's shipping sweep on Monday, 9th June. At about three o'clock in the afternoon, the aerodrome

RAF Oulton in Norfolk is buzzing with activity. Six crews of 18 Squadron have just been briefed to attack a German convoy which has been spotted off the Dutch Frisian Islands. Next to one of the Blenheim bombers three young men get into their flying suits. They are Flight Sergeants Ian Bullivant, Samuel 'Jock' Gallery and Bob Hind. Ian Bullivant, pilot of 'M-for-Mother', is the oldest of the three. He is 24, single and is from Hammersmith, a small town on the outskirts of London. Bullivant was the fattest pilot on the squadron and was therefore nicknamed 'Tubby'. Both the others are 21 years of age. Observer Jock Gallery comes from a little village in Scotland and WOp/AG Bob Hind grew up in Neasden, Middlesex.

A member of the ground crew, Les Deadfield, recalls this sunny day in June:

"I can remember so well meeting several aircrews who had come out to dispersal for a bombing operation. I walked with one pilot, a Sergeant Box, to his aircraft. He seemed rather quiet and was having a smoke. He offered me one but as I was not a keen smoker I politely refused, but when he failed to return later along with Sergeant Bullivant I felt rather mean and distressed.

"I saw Sergeant Box off first with his crew, because the ground staff assisted the aircrews with their final adjustments before take-off, and then I went over to the second aircraft where Sergeant Bullivant and his crew were waiting. After the pilot had made his pre-flight check round the aircraft and was satisfied, he signed the Form 700 and got up into the cockpit. I was on the mainplane waiting for him to get comfortable and to adjust the Sutton harness if it was needed. Why I remember it so well is because this fellow was such a big person. I had to literally push his chest in with one hand while I pulled the Sutton harness together to join up and lock. When it was connected the poor fellow could just about turn his head from one side to the other, he was like a 'trussed up chicken'. I felt sorry for him but he seemed quite happy and cheerful. I did admire those aircrew for their bravery."

The three flyers were veterans; Bullivant had successfully completed 22 trips, Gallery had done 18 and Hind 10. Gallery was a survivor of the *Blitzkrieg* in France, when the squadron was based on the continent. Within three weeks in May 1940, 18 Squadron had lost almost all her aircraft and crews over France, Belgium and Holland and was withdrawn from the Battle. On 21st May 1940 the three surviving crews arrived at Watton; Jock Gallery was one of these men. 18 Squadron was now re-equipped with new aircraft and crews and two of the airmen posted to the squadron were Ian Bullivant and Bob Hind. Hind was a good all-round sportsman. During his training as WOp/AG he excelled in athletics and rugby, he even won two cups. Because he considered himself looking too boyish, he grew a small moustache. The Sergeants Ian Bullivant and Bob Hind were assigned to different crews, as was Jock Gallery.

From July to November 1940, the three men flew on operations against the usual Bomber Command targets of this period. They attacked invasion barges at Dunkirk and Ostend, Antwerp and Calais, industrial targets in the Ruhr, flew raids against enemy airfields, etc. After these three months they were posted to 13 OTU at Bicester, to rest and train new Blenheim aircrew. Bob Hind was nominated in May 1941 to go to Canada and train as a pilot. However, as he had not received any positive news on this by the end of the month, he was posted back to his old squadron to fly on operations again as WOp/AG. A cruel act of fate, but 'Man proposes, God disposes', as Bob Hind's sister wrote to the author half a century later. Thus it came to be that on 1st June 1941 Bullivant, Gallery and Hind crewed up together in 18 Squadron.

One day later, on 2nd June, they flew their first operation to northwest Germany, but had to abort due to lack of cloud cover. This was repeated on 4th June, when Bob Hind had trouble operating his gun turret and Ian Bullivant decided to return early to Oulton. Target on this day was Alkmaar airfield in northern Holland.

Then the 9th June arrived, a warm and sunny day. As the last of six Blenheims, Flight Sergeant Bullivant pulled V6428 from the grass airfield at 15.18 hours. Flying in close formation, the bombers passed the Norfolk coast a few minutes later and descended to just above sea level. The sea was calm but the crews spotted some storm-clouds floating on the horizon. It was going to thunder that evening.

After flying at nought feet for about half an hour the Blenheims were suddenly swallowed up by a vast fog bank that stretched out over the surface of the North Sea. This caused the formation to split into two vics. The treacherous thick fog, so close to the water, proved fatal to one of the aircraft. V6427:B of

Sergeant Box and crew disappeared in the sea. Thereupon the two Blenheims of Box's vic turned round and flew back to base. The body of Sergeant Leslie Box was found floating off Texel on 3rd July and was taken to Den Helder by the motor vessel 'Maso'. Two days later he was buried at Huisduinen cemetery. After the liberation of Holland in 1945, his mortal remains were re-buried at Bergen-op-Zoom. No trace was ever found of his observer or WOp/AG and they rest at sea. Pilot Officer Paul Molloy is commemorated on Panel 33 of the Runnymede Memorial, Sergeant George Bass on Panel 39.

Of the original formation of six, only three bombers now remained, pressing on eastwards despite the thick fog for some 100 miles. Their daring paid off. Suddenly they were again flying under a clear blue sky. Soon after, the crews started their *Beat* line off Ameland. One of the men then detected wisps of smoke on the horizon -the German convoy! The ships were steaming in spread-out formation just north of Schiermonnik-oog. Skimming the waves the British bombers sped towards the convoy and each crew selected his own target ship. At exactly 17.00 hours the attack commenced. The gunners on board the enemy vessels however were wide-awake and a seemingly impenetrable curtain of exploding *Flak* shells greeted the Blenheims. Despite the ferocious defence, Pilot Officer Watson bombed one of the ships, which he claimed as damaged. The *Flak* now concentrated on Bullivant's aircraft and it was simply impossible to escape unscathed. A number of shells exploded in and around 'M-for-Mother' and then another danger loomed. A Flight of Bf109s of *3./JG 52*, escorting the convoy, swiftly came to the rescue of the ships and *Feldwebel* Heinz Ahnert immediately attacked 'L' of Sergeant Wood. He managed to escape but the German pilot then spotted Bullivant's damaged Blenheim. After a sharp turn Ahnert was on Bullivant's tail and the other two Blenheim crews, powerless to help, watched the Messerschmitt pumping cannon shells into the bomber. Before speeding home at plus 9 boost, Watson, Wood and their crews watched V6428, seemingly still under control, was slowly circling round. Possibly, Ian tried to ditch the aircraft on the surface of the sea, but none of the three men survived the crash.

Three months later, in the first week of September, Ian Bullivant's body washed ashore on the banks of the Lauwerszee near Oostmahorn. His unopened parachute was still attached to his back. On September 11th, 1941, he was buried in the cemetery of the Reformed Church at Anjum, where he still rests. After the war, his parents had 'In Loving Memory Of Ian Arthur' engraved on his headstone.

The two other crew members of 'M-for-Mother' were never found. They have their graves at sea. The names of Jock Gallery and Bob Hind are remembered on Panel 36 of the Runnymede Memorial. They are two of the 20.456 missing RAF aircrew during WWII.

At Oulton, Les Deadfield and the other ground crews waited in vain on the return of the two missing Blenheims:

"When all six of the aircraft had got into the air and were on their way, it was then that we ground staff were left with our own thoughts until we got a signal telling us they were on their way back. When at last only four returned we waited long into the night hoping to hear that they had landed on another 'drome, but when it was known that they had crashed it was most distressing to learn that the missing two were the crews I had seen off. But that is war and it was just a matter of waiting for new crews to come along. It was because of incidents like that, that we really didn't get to know the names of aircrews unless they were very lucky and they needed an awful lot of that".

On virtually every day in June, formations of 2 Group Blenheims were sent off on low level ship-hunting sweeps in the enemy shipping lanes. However, the effectiveness of the shipping *Beats* declined. The crews had achieved some promising successes during April and May, but in June the number of successful shipping strikes off the Dutch coast fell dramatically. Only one vessel was sunk, but this was a neutral Dutch fishing ship. The Blenheim crews fought against ever-increasing odds. The defences of the German coastal convoys were strengthened with more *Flak*-ships and standing patrols of Bf109s and Bf110s. This made it almost impossible for the gallant British crews to turn the odds in the shipping campaign in their favour. On 4th June, Air Vice-Marshal Stevenson commented to Air Commodore Lees of HQ Bomber Command on this:

"*Beats 8, 9* and *10* (Dutch coast and Frisian Islands shipping lanes, T.B.) are the most profitable from the point of view of finding ships, but they are also the warmest."

The operations on two further days in June will show the impossible situation for the Blenheim crews and the impact that the losses had on the next of kin of those who failed to return.

On 15th June 1941, 23 Blenheims of 2 Group were dispatched on sweeps off the Dutch and German coasts but most of the crews turned back because of lack of cloud cover. Five aircraft of 107 and 110 Squadrons went to *Beat 9* (Texel-Ijmuiden) and six of 105 to the Scheldt Estuary (*Beat 10*), all in the early evening. Led by their new CO, Wing Commander Hughie Edwards, 105 Squadron found a convoy of eight ships off The Hague. Edwards bombed a 4,000-ton merchantman, Sergeant Jackson attacked another large ship. A gaggle of ten German *E-Boats* was seen nearby, and had been avoided by most of the crews, but Flying Officer Watts, on his first operation with the squadron, mistook the heavily armed and manoeuvreable craft for merchant shipping. He went in low, and although he probably hit one, his aircraft was hit by *Flak* and burst into flames before turning over and diving into the sea with the loss of all on board. Also, V5887 of 114 Squadron - probably on a Coastal Command detachment - was shot down by a *Flak*-ship off the Hook of Holland. Sergeants Dowsey and Duffield were picked up by the Germans alive, but the observer, Pilot Officer Starkey still remains missing.

Meanwhile, in *Beat 9*, a crew of 110 Squadron attacked a 5000-ton cargo vessel escorted by five *Flak*-ships off Den Helder. Another of the formation just disappeared in the North Sea West of Bergen aan Zee. Flight Sergeant Guesford and crew of 110 Squadron were killed. Mrs. Irene 'Pat' Collins, tells about her husband Arthur Guesford, whom she married in January 1940:

"I was sixteen and, as the old song goes, 'I was too young to fall in love, and I was too young to know'. But I did! Arthur and I met at a cycling club rally and he was tall, dark and handsome and with a lovely ready smile. He had a lock of straight black hair which fell across his forehead and he would be seen to throw his head back to get the lock back into place. We were together all our spare time.

"With the threat of war hanging over us in 1938, Arthur joined the RAF reserve and learned to fly in Tiger Moths and Avro Ansons. He would fly over our house and I always knew it was him. Although he could not master driving a car, flying came second nature to him. He loved the life and in September 1939 he was called up to learn to fly bigger 'planes. A little later it was rumoured that he may be sent to Canada to train and it was his wish that if this happened and we were married I would be able to go to Canada with him and be safe. My father was not happy about this but we were able to persuade him. So, on January 20th 1940 we had a fairy-tale wedding in the little church where I had attended Sunday school and which was right on the edge of RAF Rochford (Southend Airport) where he had learned to fly. He was not called to go to Canada and I never knew if this was all set up so that we could get married! He trained at various places; Brough in Yorkshire, Grantham in Lincs. and somewhere near Peterborough and I was able to be with him all the time.

"When he became operational I came home to mother who was very proud of him and loved him like a son. He was now flying Blenheims from somewhere in Suffolk but he got home as often as he could. He was offered a commission many times but, because his crew had not been offered one, he declined. He had flown 32 sorties and was due to rest when he came home for 24 hours leave and said he could tell us nothing much except that the 'powers that be' had something special for him in a day or so. When he was due to return to base we walked to the bus stop together and met two friends in uniform who were also waiting for a bus. We stood talking and the men were smoking when we suddenly realised that Arthur had lit his cigarette from a third light of the match. Nothing was said but for the RAF this was a very bad omen - two days later he was reported missing, presumed dead. I didn't want to believe it but I knew he was dead. My mother worried endlessly for me and I could not go out without someone wanting to come with me. All I wanted was to be left alone.

"The war was dragging on and I felt I was wasting my time so I decided to join the Land Army and be of some use to the War Effort. This worried my mother but she began to understand that I had to be occupied. I enjoyed my work and met a whole lot of different people and made many new friends. Some weekends I was able to go home and see my family. Still Arthur's body or 'plane had not been found and in time, for official purposes, he was declared dead. This was a fact that I had known all along! But not my mother; she still felt he might be found and she still worried for me. She was not a religious woman but she was a Christian in every sense of the word. She would get her grocery rations every week from the same shops. It was not her way to buy from 'under the counter' - there was a war on and reductions were necessary, she would not pay 'over the top' for black market goods!

"She lived in a small community with very few shops but one day she saw a shop that had been closed since before the war had suddenly been re-opened. She did not go into it but continued to buy her provisions from her usual shop. The following week she found herself looking into the new shop window and was drawn by some 'force' to go inside. There was nobody in the shop and no-one to serve her. She waited for some time as though compelled to stay where she was. Eventually a lady appeared from the back of the shop holding her head and looking far from well. My mother was concerned for her and asked if she could do anything to help. The woman said "I have a headache but it is not a normal headache. I have a message to pass on. Someone has been trying to send a message through me for two weeks". My mother was a bit startled and went to leave the shop but the woman stopped her and said, 'Do you know a young man in a blue suit? You won't have seen him for some time but you would know him as he has black hair with a lock that sometimes falls over his forehead. He says you are not to worry any more about him. He is in a wonderful place and can watch all that goes on and is happy.' My mother realised who she was talking about and said that she recognised the young man in the blue suit and with black hair. The woman told her again that she was not to worry any more and that everything would be all right and, having given the message, she herself felt better. My mother went home and strangely felt better and more relaxed.

"The following week she thought she would go to see the lady who had given her the message. She walked across the road only to find that the shop was empty, not a thing inside and nobody about! The shop had been open for just two weeks. It was sometime after this that I was informed by the Air Ministry that Arthur's Blenheim had crashed at sea on June 15th. 1941 and that his body had been recovered on August 16th. of that year and that he was properly buried in grave number 263, Kerkeby Cemetery on the Isle of Romo, Denmark."

On the 16th June 1941, 25 Blenheims were dispatched on shipping sweeps: all went to the Dutch coast. Six crews of 139 Squadron and one of 18 Squadron went to *Beat 9* (Texel). Two aircraft, both of 139 Squadron, were intercepted by Bf109s of *1./JG 52* on the way to the target area. T1832 was shot down into the North Sea with the loss of the whole crew and V6332 limped back to England, only to crash-land near Norwich and both the pilot and observer were killed. Three remaining crews attacked shipping off the Frisian Islands, but no ships were damaged or sunk.

Five crews of 105 Squadron went to Terschelling and attacked fishing vessels off the island. None were sunk and all aircraft returned safely. A third strike force, seven aircraft of 18 Squadron, went to *Beat 10* where two of the crews found a north-bound convoy of four merchantmen and a *Flak*-ship off Flushing. Sergeant Wood and crew attacked an 1,800-ton cargo ship but no results were observed. The second Blenheim, V6512 WV-K of Pilot Officer Watson and crew, went in to attack the leading ship of the convoy, a 3000-ton cargo vessel, but their aircraft was shot down by accurate *Flak* before dropping the bombs.

Finally, six aircraft of 21 Squadron went to *Beat 7*. Off Borkum, three crews attacked fishing ships which they identified as 'squealers', and claimed two sunk. When pulling up over one of the target ships, V6034 hit the mast of the ship and cartwheeled into the sea minus one wing. This was a sad loss for 21 Squadron, as Flight Sergeant Reg Leavers DFM and his crew were almost tour-expired. They had remarkably survived three months of anti-shipping operations with the squadron. They had fought in the campaign from the very first operation by 21 Squadron on 26th March. The crew even survived a detachment on Malta where they attacked Rommel's supply ships on their way to North Africa. On 18th April, Sergeants Leavers and Overheu (observer) had each been decorated with a well-deserved DFM. By June, they were one of the most experienced anti-shipping crews in 2 Group. Reg Leavers' body washed ashore on the Northern coast of Groningen province and rests in Baflo Protestant cemetery near the coast. Sergeant Overheu DFM has no known grave, and Sergeant Phelps the WOp/AG was interred at Sage, Northern Germany. Peggy Stanton was Reg Leavers' fiancee:

"Early in 1941, April to be exact, I knew he was going on a special mission but naturally did not know where. Squadron Leader Atkinson (Attie for short) had to pick six of the best crews to go to Malta to establish a squadron there. They were the first to go from 21, whilst there Reg and his crew were awarded the DFM. When they returned they were given 10 days leave and I was so shattered to see him very drawn and seemed to have aged a 100 years; apparently it was hell out there. That was the last time I saw him.

"We had arranged to marry on his next leave which would have been June. On his return they were on daylight bombing of ships day after day. I received a letter from him saying he would be home on leave in June and by that time they would have done their share of ops and he would be coming off operations and would have been an instructor. In fact, they had done over their share of ops and the terrible part of the whole thing is that he should never have been on that last raid but crews were being lost so fast, at the last moment a crew went sick and Reg and his crew had to take their place. Six crews went on that raid from Watton, Reg and his crew did not return and instead of arriving home on leave we received the telegram saying he was missing, believed killed. I don't have to tell you just how shattered I was, we just lived in hope that he might have been taken prisoner. It was not until August we heard that his body had been washed up and he had been buried at Baflo (Den Andel) near the town of Groningen.

"Even after all these years I never really got over it, he was well loved and a wonderful person and I know we would have been very happy together."

What was the result in ships damaged and sunk off the Dutch coast on these two days, the 15th and 16th June 1941? None. On the debit side, however, seven Blenheims were lost with only three survivors. This set the trend for the remaining months of the daylight shipping campaign.

So far, we have mainly looked at the Blenheim operations to the Netherlands and the Dutch coast area. However, on raids to Germany, the crews often flew over, or flew north of, Dutch territory, where German fighters laid in ambush. This brings us to 2 Group's operations on 30 June 1941. On this day, 2 Group dispatched 46 Blenheims to enemy territory. Ten aircraft of 18 and eight of 139 Squadrons went on *Circus 27* to Pont-á-Vendin power station. Seven Blenheims of 107 Squadron flew to the German Frisian Island of Sylt as a diversionary raid for the second attempt of 'Operation Wreckage', and six Halifaxes went to Kiel. 'Wreckage' was the code-name for a daring daylight raid on Bremen, which was to gain VC fame for Wing Commander Hughie Edwards four days later. On this second (and failed) attempt, 21 Blenheims of 21, 105 and 226 Squadrons abandoned the operation due to the formation being spread out in a bank of sea fog before reaching the target. Returning individually at zero feet, some Blenheims bombed shipping off the Dutch Frisians. For example, Flight Lieutenant Anthony Scott and crew of 105 Squadron attacked a ship in Terschelling harbour. Another Blenheim of Pilot Officer Waples and crew of 21 Squadron was badly shot up by Bf109s off Terschelling on the way back from Bremen and crash-landed at Marham. Waples' WOp/AG claimed one Bf109 shot down into the North Sea off Terschelling as he saw large pieces of the fighter's wing falling away. However, German records do not confirm this claim.

Pilot Officer Bill Edrich flew one of the Blenheims of 107 Squadron on the diversionary raid to Sylt, and has every reason to vividly remember this trip:

"Wing Commander Petley led us up to Driffield where we learnt that the first six Halifax four-engined bombers ever to operate were to raid Kiel next morning. We were to support them with a daylight raid on Westerland, the fighter airfield on the island of Sylt. Sylt was renowned for its formidable defences and we were to create a major diversion, drawing off the fighters from the Halifax raid.

"The role of decoy naturally disturbed us, but the station commander at Driffield did his best to cheer us up. Perhaps with his tongue in his cheek he told us it was no accident that the raid was timed for midday Sunday. At that time, he assured us, the German fighter pilots, creatures of habit, would be enjoying a pre-lunch lager. This inspired planning was nullified when the operation was postponed until Monday.

"Seven of us took off at 10 o'clock next morning, leaving Petley and one other unserviceable Blenheim behind. Squadron Leader 'Zeke' Murray, a New Zealander, was leading, and we flew at extremely low level for the entire North Sea crossing, a distance of 360 miles, relying on dead reckoning and on what drifts the navigators could get from the wave-tops. I was No. 3 to Zeke in the leading vic of three, with a box of four behind us, and the long crossing at low altitude demanded intense concentration. Several times I felt my back stiffen up, but it was impossible to relax.

"At length, straight ahead of us, we could make out the coastline of Sylt, flat and featureless, a bleak panorama of lonely sand dunes. So far we had not been seen. As we lifted over the sand dunes we saw that we were crossing the narrow extremity of the island 10 miles south of the central bulk. Soon we were over the sea again, between island and mainland, and as Zeke altered course to the north we followed. At once the gun flashes began sparking off at us, to the left from the island, and to the right from the mainland, and straight ahead from the causeway which connects the two. I have seen paintings of naval battles, with gun flashes, illuminating the scene and the water being thrown up on all sides by shell bursts, but never have I seen such an inferno of fire-power as was directed at us in the next few minutes. We not only had to fly through this hail of metal: we had to fly through the plumes of water too.

"I shut my mind to everything and concentrated on Zeke's port wing-tip to my right. In close formation we might present a better target, but I knew that the heavier guns would have difficulty in ranging on us at low level. And all my experience had convinced me that to lose formation over the target was fatal. We began to switch into line abreast for our bombing run. Our bombs had eleven-second delay fuses and we all wanted to be clear of the target before they went off. Over my right shoulder I caught a glimpse of a Blenheim from the box of four behind us. It was flying higher than the rest of us, and for a moment it looked like a wild duck that has just been hit and is about to drop. When I looked again seconds later it was gone.

"We crossed the causeway but I was hardly aware of it; seven of us had begun the bombing run. There were four of us left. I turned to port in the direction of the airfield, and once over the island the *Flak* thinned out a little. I knew where the airfield was, but I couldn't pick out a single pin-point. We were so disorientated from the pasting we had received, and the whole picture was so much more complex and confused than those strikingly clear 'stills" we'd seen at briefing, that we simply dropped our bombs on the most likely looking building and hared out to sea as fast as we could. That was how it was. You can call it indiscriminate bombing if you like.

"Now we strove to get back into tight formation before the fighter attack that we knew must come. I knew in my mind's eye where Zeke was and soon I slid back into position to his left. I saw another Blenheim zoom erratically into the No. 2 position, and then I saw a fourth Blenheim to port and astern, intent on catching us up. Soon we were in a box of four, flying low so as to show nothing but our top camouflage to any pursuing fighter. No one seemed to be chasing us. Four of us, at least, had got away with it. When we were 100 miles from Sylt I lit a cigarette and relaxed. Then I heard a shout from Ernie, 'Snappers!'

"I had forgotten the fighters at Terschelling, on the Frisian Islands. Four of them, Bf109s, were hurrying up towards us from the south. Zeke coolly turned our formation northwards, drawing the fighters further away from their base. We knew their range was limited. But the Bf109s hung on. Zeke's gunner took control of the voice radio to direct the fire-power of the four Blenheims, and we prepared to put into practice the tactics we had rehearsed so often. The principle was that when bombers are being attacked by fighters of superior speed, the best defence is to turn into the direction of attack, thus making it difficult for the fighters to get a good stern view.

"We tried this as the Germans began their attack, but they didn't fall for it. Two of them took up position to the port rear, two to the starboard rear. As the port pair attacked with cannon and machine-gun and we turned left to make them miss and overshoot, the starboard pair automatically fastened on our stern. 'Bandit port five o'clock, half a mile. Hold it...Hold it..Fire!' The Blenheim juddered as Ernie opened up, and we sniffed the rank stench of cordite. Ahead of me I could see the water bubbling, and foaming as the bullets from the '109 churned up the sea. Had it not been for Zeke's gunner and his clear and timely directions we would never have survived that first attack, let alone those that followed. We couldn't match the fire-power of the '109s, but four Blenheim turrets firing simultaneously, switching rapidly from target to target, kept the German pilots at arm's length.

"Every now and then I could see spluttering little spurts on the metal surfaces of the other Blenheims where hits were being scored. I guessed the same thing was happening to us. One cannon shell burst with a little pink explosion on the rear of Zeke's port engine nacelle. It left a jagged hole, and as I watched the fluid streaming down the fuselage and spraying off the tail I knew his port inner petrol tank had been hit. 'My guns have packed up!' It was Ernie Hope from the turret. Soon, in all four Blenheims, the guns were either jammed or out of ammunition. With four badly mauled aircraft, greatly reducing our ability to manoeuvre, we were left with evasion as our only hope.

"Mercifully three of the '109s were giving up the chase and turning back for Terschelling. But the fourth was coming in for the kill. The German pilot was approaching from the port rear, and we could not shake him off. Reassured by the absence of answering fire, he came in closer and closer. We were sitting ducks. Yet still he did not fire. As he overtook us he banked above me and I looked straight up into his face. His look of exasperation was

136

unmistakable. He too had run out of ammunition. With a shrug of the shoulders he turned away and headed south. (This German fighter pilot was *Oberleutnant* Karl-Heinz Leesmann, CO of *I./JG 52*, who was the last of his unit to return to base at Bergen/Alkmaar after the prolonged fight with the Blenheims. Leesmann claimed two Blenheims shot down of Edrich's formation -confirmed by the German High Command as his 21st and 22nd victories!-, but all British aircraft returned to base. Leesmann was awarded the Knight's Cross after this battle, T.B.).

"I called up Zeke to tell him about his petrol tank and to suggest that he switch off his port engine. This reduced his speed to 130 miles an hour, but the rest of us closed in and escorted him back to the Yorkshire coast. Nothing was ever more welcome than the sight of Flamborough Head. I suggested that in view of the damage we had all sustained we should land singly, instead of in our usual formation, with Zeke going in first. Both Zeke and the second Blenheim crash-landed, but the remaining two of us landed normally. Soon we were grouped around one of the crashed aircraft, talking excitedly about the trip.

"While we were doing so a lone Blenheim, obviously in trouble, staggered over the field. It was one of the three missing aircraft, piloted by a sergeant pilot named Leven. We had lost two aircraft on the run in, and one of them had slewed into Leven, chewing up his ailerons and his flaps on one side. Somehow Leven had recovered and escaped into cloud; his was very probably the aircraft I had seen lurching like an injured bird. He had kept the Blenheim straight and level by holding the aileron control in the vertical instead of the horizontal position, but it had been such a strain that he had borrowed a leather belt from his navigator and strapped up the controls. He had then skipped from cloud to cloud and eventually came back to Driffield. He received an immediate award of a DFM. 'Are all your trips like this?' asked the highly impressed bomber crews based at Driffield. 'Most of them', we said laconically."

One day after Edrich's narrow escape, on 1st July, a new Bomber Command directive *BC/S.23746* came into effect. 2 Group was now instructed to do everything in its power to contain the German fighter units in the west and if possible urge the enemy to reinforce them. Thus, 2 Group was to spearhead British aid to Russia which had been invaded by the *Wehrmacht* on the 22nd June. *Circus* operations were to be executed in the Pas de Calais and Lille areas on a heavy scale, whereas the anti-shipping operations now became a secondary rôle for the Blenheim crews. Also, deep penetration daylight raids into Germany were to be undertaken: this would directly lead to the famous Bremen and Cologne raids of 4th July and 12th August. Finally, cloud cover attacks were to be made on the Kiel Canal and towns in northwest Germany.

To start off, on 1st July Bomber Command dispatched 39 Blenheims and 6 Stirlings to various targets, mostly in northwest Germany. For example, 139 Squadron sent six crews to Kiel, but they ran out of cloud cover about five miles from the target, so the operation was aborted. Only six out of the 45 aircraft bombed targets, the cost was two Blenheims lost. V6396 of 21 Squadron, flown by Squadron Leader Doug Cooper DFC, who was one of the Blenheim pilots engaged in the first scrap with Bf110s on 10th January 1940, was shot down near Kiel and V6258 of 139 Squadron was shot down by a Bf109 off Vlieland. Sergeant Fenton and crew were rescued by the Germans, and were among the very few crews to survive a Blenheim crash in 1941. Also, a Stirling of 7 Squadron was shot down by Bf109s off Texel.

One of the few Blenheim crews to successfully complete their sortie on 1st July 1941 was Squadron Leader Roe and crew of 18 Squadron. Pilot Officer Sherring was Roe's WOp/AG, and he recounts his exciting adventures on a Borkum sweep, and its aftermath:

"We took off at 9.00 for op. No.30, a shipping sweep to Borkum. Roe was a wonderful pilot to fly with, he had such perfect control of the aircraft, and was in a different class to anyone I have ever flown with. He was also very confident, and pretty mad, and he meant to find me a ship if he could. We did our ordinary three minutes sweep without seeing anything, still nothing except a buoy, which we all tried to sink by gunfire. Finally, Roe ran straight down the sands at Borkum. You could see the separate tiles on the roofs of the houses. There were men digging worms on the foreshore in blue jerseys. They just stood and gaped. Roe after nearly a quarter of an hour of this, packed up and headed for home. We must have searched about 50 miles of coastline. Visibility had been poor all through the trip, which I should think accounts for why Borkum, heavily defended, did not open fire on us.

"After coming home, I was definitely now on rest, and Flight Lieutenant Petley and Flight Lieutenant Tony Richardson fixed me up as gunnery leader of 107 Squadron at Massingham, so I came back to Raynham. By this time it was a completely strange and new 18 Squadron, with no old faces at all, and I was glad to leave".

Indeed, 18 Squadron was among the 2 Group units that suffered very heavy casualties during the anti-shipping campaign. By 1st July, when Pilot Officer Sherring left the squadron, twelve aircraft and eleven crews had been lost, excluding losses on *Circus* operations and during training flights. Of the 33 missing aircrew, only one man was made PoW. Sergeant WOp/AG Monty Scotney was one of the replacement crew members to reinforce 18 Squadron in the Summer of 1941. One of his first trips was a shipping sweep in *Beats 8* and *9*, off the Dutch Frisian Islands on 5th July. The only shipping encountered on the *Beat* were a gaggle of six heavily armed R-boats, which the crews wisely did not attack. 18 Squadron's return to Oulton has always stuck in Scotney's memory:

> "On our return (and we all came back safely) an aircrew Squadron Leader who had not flown this sortie, remarked in my presence: 'I'm surprised they all got back, I thought we'd have lost at least two'. I remember thinking it was an unfeeling, not to say callous remark to have made. I can see why he made it; flights to the Frisian Islands were mostly lengthy, and without fighter protection. Spitfires and Hurricanes just did not have the range. We relied for our safety on being undetected, and hoped to achieve this by keeping very low for the entire outward journey (below radar, not above fifty feet), and by making use of low cloud and mist in the target area. Even if heavily defended shipping was not attacked, there was a danger from enemy fighters. I was always apprehensive about meeting up with Bf110s which were armed with cannons and could stand well away whilst producing devastating fire".

Until now, we have focused our attention mainly on the anti-shipping campaign of 2 Group. Yet, Coastal Command Blenheims also contributed their might to the campaign - at night, that is. During practically the whole of 1941, crews of 53 and 59 Squadron flew their 'armed shipping recces' off the enemy coasts. Usually, two, three or four aircraft were dispatched every night to monitor the German shipping traffic and if possible, demolish one or two vessels in a surprise attack from mast-height. Moreover, the Coastal Command fighter Blenheims of 235 Squadron flew anti-shipping patrols in daylight.

As an example of the Coastal Command Blenheim anti-shipping operations in 1941, we now look at the events on the night of 7/8th July 1941. Four Blenheims of 53 Squadron flew anti-shipping patrols in the area from Borkum to Walcheren. One of these aircraft found and attacked a 4,000-ton ship in a convoy off Ameland, around 00.20. Pilot Officer Terence O'Brien was the pilot of this Blenheim, PZ-Z:

> "It was a thinly clear night, and climbing away from the satellite field (Docking, the satellite airfield of Bircham Newton, T.B.) I could see the

shimmer of moonlight on corn that was rippling in a gentle breeze, and the reed beds in the broads showed up like pallid veins on a huge dark leaf.

"We climbed gently as we crossed the North Sea, and saw a shooting star come sweeping up from the eastern horizon to streak right across the sky in a great rainbow arch to disappear below the opposite horizon, and I half expected to see it rise again in the east on another scintillating circuit of our world. When within sight of the Dutch coast at about five thousand feet I happened to look back on the port side and there on the silver ribbon of moonlight were set out three lines of ships. We had missed them in passing because we were flying down moon. You see best at night when looking up moon, the difference with ships particularly is that they stand out clearly in the lane of moonlit sea, black silhouettes sharply defined by the silver background; looking down moon it is difficult to see even a wake-producing target.

"There were four ships in the centre line, the escort in the two outer lines comprised two destroyers and three very small vessels I guessed from the wakes to be motor-torpedo boats (MTBs). We kept steadily on course towards the coast, as if en route to some continental target and uninterested in marine activities, but called the gunner with the information and warned him to keep a specially keen lookout for night-fighter cover. We continued on course until about four or five miles past them, by then over a grey curve of beach sands, and then made our move. With throttles almost closed, bombs now fused, we slanted back down in a semicircular turn that left us heading up moon and on a line we reckoned to bring the convoy directly ahead of us in the silver shaft of sea.

"They came up exactly as planned. We were still a few hundred feet above sea level, planing down fast, when we saw the three lines directly ahead - merchant ships in the centre, MTBs nearer to us, destroyers on the far side. We steepened the dive until almost within prop-tip touch of the deep blue silvered surface, then slammed on full throttle, together with the boost, and charged in towards the second merchant ship in the centre of our moonlit track. You do not just drop the bombs in such attacks, there is a feeling of positively ejecting them when you pull up sharply at the moment of release to hurl them against the black wall of the ship's hull. We passed so low between the masts we could have cut their aerial, and I saw clearly a light move quickly across the forward hatches, far too quickly to have been carried. Thrown? We dived down to sea level on the far side, skimmed through the gap between the two destroyers and then away down the moonlit trail across the calm sea. Not a single shot was fired at us.

"The bombs were fused at ten-second delay by which time we were nearly a mile away. I am sure at least one of the four 250 lb bombs must have skipped into the ship's side, and the fact that the gunner declared only that he 'thought' he saw a flash made no difference to that conviction. A bomb that explodes inside the hold of a ship might well show little or no external flash, particularly to a viewer a mile away at very low level. I considered it a copy-book attack.

"The Controller in the Operations Room did not think so. He was a namesake, Charles O'Brien, a first-war pilot and at de-briefing he told me we should have gone back to observe results. I just shrugged, but he kept on nagging about it so finally I told him that if he considered the record so important he should fly out himself to the awakened escort and look around. He became testy at this, said he would 'speak with' my Commanding Officer. There was no chance of any useful dialogue after that and we parted in scowling antagonism. He had said nothing that persuaded me we should have hung around to check results; we would not only have come under fire from the escort ships but also probably from German night-fighters normally associated with these convoys. The essential job had been done; a big ship had been hit, His Majesty's aircraft and crew were back at base ready to do another strike. That was the way to win wars, surely?"

With directive *BC/S.23746* coming into effect on 30th June, the 2 Group anti-shipping campaign was now largely taken over by Blenheim and Hudson squadrons of Coastal Command. However, the 2 Group daylight anti-shipping operations were continued throughout the Summer and Autumn of 1941, despite horrible losses in aircraft and crews. Only on 30th August, Air Vice-Marshal 'Butch' Stevenson was directly ordered to conserve his Blenheim force through Directive Ops. 240.

An overall look at the daylight anti-shipping campaign during this period shows firstly the declining effectiveness of the 2 Group Blenheim attacks on enemy shipping off the Dutch coast. Between 13th April and 30th May, 171 ships had been attacked in this area, but in June and the first week of July 182 sorties resulted in only 47 bombing attacks. Only one of these strikes was successful. On 20th June, the *IJM209*, an Ijmuiden-based Dutch fishing vessel, was sunk off Den Helder by two 18 Squadron crews. No other ships were sunk or heavily damaged during this period. But the losses among the Blenheim crews of 2 Group were heavy. No less than 22 Blenheims were lost in the Dutch coast area in June and the first week of July, plus one Coastal Command aircraft. The very slender chance of surviving a crash during the high-speed low-level attacks becomes painfully clear from the statistics; only five crew members were taken prisoners of war by the enemy. The large majority of the 66 airmen who were lost during these sweeps are still missing and commemorated on the Runnymede Memorial for the Missing of the RAF.

The results in ships damaged and sunk were overstated by 2 Group HQ probably to justify the serious losses in aircraft and crews. The 7th July shipping strike may illustrate this proposition. Five Blenheims of 105 and six of 139 Squadrons attacked a German convoy off The Hague in the early afternoon. The crews claimed to have scored hits on three vessels of 4,000 tons, one of 2 or 3000 tons and two of 2,000 tons. A press release issued by 2 Group HQ stated that those six ships were left by the Blenheim crews 'either sinking or thoroughly alight'. The truth however is a sad one. Of the eleven Blenheims that attacked the convoy three were shot down by ship's *Flak* and Bf109s and no ships were sunk or heavily damaged during this strike. The only ship in the convoy that was in fact hit was the *Delaware*, a Danish merchantman. No less than eight 250-pound bombs struck the vessel. Of these bombs, only two exploded and caused little damage. Four Danish sailors were killed in the blast and one was injured, but the ship sailed on under her own steam.

Non-exploding bombs was one of the many problems that the Blenheim crews experienced on their low level attacks. German reports clearly indicate this happened on many occasions during 1941 and 1942. A second example of this occurred during the attack on 14th September 1941. Off the Hook of Holland, the steamer *Bullaren* was hit by three bombs from an 18 Squadron aircraft and all three failed to explode. It is a sore conclusion that the Blenheim crews braved the hell of an enemy convoy time and again, only to see that their bombs hit the shipping targets and then, on many occasions, fail to explode. German ships regularly put into Dutch ports to have duds removed from their bowels. These bombs were virtually all dropped at very low level and from very short range. It appears that the eleven-second delay 250lb SAP bombs that the Blenheims dropped on their low-level shipping strikes often failed to arm before hitting their target ship. The firing mechanism of the bombs needed a certain amount of time to become 'live'. When the Blenheim crews pressed home their attacks until it was almost too late to clear the ship's superstructure - the only way to be certain of a hit -, the bombs often were not in flight long enough to arm. The sad conclusion is that the more 'press on' the Blenheim crews were, the less chance they had of actually damaging or sinking a ship. Although this problem had been recognised by Blenheim crews in 1940, the powers that be did not take any appropriate measures. A simple but effective measure would have been to give the bombs a shorter activation time, but this was not done during the anti-shipping campaign in 1941. The problem was again recognised in June 1941, but the Inspector General recommended not to reduce the fusing time as this would gravely endanger the safety of the attacking Blenheims. Instead, bombs should be equipped with some form of spoiler to anchor them in the ship's fabric. Yet, nothing came of it. When the Canadian Hudson crews of 407 'Demon' Squadron started their night shipping strikes in the Dutch coastal shipping lanes in September 1941 they experienced the same problems, but even then no action was taken to counter this serious situation.

Chapter Six

'The Charge of the Light Brigade'

Two raids against Rotterdam harbour.
16th July and 28th August 1941.

Rotterdam harbour was of great strategic importance to the Germans. Not only was it a port for transhipment of raw war materials like Swedish iron-ore, which was shipped over the Rhine directly to the steel mills in the Ruhr Valley, but it also served as an important ship-building and maintenance port. The importance of this port for Germany's war industry may be illustrated with the fact that some 3,000,000 tons of Swedish iron ore reached the port each year during 1941-43, plus some 850,000 tons of other essential war materials. Despite the fact that the Germans had set up a very strong defence of *Flak* batteries, searchlights and fighter units in and around the city, the Rotterdam harbour and docks area was a tempting target for the Royal Air Force. During 1940 and the first half of 1941, Rotterdam had been raided dozens of times mainly by RAF heavy night bombers.

In accordance with Churchill's Maritime Directive, a daring daylight bombing raid against Rotterdam harbour was planned for July 1941. Photographic reconnaissance and Dutch resistance reports had revealed that the 17,000 tons vessel 'Strassbourg' was moored at the quay of Rotterdam harbour; this big ship was to be the main target on the raid. The *Strassbourg* was the former Dutch liner *Baloeran*, which had been confiscated by the Germans and was now in service as a hospital ship. Additionally, a large number of merchant vessels and warships were present in the Dutch harbour in early July. One of these was the 10,500-ton *Oranjefontein*. The Blenheim crews of 2 Group had to neutralise them, and the job was planned for the 16th July.

The Blenheim crews practiced hard on low level formation flying, and at last the great day arrived. By 15.35, the first wave of bombers left Watton, led by Wing Commander Webster, the

CO of 21 Squadron. The force consisted of 18 aircraft of 21 and 226 Squadrons. The second wave, consisting of 18 Blenheims from 18, 139 and 105 Squadrons had taken off from Horsham St. Faith some 20 minutes earlier. This formation was led by Wing Commander Tim Partridge, CO of 18 Squadron.

The two waves of 17 and 18 aircraft (Flight Lieutenant Campbell-Rogers of 226 Squadron had dropped out of the first wave due to hydraulic problems) crossed the North Sea at wave top height and just to the southwest of Rotterdam a landfall was made. At 17.00, the first wave of Blenheims approached the target area, followed a few minutes later by the second wave. Each crew selected a suitable target and ships, harbour installations, storage buildings and railway lines were bombed and machine gunned in a widespread area. Among other buildings, a dock used by Wilton-Feyenoord ship-builders was left on fire. It was a miracle that none of the Blenheims collided as the sky over Rotterdam was full of wildly weaving bombers that braved a fierce barrage of *Flak* during the whole of the raid. Four Blenheims fell victim to the enemy gunfire which was considered to be a light toll to be paid for such a daring raid in broad daylight. In the first wave, 21 Squadron's Sergeant Bevan and crew in V6240 were hit by gunfire from *Flak*-ship *Vp1107* in the Waalhaven harbour. The stricken aircraft hit a crane, lost a wing and, after an explosion, swerved into the Waalhaven. The second wave lost three aircraft. V6267, flown by Wing Commander Partridge, was mortally hit and, in a desperate last attempt to crash-land the damaged aircraft, Tim Partridge tried to ditch his aircraft in the Noordsingel. He failed to achieve this and the Blenheim cartwheeled into the side of the canal. A second aircraft of 18 Squadron, Z7496 with Sergeant Rost and crew, crashed near Delft, and, finally, Squadron Leader Sydney-Smith successfully belly-landed Z7362 of 139 Squadron in the centre of the city. His crew survived to be taken PoWs, but the nine other men died in the remains of their Blenheims. Pilot Officer Adrian White, the observer in Squadron Leader Sydney-Smith's crew recalls:

"We were a 'scratch' crew, in so far as we had not flown together before, but had been thrown together for this particular operation. My usual pilot was not available, so I was partnered with Squadron Leader Sydney-Smith. He had just returned from a tour of duty in Malta where he had earned a DFC for attacks on enemy shipping, and was about to go on a well deserved leave. Our WOp/AG, Flight Sergeant Ted Caban, was equally unfortunate, having been posted to our squadron as a gunnery leader (instructor), in a non-flying capacity, after having completed a tour of operations. He had been decorated with the DFM for shooting down an enemy fighter. As he was only armed with a single machine-gun, whereas the German fighters were equipped with at least two machine-guns, in addition to a shell-firing cannon, this was no mean achievement."

Squadron Leader Eric Sydney-Smith takes over the story of the 16th July, 1941 raid:

"I remember very well the run-up to Rotterdam docks, a bright sunny day with occasional people waving at us, and a Bf109 on some satellite airfield taxiing out for take-off, a rather unpleasant sight. As we came across the docks, everyone looking for his own target, we were lucky (?) enough to be running practically broadside on to a cargo ship, quite a good sized one, loaded, which was manoeuvring or being towed, across the docks. It only needed a very slight adjustment to course to cross right over it, practically amidships. I had to lift the nose a bit to get over it just after letting the bombs go. On the other side I immediately put the nose well down again towards the water and then saw that we were flying straight into the guns of a *Flak*-ship moored about five hundred yards away on the far side of the dock. I could see the ship sparking from end to end with gunfire and I could hear and feel some of it hitting us. Within a few seconds Ted (Caban, WOp/AG) called on the inter-com to say that the port engine was on fire and that he had been injured. I took a quick glance at the engine and saw that thick black smoke was pouring out from the whole topside of the engine cowlings. I got busy at once opening the cowlings and switching whatever it was to put the fire out. I probably switched the engine off, but we did not have feathering props then and the propeller kept on turning. All this had only taken a very few seconds and when I looked up again, out of the cockpit, I saw what looked to me like a church tower. It seemed to rise well above us and it was so close that my first reaction was that there was no way to avoid it and that perhaps we would crash into it and be held up there. However, in the micro-seconds necessary for my mind - subconsciously - to analyse this idea, it rejected it and without any calculated intention, I heaved full back on the controls and we went straight up and over. If there had been a weather-cock on top, I doubt if it would have still been there afterwards. We came down on the other side, now with only one engine working, practically stalling, and carried on over the roof-tops flying tail-down and nose-up with a nasty sinking feeling. We were still heading northeast. We were too low and too slow to try a turn and I felt the safest way to find a space in to which we could do a wheels-up crash-landing would be the countryside on the other side of the city. But I felt it had to be soon, as we would either blow up or crash among the roof-tops.

"Suddenly there was an almost blank area ahead of us. It might have been about the area of a football pitch. I cut the engine that was still running, I forget whether I put the flaps into the 'down' position, but they would not have worked anyway, turned slightly left and then right, side-slipped to the right and straightened up at the last moment into a straight and level position. We did not seem to hit the ground, it was of cleared bomb-damage, very hard and we bounced along it for a comparatively short distance before coming to a stop with the fuselage still more or less in one piece and upright. I was unhurt except for a very slight bump on my forehead though my straps had held. Both wings, with their engines, had been cleanly torn from the fuselage and left behind and the fire had gone out.

"I was not wearing my jacket, nor collar and tie, but in shirt-sleeves. I unclipped my harness and the aircraft rescue axe and climbed out of the cockpit and down onto the port wing-stump to go and get Ted out of his gun-turret position. Almost as I stepped to the ground crowds from the streets around the bombed area were rushing towards the plane and within a few seconds, before I had any time to do anything, the first man to reach me snatched the axe from my hand and started attacking the turret (not in a hostile sense, but to get Ted out). A few seconds more and the crowd was so thick around the plane that I couldn't get anywhere near it. I went round towards the nose and over the heads of the crowd, on tip-toe, I saw Adrian being attended to. I had the impression that he was smiling with an assuring air and I thought that he had a broken leg. In any case he was being looked after and I was being pushed further and further back from the plane by the crowd. No-one paid any attention to me so I decided to clear off."

Pilot Officer Adrian White, the observer in the nose of Z7362 continues:

"I was sitting in the perspex nose of the aircraft and was catapulted through the perspex to land some distance ahead of the crashed plane to lie, like a fish out of water, completely stunned and breathless. On coming to my senses I found a crowd around me, some kind person having cut off my collar and tie to help me regain my breath. The next thing I knew was being conveyed by the Germans in an open car, through jeering crowds, to a military hospital. I remember, such were the demonstrations of hostility to my captors by the Dutch population, that one of my guards stood up in the car, threatening the crowd with his gun, whilst I sat in the back with another guard holding a pistol to my ribs. I was only lightly injured and, after a few days in hospital, was transferred to the *Luftwaffe* reception centre at Dulag Luft. Flight Sergeant Caban was more seriously wounded, a cannon shell having exploded under his foot. When I last saw him he was still in hospital, having pieces of shrapnel removed."

Squadron Leader Sydney-Smith:

"I walked quickly to the nearest bit of street, crossed it and walked along the pavement in a direction away from the plane. After a few moments a man fell into step beside me and started talking in a low voice. He said, in English, 'Are you from that plane?' I said yes and told him that I would like to try and find the American Consulate. He told me that he was a merchant seaman. The US Consulate, he continued, was back in the dock area."

Guided by the directions of the Dutch seaman and with a handful of small change he was given by him, Eric set off for the docks area. He continues:

"I arrived quite easily at the US Consulate but did not like the look of it. There were German soldiers patrolling the pavement on each side of the main doorway. It was almost on the very edge of the docks and I realised I had taken practically the identical line we had flown, so much so that in a very few moments I saw a *Flak*-ship tied up along the quayside and, out in the middle of the dock beyond it, 'our' ship, sitting on the bottom. I realised this was the *Flak*-ship which had shot us down. The crew, all talking and shouting like mad were busy cleaning the guns and putting things in order. I stood for a minute or so on the quayside, watching and listening. Looking at the *Flak*-ship, bristling with multiple pom-poms and other armament I found it hard to imagine how we had not been blown to shreds and I felt that if I had ever seen a *Flak*-ship at close quarters before it would have had a horrible effect on what the RAF discreetly called our 'moral fibre'."

Eric then decided to move out of the docks area and into the country. However, the Germans were already combing the area and he had no chance of getting anywhere. Late in the evening, he was taken prisoner of war. The manifest Dutch sympathy for the Blenheim raid and the help that the people of Rotterdam had given to Squadron Leader Sydney-Smith and his crew immediately led to German reprisals. The *Wehrmacht* Commander in the Netherlands announced that any Dutch sympathies towards downed RAF aircrew would lead to armed force. A few weeks later, five Dutch civilians were the first victims of this measure. They were murdered in cold blood after helping a downed Wellington crew in the province of Zeeland. The mayor of Rotterdam was also warned that his city would be severely punished in the event of any repeat sympathies by the people of Rotterdam towards the RAF.

Sergeant Jefferson flew as the No.2 in the second wave which was led by his CO Wing Commander Tim Partridge. Sergeant Monty Scotney, Jefferson's WOp/AG recalls the raid and the loss of Tim Partridge and his crew, with his log book entry first:

| 15.20 | Blenheim 7489 | Sgt Jefferson | Low-Level attack on shipping in Rotterdam harbour. Ship of 4000 tons hit. | 2hr.40 |

"This raid was an important first in 2 Group operations. There was a definite air of apprehension and expectancy among the crews of something big and different about to take place: engendered, no doubt, by the knowledge that our aircraft had been fitted with balloon cable cutters on the wing leading edges. Briefing confirmed the target, Rotterdam Docks, low level, two waves, each of eighteen Blenheims, our commanding officer, Wing Commander Tim Partridge to lead the second wave, and our crew to fly number two to him.

"I clearly remember waiting for the transport to take us out to our aircraft, the weather was fine, and some crew members were lolling around on the grass, others standing in small groups. One of them was Flight Sergeant Smith, who was the WOp/AG flying with the CO. I spoke to him, but I can't remember the actual conversation. Whatever his reply was, the words were among the last he spoke -two hours later he was dead. Sergeant Davies was the CO's regular air gunner, but he had been called home urgently to his critically ill father. Flight Sergeant Smith replaced him. I also recall, when we got to our plane, looking at the small, evenly spaced protuberances on the wing's leading edges. These were the cable cutters, and they looked very inadequate for the job.

"On the run in to the dock area I traversed the turret to port and took a photograph, over our port engine, of Wing Commander Partridge's aircraft. This could have been a minute or two before he was shot down. Over the target I took a second photograph, looking rearwards, of several bomb bursts. One of them must have been our 250-pounders.

"During the raid I saw no *Flak* and no fighters, although I understand the *Flak* was intense by the time the second wave of Blenheims appeared over the docks. The first eighteen alerted the defences and suffered one loss, the second eighteen lost three, two of them from 18 Sqn. Although we were flying very close, I didn't see Tim Partridge's plane go down, but my pilot and observer did. On the way back Sergeant Millns (observer) came over the intercom and said to Jefferson (pilot) - 'Did you see the Wingco go? He turned over and was on fire underneath.' Tim's aircraft hit the side of a canal."

Pilot Officer John Welch, WOp/AG with 18 Squadron, also raided the Rotterdam docks in the second wave. His adventures on the 16th July raid were published in 1942 in an Air Ministry booklet, 'We Speak From The Air' with the title 'Mast-high over Rotterdam':

"I had watched the leading squadron cross the Dutch coast only a few feet above the sandy beaches, where people waved us on, and I wondered if they had noticed the RAF unconsciously giving the 'V' for Victory sign as we flew over in vic formation. There was the astonishing flatness that I had expected and only occasionally could I feel the aircraft lifted up to miss windmills, farmhouses and villages; but most of all I was delighted to see that the country Dutchmen really do wear baggy trousers and vivid blue shirts. Cows galloped nervously about as we came hedge-hopping over the fields. Nearly everyone we saw gave us some kind of cheery gesture: but one man, evidently alarmed, was crouching against a telegraph pole. Actually we were so low that a few of my friends brought back some evidence of it. One pilot, for instance, not only cut straight through a crane cable, but got a dent in the belly of his aircraft, and some red dust, scraped from a Dutch chimney-pot, stuck to his aircraft. The same pilot had evidently been corn-cutting in between the hedges and returned with a small sheaf of the stuff in a niche on the leading edge of his wing.

"The first I saw of Rotterdam was a sky-line of high cranes over the docks. Climbing as high as the cranes themselves were fat columns of black smoke to mark the shipping that had already been successfully bombed. I was in the second formation of Blenheims to attack.

"We bombed Rotterdam at 4.55 in the afternoon. As we flashed across the docks, the observer saw 'our' ship, a bulky black hull with one funnel. We nipped across the last building and from mast-height we let our load drop. She was a medium-sized ship, I should guess about 4,000 tons. I could feel the bomb doors springing to, and then we were away over towards the town. In ship bombing of this kind, you often can't see your results, but I had a very clear view of our own results this time. There was a terrific explosion and instantaneous smoke and flames. I had seen lots of these explosions by now, but this one was by far the biggest. Over to the left we saw a good many supply vessels burning from the attack by the first wave. Elsewhere burning warehouses obstructed the view and only the bombers following on could see what had happened.

"And then on our way out of the town, with white tracers whipping under us, I saw great pillars of smoke spring up from the other enemy ships we had bombed. We had a good trip home and it had been a great day."

After the raid, the 31 remaining Blenheims flew northwest and, after re-assembling over a smoke flare that Squadron Leader Goode and crew of 105 Squadron had dropped off the Dutch coast, belted off for home. Squadron Leader Goode had also led in a Hurricane escort from Coltishall, but they were not needed on this occasion. The fighters followed the Blenheims home.

Despite the loss of four Blenheims over the target (including the leader of the second wave), the raid was deemed a success. Wing Commander Webster DFC, the leader of the first wave, was awarded a DSO. A few days after the raid, an Air Ministry communique claimed '19 ships out of action either permanently or for a long time to come, thus immobilising nearly 100,000 tons of shipping. Five more vessels, totalling between 40,000 and 45,000 tons, were severely damaged'. Indeed, Dutch reports told of 22 ships being damaged in the raid. The main target of the attackers, the *Strassbourg*, was slightly damaged. Lloyds War Records on shipping damaged and sunk in World War II lists the 5,193-ton *Hermod*, a German merchant vessel and the

5,749-ton *Knute Nelson,* a Norwegian merchantman, as damaged by the Blenheims in this raid. The German Naval
Commander in the Netherlands also listed the following vessels
as damaged in the 16th July raid: 2,653-ton *Cimbria* and
2,031-ton *Hafnia,* both Danish merchant ships. Also the Dutch
Gotha of 5,334 tons and *Oranjefontein* of 10,547 tons, the
German 8,456-ton *Treuenfels* and a gunboat that was being
fitted out were damaged. Possibly the 12,000-ton *Breisgau,* a
German merchant ship was also hit during the raid. All these
ships were slightly damaged by the 250-pound bombs and all
were soon repaired to fight another day. For example, the
Strassbourg was ready to sail by 20th July, only four days after
the raid. The lack of major damage to these ships must be
attributed to the poor capacity of the bombs that the Blenheims
dropped. The fate of the *Strassbourg* would only be sealed in
September 1943, when the ship struck an RAF air-laid mine off
Ijmuiden. Heavily damaged and lying stationary off the Dutch
port, she was torpedoed a few days later by the Royal Navy and
sunk.

A Royal Navy survey showed that enemy shipping movements
had declined significantly after the 16th July raid, but by the
first week of August the traffic was almost on the same level
again as before the raid. Therefore, 2 Group HQ planned a
repeat attack of the successful 16th July raid. The raid was
fixed for the 28th August. 36 crews of 21, 88, 110 and 226
Squadrons, the same number as six weeks earlier, were briefed
for Operation 523. In mid-afternoon, the Rotterdam harbour
area was to be attacked in the same way as on the first raid.
There were only two major changes in the plans. This time, a
Spitfire escort had to fight off any intruding German fighters in
the target area. Secondly, each bomber was armed with two
500-pound bombs, twice the capacity as on the first raid.
Possibly, Stevenson and his staff realised that heavier bombs
would probably cause much more lasting damage to the
shipping targets.

The operation however went wrong from the start; Z7299
'F-for-Freddy' of 226 Squadron lost power in the port engine
immediately after taking-off from Wattisham and crashed.
Sergeant Bill O'Connell was the pilot of this Blenheim:

"We were briefed to attack the docks and shipyard workings at Rotterdam. It was a mixed operation (crews from 226 and 110 Squadron made up six of the aircraft), and we were to rendezvous in flight along the route with aircraft from other stations. At the end of the briefing we were given the usual times, start up, take-off, rendezvous, etc. Our aircraft at Wattisham (then a grass field) were widely dispersed, and we had been instructed to taxi to the take-off position to await take-off time. This we did, and we positioned our aircraft in a position appropriate to what our flight position was going to be. I was to fly in the No.2 position, and so I took up a position slightly behind and to the right of the leader.

"By the time the aircraft were all in position for take-off, it was obvious that we would have some time to wait before take-off, so we all shut our engines down, and got out of our aircraft. We stood around in little knots in idle conversation for a couple of minutes, and then someone spotted an automobile coming towards us at high speed and drew our attention to it. Normally, this would have indicated that someone was coming to tell us that the operation was scrubbed; there would logically have been no other reason, since it had happened before on other operations. But, it was not so this time. The driver had brought the word that we were already late (10 minutes?) getting into the air, and we were to get into the air immediately, if not sooner. Someone had goofed on the times or they had been changed (a goof was the more likely explanation), so, we all scrambled for our aircraft.

"I had fixed my parachute, and started the engines, and had not had time to fix my Sutton (restraining) harness, when I noticed the leader's aircraft had started to roll. The Sutton harness would have taken 10 or 15 seconds to secure, but I couldn't spare that much time, so I started the take-off roll, hoping that I could fix it in the air with some help from Peter Saunders, my observer.

"Everybody knew that the Blenheim IV with full bomb load, full tanks, ammunition, wireless, flares, etc., was grossly overloaded. In that respect, the only differences of opinion was how much it was overloaded. My estimation in those days was that the Blenheim IV at the weight we flew them was about 4000 pounds overweight. It was a marginal aircraft to fly on one engine, even without bombs, full fuel tanks and ammunition (I tried it quite a few times).

"After we got into the air, I selected the gear up, and when we were about 20 feet off the ground I was in very good position, being just slightly behind the leader and just a few feet to his right. Without any warning whatever, the left (port) engine just quit cold (This was very unusual as an engine usually would cough a few times before quitting or the engine would just fade on you. For this reason, I felt sure that the reason for the engine failure was the breaking of a fuel feed line, probably due to the heavy hammering of the aircraft on the rough sod of the aerodrome during the take-off run). The aircraft yawed to the left and in an instant we were in the slipstream of the leader's aircraft. It is not possible to fly an aircraft in the slipstream of another aircraft at such close quarters (20 or so feet behind), and the result was that the nose of the aircraft pitched up sharply.

"This little involuntary manoeuvre was what did us in. The aircraft, with barely enough flying speed to keep it in the air in level flight, climbed to about 60 or 75 feet, started to stall and went into an incipient spin. The left wing dropped as I fought for control, and since I had to cut the take-off power on the right (starboard) engine in order to prevent the aircraft from rolling over and crashing in the inverted position, I took one hand (my left) off the control column and got the right engine throttled back. I knew we were going in.

"The aircraft was turning to the left, and we had turned through about 120 degrees as the ground came up, and by this time I had the wings once again almost level, but still left wing low. The left wing hit the ground first in an almost pancake position, and, in an instant the fuselage smashed its belly into the ground. With the impact of the fuselage, the entire aircraft burst into a huge ball of flames. For a moment, Peter and I were sitting beside each other in a sea of flames, and I knew there was no way that I could ever get out, because the control column had somehow parted from what had been the floor of the cockpit and now had my right leg pinned firmly and painfully against my seat. At this moment I was hoping that the ordeal would be a short one.

"What I did not know for those couple of seconds was that the aircraft, turning and still with some forward speed, had hit the ground and bounced back into the air again. When it hit the ground the second time, the fuselage smashed itself completely open, and the turning moment threw Peter and me out the left side of what had been the fuselage, and left us sitting side by side on the grass, about 50 feet from the main wreckage. I was still sitting in my pilot's seat. Peter hadn't fixed his restraining harness either. And that was well for both of us because both harnesses were fixed to the airframe, and we would otherwise have been trapped in the ball of flame. So, we just picked ourselves up and went to see about the fate of Robbie (Flying Officer Robertson, our WOp/AG). Peter and I both had quite red faces from the heat, so I said to Peter later, 'If anyone asks, we'll tell people that we just got back from sunny Malta a few days ago'...but no-one ever asked...

"The fuselage had broken in two, and the rear part of the fuselage, complete with gun turret, was quite removed from any other part of the wreckage. We could see Robbie's buttocks sticking out the now open part of the fuselage, just ahead of the gun turret. The explosive charge for destroying the secret IFF (Identification, Friend or Foe, the grandfather of the modern radar beacon) had detonated, and the smoke from the explosion had temporarily blinded, and perhaps confused, Robbie. He was trying to get out by attempting to make progress in the wrong direction, towards the tail of the aircraft, which was still intact. We ran over to where he was, slapped him on the backside, and told him just to fall straight backwards from where he was and we would catch him. He did, and we did. That little rescue operation was responsible for the most serious injury that resulted from the crash; Robbie somehow had hit his right knee on an unknown object when he fell backwards.

"We knew that we should clear the area as soon as possible, because somewhere in that burning inferno were two 500-pound bombs with 11-seconds delayed action fuses waiting to go off any moment, not to mention a lot of machine-gun ammunition and pyrotechnics.

"About this time the comic relief set in. The three of us, all fair athletes at that time, had started racing across the grass towards the main hangar, and I saw nothing about Robbie's pace that he had seriously injured his knee, and I never let him live it down. We must have made pretty good time (we were momentarily expecting a mighty blast or blasts behind us which inspired our running), because, after a couple of hundred yards or so, and long after we had expected the bombs to explode, the crash wagon came towards us, and stopped to pick us up. After doing so, the wagon continued on in the direction of the wreckage. I was standing on the outboard beside the driver, and I asked him where he was going. He informed me that he was going out to try to help the crew of the crashed aircraft. I told him that we were the crew, and at first he didn't believe me, and he took quite a bit of convincing that we were indeed the crew. He said later that he thought we were three aircrew who had wanted to volunteer in a rescue operation.

"Robbie was a Scotsman who seemed to live only for the humour he found in life, and he seemed to find an abundance of it. He not only found it, he created a lot of humour. I had suggested to Robbie after the crash that perhaps if we broke both his kneecaps he might do very well in the sprinting at the next Olympic games. But, Robbie had one of his own for me, which he told many times. He said he was running from the crash, and making very good time, when he was suddenly aware that a fellow had passed him showing world class speed, and this fellow was leaving him far behind. And this fellow was wearing a 40-pound pilot seat-pack parachute flapping at the backs of his legs.

"The three of us were very fortunate to get out of the crash with relatively minor injuries. But poor Robbie hobbled around for quite a few days. (He was killed in northern France on March 8th, 1942, while flying in the crew of Wing Commander Butler, CO of 226 Squadron, in a Boston in an attack on a motor lorry assembly plant at Poissy, near Paris. Their aircraft crashed in flames a few miles north of the target, after having dropped their bombs. All are buried in northern France, not too far from the site of the crash.)

"After the wreckage of our Blenheim had burned itself out, they couldn't find any trace of the bombs, which was unusual. But the next day, they found them in a little depression in the aerodrome about a thousand feet from where the aircraft had crashed. And they were complete with fusing links still in place...".

Shortly after Bill O'Connell crashed, two Blenheims of 110 Squadron had to return to base, also with engine trouble. The leader of the raid was pilot of 'Q' of 110 Squadron, which was one of the Blenheims forced to return to Wattisham and therefore the operation was aborted. The squadrons from Watton and Swanton Morley were recalled and the Spitfires of 19 and 152 Squadrons flew back to Coltishall.

After the failed beginning, the raid on Rotterdam harbour was not totally scrubbed. Half of the original force (minus O'Connell's destroyed Blenheim) were serviced and topped-up by the ground crews. Late in the afternoon, at 17.30, the 17 bombers of 21, 88 and 226 Squadrons again took off, picked up their Spitfire escort and at 18.00, 41 aeroplanes set course for the Dutch coast. As usual, they flew at nought feet to avoid detection by the German radar, some aircraft leaving their tracks on the surface of the sea.

An hour later, landfall was made. Yet, due to a small navigational error this was not made at Oostvoorne but a few miles further north off the heavily defended Hook of Holland. In addition to this severe setback, the formation of Blenheims had been spotted by a post of the German Observer Corps shortly before over-flying the Dutch coast. Swiftly, two officers of the post warned the defences of Rotterdam by telephone. These circumstances effectively took away the element of surprise and the operation was doomed to fail. The enemy *Flak* batteries and Bf109s of *JG 53* were ready and waiting for the arrival of the British bombers.

Immediately, the *Flak* batteries at the Hook put up a barrage of *Flak* that proved fatal to two Blenheims. Z7447 of 21 and L9379 of 88 Squadrons crashed in flames in the Scheurpolder. Squadron Leader Dick Shuttleworth, the leader of the raid, died at the controls of the 21 Squadron aircraft. There were no survivors among the other five airmen. Dick Shuttleworth had married his fiancee Honor only two weeks before the raid. The escorting Spitfires of 19 and 152 Squadrons nipped over the beaches, swung round and flew down the estuary. Over this area, they were also met with a fierce barrage of *Flak* and almost immediately Squadron Leader Lawson, CO of 19 Squadron, was shot down. Flight Lieutenant Cunningham took over the lead of 19 Squadron but his Spitfire was also hit by multiple pom-pom from a ship in the estuary. The engine seized up and Cunningham crashed on the beach in front of a machine gun post and was made prisoner of war.

The 15 remaining Blenheims now hedge-hopped to the east and, at 17.04 local time, arrived over the harbour area. Weaving between cranes, ship's masts and buildings each crew selected a target for their 500-pound bombs. 20-year old Flight Lieutenant Namias, pilot of Z7292 of 226 Squadron, skimmed over the water and spotted a large ship of around 10,000 tons that was moored at the quay. He skip-bombed the vessel, only just clearing the ship's superstructure, and his daring paid off. In a tremendous explosion one of his bombs knocked off the front of the ship. This was probably the *Oranjefontein* of 10,574 tons that partially sank after the raid. Little could Flight Lieutenant Mayer Namias suspect that he only had a short time left to enjoy this success; three weeks later he was dead, shot down during a convoy attack off the Hook of Holland. The *Zuiderdam*, a 12,150-ton merchant ship was hit in the engine room by a 500-pound bomb of another Blenheim crew. A fire broke out and the ship slowly sank. Dutch firemen deliberately pumped so much water into the hull that the ship capsized next day. The 12,000-ton *Westerdam*, moored close to her sister ship *Zuiderdam*, was also damaged during the raid. A 500-pound bomb exploded on the quay, forcing a 20-feet lump of concrete into the ship's hull and the ship sank slowly. It took the Germans months to repair these three big ships. It had obviously paid off to use the heavier 500lb bombs instead of the usual 250lb ones against shipping. 21 Squadron claimed hits on a 2,000 and a 3,000-ton ship and on buildings in the Waalhaven harbour. Squadron Leader Lynn of 88 Squadron hit a 5,000-ton ship, but on pulling V6032 over the masts of the ship his Blenheim was shot up by the furious *Flak*. With great flying skill, Lynn kept the crippled aircraft in the air and crash-landed at Attlebridge.

The alerted light and heavy *Flak* was murderous and three Blenheims were shot down in the port area. One aircraft, probably Z7445 of 88 Squadron, crashed into the slaughterhouse of Schiedam. Flight Lieutenant Alexander and crew were killed on impact. V6436 of 21 Squadron was mortally hit by the *Flak* from the ships in the harbour and crashed at Maassluis, exploding on impact and killing Pilot Officer Frank Orme and crew. Z7289 of 226 Squadron was hit, but Pilot Officer Johnstone managed to belly-land his burning aircraft at Kethel. They were soon made prisoners of war with only a few cuts and bruises.

Still, the carnage was not over yet. Bf109s of *JG 53* arrived on the scene and soon got entangled in fierce dogfights with the Spitfires of 19 and 152 Squadrons. One or two Messerschmitts however escaped the attention of the British fighters and *Leutnant* Hans Müller of *6./JG 53* shot down Z7435 and V5825 of 21 Squadron in quick succession. The Blenheims crashed in the North Sea just west of Rotterdam and near Roozenburg. Four men were killed and two escaped to be made prisoners by the Germans. Within half an hour, almost half of the original force of bombers were lost to the enemy defences. Only ten Blenheims, most of them severely shot up, limped back to their bases in East Anglia.

In addition to the seven Blenheims and two Spitfires of 19 Squadron lost during the raid, Sergeant Savage of 152 Squadron was shot down by fighters. There was a possibility that Squadron Leader Lawson, CO of 19 Squadron, had ditched in the North Sea off Rotterdam and was now drifting in his dinghy waiting to be rescued, so the next morning eleven Spitfires Mk.II left RAF Matlaske for an ASR Search. Off the Dutch coast, 19 Squadron aircraft searched for their C.O., but in vain. Then the Spitfires turned a bit further north, but nothing was found, except a gaggle of Bf110s from *II./ZG 76*, led by *Hauptmann* Martin Drewes. The twin-engined fighters, which were in the middle of a shooting practice, immediately engaged the Spitfires. The outcome was a very much one-sided affair: within five minutes, four British fighters were unexpectedly shot down. All four pilots of 19 Squadron disappeared without a trace. With the two aircraft and pilots lost on the Rotterdam raid, 19 Squadron thus had lost half of her front-line strength within 24 hours.

The German C-in-C of *Luftflotte 3* and Commander of the *Luftwaffe* in the west, *General* Hugo Sperrle, sent a message of congratulations to the *Flak* units at Rotterdam on 6th September 1941:

"My thanks and appreciation go to the *Flak* Group of Rotterdam and the Officers and Soldiers of the *Res. Flak post 261* and the *Res. Light Flak Battery 57*, for their wonderful and great efforts (8 Bristol-Blenheims and 2 Spitfires shot down) during the enemy raid on the evening of 28th August 1941."

21 Squadron was especially hard-hit on the second Rotterdam docks raid. A few days before the 28th August raid, Wing Commander John Kercher, CO of 21 Squadron, went on leave, and Squadron Leader Bill Edrich DFC was left in charge of the squadron. Then orders came through from Group HQ for an important raid next day, as Edrich recalls:

"We were to supply six Blenheims for a low-level strike on Rotterdam harbour. The orders specified that I was not to fly. Dick Shuttleworth was to lead. I didn't think Dick had had anything like enough experience to lead the squadron on so dangerous a raid. I was worried too about the raid's whole conception. The tactics to be employed were far too much a repetition of Tom Webster's successful raid of six weeks earlier. This time the Germans would surely be ready for us."

Edrich then went on to see if he could get permission to lead 21 Squadron on this raid, but it was no go. He continues his story:

"There was nothing for it but to throw everything into making the raid a success. But when the six Blenheims took off from Watton the following afternoon I was deeply anxious about the outcome.

"My worst fears were confirmed. Only two Blenheims got back and one of them was very badly shot up, with the rear-gunner wounded. Among the four pilots shot down was Dick Shuttleworth, whose promotion to acting Squadron Leader had come through that very day. Also among the missing was Canadian Frankie Orme.

"I had laid on nine late suppers in the Officer's Mess, but only one Officer got back. His supper remained uneaten. Late that evening I was having a brandy in the Mess and trying to pull myself together when the squadron Adjutant reminded me that Dick Shuttleworth's wife was staying at the Crown Hotel in Watton. Would I go and break the news to her? I said I would if he would come with me, anyway as far as the hotel foyer.

"There followed one of the saddest nights of my life. Dick's wife was very brave. She had already sensed that something was wrong and was packing her bags when I entered the room. She asked me if I would drive her to Dick's parents, who lived at Wroxham, just the other side of Norwich, and this I did. At about two o'clock that morning I found myself ringing the door-bell of the house. As soon as Dick's father saw me he knew what had happened. Mrs Shuttleworth senior took charge of Dick's wife, and I watched while Mr. Shuttleworth poured two large whiskies. 'You probably need this' he said, 'as much as I do.'

"It was a bleak and lonely drive back to Watton. Next day I discovered why they hadn't let me go on the raid. I had been posted to 2 Group Headquarters. My tour of operations was over. After that last tragic raid I think it was just as well for me that I was given a rest at that time. Apart from one week's leave I had been flying on operations virtually the entire summer, and I was one of the few to survive."

In August, out of 77 Blenheims that attacked shipping, 23 went missing; 19 of these were shot down in the Dutch coast area. In a total of 480 sorties, 36 were gone in a month. The Prime Minister was greatly disturbed by the losses suffered by 2 Group. Churchill stated on 29th August in one of a series of 'Action this day' minutes to the Chief of Air Staff, Sir Charles Portal:

> "The loss of seven Blenheims out of seventeen in the daylight attack on merchant shipping and docks at Rotterdam is most severe. Such losses might be accepted in attacking *Scharnhorst, Gneisenau* or *Tirpitz*, or a south-bound Tripoli convoy, because, apart from the damage done, a first-class strategic object is served. But they seem disproportionate to an attack on merchant shipping not engaged in vital supply work. While I greatly admire the bravery of the pilots, I do not want them pressed too hard. Easier targets giving a high damage return compared to casualties may be more often selected".

One day after this minute to Portal, Churchill drafted a message to the Blenheim crews themselves:

> "The devotion of the attacks on Rotterdam and other objectives are beyond all praise. The Charge of the Light Brigade at Balaclava is eclipsed in brightness by these almost daily deeds of fame".

With Churchill's profound sense of history, his comparison of No. 2 Group's achievements with one of the classic unnecessary disasters in British military history could have been no accident. Yet Air Vice-Marshal Stevenson, AOC of No. 2 Group, was unshakeable and the Blenheim anti-shipping campaign went on as fiercely as ever.

However, one lesson was obviously learnt from the so costly Rotterdam raid of 28th August. No further daylight raids by Blenheims to heavily defended harbours were carried out in the remaining months of the 1941 maritime campaign. Bomber Command continued its attacks on the port of Rotterdam by night, with Wellingtons, Stirlings and Whitleys. These raids were often successful at a far smaller cost in aircraft and crews. For example on 3/4th October 1941, 32 Wellingtons of 3 Group dropped 51.8 tons of high explosives and 5,660 4lb incendiaries on the harbour and oil installations of Rotterdam. Widespread damage was done to shipping, oil, harbour facilities, and an ammunition dump and all the 'Wimpys' returned safely to their bases in England. However, bombs also fell in residential areas near the harbour, which killed over a hundred people and wounded many more and caused widespread damage to houses in the southern and western areas of Rotterdam. This typified one of the dilemmas of Bomber Command's planners in the early war 'pioneering' years. Daylight raids by Blenheims against coastal targets had resulted in accurate attacks against military targets, but also in high casualties among these vulnerable aircraft. Similar attacks at night by the heavies of Bomber Command caused much damage at low cost, but often resulted in unavoidable and severe damage to civilian property.

Chapter Seven
Daylight Mission to Cologne

12th August 1941: Operation 77,
target Cologne power stations.

From the 10th January till the late Autumn of 1941, 2 Group Blenheim squadrons carried out 110 *Circus* operations. The main purpose of these *Circuses* was to entice German fighters into massive dogfights with the escorting RAF Spitfires and Hurricanes, the Blenheim bombers being the bait. Especially after the German invasion of Russia in June 1941, the objectives on the *Circus* raids were to tie up as many German fighters as possible, which would relieve pressure on the Russians, and to destroy as many enemy fighters in the air as possible. Targets for *Circuses* were usually railway junctions, *Luftwaffe* airfields, docks, industrial plants and power stations, mainly in northern France and Belgium. As the small groups of Blenheim bombers on these raids were protected by a mighty umbrella of fighters, the Blenheim crews welcomed *Circuses*, as Sergeant Monty Scotney, WOp/AG with 18 Squadron, recounts:

"Whilst we detested low-level attacks on shipping, which had a high casualty rate, we considered *Circus* trips a 'piece of cake' -nothing much to worry about."

Of the *Circus* campaign of 1941, a few operations stand out. One of these was the 12th August 1941 raid on the power stations of Knapsack and Quadrath, situated to the southwest and west of Cologne. Although not a *Circus* operation in the strict sense of the word since no fighter cover was provided over enemy territory on this occasion, the concept of the 12th August raid fits into this category.

Power stations had been high on the priority target lists of Bomber Command. As early as in the Autumn of 1939 operations to these targets in Germany were discussed. Apart from their industrial significance, power plants were considered ideal for air attack, being conspicuous and vulnerable targets. It was believed that turbines and boilers would easily explode when hit.

Knapsack power station had one of the largest steam generators in Europe with an output of 600,000 Kilowatts. The one at Quadrath generated 200,000 Kilowatts. For the reasons outlined above, the destruction of these two power stations was considered to be a severe blow to Hitler's war industry. Also, in the spirit of the *Circus*-type operation, the raid was intended to be a deep penetration into industrial Germany, with the aim of causing the withdrawal of German fighters from the Russian front to prevent further large-scale RAF daylight incursions of the *Reich*.

To keep losses among the Blenheim crews down and in order to confuse the German defences on 12th August, Bomber Command mounted six diversionary operations. Two high-level B-17C Flying Fortresses of 90 Squadron were briefed to attack Cologne, one more to raid Emden and a fourth to bomb De Kooy aerodrome. These were designed to split up the defences - or so it was hoped. While the Blenheims were on their way in to Cologne, six Hampdens of 5 Group would be sent to St. Omer with an escort of 84 fighters of 11 Group. Another formation of six Hampdens was to bomb Gosnay power station when the Cologne Blenheim force was on its way out again. This second diversion was escorted by no less than 114 fighters of 12 Group. Finally, six Blenheims of 226 Squadron were to raid Le Trait shipyards at around the same time as the second Hampden attack on Gosnay. All diversions proceeded according to plan, but the force bound for St. Omer aerodrome was intercepted by an estimated 150 Bf109s. Ten Messerschmitts were claimed shot down or probably destroyed by the British fighters, but six Spitfires were lost in the fierce dog fights. No diversionary bombers were lost to the enemy defences.

So to the plans for the main Blenheim raid on the 12th August. Most shipping sweeps had been suspended after the 5th and the Blenheim crews had been practicing extensively in low level bombing and formation flying techniques during the next week. At briefing early on the 12th, the target and operational procedures were at last revealed. Force 1, bound for Quadrath, was to be made up of three boxes of nine aircraft of 21 and nine of 82 Squadron and Wing Commander Kercher, CO of 21 Squadron was to lead this force. Force 2 comprised 36

Blenheims: 18 and 139 Squadrons each contributed nine aircraft, 107 six Blenheims and 114 twelve aircraft. This force was to be led by Wing Commander Nichol, CO of 114 Squadron, the big Knapsack power station was their target. Zero Hour over target was fixed for 12.30 hours, and each Blenheim was armed with two 500lb GP eleven-second delay bombs. Escort on the way in was provided by a Whirlwind twin-engined fighter squadron and six squadrons of long-range Spitfires would cover the bombers' withdrawal from the Dutch coast.

The two Blenheim formations took off between 08.55 and 09.30. Force 1 flew directly to the East coast near Orfordness, and there rendezvoused with Force 2 that in the meantime had picked up the Whirlwind fighters of 263 Squadron. The timing was excellent and according to plan (at Zero minus 82) and the large force set course for Holland, flying in loose formation low over the North Sea. When crossing the Dutch coast South of Flushing at 10.43, the Whirlwinds had to return as they had insufficient range to escort the bombers further inland. The Blenheims were on their own now, with over two hours flying ahead of them in broad daylight over heavily defended enemy territory, a frightening prospect. Nevertheless, it was a powerful and impressive sight, 54 Blenheims in formation thundering inland at low level over the flat Dutch countryside.

A few aircraft were damaged through bird strikes over the Dutch coast. Then the *Flak* woke up. The first casualty was T2437 of 82 Squadron, which crashed near the Moerdijk bridge: Pilot Officer Graham Rolland and crew were killed. Before Zero Hour, two other Blenheims were lost. V6423 of 18 Squadron crashed at Diest in Belgium, this time the whole crew was made PoW. Only minutes from arriving over target, V7451 of 21 Squadron was hit by *Flak* and crashed at Potz near Cologne. Sergeant Jim Langston, pilot of V7451, had joined 21 Squadron only a few days before the Cologne raid, and recounts his first (and last) operational trip:

"I arrived at 21 Squadron, Watton, at dusk on Tuesday August 5th 1941, after motor-cycling from my home near Painswick, in Gloucestershire, where I had spent a pleasant week's leave. But it was rather sad. The work we were doing (low level attacks on German shipping) had a very high casualty rate, and the survival rate was very, very low.

"I soon found my crew in the mess; Dave Roberts, the navigator and Ken Attew, our wireless operator/air gunner. The news was that all shipping and other operations were suspended for a week and we were to prepare for a raid on a very special target, an important power station, the loss of which would be a great blow to German industry. During this week we were to polish up our own low level bombing, low flying, and especially low level formation flying.

"The next day we took possession of our brand new Blenheim V7451 and it was a real pleasure to fly after the old ex-squadron ones we had had at Operational Training Unit. We spent every day practising our low-level bombing techniques using eleven-pound practice smoke bombs and thrilled the station with really low-level formation shoot-ups! We studied photographs of the power station we were going to attack, and hoped it was not too far inland.

"At last the great day arrived, Tuesday August 12th 1941. (The previous Saturday Wing Commander Douglas Bader had been shot down, and captured, and the previous Tuesday Pilot Officer Eric Lock, the top-scoring pilot in the Battle of Britain, had disappeared without a trace in his Spitfire). We were awakened very early and, after a bacon and egg breakfast, assembled for the briefing. What a shock when we saw the map! The ribbon stretched all the way to Cologne! The power station, 'Quadrath', was just this side of it.

"We were operating with 82 Squadron and our 18 Blenheims would be attacking the 'Quadrath' power station. We would be flying out with 36 Blenheims from four other squadrons who would be attacking the nearby 'Knapsack' power station. It was empathised that the loss of these power stations would be a great blow to German industry and they were to be attacked and destroyed at all costs. We were given our various courses, told we would have an escort of twin-engined Whirlwind fighters as far as the Dutch coast, and at what time the Spitfires would be at the coast waiting for us on the way back. We were told there would be various diversionary raids flown by other squadrons in an attempt to attract the German fighters away from us. We were very thoughtful as we left the briefing room. A lot of luck was needed if most of us were to get back. If the fighters picked us up on the way in very few of us would even reach the target, let alone get back. The formation plan showed that we were flying in three boxes of six. The leader of our box was Squadron Leader Bill Edrich, with Pilot Officer J. Corfield, and then myself on his starboard side and three others on his port side. The other two sixes were formating on either side of us.

"We collected our gear, had transport out to the aircraft, and settled in. We had trouble starting the port engine and missed our place in the stream of aircraft taxiing for take-off. We were about to transfer to the spare aircraft, as we did not want to be left behind! when at last it started, behaved itself and we taxied to take-off position. Not a hope of getting near our own formation, just an impenetrable mass of Blenheims. We were now ready for take-off and waiting for zero hour. The engines were getting rather hot and this was becoming a worry when, at last, there was movement; the first six started, then the next, until all were moving on take-off. We followed and, as soon as everyone was airborne, saw our space and moved into it.

"We did a very slow turn to the left and headed for the coast. Just as we reached Orfordness the four squadrons of Blenheims who were attacking the 'Knapsack' power station, joined us on the left, exactly in the right position. A beautiful piece of timing. With them was the Whirlwind escort, a fantastic sight! On our left were 47 Blenheims (the other six were on our right) and quite a lot of Whirlwinds. I had never seen as many aircraft flying together before, and as we were flying line abreast, so that we were all over the enemy coast at the same time, they seemed to stretch as far as the eye could see. We were now flying as close to the sea as possible, to keep below enemy radar, and this meant maximum concentration to keep position and height, but it was exhilarating and a great feeling to be part of such a large formation.

"It didn't seem long before we saw the Dutch coast ahead and we climbed to clear the sand and barbed wire. We passed over a bridge and a lot of white tracer came up, well clear of us, and then we were over the Dutch countryside. Everyone was waving, we were flying as low as it was possible to fly without hitting anything and we could see people as clearly as if we were on top of a double-decker bus. A member of the crew remarked on how attractive the girls and women were, and we all agreed, and that it would be nice to visit Holland after the war. To be waved into battle, as it were, by these people suffering under Hitler, made the risks we were taking, for their freedom and ours, all the more worthwhile.

"Our fighter escort, with its limited range, had left us at the coast to return home, and we were now on our own. Everyone was keeping a good look-out. I suddenly remembered that I had left my goggles hooked over the headlamp of my motor-cycle, and asked Dave if I could have his in case we lost the windscreen. He came back and fitted them to my helmet.

"We were still flying in line abreast with the leaders of the three vics level. For some reason the leader of the formation on our right must have got a little ahead and too close as his wing man started crowding me over, and to avoid collision I had to move over with my wing under Corfield's, who was low enough anyway, while the intruder's port wing was above my starboard wing. This was awkward and caused an anxious moment as ahead of me was a house, and I would have to climb to clear it, I cut both throttles and slowed just enough to clear both aircraft and the house. After this I kept a more open formation. No need to be too close until we attacked. Then suddenly there were no people about and nothing moved. We were over Germany.

"It was not long before Dave said we were four minutes from target, and Ken, from the rear turret, said there was no trace of any fighters and he was ready with his camera to take shots of the target as we left it. We then passed over a large area of camouflage netting and I reminded Dave to take a note of its position.

"Suddenly a loud sharp explosion shook the aircraft and it started to bank and yaw to the left; at the same time it filled with smoke and became very hot. Full right rudder and aileron had not the slightest effect, the bank was increasing alarmingly, so I cut the starboard engine to stop us going right over, and luckily it levelled with the ailerons. By this time we must have turned through ninety degrees, passing under the port members of our formation. We were at about 80 feet and I was about to get rid of the bombs, when I glanced to the left. In the distance were three stragglers; the eleven second delay fuses probably wouldn't have given them time to clear, so the bombs stayed on, not that it would make any difference to us, but having brought them all this way it would have been satisfying to leave some large holes.

"I then tried to open the hatch above my head, but I could not move it. Then the cabin filled with dense smoke and I could not see out. The heat became terrific, it was so hot that my arm and leg muscles and shoulders were tensing against it, and the thought came that when you burn to death you tense your muscles so much it helps with the pain. I then remembered the little window to the left of the windscreen used for taxiing in misty conditions, I undid the catch and opened it, the relief of the draught on my face was marvellous. I could see out and straight ahead and level with us was a row of high tension cables. I pulled the stick right back, to lift over them. Absolutely no effect, there was a crunching crash and the relief of a blast of cool air, the wires had smashed in the nose. Dave stumbled back from the front indicating to me to pull down my goggles.

"The draught from the smashed nose was blowing the flames from the centre section to the rear of the aircraft and I remember thinking that poor Ken must be getting the full blast. I could see ahead quite clearly, we were heading for a row of telephone wires, beyond which was a line of mature trees about 15 feet apart. I braced myself as well as I could and uttered the most sincere and urgent prayer of my life 'Please, please God let it be quick'. Suddenly all hell was let loose, it felt as though the whole world was disintegrating. I was waiting for the final blow, would it be quick and would I feel anything? Suddenly silence, I could not believe I was still alive. Thinking the hatch was jammed I dived for the hole in the nose, and was nearly through when my parachute stopped me. I squeezed back to remove it when I felt a kick in the shoulder, Dave had got the hatch open. I followed him through it and we dropped straight to the ground. The centre section was missing. Our first thought was to get Ken out regardless of the heat. To our surprise there was a large hole in the side of the Blenheim and through the smoke and flames we could see that there was nothing inside large enough to be a body. Ken certainly was not there. We thought he must have jumped out to escape the heat.

"We moved quickly away from the burning aircraft. We seemed to be in a series of enclosures, a sort of market garden area and orchards, there was no one about at all. We wondered what was the best thing to do. We were both bruised and shaken. My left trouser leg was torn and the knee was bleeding. Dave's hands were sore where he had burnt them opening the hatch and we both had cuts and grazes. Also we were conspicuous in flying boots and Mae Wests! Dave thanked me most sincerely for having got the plane down so well. I had to admit that I had had very little to do with it, having lost both elevator and rudder controls.

"We remembered the two 500lb bombs on board and were moving further away, when we heard a shout. Two soldiers with rifles were running towards us. We had no choice but to raise our hands high, with the fingers outstretched (as instructed if you have to surrender). Then the air raid sirens sounded the immediate all clear. The sound triggered the realization that I was not going to be killed on Blenheims, that I had a chance of being alive in a months time, and perhaps at the end of the war, and a colossal feeling of relief spread over me, a great crushing weight was coming off my mind. It became apparent, and I could hardly believe, how our very uncertain future had been wearing us down, how our fears had been driven underground by our carefree and casual manner, and just living for the day. And of course, the deaths of our friends, was costing us inside.

"I could not help this feeling of relief and I felt so ashamed and selfish at feeling it with Ken dead. Not for a moment did I relish becoming a prisoner, and had we had the choice we would certainly been whisked back to the squadron and done it again. The soldiers arrived, let us put down our hands and held us by the arm while waiting for an officer to arrive. When he arrived, he asked us if there were any bombs on board. I told him we could not tell him but he should be able to work it out for himself, which he did!

"We were led away from the aircraft to what I think was the *Flak* headquarters about 3/4 of a mile away, and given some pills and had our cuts and holes dressed. We gave our name, rank and number. They said they had found a camera, over half a mile from the aircraft. This would have been the one which was round Ken's neck. They were very courteous and very pleased to have shot us down! We had a good lunch, which we were not to know at the time, but it was a front line soldiers main meal, (and not that of non-working civilians). During the afternoon many came to see us and practise their English. We heard the expression 'For you the war is over!' several times.

"We left about tea time with some sandwiches and an escort, catching the Rhine Express at Düsseldorf, and arriving at *Dulag Luft*, Frankfurt, the reception and interrogation centre for R.A.F. prisoners in Germany, in the late evening. Here we were shown to our separate cells, our clothes taken for a thorough search, and left to our thoughts, about fourteen hours after leaving Watton!!

"In July of 1981 I was walking up the steep lane from Cranham village shop to my home, when a car pulled up. The bearded occupant said 'you don't recognise me, do you?'. But I did, it was Edgar Bircher, with whom I had been at Junior School and who had lived about half a mile from us. He joined the RAF before the war and I knew that he had been operating for some time on Blenheims. 'Yes I do' I replied 'you're the lucky devil who survived operations on Blenheims!' 'No, you're the lucky one', he said. 'I saw you hit and go down, the turret and gunner were blown completely out of the aircraft and I could not see what was holding the tail on!' and he described accurately our descent through the cables, wire and trees. He was in 82 Squadron and had seen me at the briefing but had not been able to get

167

over for a word, so that chance meeting, 40 years later, more so because I
was on foot because my car had run out of petrol at the bottom of the hill,
solved the mystery of what exactly happened when we were hit and what
had happened to Ken."

Another pilot who must have met Jim Langston during briefing
at Watton was 20 year-old Pilot Officer Walter Robinson, also a
'rookie' pilot. His crew had joined 82 Squadron at Bodney on
August 5th 1941. Walter, together with Sergeant Douglas
Attenborough, his WOp/AG, combine to give their impressions of
this, their first raid:

"We, 82 Squadron, operated from Bodney, a satellite airfield (no more than a
grass field) a few miles from the Watton RAF base. We formed a wing
together with 21 Squadron, and on this operation flew together as one unit.
My navigator/bomb aimer was Pilot Officer Kenneth Pike, and the wireless
operator/air gunner Sergeant Douglas Attenborough.

"On the afternoon of August 11th the nine aircraft of our squadron flew to
Watton for briefing and to take off together with 21 Squadron the next day.
We did not, as yet, know the target but had an inkling that a big operation
was planned. The starboard engine of my Blenheim lost power during the
short flight to Watton and I made a single-engine landing. As a newcomer to
the squadron I was, as was the custom, assigned the oldest and most worn
out aircraft, and this particular plane (T2122) had already been giving
trouble. The engineering Flight Sergeant at Watton guaranteed, however, to
have it back on top form for the next day.

"After spending the night back at our Officers quarters near Bodney we
returned to Watton early the next morning for briefing. We were to fly in
loose vics of three aircraft, at a maximum height of fifty feet. Our route
would take us across Holland and into Germany. Upon approaching Cologne
we would split into two sections, one to bomb the Knapsack power station
and the other that at Quadrath. Other squadrons were, of course, involved,
but we knew nothing of their routes."

Sergeant Douglas Attenborough, Robinson's WOp/AG expresses
his feelings during the briefing for this raid:

"The CO seeing us off on the Cologne 'do' said: 'For those of you that get
back, I'll have a good lunch waiting for you'. Being my first op I thought,
'What the hell am I doing here!!'"

Walter Robinson continues:

"At about 9.00 am we took off but, after making one circuit in order to
form up, my starboard engine again lost power and again I made a
single-engine landing - not so easily as the previous day as I now had full
tanks and a bomb load. As the plane rolled to a halt on the grass field the
Station Group Captain drove up and took Pike, Attenborough and myself to
the spare aircraft (V5634) whose engines were already being warmed up by
the ground crew. We took off again and managed to catch the squadron up

as they approached the English coast near Orfordness.

"The flight across to the Dutch coast was uneventful, apart from the sensation caused by flying literally at sea level in order to keep below the German radar screen. As we crossed the Dutch coast trouble arose, as our noisy approach caused large flocks of wild ducks to lift off right in our path. One hit my port leading edge, causing a large dent and also bending the port aileron control rod which passed just behind the leading edge. Another smashed through the starboard windscreen, letting in a strong wind. Luckily no one was hurt and we flew on although I had difficulty in controlling the lateral movement due to the damaged aileron control. The other wing man of our vic was not so lucky. The pilot, Pilot Officer Rolland was also new to the squadron. I saw his plane dip and dive straight into the sea. He had obviously been hit by the ducks and there was no hope of survival for the crew. I saw no anti-aircraft fire, at least on the way in, but I believe that more than one aircraft was lost due to collisions with the ducks (not confirmed, T.B.).

"We found the target, the Quadrath power station, quite easily and dropped our bombs. I doubt, however, if we caused much damage."

The Blenheims had pressed on at tree-top level across Holland and into Germany, losing three of their aircraft along the way. Now they approached the moment that was the reason for their being there. At a distance of about five miles, they were within clear sight of the tall chimneys of the power stations and the twin spires of the famous Cologne Cathedral, which were only a short distance east of and beyond the targets. The bombers now split into two formations and headed for their separate targets. From low level the Blenheims swept in and dropped their delayed action bombs on the targets. Accurate bombing was reported by most of the crews. Black and white smoke was seen after the attack on Quadrath, and debris was thrown into the air by the bomb blasts. 21 Squadron crews reported that the centre of the power station was set on fire. The Knapsack force also reported a highly successful attack, hits being claimed on the chimneys, coolers were hit, the power house was damaged, and fires, steam, smoke and debris were reported by the Blenheim crews of Force 2.

As expected, *Flak* was heavy and accurate over the targets. For example, all 107 Squadron aircraft were damaged by shrapnel, but they suffered no losses. 139 Squadron was not so fortunate; over Knapsack power station, V5725 and Z7448 were mortally hit by the bright red streams of *Flak* and crashed in the target area. Four men died and two were made prisoners of war.

The crews were briefed to spread out after the attack, but still to maintain box formation. Therefore, most crews sped home in pairs or in small box formations of four aircraft each. Between the target area and Holland, loose formations were again established. Some of the bombers ran into a severe rain storm over the Netherlands, which made navigating difficult. Then the Blenheims approached the Scheldt and Flushing, which was the crossing-out and rendezvous point with their fighter escort for the last lap home. In the meantime, at 11.25, an experienced Blenheim crew of 226 Squadron had departed from Ipswich to lead 30 long-range Spitfires from 10 Group (66, 152 and 234 Squadrons) to the rendezvous point over the mouth of the Scheldt to meet the returning bombers. Another force of 37 Spitfires (of 19, 65 and 266 Squadrons) was led in by a second 226 Squadron Blenheim to fly diversionary sweeps over the Islands of Zeeland province. However, when they arrived over Flushing around noon, a strong force of Bf109s of *JG 1* from Katwijk and Flushing airfields and *JG 26* from Haamstede, Woensdrecht and Wevelgem aerodromes circled overhead and immediately bounced the Spitfires and the two Blenheims. One of the British fighters was downed, crashing in the sea and killing the pilot. Other than the Bf109s of *JG 1* and *JG 26*, Bf110s of *ZG 76* and even Ju88s of *I./NJG 2*, the night fighter squadron based at Gilze-Rijen, were scrambled in an effort to shoot down as many British aircraft as possible.

At 12.45 local time, the *Flak* defences of Flushing had been alerted. Their first victim was V5859:Y of 226 Squadron. Hit by 2 cm. light *Flak* of *Battery 43/XI*, the aircraft crashed near Philippine at 12.53. Flight Lieutenant Lewis and crew were killed in the crash and their bodies were consumed in the ensuing fire. A second British aircraft, Spitfire P8446 of 152 Squadron, was also hit by the *Flak* of Battery *43/XI* and was seen spinning in at Biervliet. Sergeant George White perished in the burning remains of his aircraft. The second Fighter Navigator Blenheim then vanished, shot down into the mouth of the Scheldt by *Unteroffizer* Zick of *I./JG 1* at 13.00. Flight Lieutenant Hugh Young and crew were killed on impact.

Because the Spitfires became embroiled with their adversaries, they failed fully to protect their charges. These were the Blenheims that now arrived on the scene in small groups and as single aircraft. While a number of Bf109s fought off the British fighter cover, other German fighters pounced on the returning bombers that came in over the Scheldt at low level. The clear blue sky over Zeeland province then was transformed in a whirling mass of Spitfires, Bf109s, Bf110s, Ju88s and Blenheims.

Three Blenheims were shot down in a combined effort by Bf109s of *JG 26* and the *Flak* batteries of Flushing, between 13.18 and 13.28. V6261:M of 139 Squadron, flown by Flight Lieutenant George Herbert approached from the east at very low level over the Scheldt, when the light *Flak* battery *Hotel* at Flushing opened fire on the bomber. From a distance of one mile, seven hits were registered on the fuselage. The commander of the *Flak* post then had to stop pumping shells into the sky, as two Bf109s got on the bomber's tail. After their first pass, V6261:M came into the range of the *Light 3rd M. Flak Battery A.703*, which also scored hits on the Blenheim. She finally fell victim to one of the leading German fighter aces of the early war years, *Oberstleutnant* Adolf Galland of *Stab./JG 26* who shot her down in the mouth of the River Scheldt off Breskens as his 77th victory. There were no survivors.

Sergeant Douglas Wheatley and crew in Z7281:P of 114 Squadron were shot down a few minutes later by *Oberleutnant* Kurt Ruppert of *III./JG 26* and the aircraft crashed in the sea off Flushing. Again, there were no survivors. The next victim was V6497:U of 18 Squadron. Squadron Leader Mills ditched his Blenheim off Flushing after being hit at 13.28 hours by the fire of the light *Flak* battery *Schelde* and by *Oberleutnant* Baron Freiherr Hubertus von Holtey, of *Stab./JG 26*. The aircraft came to rest in the shallow water 800 metres from the *Flak* post and only the tail unit of the Blenheim was still visible on the surface of the sea. Mills and his crew were fortunate to get out of the sinking aircraft and took to their dinghy. A few minutes later, they were picked up by a small vessel of the German Navy, which brought them to shore at Flushing. Here they were made PoWs. Mills was slightly injured on the head. They were transported to Flushing airfield and interrogated by a *Luftwaffe* Officer.

A fourth Blenheim, V5874:P of 21 Squadron, hit high tension cables over the Dutch coast and crashed in the North Sea. Pilot Officer Jimmy Corfield and crew were killed and washed ashore on Texel Island a few days later, where they now lie at rest.

Although the Spitfires could not prevent a number of Blenheims being shot down in the Flushing area, they managed to hold off many German fighters from getting at the bombers. During the fierce dogfights that raged over Zeeland province between 13.00 and 13.30 (local time), they claimed one Bf109 destroyed, three probably destroyed and seven damaged, plus a Ju88. In fact, a Ju88 of *I./NJG 2* force-landed at Steenbergen, injuring two of the crew. A Bf109 of *2./JG 1* was shot up by a Spitfire and crash-landed near the Colijnsplaat, another pilot of *I./JG 26* made an emergency landing at Antwerpen with his shoulder shot through. The debit was six Spitfires shot down, both by the German fighters and by the light and heavy *Flak* batteries of Flushing and Wemeldinge.

It had been a very hectic half hour over the peninsula of Zeeland, with eleven British aircraft and two German fighters shot down. Sergeant Douglas Attenborough, the WOp/AG in Walter Robinson's crew of 82 Squadron, picks up his story after his crew had bombed the power station of Quadrath. While still over target, their Blenheim was hit by *Flak* that smashed out most of the perspex in Douglas' turret:

"We carried tin helmets on the raid either to put over our flying helmets or to sit on, according to whether you considered your head more vital to protect or the other part of the anatomy! Due to the smashed up turret of mine, the tin hat which I decided to wear on that day on my head went flying thro' the turret on to the target and I have always wondered if it 'conked' some Jerry on the head. Unfortunately too, at more or less the same time, I lost my Leica camera thro' the turret.

"There was an enormous quarry just the other side of the target and we dived into this, did our left hand turn in it, avoided the *Flak* and flew back to base, just a little worse for wear. Flying into a flock of geese over Holland didn't help either. We came back with another Blenheim close at hand and by accident, or our keenness to get back, we flew slap bang at 50 feet over a German aerodrome. One of their aircraft eventually came up after us and after a bit of a chase, I shot him down. I think it was a Bf109, but the gunner of our accompanying Blenheim also claimed he had done likewise, so we shared the kill, half a Jerry each! (not confirmed, T.B.) We then met heavy *Flak* at Flushing when returning to base. We got back at 1.30 pm, just the right time for the CO's sumptuous lunch! By that time my thoughts had changed, I was glad I had been on that 'do."

In all, twelve Blenheims were shot down by fighters and *Flak* on 12th August 1941, and many more Blenheims returned home damaged. However, the daylight raid on the power stations of Cologne was deemed to have been a success. Considering the nature of the raid - the first deep daylight penetration raid into Germany of the war - and also considering the heavy casualties of 2 Group on the previous daylight operations in 1941, the 20% losses of the Blenheim force was even considered to be rather low. Next day the raid made headline news in the British national press and the daring raid was a great morale booster to the British people. Although 2 Group Intelligence assumed that both power stations were effectively destroyed, photos taken during a photo recce on 21st August showed that the main targets in the power stations, the turbine sheds, were not hit during the raid.

In recognition of their leading roles in the daring raid, Wing Commanders Kercher and Nichol, the leaders of Forces 1 and 2, were each awarded the DSO. Nichol's decoration however was awarded posthumously, as one week after the Cologne raid he was shot down off Vlieland during an attack on a convoy. He is still missing, and commemorated on Panel 28 of the Runnymede Memorial.

Chapter Eight
Shipping and Fringe Targets
Phase Two:

9th July to October 1941.

We have seen how the 2 Group anti-shipping campaign was downgraded on 30th June, and that emphasis was from now on more on *Circus*-type operations in the Pas de Calais and northwestern Germany. Yet, this decision did not imply halting the daylight shipping *Beats*. On 9th July, 15 Blenheims carried out shipping sweeps off the Dutch Frisian Islands. No ships were attacked this time. On the 12th, no less than 38 Blenheims flew shipping sweeps off the Dutch coast, with seven ships attacked. One aircraft was lost, Z7487 of Wing Commander Arthur Booth, 107 Squadron's CO. Only Sergeant Scott, his observer, survived the crash in the North Sea off Ijmuiden.

On 14th July, 29 Blenheims were dispatched on coastal sweeps from Cherbourg to Holland and on a *Circus* operation to the Hazebrouck railway yards. Many targets were attacked, but R3704 and V6253 of 139 Squadron were shot down by Bf109s in the Channel after a bombing raid on Le Havre. Of this force, Squadron Leader Roe led eleven Blenheims of 18 and 139 Squadrons from Horsham St. Faith on a late-morning sweep off Ijmuiden. It was to be a successful operation. In the *Beat* area, Squadron Leader Smythe and Sergeant Dunham both hit a 3,000-ton ship and Sergeant Rost scored a direct hit on a 6,000-ton vessel. Squadron Leader Roe bombed a 6,000-ton ship, whereupon Sergeant Jefferson hit the same merchantman. Roe's vic was then bounced by two Bf109s, but the concentrated fire from the three Blenheims shot down one of the fighters into the North Sea. After completing the *Beat*, the crews sped home to Horsham; for a change they had suffered no losses! Although no *Luftwaffe* records remain to confirm the loss of a Bf109, from records it appears that the Swedish merchantman *Aspen* of

1308 tons was sunk during the attack off Ijmuiden. Sergeant Scotney was the WOp/AG in Sergeant Jefferson's crew of 18 Squadron; he gives his log book entry on this sortie first:

10.15	Blenheim 6519	Sgt Jefferson	North Sea sweep near IJMUIDEN. Merchant ship of 6000 tons attacked and hit in bows - large explosion seen. Attacked by 2 Bf109's - one shot down (confirmed).	1hr.50

"I can't recall the actual bombing of the ship, but I do remember well the attack by the '109s. After the bombing the Blenheims were strung out and all heading the same way, parallel to the coast. One Bf109, intent on pursuing a Blenheim ahead of us and off to our port, seemed quite oblivious to our presence, and flew alongside our aircraft no more than fifty yards away. I clearly remember being astonished by the pilot's lack of awareness of his vulnerability. I fired a long burst at him, and then suddenly realised that, whilst my attention was being concentrated on him, we could ourselves be the object of attack from behind. This proved to be the case. On swinging the guns rearward, I found another '109 on our tail doing a copybook quarter attack. It was close, but as far as I could tell, it was not firing - no tracer, no smoke. I fired a long burst, and the left hand Browning jammed. Using the toggle provided, I re-cocked the gun. This briefly diverted my attention, and when I looked again the '109 was nowhere to be seen. I cannot recollect seeing another '109.

"At de-briefing, on our return to base, crews of other Blenheims said that one of the '109s (either the one on our port beam, or the one behind) had dived into the sea. This was not seen by me. I've always had the feeling that these '109s were on a training flight, perhaps from an OTU and possibly even unarmed. I don't know, but in any event, how else to explain the näivety of the *Luftwaffe* pilot, who flew alongside us? No experienced aircrew would have done so."

With the first and successful Rotterdam docks raid on the 16th July in progress, five other Blenheims swept the Dutch coast without loss. Three days later, 24 Blenheims of 2 Group were dispatched on shipping sweeps, 20 of them to the Dutch coast. First off were six aircraft of 105 and six of 107 Squadrons. These left Swanton Morley and West Raynham at 11.20 for a combined sweep off The Hague. In the afternoon, eight Blenheims of 226 Squadron departed from Wattisham for a sweep in *Beat 7* (the Frisian Islands) and returned without loss. The 105 and 107 Squadron crews found an east-bound convoy off The Hague and attacked eight ships, claiming a total of

48,000 tons hit. The ship's *Flak* was murderous and V6039 of 105 Squadron was shot down into the sea near the convoy. Sergeant Ronald Taylor and crew were killed. Then Z7439 of 105 Squadron clipped the mast of his target ship and cartwheeled into the sea and again there were no survivors. As far as damage to the enemy was concerned, the Germans mention only one steam freighter, the *Hermann Fritzen* of 3845 tons damaged in this attack. Although the ship was hit by at least one bomb, it was able to proceed under its's own steam. Another merchantman, the *Ruth* was hit by one 250-pound bomb, but hardly any damage was done. A third ship in the convoy, the *Konsul Schulte* was struck by a 250-pound bomb that failed to explode and was thrown overboard by the ship's crew.

The next major Blenheim operation took place on 23rd July 1941. 12 Blenheims of 114 and 107 Squadrons went to northern France without loss, although three bombers were badly shot-up. Seventeen other crews were detailed to sweep the Dutch coast shipping lanes. Five Blenheims of 18 Squadron left Horsham St Faith at 11.45 for a *Beat* off the Dutch coast. No ships were seen but off Ijmuiden the formation was intercepted by five Bf110s of *5./ZG 76* that had scrambled from Katwijk airfield and shot two Blenheims down off Kamperduin. There were no survivors when the Blenheims crashed in the North Sea. Five men are still missing and the sixth crew member washed ashore on Terschelling island where he was laid to rest. A third Blenheim was severely shot-up and crash-landed at base with two men seriously wounded. Sergeant Tommy Thompson, a 19 year old pilot who joined 18 Squadron on 1 July 1941 recounts this *Beat*:

"On 23rd July 1941, the target was a shipping sweep off Den Haag. A formation of five aircraft led by Squadron Leader Roe DFC departed from Horsham St Faith at 11.45. The intention was for 18 Squadron to position off the coast south of Den Haag and sweep north to attack a convoy reported to be proceeding along the coast. At the same time 139 Squadron was to have positioned north of the anticipated convoy and swept south in a joint attack.

"We started our run north as planned about 800 metres offshore in clear weather and unlimited visibility. No ships were seen at the end of the 5-minute *Beat* and Roe continued on up the coast in the hope of seeing the other formation engaging the convoy presumably. After a few more miles it was obvious that the other squadron had failed to make the rendezvous and still no ships were in sight but still Roe continued on until we saw Bf110s getting airborne over the sand dunes from Ijmuiden. The formation turned onto a westerly heading pursued by five Bf110s which started to attack in pairs from the port and starboard quarters with individual stern attacks from the fifth aircraft.

"With five aircraft in V formation at absolutely 0 feet it was extremely difficult for the Blenheim wingmen to maintain position as all aircraft were at full normal power giving about 220 mph so they were either going flat out at plus 9 boost round the outside, or fully throttled back on the inside trying to keep out of the sea. The Blenheim had a boost override lever which gave plus 9lbs boost in emergency and for maximum load take-offs. The snag with this lever was that it was positioned upright and straight ahead at arms length from the right shoulder. When the hand had moved the lever down half way it had to change grip to push the lever fully down. The same performance had to be gone through shortly afterwards in reverse to take off the power. Any pause in moving the lever fully up or down could cause the engines to stop.

"As a result of these problems Nos 4 and 5 dropped slightly behind the formation and one of them was shot down into the sea. The other aircraft caught up with the formation but the No.5 Bf110 ran in from astern and raked him with cannon fire. The pilot must have been hit as out of the corner of my eye I saw him rolling hard to port towards me with the upper part of his starboard wing in tatters. To escape I jerked back the stick and climbed over the top of him before sinking rapidly back to sea level. He levelled off and went towards the coast whilst we continued to fire at the '110 as it closed up on the formation. One of the remaining Blenheim gunners must have picked off his gunner as he could be clearly seen slumped in the rear of the cockpit. The German pilot must have thought his gunner was alive as he flew slowly just forward and above the flight close enough for the 'dragons teeth and flaming nostrils' to be seen on the nose. Had the gunner been alive he could have shot the Blenheim pilots at point blank range.

"The Bf110 pulled ahead and broke off to port and the remaining attackers also turned back towards land. After my gunner had stopped cursing me for spoiling his shooting whilst avoiding the Blenheim, he said he thought he saw the damaged Blenheim being escorted back towards the coast and that one of the Bf110s had broken off its attack with smoke pouring from its starboard engine. The three remaining Blenheims closed up and we returned without further problems to Horsham St Faith. There were two wounded crew and one, Sergeant Wood, had to make a wheels up landing at base. Flight time was 2hrs 00min."

The six Blenheims of 139 Squadron that also swept the Dutch coast found a fleet of fishing ships off Kamperduin and *KW135*, a Katwijk-based fishing vessel was bombed and sunk. No opposition was encountered and all crews returned safely to

Oulton. 21 Squadron on the other hand had a bad day. Six of her aircraft scrambled from Manston for an escorted Channel Stop operation and attacked a 4,000-ton tanker between Ostend and the mouth of the River Scheldt. The target was escorted by four *Flak*-ships which put up a murderous barrage of *Flak* and four Blenheims were shot down. The tanker escaped unscathed. Nine men were killed and three escaped to become PoWs.

One week later, 2 Group had another bad day. On 30th July, 43 Blenheims of 18, 82, 114, 139 and 226 Squadrons made low level sweeps to the Kiel Canal and the Dutch and German coastal shipping lanes. Ships were found and attacked off the Frisian Islands and in the Heligoland Bight but the price was once again high, for seven Blenheims failed to return. L9249 of 18 Squadron was lost after attacking a small ship off the Frisians and R3803 and V6513 of 82 Squadron were shot down by Bf110s near their target, the Kiel Canal. A formation of 139 Squadron returning from a shipping *Beat* off northwest Germany were intercepted North of Texel by Bf110s of *II./ZG 76* that had scrambled from Leeuwarden airfield. The cannon-armed fighters had a field day; in a running battle that lasted fourteen minutes, four Blenheims were shot down into the North Sea. After expending their ammunition, all Bf110s returned jubilantly to base. There were no survivors among the unfortunate crews of 139 Squadron. Sergeant Tommy Thompson, pilot with 18 Squadron again takes up his story:

"On 30th July there was a strange coincidence. We had been briefed for a cloud cover raid on the Kiel Canal with six aircraft taking part. For an attack of that sort it was essential to have full cloud cover to escape into and if the cloud was not there the operation was to be cancelled.

"We had proceeded across the North Sea in two vics of 3 at the usual 0 feet to avoid radar and 'Squeaker boats' fitted with radios to a position north west of Heligoland when a single Bf110 was seen ahead so the formation was turned round and headed west for 5 minutes or so until the '110 turned off to the south. We turned round through north and back onto east again without further trouble. However 10 minutes later about 40 miles off the Danish coast a mixed collection of four Bf109s and six Bf110s appeared from the south behind us so we altered course towards a heavy line squall of rain. Just as we were approaching the rain six Blenheims burst out heading south. We flew into the rain which only lasted for a short distance and found we were on our own in near cloudless conditions and the '109s and '110s had presumably attacked the other formation. We headed north west towards the middle of the North Sea and turned back for

Horsham. Flight time was 3hrs 40 mins.

"We discovered afterwards that the other aircraft were from 139 Squadron on their way to Cuxhaven or Wilhelmshaven before they were jumped and lost 4 aircraft one of which V6266 was piloted by another pilot on 33 Course at Bicester."

By the end of July 1941, the average life of a Blenheim crew member in 2 Group was as little as two to three weeks. Therefore, we now let two of those young men speak who joined 2 Group in July 1941. Sergeant Ian Webster, a 21-year old WOp/AG from Aberdeen, arrived on 23rd June 1941 at No.17 OTU (Upwood), where he crewed up with John Glem (pilot) and Bruce White, an Aussie observer. Before being posted to an operational squadron, the 30 new Blenheim crews at 17 OTU had to carry out a training programme of 12 weeks. This, however, was not to be, as Ian Webster recalls:

"Some four weeks into the twelve-week course we were ordered to report to the crew room one morning and addressed by the Wingco to the effect that due to severe losses on Blenheim squadrons we would be posted immediately to various squadrons to bring them up to operational strength and would probably take part in operations and continue to train whenever possible on the squadron. Now although we had received stories of doom and disaster and a short life but a happy one from our instructors, who in some cases had done operational flying and were now being 'rested', we mainly treated this lightly as the 'old hands' attempts to frighten the pupils. But to receive such an order from the Wing Co implied that the situation really was serious and prospects for survival did not look too promising. He added that he could only grant a 24 hour leave pass in view of the seriousness of the situation. It was made clear that we had to report to our various squadrons within 24 hours of leaving the OTU at Upwood without fail.

"This was to be the only occasion that I consciously disobeyed an order and I was very aware of the consequences of my action. In view of the rather sombre outlook for Blenheim crews I was determined to see my mother once more even briefly before going to the squadron rather than our last contact to be a telegram and a letter of regret from the CO of the squadron. The train journey from OTU to Aberdeen was on average 14 hours each way so I needed at least 28 hours and would be absent without leave for at least 4 hours when reporting to 114 Squadron at West Raynham.

"My visit to my mother was a fairly normal one apart from the fact that time was very limited and I had to be on a train back to the squadron by 7 pm that evening. We had lunch at a local hotel plus a few drinks together. She was as much a friend as a mother to me. We had a walk through the town and found a shop, selling carnations which were her favourite flower and I bought her a baguet of these. She packed a food parcel for me to take back which included a bottle of whisky, bless her, and I caught my train. I thought it had all gone very well and I was very glad I had decided to break the rules and accept the punishment.

"I arrived at West Raynham airfield home of 114 Squadron about 8 hours later than I should and was interviewed by Acting Squadron Leader Judson who was due off on an op. fairly soon but he advised that he would deal with me on his return. Apart from my morale being low with the anticipation of disciplinary action to come, and which I deserved, it was lowered even further when I learned that he was actually a Flight Lieutenant made Acting Squadron Leader in order that he could deputise for the Wing Commander CO who had not returned from an operation earlier. I think the majority of new arrivals felt that if the senior aircrews of wide experience were being lost so rapidly then we novices could hardly expect to prosper for too long. There was a formula, unofficial of course, which we kept hearing form various sources that if a crew completed six successful operations then that crew had justified the expenditure in its training and equipment. So even in those days accountants were running the world.

"Acting Squadron Leader Judson did not return from the operation which gave me a strong feeling of guilt, but it was the end of the matter."

Another WOp/AG who reinforced 2 Group in July 1941 was Sergeant John Low. He recounts his introduction to squadron life with 82 Squadron:

"At the latter part of the training at 17 OTU the instructors used to like taking the Mickey out of the trainees but it was all in good fun. For example 82 Squadron was then known as the Third Eleven as twice before they had been wiped out on raids. Also the average number of ops expected was five and over that you were a veteran (in my case, my first month on a squadron).

"In fact my introduction to squadron life was as teased by the instructors. We were posted to 82 Squadron as a crew on the 31.7.41. My pilot was Sergeant Tony Trail and the third member of the crew was Sergeant Doug French (observer). On the morning of the 2.8.41 Tony, Doug and myself were welcomed to 82 Squadron by Wing Commander Burt and that was the last time we saw the CO as he went on a shipping *Beat* off the Dutch coast and was shot down. Our next CO was Wing Commander Lascelles and he 'bought it' on the 26.8.41. The next CO was Wing Commander Roe and he was our CO until the squadron was posted to SFAC and Wing Commander McMichal took over as CO. Due to the short expectation of squadron life I kept very few records of ops. etc. We knew it was a day to day life and accepted that as we were all volunteers for the positions we held."

August 1941 saw no respite to the Blenheim crews of 2 Group. On the 2nd, 24 Blenheims carried out coastal sweeps between Cherbourg and Texel. Eleven sorties went to the Dutch coast, with only one ship attacked. Wing Commander Burt, CO of 82 Squadron was shot down while attacking a convoy southwest of Texel.

On 4th, 5th and 6th August, 12, 14 and 17 Blenheim sorties were flown off the Dutch coast, resulting in 19 attacks on shipping. Then all shipping and fringe *Beats* were suspended for a week, and the crews prepared for the big Cologne raid of 12th August. Almost immediately after the Cologne 'do', maritime operations were again resumed and on the 14th, 16th and 17th August, 5, 15 and 11 sorties were flown to the Dutch coast and Frisian Islands. These resulted in 11 shipping strikes.

Alarmed by the serious losses, Stevenson now finally got what he wanted; fighter escort for his Blenheims! The AOC had repeatedly expressed his concern on the vulnerability of the Blenheim in daylight and since 11th April he had discussed the possibility of long-range Spitfire escorts on the shipping *Beats*. Yet, it took another four months before he finally had it his way. On 18th August, the first escorted *Beat* was carried out when 21 aircraft of 21, 82 and 88 Squadrons swept the Texel, Ijmuiden and Scheldt areas with long-range Spitfire escorts of 66, 130 and 152 Squadrons. Thirteen attacks on shipping were successfully executed with three fishing ships sunk off Ijmuiden and Bergen aan Zee and no losses among the Blenheim crews; a promising start of the escorted *Beats* offensive! While these operations were in progress, two *Circuses* were directed against Lille and Marquise. Blenheim V6175 of 18, and V5491 of 110 Squadrons were lost on the Lille raid.

Further operations to the Dutch coast and Frisian Islands were carried out on 19, 20, 21 and 22 August, with 26 ships being bombed. The 19th was a bad day for 114 Squadron, when a complete vic of three Blenheims was shot down by two Bf110s northwest of Vlieland during an attack on a convoy. One WOp/AG survived to be made PoW and the other eight men died. These included Wing Commander James Nicol DSO, CO of the squadron, the man who had distinguished himself on the 12th August Cologne raid. On the 20th, Bergen (Alkmaar) airfield was raided by 6 Blenheims of 21 Squadron, but only superficial damage was done. Escorting long-range Spitfires of 66, 130 and 152 Squadrons fought off Bf109s of *1.Erg./JG 3* and Bf110s of *5./ZG 76* and managed to shoot down two of these fighters. However, they also lost two of their number, both of 66 Squadron. One day later, 130 Squadron lost two Spitfires while escorting 12 Blenheims to the Ijmuiden steel-works. Pilot Officer Michael Gardener, a pilot with 152 Squadron, flew in Spitfire Mk.II P8237 on all these operations:

"The average life of an aircrew in one of the Blenheim squadrons of 2 Group, was, I remember, said to be three weeks. I remember drinking beer with some of the Blenheim crews in a pub somewhere and they were in a fairly jumpy state. No wonder! We, as escorts, were not in too much danger, except that, as we were always down at sea level, we were easy targets for the Bf109s that used to lie in wait for us on the way back after a raid.

"I have no detailed memories of these operations individually. The whole of the terror was merged in to a general picture of flying on the wave tops and turning in hard vertical turns as the 109s dived down on us as we accompanied the Blenheims. I remember spinning round and always greying out and even blacking out, and praying that when one was blind, ones judgement was good enough for the Spitfire's wing not to touch the sea. That unquestionably happened to a few. There was always an unnaturally restrained air in the mess the evening before an 'op' and there used to be overmuch use of the toilets!"

It became increasingly clear that the Blenheims, even with fighter escort, were unable to inflict major damage to the enemy's coastal convoys, while suffering dreadful losses. In answer to the increasing pressure from the RAF, the Germans had adopted very efficient convoy tactics, while the ore and coal carrying ships and tankers were flanked by *Flak*-ships and escorted by standing patrols of Bf109s and Bf110s. These odds were simply too much for the Blenheim crews, as the events on the 26th August may illustrate. On this day, 2 Group dispatched 34 Blenheims on coastal sweeps and six aircraft of 18 Squadron on a *Circus* raid to St. Omer. In all, three coastal operations were planned. Six crews of 82 Squadron left Bodney in late morning for a daring unescorted sweep in the Heligoland Bight. Two Blenheims of 110 and nine of 88 Squadrons went on a late morning shipping sweep in *Beat 7* (Frisian Islands). Finally, six bombers of 21, five of 139 and six of 226 Squadrons departed from Watton, Oulton and Wattisham at noon for an escorted sweep in *Beat 9* (Ijmuiden-Texel area). 17 ships were attacked off the Dutch coast and two of these were claimed sunk by 226 Squadron 38 kilometres north of Ijmuiden. This, however, is not confirmed by German records. The cost of these coastal operations was dreadful; seven Blenheims were lost. 21, 88 and 226 Squadrons each lost a crew off the Dutch coast and four

Blenheims of 82 Squadron were shot down off the island of Juist by three Bf109s of *I./JG 53*. 82 Squadron's new CO, Wing Commander Lascelles DFC, a cousin of the Royal Family, was killed together with the 11 other crew members. It was foolhardy to send unescorted Blenheims to a hornet's nest like the Heligoland Bight in this advanced phase of the anti-shipping campaign, knowing that the crews would hardly stand a chance when intercepted by fighters on such a long-distance sortie.

Young Canadian Sergeant Bill O'Connell flew one of the 226 Squadron aircraft on the shipping sweep off Ijmuiden on this fateful day; he was to experience his first convoy attack:

"We were always briefed to go on a shipping sweep by being given a 'start point', which would be some 4 or 5 miles off the coast, and then to proceed on a '*Beat* line' parallel to the coast for some 20 or 30 miles, during which, if we met a convoy, we would attack it. Even though ships of that period burned 'smokeless' oil (coal-fired ships had gone out of style) there was always a sort of dark haze on the horizon, which always gave away the position of the convoy, long before we could see it. So, really, the only time we went on a *Beat* line, and finished the *Beat*, was a time when there was no convoy. It was always rather consoling to approach the *Beat* line and see no smoke haze; no smoke, no ships.

"Flying on a parallel line to the coast, we were always able to approach the convoy broadside, and such was the case on this day. Our six Blenheims attacked a fairly large German coastal convoy (30 vessels in all, big and small) off Ijmuiden. I had, as crew, Flight Sergeant Peter Saunders, observer, and Flying Officer Les Harrell, the WOp/AG. I was very much aware of what we had to do and the possible consequences in my first attack on a convoy, but I was determined to do my job as best I could. The tension mounted higher in me when we finally sighted the convoy, but I can't remember whether it went even higher when the shooting started. It must have.

"What I do remember, though, was that after we had picked our ship to attack, all those black puffs of smoke and streams of heavy tracer and ammunition around us seemed to be aimed specially at our aircraft. It was the first time I had ever been the sole target for anti-aircraft gunfire. That was when I started to jink the aircraft, and moving it up and down to make a more difficult target for the German gunners. At this time I was getting nervous and a bit fearful. I then began to open fire with the Browning machine-gun in the port wing. Between bursts of machine-gun, I said to my observer, Peter Saunders, over the inter-com, 'Everyone needs a little iron each day in this system. But the best stuff for Germans is lead.' It was an inane remark, and I don't know if it was bravado or a device to help relieve pressure among us. But, I know at that time I did have some fear.

"Perhaps a couple of hundred yards from the ship, I know I had a great deal of fear, but I certainly lost none of my poise. I remember that as well as the black puffs and the tracers of the heavy machine-guns streaking past us, there were streams of light machine-gun fire coming up at us. I did not allow my poise to change, and I suddenly became very determined that I was going to accomplish my task in spite of the *Flak*, and that is when I crossed the barrier of fear - absolutely nothing else mattered but the task I was to do, and fear had flown as if on magical wings. I can remember overcoming my fear and passing almost as if over a barrier into an abnormal state of calm, alertness, and exceptional mental response and physical reaction. It was a state in which fear had completely disappeared, and I had absolutely no fear of imminent death. Moving objects seemed to slow down to slow-motion speed, and mind and physical reactions seemed to be about twice as fast as normal. I was able to do things with the greatest deliberation, and I was able to do these things at far greater speed than I could in a practice work-out. It was quite a strange experience, but it lasted only as long as the crisis I faced, perhaps something less than a minute. I stayed in this state until after I had bombed, and stayed with me while I weaved our way through the remaining ships of the convoy towards the landward side and until we were in relatively safe territory. The return to normality found me with some, but very little fear.

"I am not too sure about our losses on that day (Z7305 of Sergeant Gilbert Smith and crew was shot down during the strike, T.B.), but we did lose Flying Officer Harrell, our WOp/AG, who caught a large piece of *Flak* in the left ankle, and later had to have that leg amputated below the knee. It was while we were in that 'no engines functioning' position (after clearing the masts of the ship we attacked and stuffing the nose of the aircraft down), trying to get down to wave-top level again that this 88 mm (presumably) shell burst alongside the fuselage on the right-hand side of the aircraft. It was standard procedure for the German gun crews in the very late stage of the attack to swing their guns and set up a screen of fire behind the rigging of the ship being attacked, and there was just no way you could avoid flying through that screen of fire with dead engines.

"I didn't see or feel the burst of fire that nearly brought us down, and the first intimation that I had that all was not well was when Flying Officer Harrell said over the inter-com., 'I've been hit'. Flight Sergeant Saunders immediately crawled through the very small access to the rear of the aircraft, even while we were doing evasive action through the convoy, to minister to Flying Officer Harrell. He administered ampoules of morphine which all aircraft carried and put a tourniquet around his calf to stem the bleeding. He stayed with Flying Officer Harrell until we returned to Wattisham. Each gunner was issued a Leica camera with an automatic feed, and he was supposed to, if possible, take relevant pictures. But, we, of course, didn't get any pictures from Les since he was in shock and in great pain.

"Our aircraft was quite badly damaged by *Flak* in several places, yet, strangely, the same piece of finger size *Flak* which hit Flying Officer Harrell in the ankle was the same one that cut the main hydraulic line to his power-operated turret, spewing out all the hydraulic fluid in the hydraulic system. Since the turret and the landing gear in the Blenheim operated on the same system and used the same hydraulic fluid, there was no fluid left in the system to unlock the 'up' locks of the landing gear, and there was thus no way the landing gear could be lowered. So, we landed the aircraft on its belly with the gear up when we returned to Wattisham.

"We were credited with sinking a 7000-ton ship, but I don't recall now how we came to be credited with this, whether it was our photographs from the automatic backwards facing camera (which was installed in the floor of each Blenheim and was actuated by the same button that released the bombs, taking a picture every few seconds, until it was shut off by the navigator) or someone else's, or whether someone had seen our bombs hit the ship, but I do remember that a long-range photo-recce. Spitfire took high-level pictures a couple of hours later, and the ship was still burning and presumed to have been lost.

"Flying Officer Harrell, after many months in hospital and re-habilitation, took his honourable discharge from the RAF, and went back into civilian life.

"I found the state of going through the barrier of fear into an abnormal state of calm, alertness and exceptional mental response and physical reaction in two convoy attacks; over Le Havre on October 15th, 1941; flying a Mosquito back to England from Yerville in northern France on a feathered right engine at tree-top height against a 40 mph head-wind, with the left engine overheating, leaking glycol and slowly losing power; on November 30th, 1943, when I attacked a radar station near Ijmuiden in a Mosquito when the odds definitely favoured the German gunners by quite a wide margin. It is not a new phenomenon with fighting personnel in wars past. But, what is it? Is it a spiritual force? Do we have resources in our bodies and our minds that we have not learned to use? Is it the magical result of adrenalin? Whatever it is, it seems to defy physical laws of time and motion. My opinion is that it is something truly supernatural."

The serious losses suffered by 2 Group during July and August did not pass unnoticed by Bomber Command HQ. On 30th August, Air Vice-Marshal Stevenson was directly ordered to conserve his Blenheim force in the UK as far as possible. The requirements from Malta and the Middle East for Blenheim anti-shipping strike aircraft made this decision essential. An Air Ministry report of 29th August even called the continued Blenheim maritime daylight operations off the western European coasts 'a serious wastage'. By this time, it was realised that the remaining Blenheim squadrons had better be deployed in the Mediterranean, where they were much needed in suppressing Rommel's supply ships. Whereas overall losses in 2 Group had been 58 Blenheims in July and 51 in August (compared to the first line strength of nine squadrons with 101 aircraft and 89 fully operational crews in mid-August), the casualty rate in consequence was more than halved in September with 22 aircraft and crews lost on operations. Nevertheless, Stevenson did not fully give in and kept sending out his crews in an effort to inflict as much damage as possible to the German coastal shipping, possibly against his better judgement.

September 1941 started with an operation on the 2nd, when six Blenheims swept the Belgian coast, losing Z7274 of 139 Squadron off Zeebrugge to ship's *Flak*. The next shipping operations were planned for the 7th, when six aircraft of 110 Squadron together with six of 226 Squadron went on an escorted special shipping *Beat* off Katwijk. 110 Squadron completed the Northern part of the *Beat* without seeing anything, but 226 Squadron fared quite differently. Four crews spotted a convoy off The Hague and went into the attack. A 2,000-ton motor vessel was skip-bombed by two crews, and two others selected a 1200-ton *Flak*-ship as their target. This was a bull's eye; the 211-ton *Flak*-ship *H811* blew up after the attack. Yet, the cost for this successful strike was high.. The Blenheims were bounced by a standing patrol of three Bf109s that wasted no time and shot down Z7306 and Z7312 into the North Sea. None of the crews escaped alive, four of them are still missing. A third aircraft only just escaped destruction, as Pilot Officer Bill Gray vividly remembers:

"I did four trips attacking shipping off the Hook of Holland and adjacent area. The trip on Sunday September 7th 1941 was the most memorable and was the worst one. Six Blenheims took part in the raid. My aircraft was Z7304 'S', and my crew consisted of Pilot Officer McCarthy navigator RAF, Pilot Officer Casey WOp/AG RCAF and myself Pilot Officer Gray RCAF. It so happened that there were six merchant ships in the convoy - so each of us had a ship to attack. We made our attack at noon hour (meal time). However, in spite of a minimum gun crew on the ships, we had a 'hot' reception. The ship that our aircraft attacked was hit by our bombs and as we turned away it was on fire.

"Our aircraft had been hit as we passed over the ship and the area behind the pilot's seat (mid section) of the aircraft had been badly damaged; the fuel system was damaged and the radio equipment was destroyed. As we rounded the end of the convoy we were attacked by a Bf109, which certainly didn't add to our chances of survival. Our aircraft was damaged in the cockpit area, and the starboard side windows were knocked out. Since there was no return fire from the turret of our aircraft, on leaving the area the navigator crawled back to the air gunner's position and discovered that Pilot Officer Casey had been hit by *Flak* from a direct hit in the rear of the aircraft. Injuries did not appear to be life-threatening. The navigator came back to the pilot's compartment and reported the injuries to me.

"After leaving the area of the attack, I found that it appeared that I was the only survivor of the attack as there were no Blenheims in sight. I put on full power to both of the Bristol engines and they seemed to be in good working order. I was in a hurry to get to England. Now that we had time to assess our situation, it was discovered that the fuel lines had been damaged and that gasoline fumes were very strong in the cockpit area. The fuel supply was becoming less in both tanks but didn't appear to be disappearing very fast. We were able to return to base in England without further problems.

"On returning over the airfield at Wattisham, Suffolk, it was discovered that our hydraulic system was out of order and that there was no power to lower the undercarriage or flaps. The surface of the airfield was grass covered so I picked the largest area to land wheels up - which we did. Fortunately, there was no fire. The injuries to the WOp/AG were not life threatening and after a stay in hospital he was back on the squadron strength in a few short months.

"The other three trips were not quite as bad as the one mentioned although the opposition was quite effective. On none of these attacks on enemy convoys did we fail to lose at least two aircraft and crews. Thank God, we didn't continue in that endeavour."

The third shipping operation in September took place on the 10th, when six Blenheims of 18 Squadron left their base near Norwich on a shipping sweep off the Dutch Frisians (*Beat 7*). Two small squealers off Terschelling and Vlieland were attacked but not hit, and the raiders returned home without loss. Sergeant Monty Scotney, WOp/AG with 18 Squadron, comments:

"On this trip the weather was overcast, with lots of low cloud. We suddenly came across a fishing smack, I recall the small superstructure which was obviously the wheelhouse. I can't bring to mind actually bombing it (the target seemed too small to warrant 500lb bombs), but I certainly machine-gunned it. The results were unobserved, as we lost it in the mist and low cloud. Although it looked diminutive and harmless, these so-called fishing smacks were packed with wireless equipment, and were positioned to give the Germans early warning of enemy aircraft. We were sensitive about innocent looking fishing vessels, and would attack these. I remember feeling guilty about the machine-gunning, and thinking, 'Suppose it WAS just a fishing boat?'"

Scotney was quite right in his fears of hitting a legitimate Dutch fishing ship. On 18th August, *IJM253* and *IJM432*, two Ijmuiden based fishing cutters were bombed by twelve Blenheims of 21 and 82 Squadrons and sank off Bergen aan Zee. There were no survivors. On the same day, *IJM418* was sunk by six aircraft of 139 Squadron off Ijmuiden; a truly black day for the Ijmuiden fishing fleet. Three other Dutch fishing ships were sunk by 2 Group off the Dutch coast during the anti-shipping campaign in 1941. As Scotney mentioned, many crews had their doubts about attacking the innocent-looking vessels. However, very early on in the campaign, on 3rd April, they were ordered by Bomber Command HQ to attack any fishing vessels as these might very well be employed by the enemy as 'squealers'.

On the 11th, 12th, 14th and 15th September, nine, eleven, twelve and eight Blenheims respectively swept the Dutch coast and Frisian Islands, attacking one, five, four and six vessels. On the 15th, a 114 Squadron crew succeeded in sending the *Arna*, a merchant ship of 4,390 tons, to the bottom of the North Sea off Borkum. Also, on the 14th, the *Bullaren*, a large 10,000-ton merchantman was hit by three bombs, which were hurled into the ship by 18 Squadron Blenheims off The Hague. However, all three bombs were duds and the *Bullaren* suffered only superficial damage.

Sergeant Harry Huckins had survived a tour of operations as observer with 21 Squadron in 1940 and early 1941. A few months of 'rest' followed at 13 OTU Bicester, but Harry got so bored with instructing that he volunteered to go back on operations with his old WOp/AG Bill Bradshaw for a second tour of low level Blenheim operations. In July, 1941, they were crewed up with Squadron Leader George Lerwill DFC and Bar (who had done his first tour on Hampdens) and joined 18 Squadron at Horsham St. Faith:

"At this stage of the war we were churning out 28 crews every two weeks and not able to keep all the squadrons in full strength due to the fantastic casualties being received on the shipping strikes mainly off the Dutch coast. We got reports back at OTU that the average life of a crew were 3 raids only. Sergeant pilots who survived more than this number were promoted instantly to Flight Lieutenant or even Squadron Leader. You can imagine that these reports were a little frightening to most instructors at OTU although a lot of them never did go back on a second tour.

"It took a month or so to get George proficient on the Blenheim. We did a little practice bombing over 'The Wash' bombing range and Bill got to fire on a drogue. It was good to see that he at least had twin Brownings rather than the single Vickers on our first tour. Also, I had a single Vickers poking through the front of my position that looked like a good strafing gun.

"Our first few raids were very easy since we were to adhere to a fixed area of search and did two tips out without seeing anything but a 'Squealer' off Borkum Island which we sank in seconds. (At the time we were told they were small fishing vessels equipped with a radio in order to give more warning of any British raids. We never saw anyone on board and I have always felt guilty about this destruction of an unarmed boat but I thought it was at least good practice for me with the Vickers and four dirty great 250lb. bombs).

"Anyway, it was only a week after this raid, on 12th September 1941, that we were briefed that there was a definite report of a shipping convoy off Ijmuiden. It was a beautiful day indeed for this raid, visibility was excellent, therefore we felt confident we would make contact. We were told that the convoy was always escorted by *Flak*-ships rather than destroyers. These *Flak*-ships were supposed to have great fire power and we found out that this was definitely true. Our aircraft was in the lead of six Blenheims and we had an escort of nine Spitfires which were a very reassuring sight. George was, in my opinion, flying too high at about 250 feet. This would definitely give good notice to their lookouts. A lead Spitfire just flew right under us as much as to say 'Get down! All our lives are at stake!!' and finally George did get down to 100 feet but by this time the enemy convoy was in view. They saw us long before we got in firing range and started a murderous fire of Bofors and those black puffs of 'ack-ack' from other types of weapons, plus many lines of tracer, as an added inducement to steer clear.

"As leader, we aimed for the centre of the convoy and straight at a *Flak*-ship which threw everything at our first vic. As we were getting very close I was pumping the Vickers gun like mad and screaming to George to get down lower. I just saw our number two in flames and climbing. We were on the ship before we knew it and my salvo of bombs were overshot by 1/2 mile. There was a flash of wings as two Bf109s bored in at us but they were attacked by our great Spitfires who had jettisoned their outside fuel tanks and were more than a match for'em.

"When I got back I got a cable from home that my wife Dorothy was severely ill and pregnant. I was given the option to stay in the UK or else stay with the squadron who had just received rush orders to go to Malta. I was a little shaken at my first real shipping strike and felt there was not much future of the Dutch coast, so I opted to try my luck in the Mediterranean. I had heard that the Italian Fleet were not good at all, unlike the Krauts... We had a lot of adventures from Malta but nothing so rough as the strike near Ijmuiden. At least I survived to see my baby daughter when she was six months."

Not only the enemy posed a threat to the Blenheim crews, as Sergeant Scotney, WOp/AG with 18 Squadron, recounts. On 16th September, twelve aircraft of 18 Squadron *Beat* the Dutch Frisian Islands, when on the way back V6339 suddenly disappeared:

> "Sergeant Tracey was formating on us on the way out. At some stage he just disappeared, and no-one in our aircraft saw him go. It was presumed that for some reason he hit the sea. This was easily done at low level when turning steeply - a loss of concentration during the turn, perhaps aggravated by fatigue and constant watching of a dull, grey surface for hour after hour - wing tip touching, and that's it!"

Despite an ASR search, nothing was found of the Blenheim and her crew. Sergeant Charles Tracey later washed ashore on Texel Island, and was buried in Den Burg. Two days later, 88 Squadron lost two out of three Blenheims during a Channel Stop operation in *Beat 9*. Then, for the 20th, extensive shipping operations were once more planned. In all, 48 Blenheims operated on this day on escorted raids and sea sweeps off the enemy coasts, the majority of which took place off the Dutch coast and Frisian Islands. 22 Blenheims of 18, 139 and 226 Squadrons operated in *Beats 9* and *10*.

Six Blenheims of 226 Squadron went out on an early morning sweep off the Hook of Holland, where a convoy of fourteen ships was spotted and attacked. Four ships were claimed hit. In fact, a German merchant vessel, the *Metz* of 728 tons was sunk during this strike. The price was once again high, since two Blenheims were shot down. Flight Lieutenant Wheeler and crew had a narrow escape when Z7283:G was hit by *Flak* in one of the engines, hit the water but bounced off the waves. The whole procedure was repeated, but miraculously Wheeler managed to keep the aircraft flying and returned to Wattisham safely. Canadian Flight Sergeant Bill O'Connell has every reason to vividly remember this strike off the Hook after half a century:

> "I remember this operation, all right. But, I remember much better the aftermath, since the operation itself set me up for a double 'Whammy' and none of it was what you would call pleasant.
>
> "My crew on this operation was Flight Sergeant Saunders, navigator, and Flight Sergeant Goult, wireless operator/air gunner who joined our crew after we had lost Flying Officer Harrell on 26 August. (Flight Sergeant Goult was lost in a Mitchell operation over Northern France in the autumn of 1943 on his second tour of operations.)
>
> "Our aircraft was flying in No.2 position in a formation of six Blenheims from 226 Squadron and we could see the defensive balloons flying at 400 or 500 feet above the convoy long before we could see the convoy itself. Having determined the ship I was going to attack at a range of a couple of miles or so, we pushed the engines to full power. The formation was led by

19-year-old Flight Lieutenant Dickie Namias who was new to the squadron and operational flying. As we got closer to the convoy, the formation spread out somewhat which indicated to each pilot that no two aircraft had picked the same ship to attack, which could be done, and which could result in the most undesirable results. At a range of perhaps one and a half miles, the *Flak* (German mail) started coming at us. Almost with the arrival of the first bit of *Flak*, I noticed that Flight Lieutenant Namias' aircraft had been hit in the starboard engine, and the engine was on fire on the outboard side and clearly visible to me flying on his right side about 50 yards away, and a few yards behind him. I assumed that he could not see the fire from his cockpit, and I broke radio silence to tell him that his starboard engine was on fire. He did not reply.

"The attack continued, and after a few seconds and seeing that he had not reacted to the information I had given him, I again called him on the radio, and gave him the information once more. Again there was no response. By this time, we were on diverging tracks, and, while I was watching his aircraft, now about 75 yards away, the aircraft hit the water and disappeared in a great splash.

"I continued the attack, and I noticed that the aircraft were now quite widely spread out. After that, I saw no more of any of our aircraft until after the attack, since I was now in the leading aircraft. I have no idea what got into me or why I did it, but the instant after I had dropped my bombs, I was climbing and threw the aircraft into a vertical bank before sticking the nose down for the powerless descent to wave-top height again, where I threaded my way through the convoy and out the other side. Once inside the convoy, you were in a much safer position, because the ships were rather closely bunched for mutual defence, so there was a minimum of shooting as the Germans didn't have much of a chance to shoot at you without firing in the direction of their own ships. At this point I fully expected that we would be attacked by a squadron of Bf109s that I had seen over the convoy in the initial and intermediate stages of the attack. But they were now nowhere to be seen. It was as if they had magically disappeared, and none of our aircraft was attacked.

"On returning to Wattisham, Flight Sergeant Goult congratulated me heartily on the 'wizard' manoeuvre I had made to avoid a balloon cable on the ship we had attacked. He said we missed it by a matter of only inches and he said he could have touched it if he had been able to put his hand through the top of his turret. Until he told me, I hadn't even been aware that the ship was tethering a balloon, although it was always something to look for. I learned from that incident that it was so easy to miss a balloon over a ship, especially at a long range in a fair breeze because the balloon would not be flying directly overhead of the ship and could be easily missed in a dozen or so other balloons. I never did know why I did that vertical bank, but I was glad that I had done it.

"I have long since forgotten what evidence they used in order to credit us with sinking the ship, and I don't remember anything about our casualties, other than Flight Lieutenant Namias and crew. Nor do I remember what kind of shape our aircraft was in when we got back to Wattisham, but I would expect that it had at least a few holes in it. I would be surprised if it had none.

"The attack on the convoy near the Hook of Holland had been carried out some time quite early in the morning, and I was sitting in the Sergeants' Mess with my crew having a second breakfast (the well-known 'after-ops' bacon and eggs) when I was called to the telephone. It was the beginning of 'whammy No 1'. The CO of the squadron, Wing Commander Bobby Butler, asked me if I would like to go down to the BBC in London, and 'shoot a line' about the attack on the convoy and the ship we had already been credited with sinking. I replied that I would rather not. Less than a minute later, while I was at breakfast again, I was once more called to the telephone. And, again it was Wing Commander Butler. He informed me that, 'You HAVE to go because the AOC (Air Officer Commanding 2 Group) says so'. It seems that he was anxious to get some free publicity for the RAF, and I was 'it'.

"Accordingly, a writer for the BBC arrived on the station a couple of hours later, talked with me for several hours, and took many notes. I felt at the time like a lamb being led to slaughter. I was going to be on *BBC Postscript*. At that stage of the war, Britain was still fighting with its back to the wall, and most of the newscasts brought bad news. I am sure it was for the purpose of raising the morale of the civilians that the *BBC Postscript* news item was added. The Postscript was a very popular five-minute item that followed the regular news at noon, 6 pm, and the late news at 11 pm. It was almost always a personal story of a participant in some offensive operation against the enemy to let the folks at home know that Britain was not stagnating in its defensive posture. It might be, for instance, a sailor aboard a gun boat who had been in a brush with a German *R-boat* somewhere, someone who had been on a mine-laying operation, a fighter pilot who had been in a successful dust-up somewhere, someone in a bomber crew who had been to a target in Germany, etc. So, there was lots of material to choose from, and the RAF, by the offensive nature of its job at that time, came in for a good many *Postscripts*. There was a different Postscript for each day. These were interesting to the civilians because many of the items never reached a newspaper, since they were trivial items in terms of the news. And, being eye-witness descriptions made them very popular.

"And so it was that I arrived next morning at BBC headquarters in London in a chauffeured BBC limousine, about to embark on my career as a radio correspondent. I was there in plenty of time to practice reading 'my' eye-witness account of the incidents which were to be recorded on a disc for broadcast on the Postscript. The script turned out to be absolute fiction, which even included crew conversations which never took place. This made me wince. But, I had no choice but to try the job because I would have to have a pretty good excuse for the AOC when I got back to Wattisham, if I struck out totally. I did not then nor have I ever had any training in drama, and this obviously was required for the job. I was coached, re-coached, cajoled, threatened and subjected to all manner of persuasion through about eight attempts to make a suitable presentation. And they were all without fruit. By this time, it was deemed to be too late to catch the noon *Postscript*, so we broke for lunch. I was told to return after lunch.

"Having no stomach for the job I was supposed to do, I decided that if I were to oil my tongue and my tonsils with a few drinks, I might be able to get rid of some of my dramatic inhibitions and go back and do an acceptable job with the lies they wanted me to transmit to all of Britain. The result was predictable. When I arrived back at the BBC studio after lunch I was 'smashed'. I hardly knew where I was. Within about one minute I had been dismissed. They were very nice about it, however. The man in charge told me they didn't need me any more because they could make an acceptable presentation on a disc using the right parts of the ones I had loused up in the morning. But, I knew he lied, and I didn't care. I was free. And they were decent enough to send me back to Wattisham in another limousine. I had failed miserably in my debut as a radio correspondent.

"Actually, the same script was read by another Canadian, a man by the name of Matthew Halton, who was a well-known BBC War Correspondent of the time. I am sure he didn't know he was reading a script that was mostly a bunch of lies. What the script did have was an almost accurate but much over-blown description of the loss of Flight Lieutenant Namias and crew. This set the stage for 'whammy No 2'.

"Flight Lieutenant Namias came from London, and his parents had a home there. They, of course, by the time the Postscript came on the air, had been advised that their son was missing in action. For most British people of the time, the BBC news was a big item of the day, so when they heard the *Postscript* to the news, they didn't have to be geniuses to know that the aircraft described as crashing in the *Postscript* was Dickie's aircraft. So, they telephoned Wing Commander Butler, and wanted to know if the pilot who had seen their son crash into the sea could come and visit them. So, very early the next morning, I was roused from my sleep, and told that I had to go to London to visit the parents of Dickie Namias. I was off again.

"The parents lived in a palatial home in London (with a complement of at least some servants) and I had been invited to dinner. The father proved to be a very level-headed person and a very fine gentleman. The mother, although a fine lady, was very distraught, and wanted only that I tell her that her son was miraculously well, and would be returning to them soon. To spare her feelings, I stretched the truth, and told her that many aircraft had crashed into the North Sea, and many airmen had been picked up by rescue vessels, and I lied when I told her that there was a chance that Dickie would be picked up as well. The father took the situation in, and he realised my awkward position. After another emotional outburst by the mother, I was most uncomfortable. The father, seeing this, asked me if I would have a game of snooker with him in the billiards room. I agreed, and it was here that I told him the honest truth about Dickie, and that he would never be coming home. It was hard on me to tell him, but I knew I had to do it. He was grateful for my honesty, and apologised for Mrs. Namias, which was unnecessary, and he told me that he would undertake to tell Mrs. whatever information he thought was necessary in a time to come. He promised me that there would be no more discussion about Dickie, and asked me if I would honour them by staying for dinner. At an opportune time shortly after dinner, in the absence of Mrs. Namias, he showed me out a side door of the house. He was a very understanding man. He had made things so much easier than they might have been. I left feeling very sad for both of them.

"A couple of weeks later, I received a cheque from the BBC in the amount of something like five pounds for my dramatic debut with them. This was totally unexpected. I had picked up my mail at the sergeants' mess before leaving the station with Peter Saunders on a day off. We had to change buses on our way to Ipswich. We changed at Stowmarket, and it was here that I opened the 'surprise' bonus from the BBC. I felt as if I had been betrayed, and I was so disgusted I tore the cheque into very small pieces and, to Peter's dismay, I threw it into the fresh breeze that was blowing down the main street.

"The train of events that followed that shipping attack left me wishing that there never had been a convoy off the Hook of Holland, and it consolidated my opinion that there was a lot more to war than mere bullets."

The second operation on 20th September was mounted at 11.54, when six Blenheims of 139 Squadron took off from Horsham St. Faith for *Beat 9*. This time, neither ships nor enemy fighters were encountered and all aircraft returned safely. The last operation was commenced only a few minutes after the second, when twelve Blenheims of 18 and 139 Squadrons left Horsham St. Faith at 12.04 for *Beat 9*. Eight crews of 18 Squadron found a motor vessel of some 2-3,000 tons in a convoy off the Dutch coast near Zandvoort, with a tanker of the same tonnage. All aircraft went into the attack at around 13.00, claiming hits on the tanker and on a *Flak*-ship. Blenheims 'Q' and 'H' were damaged by *Flak*, but managed to return to base. After the attack, 'F-for-Freddy' (a veteran of 34 ops.) of 19-year old Sergeant John Nickleson and crew was seen to be in serious trouble with its starboard engine blazing, and crashing into the sea. There were no survivors. This aircraft and crew, in fact, were the ones that had dropped Douglas Bader's artificial leg on 18th August during *Circus No. 78* over Gosnay in France.

Sergeant Monty Scotney, the WOp/AG in Flight Lieutenant Jefferson's crew of 18 Squadron recalls this loss:

"This sortie was led by Squadron Leader Lerwill, and we went out, as usual, at very low level, literally at wave-top height. We came upon the convoy, rather strung out as I recall, and I remember feeling extremely relieved that my pilot chose to attack a merchant ship on the end of the line, away from the centre, that is, where the *Flak* was likely to be most concentrated. The crew lost I knew - Sergeant Pearson was married, a family man, and he was somewhat older than most aircrew, about 28. I got to know him well, and when he was operating and I wasn't, he gave me his wallet to send to his wife should he not return. When Sergeant Nickleson and crew were lost, I saw, very clearly, one of their wing-tips sticking out of the sea. I took a photograph of it with the Leica camera supplied to WOp/AGs, but it did not print out".

After the 20th September operations, there was a lull in anti-shipping sweeps off the Dutch coast and Frisian Islands. 2 Group Blenheims were now mainly employed on *Circus* operations to northern France. By October 1941, it was decided by the C-in-C Bomber Command, Air Marshal Sir Richard Peirse, that the Blenheim was totally unsuited to the daylight anti-shipping task, a sentiment which was echoed whole-heartedly by the crews themselves, reflecting on the high rate of casualties for the meagre results obtained. A directive to this effect was issued on 6th. October 1941. Statistics issued by No. 2 Group for August revealed that out of 77 attacking aircraft, no less than 23 had been lost, 19 of these off the Dutch coast. Yet, this was not the end of the shipping sweeps for 2 Group's Blenheim crews. The first shipping sweep of October was mounted on the 11th, when eleven Blenheims were dispatched to the Dutch coast. However, the fighter escort didn't show up and the operation was abandoned without loss. The very next day, a force of twelve Blenheims did complete a shipping *Beat* between Scheveningen and Ijmuiden, but during a convoy attack near the end of the *Beat* line, two aircraft of 82 Squadron were shot down by *Flak*-ship *Vp1107* and three others were badly shot-up. No ships were damaged or sunk on this occasion. In a discussion between the AOC of 12 Group Fighter Command and Air Vice Marshal Stevenson on the 13th October, the latter commented on the enemy convoys' *Flak* defences:

"Casualties from *Flak*-ships' fire in convoys off the Dutch coast is assuming serious proportions. Two aircraft were shot down in yesterday's attack, while a further three were damaged and lucky to get back. I must ask that the procedure originally adopted by close escort squadrons of eight gun fighters accompanying Blenheims in the Channel Stop is adopted off the Dutch coast. The fire of eight-gun fighters on unprotected gun positions in *Flak*-ships was shown by experience to be effective, thus enabling the bomb attack to be carried out with acceptable security from *Flak* fire".

This tactical concept, in fact, had been discussed between 'Butch' Stevenson and H.Q. Bomber Command repeatedly from June 1941. Yet, nothing materialised from these talks for the time being, not with the 2 Group Blenheims anyway. On 16th December 1941, this concept was tried out for the first time in a combined strike off the Hook of Holland by Beaufort torpedo-bombers together with cannon-armed Beaufighters and long-range Spitfires.

The next anti-shipping operation was a disaster. Before the break of dawn on 15th October 1941, twelve crews of 114 and 139 Squadrons were briefed for unescorted and thus suicidal sweeps off the Dutch Frisians islands. First off were six aircraft of 114 Squadron at 07.45 for the eastern half of *Beat 8*. As usual, the force split up into two flights of three aircraft each at the start of the *Beat* line. Z7500 (Sergeant Whittle and crew) was unable to maintain formation in the first vic due to engine trouble and returned to West Raynham. Sergeants Davidson and Balzer pressed on and were not seen again. They fell victim to Bf110s of *5./ZG 76*. Sergeant Christian Balzer washed ashore eleven days later and was buried at Harlingen. The other five men are still missing. The second vic attacked a large convoy of 18 ships off Schiermonnikoog, but no results were observed. Although the convoy put up an enormous amount of *Flak*, the Blenheims escaped with only a few bullet holes.

Six Blenheims of 139 Squadron took off at 07.58 for an anti-shipping sweep in the Western half of *Beat 7*. A vic of three aircraft attacked a large convoy of 15-20 ships 16 kilometres north of Ameland, claiming one hit on a 4,000-ton merchantman. The second vic of three Blenheims went further east and found an east-bound convoy southwest of Heligoland. They went in to attack but only one crew scored a hit, which was a dud. One of the brave Blenheim crews was shot down by ships *Flak* into the North sea and then a flight of Bf109s rushed into the scene, which had been called in by the convoy. The two remaining crews didn't stand a chance and were both shot down. Squadron Leader Stubbs and eight other men are still missing.

Sergeant Eric Atkins and his crew had only recently joined 139 Squadron at Oulton fresh from OTU, and on 15th October

the names of his crew appeared on the Battle Order for the first time:

"In September 1941 I had just finished my operational training on Blenheims at 17 OTU. I had less than 200 hours in total, flying all types. At OTU I met my crew, Sergeant Jock Sullivan observer and Sergeant Bill Harrison wireless op/air gunner. At the airfield, Oulton, Norfolk we flew on some practice bombing trips and then our names suddenly appeared on the Battle Order.

"We had to attack shipping in the *Beat* area, just off Nordeney, part of the Frisian Islands, some 1000 kilometres there and back from Oulton. We understood there were at least five enemy airfields within the nearby land area and the coastal area itself was bristling with guns. The shipping would themselves be defended by *Flak*-ships. The weather briefing told us that it was likely to be poor, with low cloud and drizzle most of the route. It was our first operation and whilst it was good to have all the training behind us and do the 'real thing', we couldn't help being apprehensive at having chosen a first operation which demanded very accurate low level flying all the way, in bad weather and on a difficult target.

"We set off in two vic's of three Blenheim aircraft. We had to fly very low over the sea, in formation, to escape the enemy radar and the sea spray was obscuring the windscreen. The cloud and rain reduced the range forward that we could see and there was an almost hypnotic effect of the sea waves rushing past below us and the wisps of cloud and I had to blink hard to keep my eyes in focus on my height and the nearby Blenheim. We were not the leading crew, but, Jock, my navigator was constantly checking the course in case we got separated or we had to take over. I was concentrating on my instruments and the other aircraft when I suddenly heard the clatter of guns on our starboard 'free' side. 'What the hell's that?', I shouted. 'Sorry Skipper', said Bill, 'just testing my guns!'. As we approached the area my vic made straight for the *Beat* and the other vic turned more north, which put them onto another adjacent *Beat*. They disappeared from sight and we concentrated on the sea and cloud ahead of us. A small ship appeared on the starboard side of us - this was a 'squealer' and Bill gave it a blast of his guns as we went past. They were there to warn the ships and fighters of our coming. We couldn't interrupt our route and destroy the ship, so we hoped that Bill's guns had done it some damage and it hadn't squealed on us!

"We turned slightly more north onto our *Beat* and I muttered to myself....'Bloody weather, even if we see a ship, we could lose it in the drizzle and low cloud and turning and attacking at these low altitudes over sea is no bloody good'. But just then the leader shouted, 'Tally Ho, two ships ahead!'. There they were, with two *Flak*-ship escorts. We couldn't gain much height and we just split up and made our own attacks. I opted for a beam attack. I had lost sight of the other Blenheims. Just as I was lined up and dropping the bombs, Jock yelled, 'Mind the Blenheim on your port!' I wrenched the aircraft a bit higher and he went underneath me. Bill said he saw the bombs make a 'near miss' and he was blasting away with his guns on the ship behind us.

"As I had gone over the enemy ship, I seemed to be staring into the barrel of the Oerlikon gun, firing at us and into the eyes of the gunner! I remember thinking how tidy and rehearsed the enemy seemed to be in meeting the attack -no panic, just a hardened reaction to the attack. We made a vain attempt to turn around and attack again with our guns, but the weather was closing in and our attack was at the wrong angle. However we might have done some damage with our guns and the bombs were near enough to have given them a good shaking. Perhaps the others had done better. The leader called us to 'Form up, return to base.'

"All three Blenheims soon found one another and set off in formation for home. The idea was that the other vic of three were supposed to have joined us about this time, but there was no sign of them. But they had gone farther than we had and it also depended on what they had met.

"When we reached base there was still no sign or sound from all three of them. And that is how it ended - they never did return. All three -9 airmen - were posted 'missing'. A loss rate of 50% on your first operation is rather daunting! I remember thinking, they were more experienced than us, what chance have we got! But the first rule of survival is 'I'm all right, look after yourself!' Our first operation was behind us. But the memory of that tightly packed drama and the loss of our comrades weighed heavily on our mind for days afterwards. We never did find out what happened to them."

In fact, Atkins' vic of 139 Squadron had attacked a large convoy north of Ameland, with a 4,000-ton merchantman claimed hit but this is not confirmed by German records. In mid-afternoon of this day, 12 Blenheims mounted an escorted *Circus* raid on Le Havre. Although the docks area was hit, a fierce dogfight developed with Bf109s over the target and Z7493 and Z7494 of 226 Squadron were shot down. It had been another hard day for 2 Group. The heavy losses on the 15th should have signalled the definitive end of the daylight shipping sweeps, but a few more were mounted. On 20th, 21st, 22nd, 24th and 26th October, 42 Dutch coast sorties were flown by 2 Group Blenheims, resulting in nine ships attacked. Only one was successful; the *Hilda*, a Norwegian merchant ship of 1,676 tons was sunk by an 82 Squadron crew off Ijmuiden on the 21st. Four Blenheims and an escorting Spitfire were lost on these sweeps.

Then the day finally arrived of the very last operation by 2 Group in the maritime campaign. The honour fell to 114 Squadron, when at 13.04 on the 27th October six Blenheims took off from West Raynham for an escorted shipping sweep off Den Helder. Wing Commander Jenkins, the squadron CO led the operation. His vic of three aircraft ran into a convoy off

Texel and each crew selected a ship to attack. One of these was left on fire; it was the 1,396-ton *Gunlog*, a Danish merchantman which sank soon after. However, a Rotte Bf109s of *4./JG 53* arrived on the scene and two bombers were shot down within a few minutes. The third Blenheim was also in trouble, but Wing Commander Jenkins was able to shake off the fighters. Escorted by Sergeant Richard Johnson's Spitfire of 152 Squadron, he nursed his crippled bomber back to base. Sergeant Denis Shanahan, observer with 114 Squadron, recalls the 27th October sweep:

"My pilot and WOp/AG, Sergeant Jack Whittle and Sergeant Frank Hoblyn, and I joined 114 Squadron on 19th September 1941 and luckily missed most of the anti-shipping attacks carried out during the summer of that year, being involved in other types of operations. Our first take-off on a shipping attack was at 08.00 on 15th October which was abandoned after 30 minutes due to engine failure.

"The only other anti-shipping sortie is that of the 27th October when six Blenheims took off from West Raynham at 13.05 to find shipping reported off the Dutch coast. We were supposed to have been escorted by a dozen or more Spitfires but, in the event, only four joined us. Halfway across the North Sea we split into two groups and our group headed for the southern end of the *Beat* line around Noordwijk aan Zee while the other group headed for the centre point of the *Beat* led by the squadron Commander Wing Commander J. Jenkins. Both groups then turned Northwards each covering half the *Beat*.

"We didn't encounter any shipping and turned for home at low level. The other group were attacked by Bf109 fighters who destroyed two out of the three Blenheims and only Wing Commander Jenkins, although damaged returned to base. Meanwhile our group ran into thick fog off the English coast and we climbed to about 1,000 feet and after a few minutes were heavily engaged by anti-aircraft fire from a British convoy (of which we had no warning) and one of our escorting Spitfires was destroyed and the leading Blenheim was hit badly and crash-landed on the Norfolk coast without serious crew casualties.....Not all our casualties were due to enemy action!"

With this final operation completed, the 'Bloody Summer' was over at last, to the great relief of the surviving Blenheim crews. On 25th November 1941, the Blenheim 2 Group anti-shipping campaign was officially halted, mainly because of the crippling losses suffered by the Blenheim squadrons on these operations. Only in emergencies, like on the 12th February 1942 'Channel Dash', was Bomber Command to assist Coastal units in the anti-shipping work after November 1941. What were the results in ships heavily damaged and sunk for the grievous losses in aircraft and crews? 2 Group claimed no less than 590 ships successfully attacked between March and October 1941, totalling 1,303,000 tons. An Air Ministry assessment sub-committee estimated that 107 of these enemy ships were destroyed or seriously damaged, totalling 355,000 tons. Another 70 vessels were assessed as slightly damaged. If these figures were true, they would represent a serious loss of at least 20% of the German-controlled merchant fleet of over 500 ships, totalling over one million tons, which was employed between Norway and Rotterdam. Thorough post-war research covering this period, however, shows a loss of only 29 ships, totalling 29,836 tons, with another 21 seriously damaged (43,715 tons). This meant less than 8% of the total North Sea fleet lost or temporarily out of commission.

The figures for the Dutch coast and Dutch Frisian Islands area show that between March and October 1941, the Blenheim crews of 2 Group sank 11 ships, totalling around 17,000 tons. This does not include six Dutch fishing vessels sunk. Medium and heavily damaged were another 12 ships, totalling 70,562 tons. Each of these damaged ships, however, was repaired and largely in action again within one or two months. Only two 12,000-ton ships, the *Zuiderdam* and her sister-ship *Westerdam* were so severely damaged during the second Rotterdam docks raid of 28th August that it took the Germans over a year to complete the repair work. When looking at the total figures of around 4,000,000 tons of imported goods and some 4,500,000 tons exported through Dutch harbours in 1941, notably through Rotterdam, the loss of these ships must be considered as negligible.

And what was the cost in aircraft and crews during the daylight anti-shipping and fringe targets campaign? 2 Group lost 170 Blenheims in the campaign between March and October 1941. 111 of these aircraft were lost in the Dutch coast and Dutch Frisian Islands area. These figures do not include losses during Malta detachments and 19 Blenheims lost on *Circus* raids to North Western France and Belgium. Total Blenheim losses suffered by 2 Group during 1941 were 276 aircraft. And what about the rôle of Coastal Command

Blenheims in the anti-shipping and coastal targets campaign? Between March and November 1941, a few hundred sorties were flown, mainly by night, and 49 attacks were carried out in the Dutch coast area by Blenheims of 53, 59, 235 and 500 Squadrons. No ships were heavily damaged or sunk. The price however was high: 22 Blenheims were lost during these Dutch coast operations.

Air Vice-Marshal Stevenson's twofold goals of halting the German coastal shipping between France and Denmark, and pinning down a large portion of the German fighter arm in the West to counter the Blenheim threat, both had not materialised into positive results. Taking this into consideration and comparing the statistics of lost Blenheims with the results in shipping and coastal targets damaged and destroyed leads to the conclusion that the 2 Group and Coastal Command Blenheim anti-shipping and fringe targets campaign was on balance a strategic and tactical failure. With hindsight, we must also conclude that the Blenheim daylight maritime campaign should have been halted at latest by July 1941. Between March and July losses rose alarmingly, with a peak in July, when forty 2 Group Blenheims and crews were lost on shipping sweeps between France and Norway in just one month. In fact, losses were so heavy on the anti-shipping raids that no aircrew in 2 Group had been able to complete 200 hours (or 50 sorties) on operations by November 1941. The experienced backbone of the Group had almost been completely wiped out. Moreover, many of those crews that survived were shattered by their experiences. Even when Basil Embry took over command of 2 Group in May 1943, he noticed the after-effects of the 'Bloody Summer' of 1941:

"The Group had not recovered from the effects of its heavy casualties during the period when its Blenheims were used for low-level strikes on heavily defended ship targets. To have to carry out specially perilous missions as normal routine, day in and day out, without any positive object other than inflicting damage on enemy shipping was making a very heavy demand on aircrew, bearing in mind that the chances of surviving a full operational tour was very slender. Low-flying tactics on heavily defended ships by slow-flying aeroplanes employing the same tactics for months on end was unimaginative operational planning.

"Air Vice-Marshal Lees had quite rightly put a stop to these operations as a matter of routine shortly after he assumed command in December 1941, but they had left a deep impression on the Group and a feeling of scepticism in the minds of many of the aircrew."

During a Station Commanders conference at 2 Group HQ on 3rd November, presided by the Group's AOC, Air Vice-Marshal Donald Stevenson, the end of the employment of the Blenheim in daylight bombing operations from Great Britain was stated as follows:

"With the very limited speed and manoeuvreability of the Blenheim and the weak tactical approach which must be used to give a reasonable chance of hitting, it was obvious that the time during which the Blenheim could be used for the attack of shipping was very limited. That point had been reached during September in the *Channel Stop*... At least sixty six per cent casualties were incurred every time a ship was attacked... A similar tactical situation has been brought about by our incessant attacks on shipping off the Dutch coast and in the Heligoland Bight... it is normal to lose a third of the force if engaged against convoys off the Dutch coast.

"It was agreed that the attack on shipping by Blenheims of Number 2 Group was now an almost impracticable operation of war. Results could be got, but only at great cost, since the enemy shipping was well organised and fully prepared to take on this form of attack... Since fringe targets were also now well defended from air attack -as for example the steel works at Ijmuiden and other important coast-wise objectives -it is obvious that the day of the Blenheim as an effective day bomber is over."

Air Vice-Marshal Donald 'Butch' Stevenson was removed from his post in December 1941 and sent overseas to command the RAF in Burma. Many of his own Staff considered him to be a ruthless and unfeeling man who threw crews away on suicidal operations. Also, in the final stages of the anti-shipping campaign there had been considerable doubt at Bomber Command H.Q. on the accuracy of Stevenson's shipping claims. Perhaps the judgment on Stevenson was too hard. Not only were the anti-shipping strikes a dangerous business under the best of circumstances, but Stevenson was acting under direct orders from Winston Churchill. The Prime Minister had ordered 2 Group's AOC in his March 1941 'Battle of the Atlantic' Directive that all coastal shipping in the North Sea was to be halted. With the meagre resources at his disposal, outdated, vulnerable Blenheims with small payloads, one could easily argue that Stevenson faced an impossible task in early 1941. But on the other hand, Stevenson must have realised by July 1941 that his Group was unable to fulfil Churchill's orders, and that his Blenheim crews were wasted in an impossible task.

Lord Sam Elworthy, CO of 82 Squadron in the first months of 1941 and serving at 2 Group HQ from May of that year is mildly critical in his comments on Stevenson:

"He was a capable officer who many of his superior officers thought would rise to the top of the RAF, which, in fact he certainly did not. Very ambitious and keen to make his mark as an outstanding operational Group Commander, he overreached himself."

A man in a perfect position to assess the effects of the 2 Group and Coastal Command anti-shipping campaign of 1941 was *Grossadmiral* Erich Raeder, the C-in-C of the German Navy. From his words, one must at least conclude that the British forces, by virtue of the combined efforts of the RAF anti-shipping and minelaying campaigns, and by the attacks of small surface Royal Navy craft, were posing a real threat to the German coastal convoys by the end of 1941. Raeder warned Hitler during a conference at the *Führer* HQ *Wolfschanze* on 13th November 1941:

"The air superiority of the enemy in the west leads to a growing threat to our sea transports and to their escorting naval forces. Apart from attacks by aircraft and MTB's, the enemy now makes more use of mines as well.... An extreme effort has been demanded of men and materials of the insufficient number of escorting vessels, which has led to great physical and mental pressure on the men.

"Despite the very difficult circumstances, by making use of all available escorting forces it has up till now been possible to keep open the shipping lanes. (During October in the west, 139 convoys totalling 542 merchantmen carrying 1.2 million tons of cargo. During air attacks 18 aircraft were shot down. Own losses: 2 merchant ships and 1 dredger sunk, 16 escorting vessels partly heavily damaged). Losses have reached the limit of what we can take.

"The only way to counter this situation at sea is reinforcing the Fighter Groups of the *Luftwaffe*, which is a pressing necessity. However, according to the information received from the Luftwaffe this cannot be realised in the near future."

The Lockheed Hudsons of 407 (RCAF), 320 (Dutch), 53 and 59 (RAF) Squadrons took over the anti-shipping campaign from the Blenheim crews. Their 'hit and run' attacks were mainly executed under cover of darkness, and were quite successful at first. Especially the Canadian 407 'Demon' Squadron wrought havoc among the German coastal convoys, but at a high price. This squadron alone lost 24 Hudsons during attacks off Dutch coast in just over one year. In June 1942 losses on the low level

Hudson shipping strikes averaged 25%, and these tactics had to be aborted. Coastal Command now reverted to medium level bombing attacks. These, however, were far less effective in ships damaged and sunk.

Only with the advent of the Beaufighter Strike Wings in 1943 and '44, the RAF was at last able to suppress the German coastal shipping to such a degree that the British aircraft largely denied the enemy her use of the coastal shipping lanes. The combination of minelaying (or 'Gardening') by the 'heavies' of Bomber Command off the enemy coasts at night, together with the devastating strikes by the North Coates and Langham Beaufighter Wings at day, proved to be fatal to the German coastal merchant shipping. This, however, was all in the far-away future by the time the Blenheims were taken off the anti-shipping operations at the end of 1941.

Pilot Officer Bill O'Connell, pilot with 226 Squadron, was heavily involved in the Blenheim shipping attacks in 1941. He vividly remembers the end of the campaign and the conversion of his squadron onto American Douglas Bostons:

"When we got the Bostons, we were in seventh heaven. With their much higher airspeed on the attack (330 mph at maximuim power for three minutes) and greater manoeuvreability, we began to feel that we were surely going to have a higher survival rate among the flight crews, particularly with respect to attacking convoys where our losses in Blenheims ran just over an average rate of one-third for each attack. The Blenheim had adapted well, but it could not compare with the Boston. Maximum speed of the Blenheim was 260 indicated airspeed, and it was generally a sloppy aircraft to fly by comparison to the Boston.

"While everyone hated the shipping sweeps on account of our high losses, we resolved that we were going to be much happier flying the Bostons. But after the squadrons (226, 88 and 107) had had the aircraft for a few weeks and the Blenheims were long gone, a very important discovery was made at Central Test and Development Unit that sent all 2 Group aircrew into celebrations. It was discovered that the Boston had one fatal flaw during shipping attacks: the bombs could not be released when the fore and aft axis of the aircraft was more than 4 degrees above the horizontal. And, best of all, there was no modification that could be incorporated into the bomb-carrying and release systems that would make it otherwise. It was concluded that the Bostons would be sitting ducks, having to make an almost level, long run-in on a convoy at an altitude of nearly 100 feet above the water. So, we would attack no more convoys, and there was much jubilation about this.

"But, our jubilation might have been a bit too soon, because almost immediately rumours (someone's idea of a joke?) started that we were going to give up the Bostons and go back to the Blenheims. I never heard that the rumour was denied, so we got nervous again. Anyhow, the rumour faded over the horizon into the land of impossibility, and everyone forgot about it, and we would see no more coastal convoys. The rumour had made sense while it circulated because the Blenheim could release its bombs in a very nose high position, which was necessary when releasing the bombs in an attack on a ship (to clear the top of the rigging of the ship while almost simultaneously releasing the bombs). So the Boston as a ship killer died on the vine. After the Boston struck out and flunked completely as a replacement for the Blenheim on shipping sweeps, attacking convoys became the almost exclusive domain of RAF Coastal Command, and we on 226 Squadron were very happy about that".

Chapter Nine
Pause for Evaluation

Blenheim aircrews' evaluation of the daylight anti-shipping and fringe targets campaign of 1941.

A number of 2 Group Blenheim aircrew recall their thoughts on the effectiveness of their anti-shipping attacks throughout the 1941 campaign. They also reflect on life in the Blenheim squadrons and on their morale during this period when their chances of successfully completing a full tour of low level daylight operations on Blenheims were very slender.

Sergeant Wilf Hepworth flew on ops as an observer with 139 Squadron during the first half of 1941:

"In the first few weeks of our operations I don't think we had received any serious training on attacking shipping. Our attention was concentrated on flying above cloud cover and then when approaching the search area, to inch down below the cloud and begin looking for enemy ships along the area of our search. The first time we attacked a ship (on 30th April 1941, off Borkum, T.B.) was nearly our last. We attacked from 800 feet a 2/3000-ton German ship, narrowly missing it but one of it's guns hit us with a shell on our elevators - it made a large hole but failed to explode.

"I was always content to be a member of a Blenheim squadron, even though it was the only bomber we had in 1941 with a (maximum) speed of 260 mph. Our crew only once did a night bombing trip (against Emden) in midwinter, flying at 15,000 feet. It was perishing cold, the engines froze and we dropped 6,000 feet before they started again. We were happier flying in daytime!

"I think that almost every one involved in 139 (and that goes for other squadrons too) were pleased to be in 2 Group. Our crews were mostly in the 19 to 25 age group and keen to tackle anything that was put to us - we had every confidence in our senior officers leading us. Naturally, most of us had apprehension at briefing times - to me, and a lot of my colleagues, saying a silent prayer before take off was conductive to settling down to what was ahead. Once we were airborne our earlier apprehension left us.

"Additionally, Bf109s & '110s were rather disconcerting, especially knowing that they were up to 100 mph faster than us! When the Air Vice-Marshal gave the whole Group a written pep-talk circa March/April with the prophetic statement that he didn't care if he lost 80% of his crews

206

and aircraft as long as we got results, - even that didn't depress us and I can say for sure that our morale was always strong! I can still mentally see the school board and easel on which it was pinned in the 139 Squadron crew room. This edict was sent to all of the squadrons in 2 Group."

Sergeant Bob 'Smudge' Coles flew as an observer with 139 Squadron from February till 7th May 1941, when his Blenheim crashed in the Waddenzee off Friesland province during a night shipping sweep:

"I would say that our crew's morale was very high, possibly because although we thought shipping attacks hazardous, the squadron had not suffered serious losses in that period. There was a definite 'buzz' in daylight low level operations and preferable to the option of heavy bomber, high level night operations of our other colleagues. I don't remember contemplating not finishing a tour of ops. because the work was too dangerous. I guess we all assumed 'It won't happen to me'. In truth, I believe we thought aircrews engaged on this type of op. were 'something special'. And I still think so! We were very young and welcomed the challenge, but on the other hand I do remember my feelings of relief when in hospital in Amsterdam that whatever else the immediate future held for me, I wouldn't have people shooting at me for the time being!"

Sergeant Ken Whittle served as a WOp/AG with 139 Squadron from November 1940 till May 1941, and comments on the Blenheim as a shipping strike aircraft:

"The Blenheim was outdated and outclassed by September 1939, ill equipped for the normal requirements of a modern air war. To attack heavily armed ships and convoys with general purpose eleven-second delay 250lb bombs was potentially suicidal. No forward attack protection for the navigator and pilot, while the shoulders and helmeted head of the WOp/AG was completely unprotected. The pilot was afforded a little ineffectual protection from his instrument panel and controls: the armour plating behind his seat of little use. The crew's protective armour was behind them for fighter attacks, on shipping strikes we had no forward attacking protection! Never was an aircraft so ill equipped for shipping strikes. The navigator, sideways seated at the navigational table in the Blenheim's perspex nose, was subject to a terrifying experience on the bombing run in. There was no torpedo delivery turn away from the target; the bombs had to be delivered and released at wave-top height, at the ship. The odds against surviving three shipping contacts were slim; an attack against a convoy needing the devil's own luck, or a miracle, to survive."

Sergeant Mike Henry, WOp/AG with 110, 101, 21 and 107 Squadrons during 1940-41 flew on anti-shipping operations from April 1941 and even survived operations from Malta against Rommel's supply ships in the Summer of 1941:

"On the 15th April, I flew on my first daylight sortie, a shipping sweep at nought feet off Le Havre. That trip was the overture, in pianissimo, to a series of low-level daylight attacks on enemy shipping which made everything we had so far experienced seem like a picnic.

"During that phase of the war, Blenheim squadrons of No 2 Group incurred heavy losses. Actual strikes sometimes resulted in losses as high as 75 per cent. The method of attack found to be most effective provided ship's gunners with reasonably simple targets. The aircraft's position low on the water, gave the defences the opportunity to correct their aim by means of the splash pattern on the water. Complete surprise was out of the question. Air gunners couldn't contribute their fire on the run-in because they couldn't fire forward. The pilot's single fixed gun helped a little but the desirable raking of decks was impossible. The only evasive action that could be taken was a gentle undulation which, while dangerous at nought feet, gave us scant protection - at best a little psychological comfort. Even the best of pilots could be unlucky enough to get one between the eyes in which case it was 'curtains' for the rest of the crew.

"The whole attack would last no more than 30 seconds plus a minute or two on the run-in and out, when the heavy calibre guns would have their say. But in that short space of time when all hell was let loose, one could die suddenly, receive some nasty jagged holes, acquire a galloping twitch or develop a craving for copious draughts of brandy without soda. Once experiencing that type of sortie, those that followed filled one with foreboding. We virtually lived on borrowed time."

Flying Officer Ralph Fastnedge served as an observer with 139 Squadron during 1940 and the first half of 1941. Then he was posted as a junior staff officer to 2 Group H.Q. He comments on morale with his squadron and on Air Vice-Marshal Stevenson, AOC of 2 Group in 1941:

"My impression of morale was that it was good. Not all operations were particularly dangerous. Often we flew singly at night, or if by day in cloud. There were no recriminations if the bomb load was brought back. The ground crew attached to my aircraft was splendid and most trustworthy.

"I was a very junior officer at 2 Group Headquarters, but I do know that Stevenson was himself very hard pressed. There was urgent need for home propaganda at that time."

Sergeant Ken Collins, observer with 82 Squadron during the first half of 1941 and taken PoW on 27th May during a Malta anti-shipping detachment, reflects on the low level Blenheim daylight operations, stress and morale:

"We did think that the daylight operations were dangerous as the Blenheim, although our fastest bomber at that time, was not fast enough to escape fighters. The operation's success depended very much on the skill of the pilot and his low-level flying capabilities. Ted Inman, my pilot, was superb and it was only because of this that we got away from the enemy aircraft; the Messerschmitts could not depress their noses sufficiently to allow their guns to bear on our Blenheims without flying into the sea.

"As far as stress is concerned I don't think we thought about it. We, as a crew, held a firm Christian faith and put our lives in God's hands every time we flew and this may have helped. When I said to Ted Inman that we seemed invincible he replied 'We've got to go sometime' and we both felt that the Malta visit would put an end to our operational career somehow or other. Our parents felt that too, as I found out after I came back from PoW days. In our case, we had expected to be 'rested' for we had already carried out more than 30 ops. and we were not very pleased when we were told we were off to Malta. The chances of surviving a tour were not very high and we were fortunate to keep going as long as we did."

Sergeant Jim 'Dinty' Moore served as a WOp/AG with 18 Squadron during the second half of 1940 and the first half of 1941. He recounts how he coped with the stress of the daylight shipping *Beats*:

"First of all, there can be no generalisation, we all coped with this in our own way. For myself, I allowed myself to be convinced it would be others who would fail to return from operations, not I. It was not until my tour ended I truly realised how close to death I had been. I had a very courageous, determined and competent pilot and a reliable and likeable observer. Despite the pressures we had a good squadron in which morale was high and we took a pride in, as we saw it, being the only part of the Armed Forces in the United Kingdom who were carrying the war to the enemy, in daylight. Remember, we were young and high spirited and treated everything as a joke as, for example, when a crew failed to return they had 'got the chop' or 'gone for a Burton'. I suppose we were avoiding the mention of death. We never mourned the loss of a colleague for very long, just being thankful we were still alive. Sounds terribly selfish but that's the way it was."

Squadron Leader Doug Cooper, pilot with 21 Squadron and PoW on 1st July 1941, comments on the stress of daylight Blenheim shipping strikes in 1941:

"My second tour of operations commenced on 20th February 1941 when I was posted to 21 Squadron at Watton in Norfolk. It was from this base that I took part in operations off the Frisian Islands as well as night attacks on Rotterdam, Hamburg, Bremen and Lorient. It was a fairly intensive period of operations and, as most of the sorties were in broad daylight at wave top height, the stress was considerable and casualties very heavy. I lost many friends.

"On the shipping strikes it was decided that the pilot had the best chance of bombing accurately and a bomb release button was mounted on an angle bracket on the control column to permit this. On one occasion one of my pilots returned from a shipping attack and complained that the angle bracket had given way when he pressed the bomb button. I attempted to bend it back into its right angle shape with two hands without success and had to get it replaced. On the next raid, on running up to the enemy ship, I pressed the bomb button WITH ONE THUMB and the damn bracket bent as though it was made of putty! A slight indication of the stress we were experiencing."

Sergeant Monty Scotney served as a WOp/AG with 18 Squadron, from June till November 1941:

"I have to say that in terms of shipping sunk or damaged we were not successful. But it should be remembered that Germany had just attacked Russia, and needed a vast quantity of weaponry, material and men, as well as aircraft, in that area of conflict. Inasmuch as we posed a threat to movement of supplies by sea, and therefore made it incumbent on the enemy to deploy fighters and manpower in defence of their shipping, perhaps, strategically, we were successful. Let the historians decide.

"Our losses in 18 Squadron during my whole tour were high. On three occasions aircraft in formation next to us were shot down. On two raids we lost two out of eight, and two out of six. Other losses occurred: my pilot, for example, went from Sergeant to Squadron Leader in just over seven weeks. In terms of promotion, it was stepping into dead men's shoes. Losses were high, and, in the main, the shipping attacks were disliked and feared by crews. But I never heard, at any time, rumblings of discontent. We were told to attack enemy vessels, which always were heavily defended, and we did.

"Morale is defined as having elements of discipline, confidence, pride, fixity of purpose, and faith in the cause, etc. To youngsters of twenty the two paramount factors were discipline and confidence; we did what we were told to do, and we felt confident about coming back. FTR was always to be someone else's fate, the 'it can't happen to me' syndrome, I suppose. I don't think any of us had positive feelings of pride in what we were doing, nor did we have much idea of its strategic purpose.

"Poor morale in any fighting unit can arise from a combination of prolonged extreme danger and loss, and insupportable living conditions, plus no relief from either in prospect, such as at trench warfare, Verdun, etc. Aircrew rarely experienced all these. Operations were dangerous, very often highly so, but back to warmth, comfort and good food before the next exposure. As for the way ahead, there was always the completion of the tour to aim for. The morale of 18 Squadron was good, and I believe this pertained throughout 2 Group. Fear and worry - yes. Murmurings of discontent - no."

Sergeant Jim Langston joined 21 Squadron as a pilot in the first week of August 1941, only to be shot down and made PoW on the 12th. He comments on his feelings about the high casualty rate in Blenheim squadrons in 1941:

"Firstly at EFTS (Elementary Flying Training School) I gave my first choice as fighters, and second flying boats. Being posted to a twin engined Service Flying School I realised I was most likely destined for twin engined night bombers (there were no four-engined bomber aircraft then) and when I was posted to Bicester on Blenheims I was very pleased, because you were first pilot and captain straight away. I did a conversion course on to Blenheims, using the short nosed Mk.I, which had dual control, and then straight on to the Mk.IV with a crew.

"We had not been at Bicester long when we heard that four crews from the course which had left just before we arrived were missing. And then the next course, several members we had got to know well left, and in a week they would start to go missing, or we would hear that they had been killed. And then my school friend MacKillop (pilot 105 Sqn., KIA 4th July 1941, T.B.) was killed on the Bremen raid, and we realised that most went on their first or second operation, and we did not hear of anyone reaching four. And then my school friend Pete Brown went missing and we never heard what happened to him, or other details (Pilot Officer Peter Brown, observer 139 Sqn., MIA 30th July 1941 off Texel, T.B.). There were four of us who had been at school together, two were killed within fourteen days of leaving OTU, and two were PoW within fifteen days of leaving OTU, they being two of the very few survivors from the Cologne raid.

"So by the time we left OTU we knew what the score was, but just did not think about it and just lived for the day. What mattered was what you were doing tomorrow and you thought no further ahead. And inwardly you thought perhaps you might have luck and survive, but you didn't really think so. But you drove the fear right underground and lived for the moment. We were really pleased to be in a position to have a go at the Germans. It was almost a privilege. We had been at EFTS when Coventry was bombed and it made us want to get into action as soon as possible for retribution. None of us thought we would become a prisoner......we would either survive or die."

Sergeant Ian Webster flew on daylight ops as a WOp/AG with 114 Squadron during the second half of 1941 and on night operations in the beginning of 1942:

"On the matter of coping with stress of operations I think it is true to say that every aircrew member had the private thought that death would never happen to them, perhaps to others but never to them, but many including myself wrote a letter to next of kin to be sent only if we did not return. It was only to take the sting out of the telegram with the bad news and the letter from the CO rather than nothing. The letters in the main I believe were in a similar vein; thanking the loved one for the life they had shared, to say sorry for inflicting the sadness, and to emphasize that this is what you had wanted to do."

Flight Sergeant Kenneth Wolstenholme, pilot with 107 Squadron in 1941 comments on morale in his squadron during the anti-shipping campaign:

"The severe losses suffered by 107, mainly during the low level attacks on shipping, put morale under a terrific strain, but I cannot recall morale dropping to danger point."

Bill Edrich, Captain of the England cricket team, served as a pilot with 107 Squadron during the Summer of 1941. He portrays the atmosphere in his squadron during the daylight campaign of 1941:

"In the 'here today, gone tomorrow' atmosphere of squadron life in wartime, parties were a necessary antidote to the neuroses of anxiety and depression. These parties were largely stag. Women certainly came into our lives, but few lasting attachments were made. The real buttress to morale came from mess life, and the feeling that if the other fellow could take it so could you. When there were losses we closed our ranks.

"Another source of strength was regimental pride. We were 107 Squadron, the daylight boys; yet our fiercest rivalries were not with the heavy bomber crews or the fighter squadrons, but with the other Blenheim squadrons who were doing the same job as ourselves. Each squadron wanted to be top squadron, and during Guest Nights the rivalry came very near the physical. Every month one Station in the Group would hold a Guest Night to which the other Stations would be invited, and the horseplay sometimes got out of hand. I remember finishing up one night at the bottom of a High Cockalorum scrum - a massed pick-a-battle between squadron and squadron - and the neck injury I received was still giving me trouble nine years later.

"A more restful relaxation came from our visits to the Crown Hotel in Fakenham, about eight miles from our base at Little Massingham, near West Raynham. There were three attractive young daughters of the proprietors, 'Pop' and Mrs. Myers, who were nicknamed 'The Crown Jewels'. The girls played records and we danced, and when closing time came the police turned a blind eye."

Flight Sergeant Bill O'Connell flew on operations as a pilot with 226 Squadron during the second half of 1941 and 1942. He comments on life and morale on his squadron:

"In the summer of 1941, our losses in 2 Group on shipping sweeps were quite high, and I often wondered if our losses were worth what we were accomplishing; and I wondered whether or not we wouldn't have been better off and accomplishing more doing operations of some other sort. It, however, never occurred to me to try to get out of 226 Squadron, or 2 Group, by any devious means (which was sometimes done), and I had resolved to see my tour through to the end, if I were lucky enough to make it.

"Each of us, I think, dealt with the fear in his own way. I remember feeling quite oppressed (not depressed) at times, especially during long periods of 2 or 3 weeks between operations, which, really, put the end of a tour of operations further down the road. It was something that I never heard anyone talk about, but I am sure that everyone thought a lot about it. Many of our friends had 'bought it' (passed on to Valhalla) and, we just simply accepted matters of this kind with a shrug. Almost to a man, we drank a lot of booze, and I think the reason for that was that it did relieve a lot of the tension, and it created a lot of camaraderie which, I suppose, lent an ambience of devil-may-care assurance. I don't think that even a couple of weeks leave did very much for me in the way of relieving the oppressed feeling I continually had. It seemed to be always there.

"We graduated from 13 OTU at Bicester, Oxon, in June, 1941, with about 20 other crews. All were posted to squadrons of 2 Group and based in Britain. By September, 1941, I felt that I was perhaps only half way through a tour of operations, yet, apart from a few crews who had been subsequently posted to the Middle East, we were the only crew left out of our course. When I realised this, it brought to mind a statement made by one of the flying instructors at OTU that life expectancy on a 2 Group squadron was about six weeks. While he was just about right on, I thought he had been basely crass and terribly stupid for saying it.

"We had a few cases of pilots or crew members, who, after a very few operations decided that they had had their fill of operations, and went straight to the CO, and told him that they were through with operations. These people were just quietly posted elsewhere - to gunnery schools, Training Command, ground jobs, etc., where there was no shooting in anger. It was a court-martial offence to go LMF (Lack of Moral Fibre), but none was ever pressed to my knowledge. I couldn't help but feeling sorry for these people, because I always felt that their decision was something that they would have to live with in their own conscience for the rest of their lives. That would have been something that I could not have contemplated. One can never hide from one's own conscience.

"The other thing comes to mind on the subject of fear. As I mentioned before, we never talked about our fear or our dark forebodings, because fear is something that is very contagious, and spreads very rapidly in dangerous situations. On the other hand, I always felt that we had an obligation to control our fears and, outwardly at least, maintain a calm mien, which likewise is contagious. Most of the chaps were able to do this without any show of bravado, and I suppose we were supporting each other with this attitude. One of our chaps, a good friend of mine, openly admitted to me one time that immediately after every pre-operational briefing, he was so nervous that he had to go to the wash-room and puke before leaving the operations room to go to his aircraft. He did it every time without fail. And, he finished a tour of operations. One can't help but admire guts like that.

"So, we just lived from day to day, had fun while we could, played outrageous pranks, and laughed a lot. The threat of sudden death was not at this minute, so I would just defer any thought of that possibility until a more appropriate time, which would in all likelihood be over a target somewhere when I would be too busy to even consider the proposition. I never brooded about it, and managed to be optimistic most, if not all, of the time. But, I always had that oppressed feeling."

Flight Sergeant Arthur Asker, observer with 226 Squadron during the second half of 1941 and 1942:

"I was lucky in that 226 Squadron came into the anti-shipping phase later in the war than most other Blenheim squadrons, and thus had a shorter time in this role. I remember that after re-equipping with Blenheims (after our old Battles) we moved into RAF Wattisham where 107 and 110 Squadrons were based. The losses that they were experiencing made our hair stand on end, and the other Blenheim squadrons were suffering just as badly. They were all experienced Blenheim crews, whereas none of us had many hours 'on type', so we were literally thrown in at the deep end. I salute those who had been carrying out these sorts of attacks for longer than we had, because sustaining such losses as they had, required the highest morale."

Pilot Officer Douglas Attenborough served as a WOp/AG with 82 Squadron during the second half of 1941. His comments on the survival rate on Blenheims are brief and to the point:

"Yes, the summer of 1941 was fairly hectic, 4 ops or 3 weeks on a squadron and you had 'had it'. How we ever got through 26 I just don't know, with 'luck and a prayer' I guess! However, my morale never suffered, I just kept making a new will every time I flew. We never discussed the unsuitable employment of the Blenheim but I think secretly we all felt the damage we were doing was very light compared with our losses."

Sergeant Ivor Broom flew on operations as a pilot with 114 Squadron during the anti-shipping campaign in 1941 and later gained fame during his stay at Malta. He comments on the shipping strikes and morale:

"The losses were extremely high, but I suppose it was good arithmetic in war if you sunk or damaged a ship for the loss of one or two crews on each attack. Strange though it may seem, I do not recall that the losses had any bad impact on morale. We were all very young with the great confidence of youth, and I am sure every pilot thought it would never happen to him."

Sergeant Denis Shanahan, observer in 114 Squadron:

"I joined 114 Squadron on 19th September 1941 and luckily missed most of the anti-shipping attacks carried out during the summer of that year. Our opinion of the daylight shipping strikes was that they were a complete waste of aircraft and crews and this was echoed by most of the squadron, but we understood that the operational requirement for these attacks came from very high level. Surprisingly our morale was very good due largely to the excellent command and leadership we had."

Dr. Frederick 'Doc' Buckler served at Watton as the 21 Squadron Medical Officer from May 1940 till May 1941 and thereafter as Squadron Leader Station MO. He tells us of the effects of the shipping strikes on the Blenheim aircrews' morale:

"Due to the heavy losses on shipping strikes there was quick promotion within the squadrons; from time to time a few senior regular officers were posted in as Squadron and Flight Commanders, but many young Pilot Officers left the squadron as Flight Lieutenants or even Squadron Leaders at the end of their tour. I think this rapid promotion helped their morale which was surprisingly high throughout, but it was generally accepted that the shipping strikes were far too expensive and went on far too long. I have the impression that Station Commanders became worried about the losses, and I have always understood that they pressed the AOC to stop them. The sad thing was that very keen young men came into the squadrons, and were lost before they ever had time to prove their ability. These young aircrew were volunteers determined to fight the enemy, and anxious to get going.

"They saw their fellow crews shot down, or hit the water but they accepted this, and it did not seem to cause depression. It now seems that these were unnecessary losses of good men, whose skills, ability and bravery might have been better used at a later date with more modern aircraft.

"Although the large majority of aircrews were very brave, they were well aware that the chances of completing a tour were slender, but many thought that they might well end up as PoW. From time to time aircrew used to give me letters to their wives or parents, and ask me to post them if they failed to return. I was always happy, when able to hand them back a few hours later, but sadly I had to post a number of them.

"I must emphasize that the important point to remember is that the spirit of the aircrews was that we must attack the enemy at all cost and defend our country, which of course at that time was very true. This country owes a great debt to the RAF"

Chapter Ten

Night Intruders and Battlecruisers

Blenheim night operations against Luftwaffe airfields, December 1941 till August 1942 and the 'Channel Dash' of 12th February 1942.

November, 1941, was a month of contemplation for the planners of Bomber Command regarding the operational employment of the remaining Blenheim squadrons in 2 Group. The daylight anti-shipping campaign was terminated and *Circus* operations were halted after the 8th due to the bad winter weather and high fighter escort casualties against the new FW190s. The end of the year saw a number of 2 Group squadrons busy converting onto the more modern Boston light bomber. Besides, rumours had already gone round for a number of weeks that the 'Wooden Wonder', the Mosquito, was going to equip some squadrons in 2 Group. Yet, for the time being this was a pipe-dream. Bomber Command HQ decided to convert three Blenheim squadrons to night operations. These were 82, 110 and 114 Squadrons.

The *Luftwaffe* employed dozens of airfields in the Low Countries and in France for her bombers, night fighters and for her Training Command. In order to disrupt the flying from these aerodromes, Havocs of 11 Group had been operating already for a few months over Belgium and northern France. However, these intruder aircraft lacked the necessary range to cover the bases in France south of Paris, where reserve training units were based. Above all, the airfields in the Netherlands were out of their range. The Blenheims squadrons of 2 Group were now ordered to intrude on these airfields at night. A list of twenty bomber bases, a dozen night fighter airfields and six training fields in these areas was sent to 2 Group and in December the Blenheim crews started training for their new intruder rôle. A recent increase of German mine-laying activities from Soesterberg, Schiphol and Leeuwarden made these three airfields the main targets for the Blenheim night intruders.

British intelligence watched the *Luftwaffe* flying activities closely from these aerodromes. Whenever signals were received that indicated night flying activity from one or more of these bases, Blenheims were to be despatched to counter it. The intention was to be as much of a nuisance to the night flying programmes as possible, preventing taking off and landing by bombing the aerodomes and shooting up the enemy aircraft when taking off or landing. This type of Blenheim operation had already taken place during the second half of the Battle of Britain, but now the intruder offensive was to start in earnest. The Blenheim crews were to fly on the main *Luftwaffe* flying routes over the Netherlands, at rather low level of some 1,000 feet. This was meant to be a safety measure, but on the other hand, the Blenheims were an easy target for the German searchlights and *Flak* when flying at this height. Sergeant Eric Ramsay, observer with 114 Squadron, gives us a clear impression of the operational procedures during the Blenheim intruder operations:

"When I joined 114 Squadron on February 6th 1942, most of the daylight Blenheim operations on shipping were finished. Apart from a trip to Herdla in Norway and an attempt to bomb the Scharnhorst and Gneisenau in the English Channel on February 12th, all our operations were night intruders.

"We had no radar on the Blenheim and we found navigating to a small aerodrome at night, over blacked out Europe, not easy unless they were operating. It was complicated by the German's efficient use of decoy airfields. Whenever possible I would plot our course via the Zuyder Zee, where I found pin points comparatively easy to locate. We normally flew at about 1,000 feet which was probably the best height for night navigation and bombing accuracy in a Blenheim. The aerodromes against which we operated were Leeuwarden, Soesterberg, Ardorff, Vechta, Venlo, Twente and Schiphol. During the time I was with 114 Squadron we lost about 15 aircraft, but some of the crew members may have been taken prisoner.

"In general we found that the most hazardous aspect of these operations was the possibility of being caught in searchlights. At 1,000 feet we were not bothered by heavy *Flak*, but when we were caught in searchlights the menace of night fighters was a real hazard - or so it seemed. There is not a lot of room to manoeuvre nor much chance of baling out at 1,000 feet".

As Sergeant Ramsay mentioned above, a factor that complicated the Blenheim intruder attacks in 1942 was the widespead use by the *Luftwaffe* of dummy airfields. The enemy had constructed full-sized dummy fields close to almost all their aerodromes. These were complete with dummy runways, wooden aircraft, flare paths, etc. The Blenheim crews regularly mistook these for operational airfields and dropped their bombs on the dummy bases. Flight Lieutenant Alec McCurdy, pilot with 18 Squadron comments:

> "When the Germans got warning of our intruder 'planes they would turn out the dim lights of their airfields' flarepath and turn on a brightly lit dummy flarepath, a little distance away. There they would simulate night flying by giving 'planes in the vicinity green and red lights, and perhaps light up fires to imitate aircraft burning on the ground. If these ruses failed they might try to confuse the 'plane overhead by switching off the first dummy and turning on another bright dummy.
>
> "After this if the 'plane still did not bomb, the Germans could well question whether the 'plane overhead really was hostile. Was it one of theirs in difficulty, perhaps lost? If so, they would switch on their real dimly lit flarepath and recommence flying."

Squadron Leader Bob Iredale, pilot with 114 Squadron in 1942, gives his impressions of the Blenheim in the new intruder rôle:

> "The Blenheim was a very good aeroplane but if you got into difficulty over enemy airfields at 1,000 or 1,500 feet, which was the height we flew for intruding, the low speed (180 mph) and the rate of climb (400 feet per minute) made it difficult to change altitude and direction quickly enough to throw off searchlights and *Flak*. I was in similar circumstances during my Mosquito tour and it was quite another matter.
>
> "When we started night intruding in January 1942 it was learning as you go. We experimented crossing the enemy coast at different times after sunset and different heights from 800 to 2,000 feet. When we had a hard time at a particular height we'd try another. We were the experimenters of the tactics!
>
> "I know we lost a lot of Blenheims. I completed ten missions, all over Dutch airfields, and consider myself very lucky to have survived".

82 Squadron was the first unit to finish the night intruder training programme in late December. Six crews were briefed for the first operation on the afternoon of the 27th. Reports had been received that the enemy had posted some sixty Dornier Do217 bombers to Soesterberg airfield and the Bodney-based Blenheim crews were to counter this threat. Wing Commander Roe successfully led the crews to the 'drome near Utrecht in the early evening and found the airfield buzzing with activity. The British crews mingled with the Luftwaffe bombers in the circuit and two Blenheims engaged Do217s with their machine-guns. Then all crews dropped their bombs on the airfield. All six

Blenheims returned home safely, the last landing at 21.45. Still, there are no clues that major damage was caused to Soesterberg airfield and it's Do217 bombers during this first intruder attack.

The Blenheims from Watton and Bodney flew only a few more night sorties to the Netherlands during the last days of 1941 before winter set in. Weather conditions during the winter of 1941/42 were so bad that operational flying was all but possible. This was to hamper night intruder operations until March, 1942. In the third week of January, 1942, 110 and 114 Squadrons were ready for intruder operations and, together with 82 Squadron, these units flew 69 sorties in the remaining weeks of January. Only very few of these however were effective, mainly due to the bad weather. On the debit side, both 82 and 114 Squadrons lost two aircraft and crews over Holland; all twelve men were killed. At least two of these Blenheims were shot down by light *Flak* while flying low near their targets, which emphasized the vulnerability of the Blenheim to the enemy defences when operating at this altitude.

At this time, there was another matter for the RAF to look after. On the night of the 11th February, 1942, the German battlecruisers *Scharnhorst* and *Gneisenau*, together with the heavy cruiser *Prinz Eugen*, had escaped undetected from Brest harbour, and now steamed up north through the Channel. The German general staff had decided to sail these ships north as the units had already been bombed some 300 times in Brest harbour by the RAF and it was deemed strategically better to employ the battle ships in the Battle of the Atlantic from a Norwegian fiord. Sailing the ships around the British Isles was out of the question, as this route would exclude fighter protection for the capital ships. Therefore, Hitler decided to pull off a daring feat by sailing the three ships through the Strait of Dover, right under the nose of the unwary British. Under a strong escort of fighters, destroyers and minesweepers the warships steamed up the English Channel, hugging the French coast. The prevailing weather conditions (mist, driving rain and low cloud) made it possible to pull this off undetected. The British finally got a fairly clear picture of what was going on by mid-day on the 12th and the RAF was called in to try to stop the advance of the German fleet. First, six Swordfish torpedo-bombers of 825 Squadron, Fleet Air Arm, tried to attack the ships off Calais in a very gallant but fruitless effort; the aircraft were all shot down by Bf109s and FW190s of *JG 2* and *JG 26*.

Throughout the day, there were two distinct disadvantages that prevented a coordinated and successful attack by the RAF and Royal Navy. First, although a sailing had been expected for some months, the speed of the breakout took the British by surprise and a well-coordinated operation was therefore impossible. Secondly, the weather conditions off the Low Countries (the position of the fleet by mid-afternoon on the 12th) were very bad indeed. Consequently, of the approximate 300 RAF bombers and torpedo aircraft which flew out to the Dutch coast to attack the German ships, only a handful caught a fleeting glimpse of the enemy. None of the British aircraft was able to execute a successful attack, although a number of crews tried to bomb the ships against all odds.

2 Group's tribulations during the Channel Dash were typical of the failure of the RAF operations on this fateful day. 37 Blenheims and 10 Bostons were dispatched on *Operation Fuller*. Only one Boston caught a momentary glimpse of the ships, but did not bomb. 110 Squadron contributed 13 Blenheims and these, led by Wing Commander Cree, took off from Wattisham and headed for the Dutch coast. Only one crew saw the ships but failed to bomb due to the atrocious weather conditions. One other crew failed to return when Z7433 was shot down by a Bf109 of *5./JG 1* providing fighter cover for the German battleships. The Blenheim crashed in the North Sea 90 kilometres west of Texel; Sergeant Reynolds and crew are still missing.

Next came 114 Squadron. Wing Commander Jenkins led six aircraft to the Dutch coast but, due to very bad weather, only Jenkins sighted and bombed a battlecruiser with his two 500lb armour piercing and four 40lb bombs. Sergeant Shackleton in Z7307 overflew the convoy no less than five times, but was unable to drop his bombs because of the very poor visibility. He returned to base only when his port engine began to fade on the fifth run-up to the ships. This was a very courageous act, as the *Flak* over the convoy was murderous. In the words of Sergeant Bert Waller, WOp/AG in a 144 Squadron Hampden, whose crew was one of the very few to bomb one of the battle cruisers: 'It was an amazing sight to see the grey cloud all around us turn blood red with anti aircraft fire.' Sergeant Lawrence Hewlett, another WOp/AG with 144 Squadron comments on the *Flak* defences of the ships when his crew bombed one of the ships: 'I had a vivid impression that the battleships seemed to be 'on fire', but this was an illusion as it was in fact the mass of guns firing at us. They threw everything at us'. Pilot Officer Drysdale of 114 Squadron was known to have been over the ships, but nothing further was heard of him and his crew. Blenheim T1922 crashed into the North Sea off the Dutch coast, possibly due to pilot error at very low level.

82 Squadron then dispatched 12 aircraft, but no one saw a thing. In fading daylight, three more crews of 114 Squadron and three of 110 left for the Dutch coast in a final attempt to raid the fleet. The 114 Squadron crews located the enemy, bombed through a gap in the cloud and claimed a possible hit on the port side of a warship. 110 Squadron saw nothing and went home frustrated but relieved to have survived.

Sergeant Denis Boissier, observer with 82 Squadron at Watton recalls the Channel Dash:

"Being assembled at the Flights, we knew something big was in the air, but nobody told us until about lunchtime. Being fairly 'green' we were thinking a raid on Brest likely (bad news!). Our aircraft were loaded with 500lb armour-piercing bombs which meant high altitude to get sufficient velocity to penetrate steel plate from maybe 8,000 feet. We were later given the target, take-off time, a vector to fly on, and the instruction to leave the target area by 4.30 pm at the latest.

"While warming up, we noticed two Beaufighters landing and we later found that these two pilots knew more than we did, and deliberately over-heated their engines....they were still there when we returned. It was a very cold day and I had the electric heating connected up throughout my jacket, boots and trousers for take-off. Off we went in a loose formation and the adrenalin started pumping, and first off came the heating. Then the very hot trousers came off and I was still sweating as we approached zero time of 4.30! There was considerable light cloud over the target area, the clouds were down to about 3,500 feet and the bombs would be useless anyway. We stayed just under the cloud base but felt very naked at times as the German fighters were whizzing all over the place; the 'planes that shot past were out of sight in a split second, and we always felt they were '109s and '110s. 4.30 came...4.32 and I pointed to my watch so that Dutchy Holland (pilot) was aware that I felt we'd done enough!

"Eventually, he turned back at 4.35 - the longest five minutes of my life!

By now we were on our own and headed back for base on a guesswork basis - looking for a landfall. The visibility was closing down but we all felt OK. The skipper saw land and we felt pleased when suddenly a voice came from Bill Shipton (WOp/AG) 'Look out -we're in the middle of a balloon barrage!' I looked up and sure enough we were over Harwich and I prayed that those funny things on the leading edges of the wings would do their stuff with a loud bang. But Dutchy did the wise thing and just kept going (actually we were all petrified!) - we got clean through.... The next morning we went out to see if we could find any survivors, but found no signs of anything."

During the 'Channel Dash' operations, none of the three German capital ships were hit by bombs or torpedoes dropped by the RAF attackers. The only damage done to the *Gneisenau* and *Scharnhorst* was caused by RAF air-laid mines. Off Terschelling, both ships struck magnetic mines but were able to carry on with the voyage under their own steam. On the debit side, apart from the six Swordfish and a number of fighters shot down, the RAF lost 21 bombers and torpedo aircraft to *Flak* and German fighters off the Dutch coast. No. 5 Group especially suffered. Of the 64 Hampdens dispatched, nine were shot down and one crashed on return in England. It had been a black day for Great Britain and for the RAF.

Shortly after the 'Channel Dash', the Blenheim night intruder force received a serious blow, even before the campaign had had a real chance to get off on a good start. Because the strategic situation in the Far East took a turn for the worse (the Japanese forces advanced much more rapidly than expected after Pearl Harbour), 82 Squadron was now relieved of its intruder commitments in the UK and posted to India. The long and distinguished service of 82 Squadron in 2 Group had finally come to an end. The same fate befell 110 Squadron, which left 114 Squadron to continue the night intruder offensive alone. Obviously, only one squadron of Blenheim intruders could accomplish precious little.

In February, 1942, a handful of Blenheim intruders left West Raynham to attack enemy airfields in the Netherlands on just two nights. Only two sorties were succesfully completed (both on the night of the 16/17th). However, no damage was inflicted on this night. Bad weather prevented further operational flying during the month. As a result of the 'decapitation' of the Blenheim intruder force, 114 Squadron aircraft flew a mere 30 sorties during March, of which 11 were aborted and 16 resulted in bombing and strafing attacks. No major damage resulted from these attacks to German aircraft and aerodromes. On the debit side, three Blenheims and crews were lost over the Netherlands.

The night that saw the most activity during March 1942 was the 26/27th. Eleven crews of 114 Squadron were briefed to intrude on the aerodromes of Schiphol, Soesterberg and Leeuwarden in Holland. Visibility was good and five aircraft located Schiphol, all claiming hits. Two Blenheims found Soesterberg and one located Leeuwarden, but no hits were observed during their attacks. It was a rough night for the crews of 114, as Australian Squadron Leader Bob Iredale recalls:

> "It was a bad night as *Flak* and searchlights were intense over Schiphol airfield. I was hit, and on reaching base found we had 85 holes over the fuselage. We were caught in the searchlights for 20 minutes before finally getting out of range."

Two Blenheims failed to return from 114 Squadron. Z7307:L of Flight Sergeant Bill Popplestone and crew were shot down by *Oberleutnant* Paul Gildner of *II./NJG 2* and crashed into the Waddenzee North of Wieringen. Popplestone and his WOp/AG Cyril White were both washed ashore and were laid to rest in the Harlingen war cemetery. The second Blenheim lost was Z7700:Q of Flight Lieutenant Martin Bury and crew. This aircraft disappeared without a trace in the cold and grey waters of the North Sea off the Dutch coast. Martin and his crew are commemorated on the Runnymede Memorial, on panels 65, 78 and 80. Nancy Bury, Martin's wife, tells us of the dreaded telegram that informed her of the bad news:

> "It was a day in March 1942. I was sharing a flat in Yorkshire with a girl friend, we were both working in the neighbouring town of York. I had a son aged five who was a weekly boarder at a local school and my husband was a pilot in the Royal Air Force. On this particular day I returned from lunch to find an orange envelope on my typewriter. I have never liked telegrams but it had to be opened and read. The message it contained was short and straightforward: - 'We regret to inform you that your husband, Flt/Lieut Martin Bury is missing on operations'. The words became blurred and I could not take them in at first but gradually something inside told me that during the last hour the whole course of my life had been changed.
>
> "My husband had been with a squadron since the beginning of the war, some of whom I had got to know quite well and a nicer bunch of chaps it

would be hard to find, and in no time at all I had letters from his close friends saying they would be coming to see me to tell me all they could find out about this particular sortie which turned out to be a night bombing raid on Schiphol Aerodrome in Holland. The very next weekend they came but they had no definite news. Again I was lucky, as I was sharing a flat with a very close girl friend who could not have been more helpful and supportive. But my first thoughts were 'I have got my son', the son we had both wanted and adored, now aged five. Too young I felt to say much to at this moment, but if the worst had happened to Martin it was a very big reason for me to go on living and this gave me enormous strength.

"My friends from the squadron kept in constant touch and so time went by and I carried on hoping there would be good news. Alas, none came, and after six months Martin was presumed killed. The system was that the RAF put people on the missing list for six months after which they were presumed killed. Luckily I had plenty to occupy my mind and lots of good friends, I also had my work and a good reason to go on living. And so the years rolled by and time does heal up to a point. I have not re-married although I have had one or two close friendships and many difficulties to overcome.

"Strangely enough the old orange envelope is no longer in existence."

Sergeant Eric Ramsey, observer with 114 Squadron, sat down to write in his diary on 27 March 1942:

"Two of our kites did not return last night. Beachy and Tommy Crilly were good guys, and so was Pop. This is my first experience of losing pals with whom I'd been drinking and joking the night before, and it's rather shaken me. It doesn't seem to affect the older members of the squadron, I guess its just the way it goes".

Sergeant Ian Webster, WOp/AG in 114 Squadron, well remembers Flight Sergeant Popplestone:

"Bill was a good-natured chap, pleasant features and a moustache of sorts, in order I suppose to make himself look older than his 22 years. He had a pleasant Canadian accent but I used to say to him that Popplestone could not be a real name. Had he made it up in case he got any English girl into trouble? He would respond in kind suggesting that in view of my Scottish accent I should try to learn how to speak English and did we still eat missionaries up in Aberdeen. I believe the world would have been a better place had we not lost so many good men in those days."

The very next night, on 27/28th March, both 114 Squadron and 2 Group received a severe blow. At 19.20, the squadron dispatched eight Blenheims to intrude on Schiphol and Soesterberg. Two aborted the operation on the way in, but three aircraft reached Schiphol and bombed the airfield. At debriefing, the crews reported large smoke clouds over the base after their bombing attack. Two other aircraft flew further inland and

qn shipping sweep with Spitfire escort off The Hague 1941. *(via M. S. Scotney)*

Sqn crew at Mersa Matruh, Egypt, just after landing. *(left to* Sgts Sullivan, Atkins and Harrison, early 1942. *(Eric Atkins)*

eim T1945 of 2 OTU on the beach at Texel, 27.8.1941. *Bakker)*

f110s of II.ZG 76, the Haifisch Gruppe, on patrol, 1940–41. *an Kampen)*

Sgt Kenneth Hood, observer with 226 Sqn, was killed off the Hook of Holland on 20.9.1941. *(Molly Lewey)*

226 Sqn at Wattisham, August 1941. *(left to right)* P/O Bill Gray (pilot RCAF), P/O McCarthy (observer) and P/O Casey (Wop/AG RCAF). *(Bill Gray)*

Sgt Tommy Thompson, pilot with 18 Sqn at Blickling Hall, July 1941. *(Tommy Thompson)*

Above: On 14.9.41, S/L Jefferson and his crew attacked this 10,000 ton ship off the Hague. The photo was taken after bomb release as T7308 climbed to clear the masts. *(M. S. Scotney)*

Below: Ship on fire off Holland, 1941, hit by either 21 or 82 Sqns. *(Paul Lincoln)*

Above: Jinking wildly, S/L Jefferson's 18 Sqn Blenheim runs in at sea level to attack a convoy on 14.9.1941. The photo was taken by the observer in another aircraft using a hand-held F-24 camera. *(Monty Scotney)*

Below: H811, a German coastal guard vessel of 211 tons, sinks off the Hague after an attack by two 226 Sqn Blenheims on 7.9.1941. *(Otto Keller)*

114 Sqn, 1941–42. John McCaul (Canadian navigator), Bobby Iredale (Australian pilot) and Sgt John Townsend (British air gunner). *(John Townsend)*

18 Sqn aircrew at Wattisham, summer 1942. *(Alec McCurdy)*

18 Sqn, Wattisham, summer 1942. S/L Hugh Malcolm (on motor-cycle) was killed in action in North Africa on 4.12.1942, and was awarded the Victoria Cross. *(Alec McCurdy)*

114 Sqn crew, spring 1942. *(left to right)* John Glen (pilot), Bruce White (RAAF observer), Ian Webster (Wop/AG). *(Ian Webster)*

Blenheim V5458:O of 114 Sqn failed to return from a sortie to Leeuwarden on 24/25.4.1942. *(via Bill Burberry)*

Sgt Bill Burberry of 114 Sqn at West Raynham, May 1942. *(via Bill Burberry)*

114 Sqn aircrew. *(left to rig* Molesworth (pilot) and De *(observer). (Bill Burberry)*

114 Sqn aircrew, late 1941: *(left to right)* Sgt J. A. Willis (observer), P/O B. J. Adams (pilot) and P/O F. W. O. Street-Porter (Wop/AG), all missing in action on 14/15.1.1942. *(Bob Willis)*

F/L Martin Bury,114 Sqn, missing off Dutch coast 26/27.3.1942. *(Nancy Bury)*

114 Sqn aircrew just back from 'Channel dash' operation on 12.2.1942. *(left to right)* S/L Newbu W/C Jenkins (KIA 27/28.3.1942) and F/O Brancker (KIA 27/28.3.1942). *(Eric Ramsey)*

...heim OTU aircrew, Bicester, May 1941. Front row 2nd from right is Jimmy Corfield, KIA ...1941. Back row, 5th from right, is Sgt Ivor Broom, who retired as an Air Marshal. *(Bill Corfield)*

...heim PoWs at Oflag XXI Autumn 1941. *Left to right:* ...Jack Stephens (107 Sqn) U/K, S/Ldr Douglas Cooper ...Sqn), S/Ldr Ken Doran (110 Sqn) U/K, U/K. *(via Doug ...er)*

Left to right: Sgt Scotney (Wop/AG), S/L Jefferson (pilot) and Sgt Ralph Milne (observer), 18 Sqn Blenheims 1941. *(via Monty Scotney)*

...re: On 16.6.1941 Blenheim V6034:D of 21 Sqn clipped the ... of the target vessel, losing half of the outer wing section. ...eavers and his crew died seconds later when the aircraft ...ed into the North Sea. *(Jim Langston)*

...t: Sgt Arthur E. Guesford married Miss Irene 'Pat' Collins on ...1940. He was killed on 15th June 1941 while flying as a pilot ...110 Sqn and is buried on Romo Island, Denmark. *(via Mick*

Above: The Dutch 'Oranjefontein', again photographed by 21/B on 16.7.1941. *(Pieter Bergmann)*

Below: Blenheim 'U' of 139 Sqn at low level over the bombed-out centre of Rotterdam, with burning dock targets in the background. *(Pieter Bergman)*

Above: The Norwegian 'Knute Nelson' photographed at Rotterdam by Blenheim 'B' of 21 Sqn, 16.7.1941. *(Pieter Bergman)*

Below: The run-in to the Rotterdam docks (on the horizon). This aircraft, V6267 of 18 Sqn, flown by W/C Partridge, was shot down and the crew killed. *(I.W.M.)*

Clockwise from top left: Remains of V5859:Y of 226 Sqn (F/L Lewis and crew), which fell to Flak near Philippine on 12.8.1941. *(Hans van Soest)*

Sgt Jim Langston, pilot with 21 Sqn. Photo taken on 5.8.1941. He was taken prisoner on 12.8.1941. *(Jim Langston)*

The victory board of the Rotterdam Flak defences. It shows five Blenheims and one Spitfire shot down on the Rotterdam docks raid of 28.8.1941. *(Luit van Kampen)*

Target photo of Rotterdam docks, taken by 487 Sqn Ventura on 28.3.1943. *Tom Sheehan)*

Blenheim Z7289:R of 226 Sqn, lost on Rotterdam raid 28.8.1941. *(Douwe Drijver)*

Quadrath power station under attack, 12.8.1941. *(Don Bruce/Ab Jansen)*

Wreckage of unidentified 18 Sqn Blenheim, possibly at Zeeland. *(G. Zylstra)*

Blenheim V6339 of 18 Sqn vanished into the North Sea with Sgt Tracey and his crew on 16.9.19
(via M. S. Scotney)

successfully bombed the runway of Soesterberg. A third crew was not so successful. Z7276:N, flown by 114 Squadron's CO, Wing Commander Jenkins, was shot down by the *Flak* defences of Soesterberg, and at 22.28 the Blenheim crashed in flames on the grounds of the estate *Djimat* at Zeist near the aerodrome. Wing Commander Fraser Jenkins DSO DFC, F/O Paul Branker DFC & Bar MiD, and WOp/AG Flight Sergeant Charles Gray DFM were killed on impact. They were buried at Amersfoort a few days later.

The loss of Wing Commander Jenkins and his crew is the more tragic as the trip to Soesterberg was the final sortie of their second tour of operations. Jenkins and his crew had flown operationally in Blenheims since November 1940. Flight Sergeant Gray, then serving with 110 Squadron, had been decorated with an immediate DFM for shooting down an enemy aircraft over Amiens-Glisy in France. Jenkins was educated pre-war at Cambridge, where he became a member of the University Air Squadron. He was commissioned in the RAF Volunteer Reserve in 1938. In 1941, Jenkins and Brancker developed into two of the most respected and leading personalities in 2 Group. During the shipping campaign, Jenkins, then serving with 18 Squadron, had led a considerable number of shipping strikes and was awarded the DFC in July. On the final shipping beat of the campaign (on 27th October 1941) he was the only one from a formation of three to return from a strike off Den Helder. Within six months he was promoted to Wing Commander and was awarded the DSO to his DFC for gallantry in leading 114 Squadron on a daring daylight raid to Norway on 27th December, 1941. Brancker had joined the RAF early in the war and gained his first DFC in July 1941 for active service with 18 Squadron. A lovable, heavily built man with a reputation of sporting the largest nose in 2 Group, he was the observer who had perfectly navigated the formation of 114 Squadron to Vaagso airfield on 27th December 1941, which earned him a Bar to his DFC. Brancker, who was declared 'totally unfit for all types of Service flying' by an RAF Medical Board shortly before the war due to his astmatic affection, had his plans all worked out for after the war. He intended to pick up his pre-war job as an insurance agent and he wanted to run a hotel. It was not to be, for Paul Brancker was killed shortly before turning 31. Sergeant Ian Webster, WOp/AG in 114 Squadron, well remembers Wing Commander Jenkins and his crew and the day they were lost:

"To me there was something quite special about the crew when we first met them. I don't know how long they had been on the squadron but we knew that they had been operating for some time previously in the days when survival in 2 Group was none too easy. Wing Commander Jenkins appeared to me to be a quiet person. At first I thought he may have been in need of a break from operations and a rest from the constant strain of loss of aircrews and dealing with next-of-kin and all the problems that beset a CO of a squadron, but as time went by it became apparent that it was, in fact, in his nature to be relaxed and calm.

"As a new crew on arrival we introduced ourselves to him and he listened with interest to what we said, and asked relevant questions and gave a feeling of assurance that if you were to survive this would be the person who would make it possible. I know John Glen my pilot felt as I did, a complete confidence in Wing Commander Jenkins as a man, and a pilot and CO. It was the feeling with every trip that Wing Commander Jenkins led and that we were on, that there was an improved chance of survival. Obviously, we did not use the Officers Mess so we have no idea how he was when off duty but we were aware that he was held in high regard by the more junior officers with whom we did socialise. Paul Brancker the observer was an extremely friendly person to all, irrespective of rank and an expert in his capacity as observer so it was easy to understand why Wing Commander Jenkins had selected him for his crew. Flight Sergeant Gray was a serious young man who took his duties as the Wing Commander's gunner with a great sense of responsibility and I'm fairly sure that he was in the Regular Air Force prior to wartime and for him it was a career which he hoped to follow after the war. So he was a likeable chap in many ways and certainly less flippant than those of us who were in only for the duration.

"It was therefore a severe shock to all of us when the crew failed to return from an intruder operation. I had accepted the loss of collegues over the months with sadness, but with resignation, but this was an extremely personal loss for all of us. There was always the hope that they had survived and might be PoWs."

The hazardous nature of the night intruder operations to *Luftwaffe* aerodromes is vividly illustrated by Flight Sergeant Eric Atkins' story. 'Tommy' Atkins and his crew (Sergeants Jock Sullivan and Bill Harrison) had recently returned from Malta and the Middle East to the UK. They were the second crew to depart from West Raynham after Wing Commander Jenkins to intrude on Schiphol on 27th March in R3620:A:

"We were to rejoin our squadron, 139, but we found them packed up ready to go out to the Far East. We were instead, posted to 114 Blenheim Squadron. We were tired and ready for a 'rest', but 114 Squadron was in the process of changing over to night operations on Blenheims. We hadn't flown at night since Service Flying Training School on Oxford aircraft in May, 1941 and then only two hours dual. Our first night flying practice was nearly disaster - it was a pitch black night and drizzle and in the midst of circling the aerodrome there was an air-raid and all the lights were switched off and R/T communication ceased. We headed away from the area of the raid in Norfolk and got lost. These were the days before radar and *GEE* and we only had DR navigation, which wasn't much good for us on that night. After getting caught up in an air-raid over London and narrowly missing the balloons we finally asked for a 'May Day' (emergency) landing - anywhere! Lights were switched on at an aerodrome and I side-slipped quickly onto the runway. We had landed at Manston on the southeast coast, due south of our base after flying for three and a half hours. When I got back to base all my personal flying clothing had gone - taken by the squadron 'Tally-man', a gunner, who made it a habit of asking 'would be' casualties whether he could have their clothing if they 'went down'. We always treated it as a joke - some joke now!

"Twenty-five days later and after two more night flying practises of one and a half hours each, we went on our first night operation. This was an attack on Ostend Docks, which took two and three-quarter hours and was, surprisingly, quite successful and apart from *Flak* and searchlights which were mainly non-effective, passed without incident.

"On the 25th March 1942 I carried out a daylight weather recce' off the Dutch coast. Then, on 27th March, we took off at night for an intruder attack on Schiphol Airport. Intruding was not an easy task in a Blenheim, airfields were difficult to locate at night unless they were lit. Also these operations were flown entirely at between 1,500 - 2,000 feet, with a bombing height set at 1,200 feet for accuracy. Sound locators could track the aircraft easily, searchlights were very active and not easy to evade at that height, with light *Flak* all around. About this time 2 Group issued guidance on evasion of *Flak* - height would be gained or lost in a varied fashion. It was also desirable to cross the sea as low as possible to avoid radar detection.

"On the night of 27th March, 1942 we took off for an intruder operation on Schiphol - to disrupt its flying, to shoot anything down that we could and to bomb the airport. There was a moon, but it was frequently obscured by cloud at 3,000 feet. We flew low over the sea and my navigator frequently checked my altimeter and gave me a warning look as if he thought I was interpreting the rules too rigidly and getting too low! Night flying is an eerie experience until you get used to it. You seem to be cloaked in darkness, almost a separate entity from the world you are in and entirely dependent on your instruments. Your senses play you tricks - I have known a pilot to believe that he was turning to starboard, because his hand was heavily against the fuselage at that side. In fact he was level and pressing his hand there himself to back up his senses! There is only one solution - believe completely in your instruments.

"As we approached the coast we climbed to 2,000 feet and soon afterwards to 3,000 feet. Below was just pitch blackness and some low cloud obscuring our view. We saw no activity of any kind, but all the time we kept thinking - it was too quiet, fighters were homing in on us, the German radar was getting a fix on us and any moment the heavens would light up. But, nothing happened and we sped unimpeded towards the target - Schiphol. Jock, my navigator seemed confident of his navigation and kept saying how accurate the weather forecast was. I didn't query how he knew, because I could see nothing at all below -just blackness! Bill, the gunner, kept 'seeing things', but they all turned out to be non-existent, and we were soon approaching the target area.

"I reduced my height to 1,000 feet to get a better view of the ground and to prepare for the special height at which we had to drop the bombs, 1,200 feet. Suddenly we saw evidence of some activity on the ground with moving lights. Jock confirmed that it was in the region of the target. I flew over it at 600 feet and then climbed to 1,000 feet, to decide whether to bomb, or to chase the lights which might prove to be aircraft. We decided that we should bomb the airport as soon as we got a positive identification of it. I had levelled out at 1,200 feet when suddenly 'all hell broke loose'. At least six searchlights coned us and light *Flak* started bursting all round us. I varied height by 500 feet and flung the aircraft about the sky. I remained calm, but tried all options. The problem was that the searchlights reflected off the clouds and with us underneath it. The cloud made their successful coning easy, and we were desperately exposed. I couldn't get out of the searchlight beams; they clung to us in the darkness, like magnetic fingers. At last I gave up the violent evasive action and flew straight, which took me out of the beams! I had probably gone around in circles with the radius of the searchlights exposing us and the sudden straight course left them behind! Jock identified the airport and I could see landing areas. We started our bomb run. Light *Flak* and tracer bullets came at us from all sides. There was a loud bang underneath the Blenheim, but the bombs were away. Jock saw them burst in the airfield area. The aircraft seemed all right; the searchlights were now pointing their fingers not directly at us, but in a directional action which we thought was meant for their fighters. It was no time to linger - we turned for home, varying our heights from 500 to 1,000 to 500 to 3,000 feet. Over the sea we stayed down as low as possible. 'What was that loud bang?' I asked, 'Any damage?' We had no explanation.

"At West Raynham airfield, a grass landing area, we got the OK to land. At night you have a sixth sense as to whether you have made a good three point landing or only an adequate one. I remember thinking, 'This is a good one'. We touched down allright and then the world turned upside down for me! The aircraft skidded, spun and tried to loop and flung me against the airframe. A blinding light in my head and then the thought, 'What have I done wrong?', then I lost consciousness. What had happened was that on a Blenheim the wheels still protrude from the aircraft even when the undercarriage is fully retracted. The light *Flak* had burst the tyres and damaged the wheels - we had nothing to run on when I landed. The green light was still on to show the undercarriage was down. Bill and Jock were badly shaken, but no other damage; I had concussion and was taken to hospital. When I got out of hospital my crew had been posted elsewhere (both died later). I was told that I had finished my first tour of ops., immediately commissioned in the field, from Flight Sergeant to Pilot Officer and posted as an Instructor to 13 OTU on Mitchells. Later I went onto 464 and 305 Squadrons on Mosquitoes and finished three tours of ops. For me, however, my second night operation on Blenheims was an occasion I will never forget! Later, I was told that Schiphol was a target where many a good crew met their finest challenge!"

In April 1942, 114 Squadron was still the sole Blenheim intruder squadron in the UK. With the bad winter weather now behind, the squadron mounted 52 sorties that month, of which 39 resulted in bombing attacks on enemy airfields. A great improvement on the efforts in the previous months! And operations gained more importance because of the resumed German bombing offensive against British cities. In retaliation of Bomber Command's heavy raids against Germany, Hitler ordered a renewed 'Blitz' against Great Britain. Many of these *Baedeker* raids were mounted from aerodromes in the Netherlands, which made the intruder attacks by 114 Squadron of paramount importance. Reinforcement was on the way, as 18 Squadron had completed night intruder training by the end of April and was ready to resume operations.

Although there is little of importance to report on the April, 1942 Blenheim intruder attacks, 114 Squadron again lost a few aircraft and crews. The first loss occurred on 17/18th April, when six crews left West Raynham at 21.21 to attack Leeuwarden, Soesterberg and Schiphol airfields. Only two crews located Leeuwarden and dropped their bomb loads over the notorious night fighter base. The other four crews could not find their targets, but one of their number was lost. Z7430, flown by Wing Commander Hull DFC, Wing Commander Jenkins' successor as CO of 114 Squadron, was hit by light *Flak* in the nose and port engine when the Blenheim approached Schiphol airfield. Hull, who had been CO for just eight days, could hardly see anything for the glare of searchlights that kept the stricken aircraft trapped in their beams. He could barely keep the aircraft in the air and did a magnificent job by belly-landing the damaged intruder on the verge of the airfield after jettisoning the four 250-pound bombs safe. The three men were very fortunate to escape death and were made PoWs by the Germans. Hull and his observer Flight Lieutenant Baker were severely injured in the crash and were taken to hospital in Amsterdam, but the WOp/AG Pilot Officer Morton escaped with only cuts and bruises. Hull and Baker were both pre-war 'regulars' in the RAF and had survived some 50 operations together on 107 and 114 Squadrons. As Flight Commander with 107, Hull was awarded the DFC in April 1941. Shortly after returning from captivity in 1945, he was sadly killed in a crash while converting onto Mosquitoes.

114 Squadron lost a second crew in April; V5458 disappeared without a trace in the North Sea on the 24/25th while on its way to Leeuwarden. Sergeants McKenny, McIntyre and Lewis remain missing. The final loss of the month occurred on 26/27th April. Two Blenheims flew to Leeuwarden, which was bombed in bright moonlight. The third aircraft of 114 Squadron to operate on this night went to Eindhoven. Pilot Officer Bob Molesworth, the Australian skipper pulled T2430 'Q-for-Queenie' into the night sky at 22.45 and set course for the Dutch coast. Little could he suspect the events which lay ahead in the coming hours. Sergeant Bill Burberry, WOp/AG in Bob Molesworth's crew, recounts this sortie:

"I was a Sergeant WOp/AG, on 114 Squadron, flying mainly night operations against *Luftwaffe* fighter stations. Afterwards I went to North Africa to do a further 50 or so operations on Blenheims Mk.V and Boston III until the end of the war in Tunesia.

"I remember that on our night sorties usually we left the UK flying out over Southwold, making for a flashing beacon 'W-W' before setting course for our targets. Our main activity was during the moon periods when we could see the targets (we had no radar). Also, the night fighters could see us, which none of us liked. An incidental fear of ours was that the Blenheim looked very much like a Ju88 in the dark, and could thus be mistaken by our own night fighters for a German bomber.

"On the night of 26th April, 1942, we took off at 11.45 pm in Blenheim IV No. T2430. Once over the coast I tested my guns and found they would not fire. On the floor of the aircraft I stripped out the breechblocks of both guns (Browning .303), in the dark, but could not discover the fault. It could have been a malfunction in the electrical Palmer firing gear. I reported to Bob Molesworth - he said, 'Well it's a quiet night, let us take a chance', and we all agreed.

"We located the target, Eindhoven, bombed the runway (four 250lb bombs, eleven-second delay fuses) and turned for home. The sky was clear, moonlight as we left over the Scheldt estuary. After five minutes or so I asked Tim Denny, the observer, if he would like a navigational fix - he said yes, so I left the turret to wind out the trailing aerial. As I finished doing so, the aerial winder disappeared and shrapnel penetrated my right arm. I jumped back into the turret and saw what I believed to be a Ju88 at about, say 3-400 metres, firing what I supposed were cannon, judging from the damage. The radio had burst, the IFF was shattered and my parachute had been blasted away through another hole in the fuselage. The intercom was out of action, so I crawled through the bomb bay to tell the pilot. One engine had failed and it was difficult to take evasive action without going into a lethal spin.

"As we approached the Suffolk coast I shot off the identifying colours of the day. These served as an admirable target for the British anti-aircraft battery, probably at Lowestoft, and this may have damaged our other engine. In any case we were losing height, so Bob decided he would have to put the aircraft down, in the dark, wherever he could.

"We crash-landed at 03.30 at a disused airfield, Pulham, between Norwich and Diss. The aircraft caught fire and Bob and Tim jumped out and ran. I could not get out because the airframe had twisted so that I was unable to open the roof hatch. I must have shouted (I suspect I did because it was getting hot with petrol flames). Tim very bravely ran back, climbed on to the roof of the fuselage and by jumping on the hatch managed to free it and help me out. We then all jumped into a ditch and watched the aircraft explode (probably from the oxygen bottles).

"After a while farm workers came along, armed with pitchforks, clubs and so on, in the belief that we were German. Bob spoke to them, in his Australian accent, and so convinced them that indeed we were German, and they seemed to be preparing to hang us. Fortunately the farm owner came along to rescue us. I was treated in hospital for arm wounds, and recovered in time for our next operation on 30th May, the first 1,000 Bomber Raid on Cologne."

In early May 1942, 18 Squadron joined 114 in the night intruder campaign. Within a few nights, on the 6/7th, 18 Squadron suffered her first casualty when V6382 disappeared without a trace over the North Sea. Eindhoven airfield was the target for Pilot Officer Palmer and crew, but this was never reached and the three men are still missing.

A couple of Blenheim squadrons of Army Co-operation Command, 13 and 614 Squadrons, were transferred to Wattisham and West Raynham on the 27th May. The reason for this soon became apparent; a Bomber Command raid on an unprecedented scale was to take place shortly. Target for the bombers was to be either *Dace* (Hamburg) or *Trout* (Cologne). In support of the raid, 13, 18, 114 and 614 Blenheim Squadrons had to disrupt air traffic over all German night fighter bases which were situated on the route of the main force. On 30th May 1942, the go-ahead for the raid was given, which has gone down in history as the first 1,000-bomber raid or *Millennium I*. 1,047 bombers carried out a devastating raid on the medieval city of Cologne, and 49 Blenheims of 2 Group and Army Co-operation Command swarmed out to Bonn, St. Trond, Juvincourt, Vechta, Venlo and Twente. Moreover, 38 Bostons, Havocs and Hurricanes of Fighter Command were deployed against enemy night fighter bases in the Low Countries, France and western Germany.

It is hard to estimate to what extent the Blenheim intruders were successful in keeping the German night fighters away from the enormous bomber stream. Certainly, the aerodromes at Bonn, St. Trond, Venlo and Juvincourt were successfully bombed and the taking off and landing of the enemy aircraft were somewhat disrupted. Despite these successful nuisance attacks however, dozens of night fighters managed to take off from these bases and mingled with the British bombers. The situation at Venlo may be regarded as a typical example of the events on this night. Five Blenheims of 18 and one aircraft of 13 Squadrons bombed and machine-gunned this large night fighter base, the home of the crack unit *I./NJG 1*. In spite of these efforts, 10 Bf110 crews took off from Venlo and managed to shoot down twelve bombers of the 44 that failed to return from this historic raid. Clearly, disrupting the so extensive and well-organised German night fighter arm with a relatively small intruder force was no sinecure.

Two nights later, 956 bombers flew to Essen in an effort to repeat the successful first 1,000-bomber raid. Unfavourable weather however prevented a concentrated bombing attack and the city was only lightly hit. The four Blenheim squadrons, again supported by aircraft of Fighter Command, swarmed out to the enemy aerodromes. Yet, they could not prevent the loss of 33 bombers. In addition, three Blenheims were lost, two of them failing to return from Venlo.

The third and final 1,000 bomber raid took place on 25/26th June 1942. The scenario was the same as on the previous two raids. A record number of 1,067 bombers flew in a gigantic stream to Bremen and 31 Blenheims, 21 Bostons and 4

Mosquitoes faced the task of keeping the enemy night fighters at bay. Most Blenheims went to Holland, their targets the night fighter bases of Venlo, Twente, Eelde, Leeuwarden and also St. Trond in Belgium. Two Blenheims, both of 13 Squadron, were lost. Z6084 on an intruder sortie to St. Trond was shot down by a night fighter and crashed at Houwaart in Belgium and T2254 was intercepted and shot down on its way to Venlo by *Oberleutnant* Reinhold Knacke of *I./NJG1*. None of the six men survived these crashes.

Despite the gallant efforts of the British intruders over the heavily defended enemy airfields, German night fighters were active as never before. For example, fifteen Bf110s took off from Leeuwarden and reaped havoc among the British bombers. Seventeen aircraft fell to their guns over the Northern provinces of the Netherlands. Although the bombing of Bremen was fairly concentrated and *Millennium II* was deemed a success, a record number of 55 aircraft failed to return.

Sergeant Ian Webster, WOp/AG in Flight Sergeant John Glen's crew, flew in Blenheim V6431 'M-for-Mother' of 114 Squadron to Bremen. It was the crew's 21st Blenheim sortie and this time they didn't operate in the usual intruder role, but as part of the main bomber force:

"It was probably becoming difficult to maintain 1,000 on the main target plus an intruder force due to losses and damage etc. in the previous 1,000 raids, so we were briefed for Bremen. We took off at midnight. There was 10/10th cloud over Germany and on the first leg of the trip cloud tops were at about 4,000 feet. In order to avoid an attack while we still had bombs on we agreed to fly just above the tops so we could disappear into cloud as we had done on previous occasions if need be. The flight path was in a direct line probably between Texel and Den Helder for a navigational pin-point, then on to Bremen. I would think that with the number of aircraft involved there was a potential hazard in doing any dog-legs to confuse the enemy. At various points along our route we received very accurate light *Flak* and wondered why. Eventually we realised that the German night fighters would have advised *Flak* controllers of these heights and *Flak* would have had a succesful number of kills. We decided that discretion was the better part of valour and started to climb to our bombing height of 12,000 feet.

"As we approached Bremen extensive fires lit up the clouds and I saw a twin-engine aircraft silhouetted against the clouds about 500 feet below us to port flying on a parallel course. From the bulbous shape of the cockpit area I believe it was a Ju88 and I kept it in sight as we started our bombing run. We were immediately boxed by heavy *Flak* and the suspect aircraft peeled off and I lost sight of him. The bomb run seemed endless, as always, but in reality we were merely stoking up the fires started by the first waves as opposed to having a specific aiming point. We had taken a fair amount of Flak and, having dropped our bombs, set course for home. We now had time to sweat over possible damage and our chances of getting home.

"I saw only two other aircraft that night, both four-engined, on the way to the target. It may have been that the 1,000 aircraft were spread over several hours of darkness which would explain why I only saw so few, although many Lancs and Halifaxes would have been at 15,000 to 20,000 feet.

"We always felt relieved when we had cleared Germany as we had been warned from the start of the heavy bombing of German towns that aircrew who had to bale out they would probably be harshly dealt with by the civil population or police if captured by them. Apparently even lynching of aircrew had taken place and, if at all possible, you should surrender to either the German Army or *Luftwaffe* if that became necessary. Over Holland we always felt much less vulnerable because it was the feeling that if a forced landing or bale-out took place there would be help of some kind from the people. Then once across the Frisian Islands it was 'well we've got this far' let's hope we survive the North Sea crossing because the thought of ditching in the dark was not relished.

"I believe many crews and particularly air gunners, having cleared the Frisians, relaxed too soon and left themselves vulnerable to attack from night fighters who anticipated the reaction of aircrews at the apparent end of a succesful operation. This area must have proved to be very fruitful hunting ground. For my part I very much wished to survive and I owed it to Johnny and Bruce to protect their backs so I was very much on edge from start to finish on all trips.

"After our aircraft was inspected next day by the engineering officer he pointed out many holes in the wings and fuselage and both fuel tanks had been holed. Thank God for self sealing tanks."

In all, Blenheims of 18 and 114 Squadrons flew 171 night intruder sorties in June, resulting in 118 successful attacks. The costs were relatively low; five Blenheims failed to return and a sixth crashed on take off from West Raynham. During July 1942 the crews of the two intruder squadrons carried out another 108 sorties in support of Main Force raids, losing nine Blenheims in the process. Six of these aircraft failed to return from sorties to Dutch aerodromes. On 31st July/1st August, 114 Squadron completed her final Blenheim intruder sorties. This historic event was overshadowed by the loss on this night of 18 Squadron's CO. V6452, flown by Wing Commander Hartie-Jones DFC, was shot down by *Oberleutnant* Werner Streib, the CO of *I./NJG 1*, the elite night fighter unit based at Venlo. This was the final Bristol Blenheim lost on operations to the Netherlands during World War Two; the last of a long - a too long - line of lost Blenheims and their crews.

In the night of 17/18th August 1942, 18 Squadron carried out the final Bomber Command Blenheim operations over the Third Reich, when eight of her crews were briefed to intrude on Vechta, Rheine, Twente and Leeuwarden. Two crews left Wattisham at 21.20 for Twente, claiming hits on the runways of the airfield. Two other crews that had taken off at 22.18 for Leeuwarden could not locate the target and attacked Eelde airfield and Borkum instead. Sergeant Rounding in Blenheim Mk.IV Z7295 'F-for-Freddy' touched down at Wattisham at 01.45, ending the final Blenheim operation from the United Kingdom over enemy territory.

What were the results obtained by the Blenheim intruder force on the bombing and strafing attacks of aerodromes in the Netherlands during the first half of 1942? It is certain that the Blenheim attacks, combined with those of Fighter Command Havocs, Bostons and Hurricanes, were a nuisance to the Germans. Until late 1941, their night fighter force operated virtually undisturbed from their bases in the battle against the British bomber offensive. With the onset of the British night intruder offensive, their peaceful existence was over. In this sense, the Blenheim crews and their Fighter Command counterparts were a nuisance to the *Luftwaffe*, and their intruder offensive a first indication of what was in store in the coming years.

Occasionally, the Blenheim intruder crews scored a substantial success, as on the nights of 25/26th and 29/30th April and 2/3rd July 1942. On the first night, Leeuwarden airfield was effectively out for the night by bomb hits on the intersection of the runways. On the other two nights, widespread damage was caused to night fighters, buildings and installations on aerodromes in the Netherlands. However, these successes must be categorised as incidents, as on the large majority of the intruder sorties no physical damage was done to the enemy, and the flying traffic went on undisturbed on their airfields. For example Venlo, a major night fighter base, largely responsible for the defence of the vital Ruhr industry, was raided by Blenheim intruders on 1/2nd and 21st February, on 8/9th and

Map 5. Main Targets for Blenheim Operations
over the Netherlands

10th March, on 2/3rd and 5/6th June 1942, with hardly any tangible results. As a side effect of one of these attacks *I./NJG 1* lost an aircraft and crew on 5/6th June, a shot-up Bf110 making a failed crash-landing on the field, as a Blenheim intruder dropped his bombs at that same time. As a result, the night fighter crew was killed. Normally, however, the German night fighters could take off and land unhindered by intruder attacks on Venlo airfield. *I./NJG 1* based at Venlo claimed no less than 48 British night bombers shot down in the first six months of 1942. Another German aerodrome that the Blenheim intruders regularly paid attention to was Leeuwarden. At this airfield it is the same story as on Venlo. Despite a few single archievements by the Blenheims, the crews of *II./NJG 2* operated almost scot-free. This particular unit shot down 159 British bombers between January and July 1942, the period of the Blenheim intruder offensive.

As has already been shown, the handful of Blenheims, Havocs, Bostons and Hurricanes available to give the Luftwaffe bomber and night fighter arms a hard time were simply insufficient in number and striking power for the task in hand. Only in the last year of the war, would the German night fighter arm be defeated by a combination of factors. One of these was a most effective night intruder campaign by the superior Mosquitoes of 100 Group and of the Second Tactical Air Force. In 1942 however, this was still far in the future.

Blenheim Is and IVs were still employed on Air Sea Rescue duties over the North Sea during the second half of 1942, mainly from Blenheim OTUs. The final development of the Bristol Blenheim, the heavier Mk.V Bisley soldiered on in North Africa, the Middle East, and in India. It was mainly used in the ground attack and anti-shipping rôles and in the war against *U-boats*, but losses again were high. Already obsolescent when production began in mid-1941, the Bisley was finally taken off operations in these theatres of war in September, 1943. Thus, the Blenheim's chequered wartime service had come to an end.

Appendix I

Blenheims lost during operations to and over the Netherlands, 1940-42:

Listed are the following items: date - aircraft type - serial number - squadron - take off time - base - mission - fate - crash place - crew details (rank, full name, air force, age, married or not, place of origin, details of burial place or Runnymede Panel).

Notes:

Rm. stands for Runnymede Memorial for the Missing of the RAF. The number of the Panel on which the individual aircrew are commemorated is mentioned after Rm.

The times of take off are British times, the times of German fighter and Flak claims are local, Continental times.

Bracketed numbers indicate crash-sites, to be found on the maps of Blenheims lost on operations to the Netherlands.

(1)   10.1.1940.   Blenheim IV P4859 VE- of 110 Squadron.
T/o 10.18 Wattisham for North Sea shipping recce, shot down by Bf110 of *Hptm* Wolfgang Falck (*St.Kpt. 2./ZG 76*, Jever) at 12.57 200 km N of Terschelling, exploded on impact.
Crew: **Sgt. John H. Hanne** (Pilot RAF), age 26, married, of Maida Vale, London. Rm. 15.
            Sgt. George L. Williams (Obs. RAF), age 23, of Ynsddu, Monmouthshire. Rm. 21.
            AC1 Edwin Vick (WOp/AG RAF), age 19, of Morecambe, Lancashire. Rm. 26.

(2)   10.1.1940.   Blenheim IV N6203 VE- of 110 Squadron
T/o 10.18 Wattisham for North Sea shipping recce, badly damaged by Bf110s of *2./ZG 76* (Jever) 200 km N of Terschelling. and crashed at 14.25 at Manby/Lincolnshire. A/c written off.
Crew: **P/O G.H. Pemberton** (Pilot RAF), safe.
            Sgt. Quarrington (Obs. RAF), safe.
            AC1 Roberts (WOp/AG RAF), safe.

(3)   10.1.1940.   Blenheim IV N6213 VE- of 110 Squadron
T/o 10.18 Wattisham for North Sea shipping recce, badly damaged by Bf110s of *2./ZG76* (Jever) 200 km N of Terschelling and written off after return to Wattisham.
Crew: **P/O P.V. Arderne** (Pilot RAF), safe.
            Sgt. Evans (Obs. RAF), safe.
            LAC J. Tippett (WOp/AG RAF), safe.

(4)   17.2.1940.   Blenheim IV N6211 VE- of 110 Squadron
T/o 12.31 Wattisham for recce Heligoland-Borkum area, shot down by
Bf110 of *Hptm* Wolfgang Falck (*St. Kpt. 2./ZG 76*, Jever) at 16.10 off
Dutch Frisians and crashed in flames.
Crew: **Sgt. Frederick J.R. Bigg** (Pilot RAF), age 27, Rm. 12.
          Sgt. William B. Woods (Obs. RAF), age 21, Rm. 21.
          AC1 Jack Orchard (WOp/AG RAF), age 20, Rm. 25.

(5)   14.4.1940.   Blenheim IV L9465 DX- of 57 Squadron
T/o Rosieres-en-Santerre for photo recce of Muenster-Hamm-Bielefeld area,
shot down at 16.00 by Bf109Es of *JG 20* and crashed near Babberich.
Remains recovered by Dutch Air Force in May 1973.
Crew: **F/O Horace G. Graham-Hogg** (Pilot RAF), age 27, buried Arnhem.
          Sgt. John R. Proctor (Obs. RAF), age 26, of Aberdeen.
          Buried Arnhem.
          AC1 James Shuttleworth (WOp/AG RAF), age 21, of Ilford, Essex.
          Buried Arnhem.

(6)   10.5.1940.   Blenheim IV L8776 BL-K of 40 Squadron
T/o 09.05 Wyton for recce Hook of Holland-Venlo-Hengelo, shot down by
light *Flak* and crash-landed N of Venlo near River Meuse.
Crew: **F/O R.M. Burns** (Pilot RAF), injured, PoW in *Stalag*
          Luft III Sagan.
          Sgt. James R. 'Jim' Brooker (Obs. RAF), injured, PoW in *Stalag*
          Luft 357 Kopernikus.
          Cpl G. Hurford (WOp/AG RAF), injured, PoW in *Stalag*
          Luft III Sagan.

(7)   10.5.1940.   Blenheim IV L8833 BL- of 40 Squadron
T/o 09.05 Wyton for recce Hook of Holland-Hengelo-Venlo, attacked by
Ju88 soon after crossing Dutch coast and landed at base with engine on
fire at 12.20. A/c burnt out & written off.
Crew: **S/L. B. Paddon** (Pilot RAF), safe.
          Sgt. J.A.D. Beattie (Obs. RAF), safe.
          P/O W.G. Edwards (WOp/AG RAF), safe.

(8)   10.5.1940.   Blenheim If L6616 BQ-R of 600 Squadron
T/o 10.30 Manston for Waalhaven A/F, shot down by Bf110 of *3./ZG 1*
over target and crashed at Pernis.
Crew: **S/L. James M. Wells** (Pilot RAF Aux. AF & C.O. 600 Sqn.), age
          31, of Felmersham, Bedfordshire. Buried Rotterdam.
          Sgt. John N. Davis (Obs.), evaded capture, returned to England.
          Cpl. Basil A. Kidd (WOp/AG RAF Aux. AF), age 30, of Dulwich
          Village, London. Buried Rotterdam.

(9)   10.5.1940.   Blenheim If L1515 BQ-L of 600 Squadron
T/o 10.30 Manston for Waalhaven A/F, shot down by Bf110 of *3./ZG 1*
over target and crashed at Hoogvlietse Visserij near Spijkenisse bridge.
Crew: **P/O Michael H. Anderson MiD** (Pilot RAF), age 23, married, of
          Kingston near Lewes, Sussex. Buried Spijkenisse.
          LAC Herbert C.W. Hawkins (WOp/AG RAF), buried Spijkenisse.

(10)   10.5.1940.   Blenheim If L1401 BQ-K of 600 Squadron
T/o 10.30 Manston for Waalhaven A/F, shot down by Bf110 of *3./ZG 1*
over target and crashed at Piershil.
Crew: **F/L. J. Hugh C. Rowe** (Pilot), injured, returned to England.
          P/O Robert W.H. Echlin (WOp/AG RAF VR), age 36, married,
          of Ottawa, Ontario, Canada. Buried Piershil.

(11)   10.5.1940.   Blenheim If L1514 BQ-N of 600 Squadron
T/o 10.30 Manston for Waalhaven A/F, shot up by Bf110 of *3./ZG 1* over
target and force landed in Grevelingen near Herkingen.
Crew: P/O **Robert C. Haine** (Pilot), returned to England on 13 May 1940.
          P/O **M. Kramer** (WOp/AG), returned to England on 13 May 1940.

(12)   10.5.1940.   Blenheim If L1335 BQ-W of 600 Squadron
T/o 10.30 Manston for Waalhaven A/F, shot down by Bf110 of *3./ZG 1*
over target and crashed at Waalhaven.
Crew: F/O **Charles R. Moore** (Pilot RAF Aux. AF), buried Rotterdam.
          Cpl **Laurence D. Isaacs** (WOp/AG RAF Aux. AF), age 20, of De
          Beauvoir Town, London. Buried Rotterdam.
*Note: These Blenheims of 600 Squadron were claimed by the following
pilots of I./ZG 1 (Kirchhellen/Germany): Lt Wolfgang Schenk (2 claims);
Lt Reinhold Knacke (1 claim); Fw Gildner (1 claim); Lt Werner Streib
(1 claim).*

(13)   10.5.1940.   Blenheim IV L8828 BL- of 40 Squadron
T/o 15.55 Wyton for Ypenburg A/F, shot down by fighter and crashed in
North Sea off Rotterdam.
Crew: P/O **Percival J.H. Rowan** (Pilot RAF), of New Zealand.
          Buried Rozenburg.
          Sgt. **George Beardwood** (Obs. RAF), age 27, of Blackburn,
          Lancashire. Buried 'S Gravenzande.
          Cpl. **Temple F.S. Clark** (WOp/AG RAF), age 21, of Wick,
          Caithnessshire. Buried Rockanje.

(14)   10.5.1940.   Blenheim IV L8831 BL- of 40 Squadron
T/o 15.55 Wyton for Ypenburg A/F, shot down by fighter near The Hague.
Crew: Sgt. **Ivor L. Thomas** (Pilot RAF), age 24, married, of Peterborough,
          Northamptonshire. Buried The Hague.
          Sgt. **Victor Spurr** (Obs. RAF), buried The Hague.
          LAC **Harold Bridson** (WOp/AG RAF), age 20, of Douglas, Isle of
          Man. Buried The Hague.

(15)   10.5.1940.   Blenheim IV P6901 BL- of 40 Squadron
T/o 16.00 Wyton for Ypenburg A/F, shot down by fighter and crashed near
Voorburg.
Crew: Sgt. **Alfred J. Robertson** (Pilot RAF), age 26, married, of Ruislip
          Manor, Middlesex. Buried Voorburg.
          Sgt. **Francis Checkley** (Obs. RAF), age 21, of Chesterfield.
          Buried Voorburg.
          AC1 **J.A. Webster** (WOp/AG RAF), injured, PoW in *Stalag
          Luft III Sagan.*

10.5.1940.   Blenheim IV L8827 BL- of 40 Squadron
T/o 15.55 Wyton for Ypenburg A/F, badly shot up by fighters in target area
but returned to base. A/c repaired.
Crew: F/L. **Hugh Smeddle** (Pilot RAF), seriously injured, awarded DFC.
          Sgt. **Wooldridge** (Obs. RAF), seriously injured, awarded DFM.
          LAC **G.D.P. Quinn** (WOp/AG RAF), seriously injured,
          awarded DFM.

(16) 10.5.1940.   Blenheim IV L8860 WV- of 18 Squadron
T/o 16.00 Meharicourt for recce of Meuse bridges in Venlo area, shot down
by Bf109E of *Oblt* Schafer (*5./JG 27*, Boenninghardt/Germany) and
crashed at Kessel near Venlo.
Crew: P/O **Leonard T. Dixon** (Pilot RAF), buried Nijmegen.
      Sgt. Thomas A. Peach (Obs. RAF), age 24, of Smethwick,
      Staffordshire. Buried Nijmegen.
      AC1 **John Townsley** (WOp/AG RAF), age 18, of Kelton,
      Dumfriesshire. Buried Nijmegen.

(17)   10.5.1940.   Blenheim If L1517 NG- of 604 Squadron
T/o 16.30 Northolt for Ju-52s on beach Scheveningen, hit by *Flak* over
target and crashed at 17.45 in dunes of Wassenaar. Crew set fire to
aircraft before making to The Hague.
Crew: F/O **I.K.S.Joll** (Pilot RAF), safe, returned to England
      on 13th May 1940.
      LAC **Jim Pickford** (WOp/AG RAF), safe, returned to England
      on 13th May 1940.

(18) 10.5.1940.   Blenheim IV L9245 DX- of 57 Squadron
T/o 15.30 Rosieres-en-Santerre for recce of Belgium, probably shot down by
Bf109E of *Lt* Emmerich Fluder (*5./JG 27*) and crashed into bridge at
Echteld in Betuwe.
Crew: P/O **Alban Thomas** (Pilot RAF), buried Hook of Holland.
      Sgt. Penry L. Thomas (Obs. RAF), age 27, married, of Boscombe
      East, Bournemouth, Hampshre. Buried Buurmalsen.
      AC1 **Leslie F. Jordan** (WOp/AG RAF), age 27, of Victoria, B.C.,
      Canada. Buried Hook of Holland.

(19)   10.5.1940.   Blenheim IV L9245 DX- of 57 Squadron
T/o 15.30 Rosieres-en-Santerre for recce 'S Hertogenbosch, damaged by
ground fire, wounding the pilot and WOp/AG. Returned to base, but
abandoned there when Sqn withdrew to Poix on 17 May.
Crew: F/L **G.M. Wyatt** (Pilot), injured.
      Sgt W.J. Gardiner (Obs.), safe.
      Cpl **F.T. Russell** (WOp/AG), injured.

(20)   10.5.1940.   Blenheim IVf N6193 LA- of 235 Squadron
T/o Bircham Newton for dusk shipping recce Texel-Borkum area, crashed
on return at base due to engine failure and burnt out.
Crew: P/O **Patterson** (Pilot RAF), safe.
      Lt **Ogilvie** (Obs. Royal Navy), safe.

(21)   11.5.1940.   Blenheim IV L1405 WV- of 18 Squadron
T/o 08.15 Meharicourt for photo-recce of Meuse-Venlo area, shot down and
crashed in Germany.
Crew: P/O **Geoffrey F. Harding** (Pilot RAF), age 21, of Branksome Park,
      Bournemouth, Hampshire. Buried Reichswald Forest.
      Sgt. Kenneth N. Shrosbree (Obs. RAF), age 25, of Ealing,
      Middlesex. Buried Reichswald Forest.
      LAC **Roland B.H. Townsend-Coles** MiD (WOp/AG RAF), age 30,
      married, of Streatham, London. PoW, died in captivity on 15 July
      1944, no known grave. Rm. 215.

(22)   11.5.1940.   Blenheim IV L9175 VE- of 110 Squadron
T/o 14.50 Wattisham for Maastricht bridges, shot down at 17.30 by
Bf109E of *Oblt* Gerhard Homuth (*I./JG 27*) at Ballaer/Belgium.
Crew: F/O **Gordon R. Grattan** (Pilot RAF), buried Kaggevinne.
      Sgt T. Patterson (Obs. RAF), PoW in *Stalag Luft 383* Hohenfels.
      LAC **Frederick J. Allam** DFM (WOp/AG RAF), age 20, of Ilford,
      Essex. Buried Kaggevinne.

(23)   11.5.1940.   Blenheim IV N6208 VE- of 110 Squadron
T/o 14.50 Wattisham for Maastricht bridges, crashed in flames near
Fouquieres-les-Bethune/France.
Sgt G.C. Bennett (Pilot RAF), injured.
Sgt Arthur Colling (Obs. RAF), age 20, of Darlington, Co.
    Durham. Buried Fouquieres/France.
AC2 E. Hannah (WOp/AG RAF), injured.

11.5.1940.   Blenheim IV P6886 YH- of 21 Squadron
T/o 15.10 Watton for Maastricht-Tongres road, damaged by machine gun
fire over target at 16.30, a/c repaired.
Crew: P/O MacDonald (Pilot), safe.
    Sgt Sidlon (Obs.), safe.
    AC1 Robert 'Paddy' Charleton (WOp/AG RAF), age 31, married, of
    Middleton-St. George, Co. Durham. Buried Belfast.

(24)   12.5.1940.   Blenheim IVf L9189 QY-O of 235 Squadron
T/o 05.00 Bircham Newton for cover evacuation Queen Wilhelmina, shot
down by Bf109Es of *II./JG 27* (Wesel West) and crashed at Oostvoorne.
Wreckage salvaged by Dutch Air Force in August 1967.
Crew: P/O Norman A. Savill (Pilot RAF), injured, of South Woodford, London.
    PoW in *Stalag Luft III* Sagan.
    Sgt Henry R. Sunderland (Obs. RAF VR), age 23, of Berkhamsted,
    Hertfordshire. Buried Oostvoorne.
    LAC Roy H. Tyler (WOp/AG RAF), age 19, of Leicester. Buried Oost-
    voorne.

(25)   12.5.1940.   Blenheim IVf L9324 QY-P of 235 Squadron
T/o 05.00 Bircham Newton for cover evacuation Queen
Wilhelmina, shot down by Bf109Es of *II./JG 27* (Wesel West)
and crashed near the Hook of Holland.
Crew: P/O Norman A.L. Smith B.Sc.,Hons (Pilot RAF), age 25, of
    Cambridge. Buried The Hague.
    Sgt John C. Robertson (Obs. RAF VR), age 20, of Perth. Buried
    Hook of Holland.
    LAC Thomas J. Lowry (U/T A/G RAF), age 17, of Chiswick,
    Middlesex. Buried Hook of Holland.
Note: These two Blenheims were claimed by five pilots of II./JG27: Lt Hermann Kugeler,
Lt Wilhelm Wiesinger, Fw Fritz Roeckel, Uffz Karl-Heinz Bendert and Uffz Arthur
Schlacht.

(26)   12.5.1940.   Blenheim IV L9416 XD-A of 139 Squadron
T/o 04.58 Plivot for Maastricht-Tongeren road, shot up by Bf109E of
2./JG 1 over target and belly-landed at Hoepertingen/Belgium.
Crew: F/O N.E.W. Pepper DFC (Pilot RAF), safe, evaded capture.
    Sgt. T.E. Hyde (Obs. RAF), safe, evaded capture.
    AC1 Hill (WOp/AG RAF), injured, PoW.

(27)   12.5.1940.   Blenheim IV N6215 XD- of 139 Squadron
T/o 04.58 Plivot for Maastricht-Tongeren road, shot down by Bf109E over
target and crashed near Lanaken/Belgium.
Crew: F/O Andrew McPherson DFC (Pilot RAF), age 22, of Glasgow. Buried
    Heverlee/Belgium.
    Sgt Francis W. Gregory (Obs. RAF), age 23, of Halberton, Devon. Buried
    Heverlee.
    LAC Hubert F. Over (WOp/AG RAF), age 19, of Belfast, Northern
    Ireland. Buried Heverlee.

(28)   12.5.1940.   Blenheim IV N6216 XD- of 139 Squadron

T/o 04.58 Plivot for Maastricht-Tongeren road, shot down by Bf109E over target and crashed at Rekem/Belgium on W bank of River Maas.

Crew: S/L **William I. Scott** (Pilot RAF), of Aberdeen. Buried Rekem.
Sgt **Thomas W. Davis** (Obs. RAF), age 22, of Cardiff. Rm. 13. Possibly buried Rekem as unidentified airman.
LAC **William A. McFadden** (WOp/AG RAF), buried Rekem.

(29)   12.5.1940.   Blenheim IV N6219 XD- of 139 Squadron

T/o 04.58 Plivot for Maastricht-Tongeren road, shot down by Bf109E over target.

Crew: F/O **G.E. Grey-Smith** (Pilot RAF), PoW.
Sgt **Phillip C. Gray** (Obs. RAF), Rm. 14.
Sgt **Cyril Taylor** (WOp/AG RAF), age 23, of Birmingham. Rm. 20.

(30) 12.5.1940.   Blenheim IV N6229 XD- of 139 Squadron

T/o 04.58 Plivot for Maastricht-Tongeren road, shot down by Bf109E over target.

Crew: Sgt **Tom C.R. Harrison** (Pilot RAF), age 25, married, of Shoreham-by-Sea, Sussex. Buried Heverlee/Belgium.
Sgt **Norman S.D. Jones** (Obs. RAF), buried Heverlee.
LAC **Harold T. Garbett** (WOp/AG RAF), age 24, of Caverswall, Staffordshire. Buried Heverlee.

(31)   12.5.1940.   Blenheim IV P4826 XD- of 139 Squadron

T/o 04.58 Plivot for Maastricht-Tongeren road, shot down by Bf109E over target and disappeared without trace. Possibly crashed near Neerwinden; three unidentified aircrew were buried there. Later reburied at Heverlee.

Crew: F/L **Andrew W. Lee** (Pilot RAF), of Kingston, Kent. Rm. 4.
Sgt **Joseph B. Keegan** (Obs. RAF), Rm. 16.
LAC **Charles C. Child** (WOp/AG RAF), age 20, of Stanford Bridge, Worcestershire. Rm. 22.

(32)   12.5.1940.   Blenheim IV P4923 XD- of 139 Squadron

T/o 04.58 Plivot for Maastricht-Tongeren road, shot down by Bf109E over target and crashed at Herstal/Belgium.

Crew: S/L **T.G. Tideman** (Pilot RAF), evaded capture, safe.
Sgt **Hale** (Obs. RAF), evaded capture, safe.
LAC **John Rooney** (WOp/AG RAF), age 20, of Newcastle on Tyne. Buried Herstal/Belgium.

(33)   12.5.1940.   Blenheim IV N6224/N6225 of 139 Squadron

T/o 04.58 Plivot for Maastricht-Tongeren road, badly shot up by Bf109Es over target and written off after return to base.

Crew: W/C **Louis W. Dickens AFC** (Pilot & CO 139 Sqn. RAF), safe, awarded DFC.
Sgt **Payne** (Obs. RAF), safe, awarded DFM.
AC1 **Crowley** (WOp/AG RAF), badly injured, probably PoW.

(34)   12.5.1940.   Blenheim IV L8733 OM- of 107 Squadron

T/o 08.10 Wattisham for Maastricht bridges, shot down by *Flak* in target area.

Crew: P/O **Stanley G. Thornton** (Pilot RAF), age 24, of North Sydney, N.S.W., Australia. Buried Heverlee/Belgium.
Sgt **Kenneth Mellership** (Obs. RAF), age 25, of Bridlington, Yorkshire. Buried Heverlee.
AC2 **John R. Mayor DFM** (WOp/AG RAF), age 28, of Burtonwood, Lancashire. Buried Heverlee.

(35)   12.5.1940.   Blenheim IV L8748 OM-K of 107 Squadron
T/o 08.10 Wattisham for Maastricht bridges, shot down by Bf109E on
return and crashed in Belgium.
Crew: F/O R.C. Rotherham DFC (Pilot RAF), safe, returned to England.
Sgt R. Brown (Obs. RAF), safe, returned to England.
LAC C.E. Coote (WOp/AG RAF), injured, PoW, in
Stalag 357 Kopernikus.

(36)   12.5.1940.   Blenheim IV P4905 OM- of 107 Squadron
T/o 08.10 Wattisham for Maastricht bridges, shot down by Bf109E on
return and crashed at Bettenhoven/Belgium.
Crew: F/O W.H. Edwards DFC (Pilot RAF), escaped capture,
returned to England.
Sgt V.G.L. Luter (Obs. RAF), PoW, in *Stalag 357* Kopernikus.
LAC William E. Palmer (WOp/AG RAF), buried Bettenhoven.

(37)   12.5.1940.   Blenheim IV P4914 OM- of 107 Squadron
T/o 08.10 Wattisham for Maastricht bridges, shot down by Bf109E on
return and crashed at Voroux-Goreux/Belgium.
Crew: P/O Osborne H. Keedwell (Pilot RAF), age 26, of Levin, Wellington, New
Zealand. Buried Voroux-Goreux.
Sgt Leonard J. Merritt (Obs. RAF), age 27, married. Buried Voroux-
Goreux.
AC2 Leslie A. Berridge (WOp/AG RAF), age 22, of Cranford,
Northamptonshire. Buried Voroux-Goreux.

(38)   12.5.1940.   Blenheim IV N6151 LS- of XV Squadron
T/o 07.50 Alconbury for Maastricht bridges, shot down by *Flak* around
09.15 in target area.
Crew: Sgt F.R. Pepper (Pilot RAF), PoW, in *Stalag 357* Kopernikus.
Sgt R. Booth (Obs. RAF), PoW, in *Stalag 357* Kopernikus.
LAC J. Scott (WOp/AG RAF), PoW, in *Stalag 357* Kopernikus.

(39)   12.5.1940.   Blenheim IV L8849 LS-S of XV Squadron
T/o 07.50 Alconbury for Maastricht bridges, shot down by *Flak* around
09.15 over target and crashed at Beverst.
Crew: F/O Peter N. Douglass (Pilot RAF), buried Heverlee/Belgium.
Sgt Wilfred O. Shortland (Obs. RAF), age 28, married, of Limbury,
Bedfordshire. Buried Heverlee/Belgium.
Sgt W.E.M. Davies (WOp/AG RAF), PoW, in *Stalag Luft III* Sagan.

(40)   12.5.1940.   Blenheim IV L8847 LS- of XV Squadron
T/o 07.50 Alconbury for Maastricht bridges, damaged by *Flak* at 09.16 over
target and crashed in flames at Borgharen.
Crew: F/O Thomas G. Bassett (Pilot RAF), age 22, of Te Kopuru, Auckland,
New Zealand. Buried Maastricht.
Sgt Neville C. Middlemass (Obs. RAF), age 26, of Sheffield.
Buried Maastricht.
LAC William T. Cavanagh (WOp/AG RAF), age 22, buried Maastricht.

(41)   12.5.1940.   Blenheim IV P6911 LS- of XV Squadron
T/o 07.50 Alconbury for Maastricht bridges, shot down by *Flak* around
09.15 in target area and crashed in woods at Munsterbilzen/Belgium.
Crew: F/O Albert E. 'Bertie' Oakley (Pilot RAF), age 25, of Sydney, N.S.W.,
Australia. Buried Munsterbilzen/Belgium.
Sgt Douglas J. Avent (Obs. RAF), buried Munsterbilzen.
LAC Denis V. Woods (WOp/AG RAF), age 19, of Normandy, Surrey.
Buried Munsterbilzen.

(42)   12.5.1940.   Blenheim IV P6912 LS- of XV Squadron
T/o 07.50 Alconbury for Maastricht bridges, shot down by *Flak* around
09.15 in target area, crashed in flames in Kattevennen near Genk/Belgium.
Crew: P/O **Claude R. Frankish** (Pilot RAF VR), age 25, married, of Wanganui,
Wellington, New Zeland. Buried Leopoldsburg/Belgium.
Sgt **Edwin G. Roberts** (Obs. RAF), age 26, married, of Christchurch,
Hampshire. Buried Leopoldsburg.
LAC **Ernest W.L. Cooper** (WOp/AG RAF), age 20, of Bedminster Down,
Bristol. Buried Leopoldsburg.

(43)   12.5.1940.   Blenheim IV P6914 LS- of XV Squadron
T/o 07.50 Alconbury for Maastricht bridges, shot down around 09.15 by
Flak over target, crashed in flames on bank of Albert Canal at Gellik/
Belgium.
Crew: Sgt **Hubert R. Hall** (Pilot RAF), age 27, married, of Trimly St. Martin,
Suffolk. Buried Hotton/Belgium.
Sgt **Edward R. Perrin** (Obs. RAF), age 23, of Woodford Green, Essex.
Buried Hotton.
LAC **Patrick J. McDonnell** (WOp/AG RAF), age 23, of Ash Vale, Surrey.
Buried Hotton.

(44)   12.5.1940.   Blenheim IV L8851 LS- of XV Squadron
T/o 07.50 Alconbury for Maastricht bridges, badly damaged by Flak and
fighters in target area, landed at Alconbury at 11.30. A/c written off.
Crew: F/L **P.F. Webster** (Pilot RAF), injured.
Sgt **R.A.M. Stone** (Obs. RAF), safe.
LAC **R.E. Hunter** (WOp/AG RAF), safe.
*Note: On 12 May 1940, the following Bf109E pilots claimed Blenheims shot down over
Maastricht: Oblt. Walter Adolph (I./JG 1) claimed three aircraft destroyed, Oblt. Gert
Framm (I./JG 27) and Lt. Graf Erbo Kageneck (I./JG 1) each claimed two Blenheims
shot down, Oblt. Erhard Braune (I./JG 1), Lt. Dr. Hans-Ludwig Oertel (I./JG 1), Fw.
Franz Blazytko (I./JG 1), Oblt. Gerhard Homuth (I./JG 27), Fw. Herman Richter (I./JG
1) and Lt. Borchert (I./JG27) each claimed one Blenheim destroyed.*

(45)   12.5.1940.   Blenheim IV L8861 of 18 Squadron
T/o 20.30 Meharicourt for recce Maastricht, crashed at Kanne, Belgium.
Crew: F/O **Charlie Bellis** (Pilot RAF), of Holt, Denbighshire. Buried Lange-
marck/Belgium.
Sgt **Horace D. Welch** (Obs. RAF), buried Langemarck.
LAC **Kenneth Parry** (WOp/AG RAF), age 20, of Llandudno,
Caernarvonshire.

(46)   12.5.1940.   Blenheim Mk.IVf P4834 of Special Duty Flt,
T/o Martlesham Heath, shot down a He111 30 miles off the Hook of Holland
at 10.45. Damaged by return fire and burned out on return to base at
11.00.
Crew: F/L **Christopher D.S. Smith** DFC (Pilot RAF), injured.
AC1 **A.W. Newton** (WOp/AG RAF), safe.

(47)   15.5.1940.   Blenheim IV L8856 LS-U of XV Squadron
T/o 09.58 Wyton for Dinant/France, hit by *Flak* over target & crash-landed
around 12.00 near St. Kruis (coast of Zeeuws-Vlaanderen) on way back,
due to port prop flying off.
Crew: P/O **D.S.R. Harriman** (Pilot), escaped capture, safe.
Sgt **J.R. Stanford** (Obs.), injured, remained in hospital in Belgium. PoW
in *Stalag Luft 357* Kopernikus.
LAC **Moorhouse** (WOp/AG), escaped capture, safe.

(48) 24.5.1940. Blenheim IVf L9259 QY- of 235 Squadron

T/o Bircham Newton for escort anti-shipping Hudsons, shot down at 08.30 by Bf109E of *Oblt.* Emmerich (*II.(J)/186*) off Schiermonnikoog.

Crew: P/O Michael E. 'Mick' Ryan (Pilot RAF), age 20, of Chattisham, Suffolk. Buried Schiermonnikoog.
Sgt William Martin (Obs. RAF VR), buried Schiermonnikoog.
LAC Albert G. Smith (WOp/AG RAF), Rm. 24.

(49) 26.5.1940. Blenheim IV R3613 TR- of 59 Squadron

Crashed at Dussen at Waasten/Belgium.

Crew: P/O Richard E. Shaw (Pilot RAF), age 22, married, of Danbury, Essex. Buried Nijmegen.
Sgt Gordon L. Schwind (Obs. RAF), age 21, of Crowborough, Sussex. Buried Waasten/Belgium.
AC2 Albert C. Brogan (WOp.Air), age 18, of Folkestone. Buried Waasten.

(50) 13.6.1940. Blenheim IV L8829 UX-P of 82 Squadron

T/o 15.04 Watton for Foret de Gault/France, crashed in North Sea.

Crew: Sgt Albert E. Merritt (Pilot RAF), age 22, of Camden Town, London. Buried Sage, Germany.
Sgt Neville W. Carlile (Obs. RAF), age 23, of Hunstanton, Norfolk. Buried Harlingen.
Sgt Leslie D. Nineham (WOp/AG RAF), of Woodford Green, Essex. Rm. 18.

(51) 23.6.1940. Blenheim IV R3688 OM- of 107 Squadron

T/o 13.35 Wattisham for Soest/Germany, shot down at 15.30 by Bf110 of *ZG 76*, crashed near Willemsoord.

Crew: P/O Stephen G. Esson (Pilot RAF), age 20, of Banchory, Kincardineshire. lightweight boxing champion RAF, 1938. Buried Willemsoord.
P/O James J. Tozer (Obs. RAF VR), age 20, of Finaghy, Co. Antrim, Northern Ireland. Buried Willemsoord.
Sgt George R. Murchison (WOp RAF VR), age 21, of Leith, Edinburgh. Buried Willemsoord.

(52) 23.6.1940. Blenheim IV N3593 OM- of 107 Squadron

T/o 16.50 Wattisham for Soest/Germany, shot down at 20.15 by Bf109E of probably *Lt.* Adolf Kinzinger (*2./JG 54*, Schiphol) and crashed near Sloten. *Lt.* Kinzinger was shot down by Sgt Adams during the fight.

Crew: F/L J.W.D. Stephens (Pilot RAF), PoW in *Stalag Luft III* Sagan.
Sgt William J. Barrett DFM (Obs. RAF), age 23, of Putney, London. Buried Amsterdam.
Sgt Peter E.F. Adams (WOp/AG RAF), age 23, found during recovery of wreck in 1951, buried Nijmegen.

(53) 23.6.1940. Blenheim IV L8754 VE- of 110 Squadron

T/o 17.50 Wattisham for Vohwinkel/Germany, shot down at 20.52 by Bf109E of *I./JG 54* (Schiphol) and crashed between Halfweg and Amsterdam.

Crew: P/O Thomas C. Prescott (Pilot RAF VR), age 27, of Harpenden, Hertfordshire. Buried Amsterdam.
Sgt Harold Kenyon (Obs. RAF), age 22, of South Shore, Blackpool, Lancashire. Buried Amsterdam.
Sgt Vincent J. Swallow (WOp/AG RAF), age 23, of Keenley, Northumberland. Buried Amsterdam.

(54) 26.6.1940. Blenheim IV R3776 VE- of 110 Squadron
T/o Wattisham for Soest/Germany, shot down at 10.10 by Bf109E of *Lt.*
Hans-Ekkehard Bob *(9./JG 54,* Soesterberg) and crashed in North Sea
near Rotterdam.
Crew: P/O Cyril R. Worboys (Pilot RAF), Rm. 10.
    Sgt Gerald P. Gainsford (Obs. RAF), Rm. 14.
    Sgt Kenneth Cooper (WOp/AG RAF), Rm. 13.

(55) 27.6.1940. Blenheim IVf P6958 QY-D of 235 Squadron
T/o 13.00 Bircham Newton for Zuyder Zee shipping recce, shot down at
15.00 by Bf109E of *I./JG 76* or *3./JG 21* (both Soesterberg) and crashed at
Ouderkerk aan de Amstel.
Crew: P/O Hugh S. Pardoe-Williams (Pilot RAF), age 23, of Exeter. Buried
    Amsterdam.
    Sgt Clifford W. Thorley (Obs. RAF VR), buried Amsterdam.
    P/O Edward A. Saunders (WOp/AG RAF VR), buried Amsterdam.

(56) 27.6.1940. Blenheim IVf L9447 QY-Y of 235 Squadron
T/o 12.55 Bircham Newton for Zuyder Zee shipping recce, shot down at
15.00 by Bf109E of *2./JG 76* or *3./JG 21* (both Soesterberg) and crashed at
Waverveen.
Crew: P/O John R. Cronan (Pilot RAF), age 21, of Birkenhead, Auckland, New
    Zealand. Buried Bergen-op-Zoom.
    Sgt Aubrey O. Lancaster (Obs. RAF), PoW in *Stalag Luft III* Sagan.
    Sgt Philip L. Lloyd (WOp/AG RAF), age 19, of Conway, Caernarvonshire,
    Wales. Buried Bergen-op-Zoom.

(57) 27.6.1940. Blenheim IVf N3543 QY-U of 235 Squadron
T/o 12.55 Bircham Newton for Zuyder Zee shipping recce, shot down by
Bf109E of *Lt.* Joachim Schypeck *(2./JG 76,* Soesterberg) at 15.30 and
crashed near Oegstgeest.
Crew: P/O Alan R. Wales (Pilot RAF), age 20, of City of London. Buried
    Oegstgeest.
    Sgt John W. Needham (Obs. RAF VR), age 25, of Kilburn, Middlesex.
    Buried Oegstgeest.
    Sgt Thomas C. Jordan (WOp/AG RAF), age 18, of Belfast, Northern
    Ireland. Buried Oegstgeest.

(58) 27.6.1940. Blenheim IVf P6957 QY-R of 235 Squadron
T/o 12.55 Bircham Newton for Zuyder Zee shipping recce, shot down at
15.30 by Bf109E of *2./JG 76* or *3./JG 21* (both Soesterberg) off Egmond.
Crew: P/O Peter Weil (Pilot RAF), age 20, of Burgh Heath, Tadworth, Surrey.
    Buried Becklingen/Germany.
    Sgt Sidney K. Bartlett (Obs. RAF VR), age 28, married, of Darlington,
    Co. Durham. Buried The Hague.
    Sgt Alan Kempster (WOp/AG RAF VR), of Bradford, Yorkshire. Buried
    Egmond, later re-buried Nijmegen.
Note: On 27th June 1940, the following German Pilots shot down these four Blenheims of
235 Squadron: Uffz. Wilhelm Schilling (3./JG 21); Ofw. Max Stotz (1./JG 76); Oblt.
Roloff von Aspern (Staff.Kap. 2./JG 76); Oblt. Franz Eckerle (3./JG 76); Lt. Joachim
Schypek (2./JG 76).

(59)   27.6.1940.   Blenheim IV R3731 UX-Y of 82 Squadron

T/o Watton for NW Germany, shot down at 16.20 by Bf109E of *Oblt.* Georg
Schneider (*St.Kpt. 9./JG 54*, Soesterberg) and crashed at Austerlitz/ Zeist.
During this dogfight, *Oblt.* Schneider was shot down by Sgt Clark and
killed.

Crew: **P/O Ralph A. Percy** (Pilot RAF), age 21, of Croydon, Surrey. Buried Zeist.
Sgt A.A. Stanley (Obs.), injured, PoW in *Stalag Luft 357* Kopernikus.
Sgt Andrew M. Clark (WOp/AG RAF VR), age 22, of Elgin, Morayshire.
Buried Zeist.

(60)   2.7.1940.   Blenheim IV P6895 UX-H of 82 Squadron

T/o 09.35 Watton for Dortmund-Ems Canal, shot down at 11.45 by two
Bf109Es of *I./JG 54* (Schiphol) and crashed in flames at Veenhuizen near
Heerhugowaard.

Crew: **S/L Hurll F. Chester** (Pilot RAF), of Falmouth, Cornwall. Buried
Veenhuizen.
Sgt Herbert Histon (Obs. RAF), age 29, married, of Barrowden, Rutland.
Buried Veenhuizen.
Sgt Robert J. McAllister (WOp/AG RAF), age 27, buried Veenhuizen.

(61)   4.7.1940.   Blenheim IV L8866 WV- of 18 Squadron

T/o 08.35 West Raynham for NW Germany, crashed in Brielse Maas near
Oostvoorne.

Crew: **F/L Ivor C.B. Worthington-Wilmer** (Pilot RAF), age 29, of Gerrans,
Cornwall. Buried Zwartewaal.
Sgt Jesse G. Stanley (Obs. RAF), age 24, of Shipston-on-Stour,
Warwickshire. Rm. 19.
Sgt George E. Maydon (WOp/AG RAF), age 22, of Hillingdon, Middlesex.
Buried Oostvoorne.

4.7.1940.   Blenheim IV R3769 LS- of XV Squadron

T/o 12.25 Wyton for Ruhr, damaged by Bf109Es before bombing secondary
target Schiphol A/F, landed at 15.35 Wyton, a/c repaired.

Crew: **P/O Lane-Sansom** (Pilot RAF), safe.
Sgt Abbott (Obs. RAF), safe.
Sgt Terence J. Maloney (WOp/AG RAF), age 18, buried Battersea,
Surrey.

(62)   12/13.7.1940.   Blenheim IV L9474 PZ-L of 53 Squadron

T/o 21.03 Detling for Leiden, abandoned above cloud on return while short
of fuel, a/c crashed at 02.45 near Upminster/Essex.

Crew: **W/C Edward C.T. Edwards** (Pilot RAF & C.O. 53 Sqn), safe.
Sgt Morriss (Obs.), safe.
Sgt Williams (WOp/AG), safe.

(63)   13.7.1940.   Blenheim IV R3701 UX- of 82 Squadron

T/o Watton for Amsterdam, shot down by Bf109E and crashed in North
Sea.

Crew: **F/L Peter H. Lewis** (Pilot RAF), age 26, of Weybridge, Surrey. Rm.4.
Sgt Horace W. 'Ginger' Richardson (Obs. RAF), age 19, of York. Buried
Schiermonnikoog.
Sgt James Newberry (WOp/AG RAF), age 20, of Markinch, Fife. Rm.17.

(64)   13.7.1940.   Blenheim IV R3756 UX-C of 82 Squadron

T/o Watton for Amsterdam, possibly shot down by fighters and crashed in
North Sea.

Crew: **Sgt D.A. Adams** (Pilot RAF), PoW at *Stalag Luft VI* Heydekrug.
Sgt A. Avery (Obs. RAF), PoW at *Stalag Luft 357* Kopernikus.
Sgt Arfon Evans (WOp/AG RAF), age 18, of Ton-yr-efail, Glamorgan.
Buried Hamburg.

248

(65) 16.7.1940. Blenheim IV P6933 WV- of 18 Squadron
T/o West Raynham for barges Flushing harbour, shot down at 07.30 by
Bf109Es of *II./JG 54* (Haamstede), crashed in Scheldt 10 km NW of
Flushing.
Crew: **Sgt Anthony St.J. Bunker** (Pilot RAF VR), age 20, of Barnes, Surrey.
Buried Heist-Sur-Mer/Belgium.
Sgt Peter R. Harris (Obs. RAF), buried Flushing.
Sgt John F. Hatch (WOp/AG RAF VR), age 25, of Watford, Herts. Buried
Flushing.

(66) 18.7.1940. Blenheim IV R3661 PZ-A of 53 Squadron
T/o Detling for recce Flushing harbour, shot down ca.14.00 by Bf109E of
6./JG 54 (Haamstede) & crashed in mouth of River Scheldt.
Crew: **F/O John E. Mahony** (Pilot RAF), Rm. 6.
Sgt Denys A. Keetley (Obs. RAF VR), age 22, of Southwell, Nottingham-
shire. Rm. 16.
Sgt George E. Exton (WOp/AG RAF), age 20, of Gosport, Hampshire.
Buried Klemskerke, later re-buried Adagem/Belgium.

(67) 20.7.1940. Blenheim IV R3738 VE- of 110 Squadron
T/o Wattisham for Flushing A/F, shot down at 13.45 by two German
fighters and crashed in North Sea between Voorne and Goeree. A/c
exploded on impact.
Crew: **S/L John F. Stephens** (Pilot RAF), Rm. 4.
Sgt E.C. Parker (Obs.), PoW in *Stalag Luft III* Sagan.
Sgt James V. West DFM (WOp/AG RAF), age 22, of Chasetown,
Staffordshire. Rm. 20.

(68) 23/24.7.1940. Blenheim IV R3748 VE- of 110 Squadron
T/o Wattisham for Bernburg A/F Germany, crashed in North Sea off
Burgh-Haamstede.
Crew: **Sgt Clifford C. Heyward** (Pilot RAF VR), age 27, married, of Chingford,
Essex. Rm. 15.
Sgt Leslie A.N. Walker (Obs. RAF VR), age 19, Rm. 20.
Sgt Israel Winberg (WOp/AG RAF VR), age 28, of Sunderland, Co.
Durham. Rm. 21.

(69) 24/25.7.1940. Blenheim IV R3836 PZ-X of 53 Squadron
T/o Detling for shipping patrol, crashed at 02.15 on the Koffieboon Plaat off
Ballum/Ameland.
Crew: **P/O David B. Starky** (Pilot RAF), age 20, of Opotiki, Auckland, New
Zealand. Rm. 10.
Sgt Harry W. Hunt (Obs. RAF), age 23, married, of Stoke Newington,
London. Buried Ballum/Ameland, later re-buried Nijmegen.
Sgt Bartholomew Moriarty (WOp/AG RAF), age 24, of Ballineen, Co.
York, Republic of Ireland. Rm. 17.

(70) 25/26.7.1940. Blenheim IV L9469 LS- of XV Squadron
T/o 23.30 Wyton for Eelde A/F, crashed on Boschplaat between Ameland
and Terschelling.
Crew: **P/O Charles H. Robinson** (Pilot RAF), age 21, of Wimbledon, Surrey.
Buried Nijmegen.
P/O Alexander L. McLaggan (Obs. RAF VR), age 20, of Glasgow. Rm. 9.
Sgt Leslie J. Horton (WOp/AG RAF), age 21, Rm. 15.

28.7.1940.   Blenheim IV T1828 UX- of 82 Squadron

T/o Watton for Leeuwarden A/F, shot up by Bf109Es of *II/JG27* (Leeuwarden) over target, belly-landed at base, a/c repaired to complete 54 sorties.

Crew: W/C **Lart** (Pilot & CO 82 Sqn.), injured.
        F/S **Robertson** (Obs.), injured.
        Sgt **Beeby** (WOp/AG), injured.

(71)   29.7.1940.   Blenheim IV R3619 UX- of 82 Squadron

T/o Watton for Bremen, shot up by Bf109E of *Lt.* Herbert Kargel (*II./JG27*, Leeuwarden) after attack on secondary target Leeuwarden A/F and crash-landed at 13.00 near Wittenhoek on Texel Island.

Crew: F/L **Bill Keighley** (Pilot RAF), PoW in *Stalag Luft III* Sagan.
        Sgt **J.W.H. Parsons** (Obs. RAF), PoW in *Stalag Luft 357* Kopernikus.
        Sgt **Keith D. MacPherson** (WOp/AG RAF), buried Den Burg/Texel.

(72)   30.7.1940.   Blenheim IV R3764 LS-U of XV Squadron

T/o 15.50 Wyton for Paderborn, abandoned op. due to lack of cloud cover. On approach of secondary target Flushing A/F shot down by an Bf109E of *II./JG 54* (Flushing) and crashed in flames into Scheldt near Breskens. Crew baled out.

Crew: P/O **P.F. 'Red' Eames** (Pilot), rescued by tug *Spitsbergen*, PoW in *Stalag Luft III* Sagan.
        P/O **Francis H. Jones** (Obs. RAF), age 32, married, pre-war RAF heavy-weight boxing champion. Drowned, buried Breskens.
        Sgt **Patrick Murphy** (WOp/AG RAF), age 22, of Newtown Forbes, Co. Longford, Republic of Ireland. Drowned, Rm. 17.

(73)   1.8.1940.   Blenheim IV R3898 RT- of 114 Squadron

T/o 14.15 Horsham St. Faith for Haamstede A/F, shot down at 15.50 by 3 Bf109Es of *4./JG 54* (Flushing) near target.

Crew: P/O **John D. Goode** (Pilot RAF), age 20, of Marston Morteyne Rectory, Bedfordshire. Severely injured, died at Zierikzee and buried Haamstede, later re-buried Bergen op Zoom.
        Sgt **Ernest A. Will** (Obs. RAF), buried Haamstede, later re-buried Bergen op Zoom.
        Sgt **Victor St.G. Barrow** (WOp/AG RAF), age 24, married, of Cranwell, Lincolnshire. Buried Haamstede, later re-buried Bergen op Zoom.

(74)   2.8.1940.   Blenheim IV L8780 VE- of 110 Squadron

T/o 06.40 Wattisham for Soesterberg A/F, damaged by *Flak* over target, crashed at Wattisham at 09.00. A/c written off.

Crew: Sgt **Hards** (Pilot), injured by *Flak*.
        Sgt **Cashman** (Obs.), safe.
        Sgt **Dunleavy** (WOp/AG), safe.

(75)   2.8.1940.   Blenheim IV L9422 WV- of 18 Squadron

T/o 09.35 Horsham St. Faith for Haamstede A/F, shot down at 12.00 by 3 Bf109Es of *4./JG 54* (Flushing) in target area and exploded on impact.

Crew: Sgt **John H. Davies** (Pilot RAF VR), age 24, married. Buried Bergen op Zoom.
        Sgt **Kenneth R. Bryant** (Obs. RAF VR), age 21, of Hayes Bromley, Kent. Buried Bergen op Zoom.
        Sgt **Warren S. Barrett** (WOp/AG RAF VR), age 20, of Burgh Castle, Suffolk. Buried Bergen op Zoom.

(76)   3/4.8.1940.   Blenheim IV L9475 PZ-V of 53 Squadron
T/o 19.48 Detling for Emden harbour, crashed at 01.05 in North Sea off
Norfolk coast.
Crew: F/O **Hugh C. Corbett** (Pilot RAF VR), age 22. Buried Schoorl.
   Sgt **S.E. Riddington** (Obs.), buried U.K.
   Sgt **Kenneth W. Crane** (WOp/AG RAF), age 22, of York. Rm. 13.

(77)   8.8.1940.   Blenheim IV L9472 WV-T of 18 Squadron
T/o 16.00 West Raynham for Schiphol and Valkenburg A/Fs, shot down by
Flak into North Sea.
Crew: Sgt **Jack H. Saville** (Pilot RAF VR), age 23, of Coventry. Rm. 19.
   Sgt **Frederick F. Parvin** (Obs. RAF), of Barton, Richmond, Yorkshire.
   Buried Zandvoort, later re-buried Bergen op Zoom.
   Sgt **Victor R.T. Land** (WOp/AG RAF VR), age 20, of Isleworth, Middlesex.
   Rm. 16.

(78)   19.8.1940.   Blenheim IV R3892 RT- of 114 Squadron
T/o 06.10 Oulton for Bremen oil refinery, shot down at 07.55 by Bf109E of
Uffz. Richard Woick (*7./JG 54*, Bergen), crashed in flames in Midden-
beemster.
Crew: Sgt **Kenneth H. Dobb** (Pilot RAF VR), age 19, of Ruislip, Middlesex.
   Rm. 13.
   Sgt **Anthony Stevenson** (Obs. RAF), age 25, PoW in *Stalag Luft III*
   Sagan.
   Sgt **Alexander M. Pillam** (WOp/AG RAF VR), age 18, Rm. 18.
   Note: Sgts. Dobb and Pillam have a field grave at the place of impact.

(79)   19/20.8.1940.   Blenheim IV L9419 SR- of 101 Squadron
T/o West Raynham for Eindhoven A/F, crashplace unknown.
Crew: Sgt **A.G. Chelmick** (Pilot RAF), PoW in *Stalag Luft 357* Kopernikus.
   Sgt **N.H. Martyn** (Obs. RAF), PoW in *Stalag Luft VI* Heydekrug.
   Sgt **J. Carbine** (WOp/AG), PoW.

(80)   19/20.8.1940.   Blenheim IV N3574 SR- of 101 Squadron
T/o 22.05 West Raynham for Antwerp, attacked Haamstede A/F instead
due to engine trouble. Forced to ditch on return at 00.20 off Lowestoft
alongside British destroyer as engines stopped. Seas rough and WOp/AG
injured. Pilot & Obs. tried to rescue WOp/AG before aircraft sunk - failed.
Crew: P/O **N.H. Bicknell** (Pilot), safe, awarded DFC.
   Sgt **Gingell** (Obs.), safe, awarded DFM.
   Sgt **John H. George** (WOp/AG RAF), age 21, of Claines, Worcestershire.
   Rm. 14.

(81)   24/25.8.1940.   Blenheim IV T2035 PZ-F of 53 Squadron
T/o Detling for *HOOKOS* patrol, hit two houses near Dover on return and
crashed.
Crew: F/O **Stephen C. Rochford** (Pilot RAF), age 24, of Little Berkhampstead.
   Buried Hertford.
   Sgt **William Briggs** (Obs. RAF VR), age 21 of Coventry. Buried Coventry.
   Sgt **Dennis Brook** (WOp/AG RAF), of Anlaby Common. Buried Haltem-
   price.

(82)   28.8.1940.   Blenheim IV T2046 PZ-J of 53 Squadron
T/o 20.54 Detling for *HOOKOS* patrol and Schellingwoude seaplane base,
crashed North Sea.
Crew: P/O **William E. Fitzpatrick** (Pilot RAF VR), of Brentry, Gloucestershire.
   Rm. 8.
   Sgt **Jack Bann** (Obs. RAF), age 22, of Macclesfield, Cheshire. Rm. 11.
   Sgt **Harry Dunnington** (WOp/AG RAF), Rm. 13.

(83)   29/30.8.1940.   Blenheim IV N3620 OM- of 107 Squadron

T/o 00.25 Wattisham for De Kooy A/F, shot down by *Flak II./Regiment 22*
(De Kooy) at 04.25 and crashed in flames in IJsselmeer NE of target.

Crew: F/O **Ernest R. Berry** (Pilot RAF), age 23, of Umberleigh, Devon. Buried
Huisduinen, later re-buried Bergen op Zoom.

Sgt **Alfred P. Sully** (Obs. RAF), age 20, of Otley, Yorkshire. Buried
Huisduinen, re-buried Bergen op Zoom.

Sgt **Henry Bentham** (WOp/AG RAF), age 18, of Hindsford, Lancashire.
Buried Huisduinen, re-buried Bergen op Zoom.

(84) 31.8./1.9.1940.   Blenheim IV T1940 PZ-D of 53 Squadron

T/o Detling for Pernis/Rotterdam oil refinery, shot down at 21.10 by *Flak
Gruppe 261* over target and crashed in flames at Welplaat.

Crew: W/C **Edward C.T. 'Sphinx' Edwards M.A.** (Oxon) (Pilot RAF & C.O. 53
Sqn.), age 35, of Kensington, London. Buried Rotterdam.

Sgt **Lionel L. Benjamin** (Obs. RAF VR), age 22, married, of Wembley,
Middlesex. Buried Rotterdam.

Sgt **John T. Beesley** (WOp/AG RAF), age 19, of Perivale, Greenford,
Middlesex. Buried Rotterdam.

(85)   2/3.9.1940.   Blenheim IV L8757 BL-T of 40 Squadron

T/o Wyton for Schlebusch/Germany, crashed in Waddenzee near Texel at
01.38.

Crew: F/S **Rodolphe B. 'Chiefy' Broadhurst** (Pilot RAF), buried Den Burg/
Texel.

Sgt **Arthur Marsden** (Obs. RAF VR), age 19, of Hull. Rm. 17.

Sgt **Angus J. 'Jock' Burns** (WOp/AG RAF), age 31, married. Rm. 12.

(86)   8.9.1940.   Blenheim IV R3915 UX- of 82 Squadron

T/o 12.00 Watton for recce Dutch and Belgian coasts, crashed in North Sea
off Dutch coast.

Crew: F/O **Alexander W.L. Cobbe** (Pilot RAF VR), age 21, of Wittersham, Kent.
Son of General Sir Alexander Cobbe, V.C., GCB, KCSI, DSO. Rm. 5.

P/O **Henry M. Christopher** (Obs. RAF VR), age 30, married, of Ilford,
Essex. Rm. 7.

Sgt **William H. Cassels MiD** (WOp/AG RAF), age 23, of Portswood,
Hampshire. Rm. 12.

(87)   8.9.1940.   Blenheim IV R3730 UX-U of 82 Squadron

T/o 12.00 Watton for recce Dutch and Belgian coasts, crashed in North Sea
off Dutch coast.

Crew: P/O **James M. McCausland** (Pilot RAF VR), Rm. 9.

Sgt **John B. Philpott** (Obs. RNZAF), age 30, Rm. 28.

Sgt **Ronald S. Fletcher** (WOp/AG RAF VR), Rm. 14.

(88)   8.9.1940.   Blenheim IV L8848 HA-J of 218 Squadron

T/o 15.55 Oakington for recce Dutch coast, crashed in North Sea.

Crew: Sgt **Gerald L. Clayton** (Pilot RAF VR), age 23, of Fermoy, Co. Cork,
Republic of Ireland. Rm. 12.

Sgt **Frederick C. Coish** (Obs. RAF), age 23, of Wembley, Middlesex. Rm.
12.

Sgt **Gordon Taylor** (WOp/AG RAF VR), age 20, of Barry Island,
Glamorgan. Buried Bergen-op-Zoom.

(89) 9.9.1940.   Blenheim IV T1894 GB- of 105 Squadron
T/o Watton for Dutch ports invasion barges, shot down in flames by Bf109E
of *Lt.* Waldemar Wübke (*9./JG 54*, Bergen) 15 km W Den Helder.
Crew: **Sgt Dennis D.R. Hodson** (Pilot RAF), age 24, of Reading, Berkshire.
        Rm. 15.
        Sgt Edward B. Palmer (Obs. RAF VR, of N. Ireland), age 27, married, of
        Armagh, Northern Ireland. Rm. 18.
        Sgt Rendle Green (WOp/AG RAF VR), age 21, of Oldham, Lancashire.
        Rm. 14.

(90) 30.9./1.10.1940.   Blenheim IV T2044 PZ-G of 53 Squadron
T/o Detling for Rotterdam harbour, crashed in North Sea off English coast.
Crew: **P/O Spencer R. Bevan-John** (Pilot RAF VR), age 19. Scholar of Oxford,
        of Pembrey. Buried Pembrey/Wales.
        Sgt Stanley Macquire (Obs. RAF VR), age 21, of Northampton. Buried
        Northampton.
        Sgt Harold A. Shaw (AG RAF), age 31, of Compton, Plymouth. Rm. 19.

(91) 5.10.1940.   Blenheim IV R2771 PZ-A of 53 Squadron
T/o Detling for *HOOKOS* patrol, crashed in flames near Manston returning
from a shipping strike.
Crew: **P/O K.A. Faulkner** (Pilot), seriously injured.
        Sgt Albert R.S. Hall (Obs. RAF VR), age 30, married, of Goodmayes.
        Buried Brentwood.
        Sgt G.B. Fielder (WOp/AG RAF VR), seriously injured.

27.10.1940.   Blenheim IV T2132 PZ-R of 53 Squadron
T/o Detling for shipping in Den Helder harbour, badly damaged by 3
Bf109Es of *9./JG 54* (De Kooy) in target area, landed at Martlesham. A/c
repaired.
Crew: **P/O Eric Plumtree** (Pilot), injured, awarded DFC.
        Sgt Wood (Obs.), injured.
        Sgt P.M. Kinsey (WOp/AG), injured, awarded DFM.

(92) 3.11.1940.   Blenheim IV L9392 of 248 Squadron
T/o Dyce, shot down by Bf109E of *JG 54* off Katwijk.
Crew: **P/O Anthony H.H. Garrad** (Pilot RAF), age 19, Rm. 8.
        Sgt Ernest J. Bayliss (Obs. RAF), age 21, Rm. 11.
        Sgt Harold F.J. Moynham (WOp/AG RAF), age 21, Rm. 17.

(93) 7.11.1940.   Blenheim IV T1871 XD- of 139 Squadron
T/o Horsham St. Faith for NW Germany, shot down by Bf109E of *Lt.*
Waldemar Wübke (*9./JG 54*, De Kooy) in North Sea off Den Helder.
Crew: **S/L John A.F. Mertens** (Pilot RAF), age 29, of Hammersmith, London.
        Rm. 4.
        Sgt Reginald W. Spiller (Obs. RAF), age 23, of Abercynon, Glamorgan.
        Rm. 19.
        Sgt Allan R. Merry (WOp/AG RAF VR), age 19, of Derby. Rm. 17.

(94) 10.11.1940.   Blenheim IV R3753 RT- of 114 Squadron
T/o 10.20 Oulton for Roving Commission to Dortmund, shot down by
Bf109E of *Uffz.* Eugen-Ludwig Zweigart (*9./JG 54*, De Kooy) in North Sea
W of De Kooy.
Crew: **F/O Eric H. Dawson DFC** (Pilot RAF), of Epping, Victoria, Australia.
        Rm. 5.
        Sgt John R.G. Lamb DFM (Obs. RAF), age 21, of Sharptone, Sussex.
        Rm. 16.
        Sgt William White DFM (WOp/AG RAF), age 20, of Sheffield. Rm. 20.

(95)   29/30.11.1940. Blenheim IV R2796 YH- of 21 Squadron
T/o 20.30 Bodney for A/Fs, crashed in North Sea.
Crew: **Sgt William R. Starns** (Pilot RAF VR), age 26, married, of Cambridge.
Rm. 19.
Sgt Raymond B. Stilwell (Obs. RAF VR), age 21, of Hull. Rm. 19.
Sgt George G. Moffat (WOp/AG RAF VR), age 20, of Glasgow. Rm. 17.

(96)   3/4.12.1940.   Blenheim IV N3594 UX-F of 82 Squadron
T/o Bodney for Krupps at Essen, force-landed intact at Hulsen near
Hellendoorn.
Crew: **Sgt W.H.M. Butcher** (Pilot RAF), PoW in *Stalag Luft 357* Kopernikus.
Sgt W.J.P. Sheppard (Obs. RAF), PoW in *Stalag Luft 357*.
Sgt J. Ferguson (WOp/AG RAF), PoW in *Stalag Luft 357*.

(97)   7.12.1940.   Blenheim IV T2395 PZ-N of 53 Squadron
T/o Thorney Island for *HOOKOS* patrol, crashed at Deal (U.K.) returning
to Manston.
Crew: **P/O Alfred K. Steel** (Pilot RAF), buried Sunderland.
Sgt William R. Hemsley (Obs. RAF VR), age 24, married, of Normanton,
Derby. Buried Derby.
Sgt D. Robson (WOp/AG RAF VR), seriously injured.

(98)   27/28.12.1940. Blenheim IV T2223 YH-T of 21 Squadron
T/o Bodney for Gilze-Rijen A/F, shot down by light *Flak* at Gilze-Rijen at
19.30, crashed near target.
Crew: **S/L M.L.C. McColm** (Pilot RAF), PoW in Colditz.
Sgt Cecil J. Hann (Obs. RAF), age 22, of Lytchett Matravers, Dorsetshire.
Buried Breda, later re-buried Bergen-op-Zoom.
Sgt David G. Shepherd (WOp/AG RAF), age 19, of Forfar, Angus. Buried
Breda, re-buried Bergen-op-Zoom.

(99)   31.12.1940.   Blenheim IV R3897 RT- of 114 Squadron
T/o 11.54 Oulton for Gilze-Rijen A/F, shot down by light *Flak* at Gilze Rijen
at 14.20, exploded on impact at De Moer near target.
Crew: **Sgt Leslie A. Young** (Pilot RAF VR), age 25, of Derby. Buried Breda, later
re-buried Bergen op Zoom.
Sgt John E. Brown (Obs. RAF VR), age 21, of Balsall Heath, Birming-
ham. Buried Breda, re-buried Bergen op Zoom.
Sgt Jack Coates (WOp/AG RAF), age 19, of Rossendale, Lancashire.
Buried Breda, re-buried Bergen op Zoom.

(100) 6.1.1941.   Blenheim IV V5375 UX- of 82 Squadron
T/o 15.06 Bodney for Rotterdam, crashed due to engine failure into
anti-glider obstructions at 18.25 at Strumpshaw/Norfolk on return. A/c
written off.
Crew: **Sgt Jackman** (Pilot), injured.
Sgt Thomas H. Cooke (Obs. RAF VR), age 22, of Windsor, injured.
Sgt Perry (WOp/AG), safe.

(101) 11.1.1941.   Blenheim IV T2163 UX- of 82 Squadron
T/o 14.50 Bodney for Amsterdam, crashed in North Sea.
Crew: **P/O Alfred H. Poulsen** (Pilot RAF), age 24, of Horsmonden, Kent. Rm. 34.
Sgt James Burton (Obs. RAF VR), age 30, of Edinburgh. Rm. 40.
Sgt Harold Summers (WOp/AG RAF VR), age 20, Rm. 53.

(102) 13.1.1941.   Blenheim IV T1858 RT- of 114 Squadron
T/o 08.55 Oulton for weather recce of Nordhorn airfield, shot down by
Bf109E of *Fw.* Rudolf Mickel (*1./JG 1*, Bergen) at 10.55 in North Sea 20
km NW of Bergen aan Zee.
Crew: **P/O David Lowther-Clarke** (Pilot RAF), age 28, married, of Newmarket,
      Suffolk. Rm. 33.
      Sgt Alfred R. Grindley (Obs. RAF VR), Rm. 44.
      Sgt Norman O. Allen (WOp/AG RAF VR), age 19, of Headington,
      Oxfordshire. Rm. 38.

(103) 10.2.1941.   Blenheim IV T2282 YH- of 21 Squadron
T/o 22.05 Watton for Hannover, shot down by *Flak* at Flushing at 22.03
and crashed in flames in Scheldt W of Valkenisse.
Crew: **F/L R.J. McConnell** (Pilot RAF), PoW in *Stalag Luft III* Sagan.
      Sgt E.W. Green (Obs. RAF), PoW in *Stalag Luft 357* Kopernikus.
      Sgt D.E. Bristow (WOp/AG RAF), PoW in *Stalag Luft 357*.

(104) 15.2.1941.   Blenheim IV T2125 RT- of 114 Squadron
T/o 08.35 Oulton for Flushing harbour, shot down by Bf109E of *Oblt.*
Karl-Heinz Leesmann (*3./JG 52*, Katwijk) at 10.36, crashed at Oostka-
pelle.
Crew: **Sgt Thomas E. Barnes AFM** (Pilot RAF), age 29, married, of Yaxley,
      Huntingdonshire. Buried Flushing.
      Sgt Harold S. Seward (Obs. RAF VR), age 20, of Bath, Somerset. Buried
      Flushing.
      Sgt Louis S. Walsh (WOp/AG RAF VR), age 20, of Middleton, Manchester.
      Buried Flushing.

(105) 17.2.1941.   Blenheim IV Z5902 RT- of 114 Squadron
T/o 09.35 Oulton for weather recce Den Helder area, shot down by *Flak* in
North Sea.
Crew: **F/L Michael J.C. Marks DFC** (Pilot RAF VR), age 24, scholar of Eton and
      of Christ Church, Oxford. Of Kilburn, London. Rm.29.
      Sgt Horace Teeton (Obs. RAF VR), age 28, married, of Prestatyn,
      Flintshire. Rm. 53.
      Sgt Irvine H. Adkins (WOp/AG RAF VR), age 20, of Ilford, Essex. Rm. 38.

(106) 28.2.1941.   Blenheim IV T1799 XD- of 139 Squadron
T/o 17.58 Horsham St. Faith for Flushing docks, bogged down on grass
runway on return at base, run into by L9402 at 20.32.
Crew: **Sgt Vivian** (Pilot), badly wounded.
      Sgt Archibald R. Severn (Obs. RAF VR), age 25, of Sherwood. Died of
      injuries, cremated at West Bridgford, Nottinghamshire.
      Sgt Handley (WOp/AG), slightly injured.

(107) 28.2.1941.   Blenheim IV L9402 XD- of 139 Squadron
T/o 18.06 Horsham St. Faith for Den Helder, collided at 20.32 with T1799
on return at base. A/c burnt out.
Crew: **Sgt Robert Bennett** (Pilot RAF VR), of Heaton, Newcastle-on-Tyne,
      slightly injured.
      Sgt Mills (Obs.), badly injured.
      Sgt Ernest W. Laban (WOp/AG RAF VR), age 23, of Derby, safe.

(108) 28.2./1.3.1941. Blenheim IV T1895 GB- of 105 Squadron
T/o 23.25 Swanton Morley for Wilhelmshaven, shot down by Bf110 of *Ofw.*
Paul Gildner (*4./NJG 1*, Leeuwarden) at 02.58, exploded in mid-air and
crashed at Oosterhogebrug.
Crew: **Sgt John S.H. Heape** (Pilot RAF VR), age 27, PoW, in *Stalag Luft 357*
Kopernikus.
   Sgt Sylvester Jones (Obs. RAF VR), age 26, of Manchester. Buried
Groningen.
   Sgt John Bimson (WOp/AG RAF VR), age 32, buried Groningen.

(109) 2/3.3.1941.   Blenheim IV Z5901 YH- of 21 Squadron
T/o 20.40 Watton for Rotterdam, crashed in North Sea.
Crew: **Sgt Allen Warcup** (Pilot RAF VR), age 20, of Hull. Rm. 54.
   Sgt Andrew B. Ferguson (Obs. RAF VR), age 20, Rm. 43.
   Sgt Thomas S. Courtman (WOp/AG RAF), age 21, of Thornaby-on-Tees,
Yorkshire. Rm. 41.

(110) 13/14.3.1941.   Blenheim IV R2278 VE- of 110 Squadron
T/o 20.27 Wattisham for Hamburg, shot down by Bf110 of *Ofw.* Paul
Gildner (*4./NJG 1*, Leeuwarden) at 22.48 and crashed at Tolbert.
Crew: **F/L John Dickinson DFC** (Pilot RAF VR), buried Groningen.
   Sgt Charles W. Fry (Obs. RAF VR), age 29, married, of Whipton, Exeter.
Buried Groningen.
   Sgt Robert Mower (WOp/AG RAF VR), buried Groningen.

(111) 18/19.3.1941.   Blenheim IV R3846 SR- of 101 Squadron
T/o 19.35 West Raynham for Wilhelmshaven, possibly shot down in flames
over Texel and crashed in North Sea.
Crew: **P/O Charles R. Brown DFC** (Pilot RAF VR), age 28, married, of Long
Ashton, Somerset. Buried Sage, Germany.
   P/O Gordon Collis DFM (Obs. RAF VR), age 21, of Norbriggs, Derbysh-
ire. Rm. 31.
   Sgt Godric Loughlin DFM (WOp/AG RAF), Rm. 47.

(112) 20.3.1941.   Blenheim IV R3604 UX- of 82 Squadron
T/o 11.09 Bodney for shipping sweep to *Beat A*, shot down by *Flak* from
Minesweeper *No.64* off Den Helder.
Crew: **Sgt John H. Kelly** (Pilot RAF VR), age 25, of Kendal, Westmorland.
Buried Huisduinen, later re-buried Bergen-op-Zoom.
   Sgt Graham R. Wilson (Obs. RNZAF), age 20, of Wellington City, New
Zealand. Buried Huisduinen, re-buried Bergen-op-Zoom.
   Sgt Singleton W. Adair (WOp/AG RAF VR), age 23, of Fortwilliam,
Belfast. Rm. 38.

(113) 22.3.1941.   Blenheim IV T2433 of 59 Squadron
T/o Thorney Island for shipping patrol, shot down at 07.42 by Bf109E of
Oblt. Paul Stolte (*St.Kpt. 3./JG 1*, De Kooy) off Katwijk.
Crew: **P/O David W. Date** (Pilot RAF VR), age 26, of Old Basing, Hampshire.
Rm. 32.
   P/O Eric P. Moore (Obs. RAF VR), Rm. 33.
   Sgt Basil J.O. Watkins (WOp/AG RAF), age 21, of Aldershot, Hampshire.
Rm. 54.

(114) 23.3.1941.   Blenheim IVf L9404 QY-A of 235 Squadron
T/o 15.40 Bircham Newton for *Pirate* Patrol, shot down at 18.52 by Bf109E
of *Uffz.* Hans Schubert (*3./JG 1*, De Kooy) after attack on convoy off Hook
of Holland.
Crew: **Sgt Cecil R. Evans** (Pilot RAF VR), age 20, of Kingston-on-Thames.
Rm. 43.
Sgt Eric H. Harvey (Obs. RAF VR), age 23, of Melling, Liverpool. Rm. 44.
Sgt George S.M. MacLeod (WOp/AG RAF), age 18, of Dornoch,
Sutherlandshire. Rm. 47.

(115) 23.3.1941.   Blenheim IVf Z6085 QY-D of 235 Squadron
T/o 15.40 Bircham Newton for *Pirate* Patrol, shot down with port engine on
fire at 18.52 by Bf109E of *Oblt.* Paul Stolte (*St.Kpt. 3./JG 1*, De Kooy)
after attack on convoy off Hook of Holland.
Crew: **P/O Anthony W.B. Newman** (Pilot RAF VR), Rm. 33.
Sgt Harry Willis (Obs. RAF VR), age 20, of Filey, Yorkshire. Rm. 55.
Sgt Victor S. Key (WOp/AG RAF VR), age 20, married, of Littleport,
Cambridgeshire. Rm. 46.

(116) 24.3.1941.   Blenheim IV L9389 UX- of 82 Squadron
T/o 14.10 Bodney for shipping sweep to *Beat A*, shot down by *Flak* from
target destroyer in Marsdiep, S of Texel.
Crew: **F/L Hugh J.W. Black DFC** (Pilot RAF), age 20, of Edinburgh. Buried
Huisduinen, re-buried Bergen op Zoom.
Sgt Thomas H. Cooke (Obs. RAF VR), age 22, of Windsor. Rm. 41.
Sgt Frank Archer DFM (WOp/AG RAF VR), age 21, of West Hartlepool,
Co. Durham. Rm. 38.

27.3.1941.   Blenheim IV L9386 XD- of 139 Squadron
T/o 10.11 Horsham St. Faith for shipping sweep to *Beat B*, badly shot up
during attack on convoy of warships off Hook of Holland, a/c repaired.
Crew: **P/O Eric Sydney-Smith** (Pilot RAF), age 28, safe.
Sgt Ryan (Obs.), injured.
Sgt Fox (WOp/AG), safe.

(117) 31.3.1941.   Blenheim IV R3884 YH- of 21 Squadron
T/o 11.15 Watton for shipping and fringe targets sweep to *Beat 9*, shot
down at 14.00 by *Vorpostenboot Flak* off Texel.
Crew: **Sgt Peter A. Adams** (Pilot RAF VR), age 20, of Welwyn Garden City,
Hertfordshire. Rm. 38.
Sgt Thomas R. Alston (Obs. RAF VR), Rm. 38.
Sgt Ralph E. Nichols (WOp/AG RAF VR), Rm. 49.

(118) 31.3.1941.   Blenheim IV R3900 YH- of 21 Squadron
T/o 11.20 Watton for shipping and fringe targets sweep to Beat 9, shot
down at 14.00 by *Vorpostenboot Flak* off Texel.
Crew: **P/O Dennis A. Rogers** (Pilot RAF VR), age 20, of Chopwell, Co. Durham.
Rm. 34.
P/O William L. Gourlay (Obs. RAF VR), age 35, of Edinburgh. Rm. 32.
Sgt George H. Howard (WOp/AG RAF VR), age 26, of Headington,
Oxfordshire. Rm. 45.

(119) 2.4.1941.   Blenheim IV Z5818 UX-P of 82 Squadron
T/o 14.20 Bodney for shipping sweep to *Beat E*, shot down by *Flak* during
attack on convoy W of Flushing.
Crew: **Sgt William C. Haynes** (Pilot RAF VR), age 22, of Birmingham. Rm. 44.
P/O Alan A. Ford (Obs. RAF), age 23, of Caversham, Oxfordshire. Rm. 32.
Sgt Albert Lee (WOp/AG RAF VR), Rm. 47.

2.4.1941. Blenheim IV T2118 UX-J of 82 Squadron

T/o 14.20 Bodney for shipping sweep in *Beat E*, shot up by *Flak* during attack on convoy off Flushing. A/c repaired.

Crew: **F/L Munroe** (Pilot RAF), injured.
  P/O John L. Tait (Obs. RAF VR), buried Thornaby-on-Tees.
  Sgt A. Tucker (WOp/AG), safe.

(120) 4.4.1941. Blenheim IV L9270 UX-X of 82 Squadron

T/o 12.50 Bodney for shipping sweep in *Beat F*, crashed in North Sea off Dutch coast, possibly shot down by fighter 30 km W of Bergen aan Zee.

Crew: **Sgt Albert V.M. Farns** (Pilot RAF VR), age 25, of North End, Portsmouth. Rm. 43.
  Sgt William W. Fox (Obs. RAF VR), age 19, of Stockton-on-Tees, Co. Durham. Rm. 43.
  Sgt Norman A. Geer (WOp/AG RAF VR), Rm. 43.

(121) 7.4.1941. Blenheim IV L9386 XD-T of 139 Squadron

T/o 15.43 Horsham St. Faith for IJmuiden steelworks, damaged by *Flak* over target and finished off by Bf109 of *Uffz.* Krause (*1./JG1*, probably Bergen) at 15.12 25 km W of IJmuiden.

Crew: **Sgt Robert Bennett** (Pilot RAF VR), of Heaton, Newcastle-on-Tyne. Rm. 39.
  P/O Eric R. Pierce (Obs. RAF VR), age 22, Rm. 34.
  Sgt Ernest W. Laban (WOp/AG RAF VR), age 23, of Derby. Rm. 47.

(122) 7.4.1941. Blenheim IV V5521 XD-E of 139 Squadron

T/o 15.43 Horsham St. Faith for IJmuiden steelworks, caught fire on landing at base due to *Flak* and fighter damage and crashed. A/c written off.

Crew: **Sgt Dennis** (Pilot), safe.
  Sgt Stan G. Hill (Obs. RAF VR), age 21, married, of Wavertree, Liverpool. Severely wounded, died 14/15th April, buried Norwich.
  Sgt Waddington (WOp/AG), safe.

(123) 7.4.1941. Blenheim IV V5826 XD-F of 139 Squadron

T/o 15.43 Horsham St. Faith for Ijmuiden steelworks, written off on return due to being badly shot up by Bf109s.

Crew: **Sgt Jennings** (Pilot), slightly wounded.
  Sgt Scholefield (Obs.), slightly wounded.
  Sgt Shrimpton (WOp/AG), slightly wounded.

(124) 10.4.1941. Blenheim IV N3569 UX-T of 82 Squadron

T/o 12.56 Bodney for shipping and fringe Beat to Borkum, crashed in North Sea off Dutch coast.

Crew: **F/S John M. Irving** (Pilot RAF VR), age 25, of Brighton, Sussex. Rm. 36.
  P/O John W. 'Jack' Gadsby (Obs. RAF VR), age 30. Rm. 32.
  Sgt John G. MacIlwraith (WOp/AG RAF VR), age 21, of New Southgate, Middlesex. Rm. 47.

(125) 10.4.1941. Blenheim IV V5596 UX-C of 82 Squadron

T/o 12.57 Bodney for shipping and fringe Beat to Borkum, landed at 17.30 on sand bank off Birchington 1 mile WSW of Margate. A/c written off.

Crew: **Sgt Crew** (Pilot), safe.
  Sgt Cartside (Obs.), safe.
  Sgt Drummond (WOp/AG), safe.

10.4.1941.   Blenheim IV V5634 UX-W of 82 Squadron

T/o 13.00 Bodney for shipping and fringe Beat to Borkum, damaged by
Bf110s off Dutch Frisians on way back and lost propeller over sea, landed
Horsham St. Faith. A/c repaired.

Crew: Sgt **Long** (Pilot), safe.
　　　Sgt **Nicholson** (Obs.), safe.
　　　Sgt **John G. Cameron** (WOp/AG RAF VR), age 24, of Paisley, Scotland.
　　　Buried Scotland.

(126) 12.4.1941.   Blenheim IV R3905 VE- of 110 Squadron

T/o 13.10 Wattisham for shipping sweep in *Beat B*, shot down by ship's
Flak during attack on small vessel 1 km. W of Kapelle. All three of crew
managed to get out of aircraft, but only pilot survived to be picked up by
German rescue launch.

Crew: S/L **D.B. Gericke** (Pilot RAF), PoW in *Stalag Luft III* Sagan.
　　　Sgt **Denis C. Staples** (Obs. RAF VR), age 23, married, of Wimbledon,
　　　Surrey. Rm. 52.
　　　F/S **Edward W. Rae** (WOp/AG RAF), Rm. 37.

12.4.1941.   Blenheim IV V6031 YH- of 21 Squadron

T/o Watton 16.19 for Flushing. Damaged by Bf109s over target, a/c landed
at base and repaired.

Crew: Sgt **Lloyd** (Pilot), safe.
　　　Sgt **Fairey** (Obs.), safe.
　　　Sgt **Wade** (WOp/AG), badly injured.

(127) 13.4.1941.   Blenheim IV L9247 WV-L of 18 Squadron

T/o 10.51 Oulton for shipping sweep to Borkum, shot down by ship's *Flak*
at 12.30 during convoy attack N of Schiermonnikoog.

Crew: Sgt **James M. Anderton** (Pilot RAF), age 23, of Hornsea, Yorkshire.
　　　Buried Sage, Germany.
　　　F/O **Ronald F. Tapp** (Obs. RAF VR), age 26, married, of Worthing. Buried
　　　Sage.
　　　Sgt **Ronald G. St.James-Smith** (WOp/AG RAF), Rm. 37.

(128) 14.4.1941.   Blenheim IV V5376 of No.1 PRU

T/o Benson for photo recce Dutch coast, damaged by *Flak* at Flushing and
finished off at 12.27 by Bf109 of *Oblt.* Helmut Bennemann (*Stab I./JG 52*,
Flushing), crashed near Breskens.

Crew: F/O **James K. Flynn** (Pilot RAF), age 26, married, of Armagh, Northern
　　　Ireland. Buried Flushing.
　　　F/O **William C. Hall** (Obs. RAF VR), age 30, of Ovington, Northumber-
　　　land. Buried Flushing.
　　　F/S **Robert A. Stephens** (WOp/AG RAF), age 19, of Carharrack, Cornwall.
　　　Buried Flushing.

(129) 14.4.1941.   Blenheim IV R2784 YH-Z of 21 Squadron

T/o 15.14 Watton for Leiden power station, shot down by light *Flak*,
crashed between Leiden and Oegstgeest at 17.17.

Crew: Sgt **Edgar Newhouse** (Pilot RAF VR), buried Oegstgeest.
　　　Sgt **Victor A. Cobb** (Obs. RAF VR), age 22, married, of East Ham. Buried
　　　Oegstgeest.
　　　Sgt **John M.C. Bougin** (WOp/AG RAF VR), age 26, married, of Wollaton
　　　Park, Nottinghamshire. Buried Oegstgeest.

(130) 23.4.1941.   Blenheim IV V6318 GB- of 105 Squadron
T/o 10.55 Swanton Morley for shipping sweep in *Beat 10*, shot down by
Flak from minesweeper *M1404* at 12.45 during attack on convoy off
Domburg.
Crew: **Sgt Alan H. Lister** (Pilot RAF VR), age 25, married, of Helensburgh,
       Dunbartonshire. Buried Flushing.
       Sgt William T. Heaney (Obs. RAF VR), of Cregagh, Co. Down. Rm. 45.
       Sgt Kenneth W. Porter (WOp/AG VR), age 21, of Norton, Malton,
       Yorkshire. Buried Wenduine/Belgium.

(131) 25.4.1941.   Blenheim IV V6370 GB- of 105 Squadron
T/o 05.05 Swanton Morley for shipping sweep in *Beat 10*, shot down by
Bf109 of *3./JG 1* (De Kooy) in North Sea 5 km W of Westkapelle.
Crew: **P/O Roland Needham** (Pilot RAF VR), age 19, Rm. 33.
       P/O Thomas Keightly-Smith (Obs. RAF VR), age 27, married, of Ely,
       Cambridgeshire. Buried The Hague.
       Sgt Francis H. Bridgman (WOp/AG RAF VR), age 24, of Saffron Walden,
       Essex. Rm. 40.

(132) 25/26.4.1941.   Blenheim IV TR-D of 59 Squadron
T/o Thorney Island for E-boat base IJmuiden, crashed on landing due to
undershooting base. A/c written off.
Crew: **P/O Herbert Badland** (Pilot RAF VR), age 24, safe.
       Sgt Cox (Obs.), injured.
       Sgt Ronald Henderson (WOp/AG RAF VR), age 24, safe.

(133) 26.4.1941.   Blenheim IV V6338 YH- of 21 Squadron
T/o 07.05 Watton for shipping sweep in Beat 8, shot down by *Flak* during
attack on convoy between Schiermonnikoog and Vlieland.
Crew: **W/C George A. Bartlett DFC** (Pilot RAF & C.O. 21 Sqn.), age 30,
       married, of Ealing, Middlesex. Rm. 28.
       F/O Arthur F.S. Winder (Obs. RAF VR), age 30, of Southampton. Rm. 30.
       Sgt Peter K. Eames DFM (WOp/AG RAF), age 19, of Southbourne,
       Bournemouth, Hampshire. Rm. 36.

(134) 26.4.1941.   Blenheim IV V5822 YH-A of 21 Squadron
T/o 07.05 Watton for shipping sweep in *Beat 8*, damaged by *Flak* during
attack on convoy between Schiermonnikoog and Vlieland and crashed in
North Sea on way back to England.
Crew: **Sgt Cyril F. Spouge** (Pilot RAF VR), Rm. 52.
       Sgt Arthur Jordan (Obs. RAF VR), age 24, of Hull. Rm. 46.
       Sgt Eric P. Acton (WOp/AG RAF), buried Sage, Germany.

(135) 26.4.1941.   Blenheim IV V6063 VE- of 110 Squadron
T/o 08.25 Wattisham for shipping sweep in *Beat 9*, shot down by Bf109 of
Lt. Otto Vinzent (*3./JG 54*, Eelde) N of Texel, prob. during convoy attack.
Crew: **F/L George O. Lings DFC** (Pilot RAF), Rm. 29.
       F/S Charles I. Martin (Obs. RAF), age 23, of Dublin, Republic of Ireland.
       Rm. 37.
       Sgt Stephen G. Peplar (WOp/AG RAF), age 21, of Broom, Yorkshire.
       Rm. 50.

(136) 28.4.1941.   Blenheim IV TR-A of 59 Squadron
T/o Thorney Island for shipping sweep, shot down by *Flak*-ship at 12.20
during attack on convoy off Hook of Holland.
Crew: **P/O Herbert Badland** (Pilot RAF VR), age 24, of Bradford, Yorkshire.
       Buried Rockanje.
       Sgt Albert H.H. Hazell (Obs. RAF VR), age 28, of Plymouth. Rm. 45.
       Sgt Ronald Henderson (WOp/AG RAF VR), age 24, of Scotswood,
       Newcastle-on-Tyne. Buried Hook of Holland.

(137) 28.4.1941.   Blenheim IV TR-F of 59 Squadron
T/o Thorney Island for shipping sweep, shot down by *Flak*-ship at 12.20
during attack on convoy off Hook of Holland.
Crew: P/O Sydney G. Collier (Pilot RAF VR), age 21, of Maseru, Basutoland,
South Africa. Buried Hook of Holland.
Sgt John Mingham (Obs. RAF VR), age 26, married, of Manchester.
Buried Hook of Holland.
F/S William Powell (WOp/AG RAF Aux.AF), age 22, of Leeds, Yorkshire.
Buried Hook of Holland.

(138) 28.4.1941.   Blenheim IV TR-H of 59 Squadron
T/o Thorney Island for shipping sweep, shot down by *Flak*-ship at 12.20
during attack on convoy off Hook of Holland.
Crew: P/O H.D. Norton (Pilot RAF), PoW, in *Stalag Luft III* Sagan.
Sgt W. Flury (Obs. RAF), PoW, in *Stalag Luft 357* Kopernikus.
Sgt John J. Hulme (WOp/AG RAF), buried Bergen aan Zee.

(139) 28.4.1941.   Blenheim IV TR-E of 59 Squadron
T/o Thorney Island for shipping sweep, shot down *Flak*-ship *MFLA 703* at
12.20 during attack on convoy off Hook of Holland and crashed in flames.
Crew: F/L Anthony E.R. Fry DFC B.Sc.Hons (Lond.) (Pilot RAF VR), age 23,
of Somerset West, Cape Province, South Africa. Rm.
F/S Edward Freeman (Obs. RAF VR), age 20, of Leamington Spa,
Warwickshire. Rm. 36.
Sgt John F.J. Taylor (WOp/AG RAF VR), Rm. 53.
Note: On 28th April 1941, 59 Squadron lost a whole attacking formation of 4 Blenheims
off the Hook; N3615, V5520, V5687 and V6097.

(140) 30.4.1941.   Blenheim IV V5853 YH- of 21 Squadron
T/o 05.30 Watton for shipping sweep in Beat 10, damaged by *Flak*-ship of
32nd. Minesweeper Flotilla at 07.30 during attack on convoy off The Hague
and ditched near convoy.
Crew: Sgt Maurice S. Dewing (Pilot RAF VR), age 23, of Norwich. Buried Hook
of Holland.
Sgt William H.R. Smale (Obs. RAF VR), age 26, of St. Albans, Hertfordshire. Buried Hook of Holland.
Sgt Harry Nathan (WOp/AG RAF VR), buried Hook of Holland.

(141) 1.5.1941.   Blenheim IV V6177 XD- of 139 Squadron
T/o 15.39 Horsham St. Faith for Den Helder power station and harbour,
shot down by *Flak* at 18.15 off Den Helder after attack.
Crew: W/C Igor W. Braye DFC (Pilot RAF & C.O. 139 Sqn.), age 30, of Earl's
Court, London. Rm. 28.
F/S Kenneth C. Peek (Obs. RAF), Rm. 37.
Sgt John Hutchison (WOp/AG RAF), age 26, of Glasgow. Rm. 46.

1.5.1941.   Blenheim IV T1832 XD- of 139 Squadron
T/o 15.39 Horsham St. Faith for Den Helder power station and harbour, hit
by *Flak* ca.18.15 over target, mortally wounding Pilot. Obs. flew a/c back to
base. A/c repaired to complete 49 sorties, finally shot down off Texel on
16.6.1941.
Crew: P/O Edgar R. Phillips (Pilot RAF VR), age 22, of West Hartlepool. Died
1st May 1941, buried West Hartlepool.
F/O Ralph Fastnedge (Obs. RAF VR), age 28, of Wood Green, London,
safe, awarded DFC.
Sgt John Allen (WOp/AG RAF VR), safe.

(142) 1.5.1941.   Blenheim IV V5823 GB- of 105 Squadron

T/o 12.15 Swanton Morley for shipping and fringe target sweep, hit by *Flak*
and Bf109s over Rotterdam oil tanks, crash-landed Cookley/Suffolk at
14.20. A/c written off.

Crew: **F/L Goode** (Pilot), injured, awarded DFC.
          P/O Hogan (Obs.), injured, awarded DFC.
          Sgt Rowland (WOp/AG), injured, awarded DFM.

(143) 5.5.1941.   Blenheim IVf Z5742 QY-A of 235 Squadron

T/o 08.30 Bircham Newton for shipping sweep, probably shot down by
Bf110s during attack on convoy off Borkum.

Crew: **Sgt Bernard L.T. Crawforth** (Pilot RAF VR), age 20, of Coventry. Buried
          Sage, Germany.
          Sgt Cecil D. Robertson (Obs. RAF VR), age 19, of Barrhead, Renfrew-
          shire. Buried Sage.
          Sgt William K. Blackford (WOp/AG RAF VR), age 21, of Lincoln. Rm. 39.

(144) 6.5.1941.   Blenheim IV Z5875 YH-W of 21 Squadron

T/o 06.00 Watton for shipping sweep in *Beat 9*, shot down during attack on
shipping off Texel.

Crew: **Sgt Kenneth B. Fitzgerald** (Pilot RAF), age 19, of Seaford, Sussex.
          Rm. 43.
          Sgt Nathaniel Berry (Obs. RAF VR), age 29, married, of Wandsworth,
          London. Rm. 39.
          Sgt Arthur Barron (WOp/AG RAF), Rm. 39.

(145) 6.5.1941.   Blenheim IV R3600 VE- of 110 Squadron

T/o 11.15 Wattisham for shipping sweep in *Beat 7*, crashed in North Sea off
Dutch coast. R3600 completed 48 sorties.

Crew: **F/L Edward N. Steel** (Pilot RAF), age 24, of Wellington, New Zealand.
          Rm. 29.
          F/S Ronald A. Freestone (Obs. RAF VR), Rm. 36.
          Sgt Joseph D. Bramhall (WOp/AG RAF VR), buried Sage, Germany.

(146) 6/7.5.1941.   Blenheim IV TR- of 59 Squadron

T/o 22.18 Bircham Newton for E.M.R.O. patrol, crashed in North Sea.

Crew: **S/L Gerald T. 'Ropey' Palmer DFC** (Pilot RAF), age 23, of Denham,
          Buckinghamshire. Buried Sage, Germany.
          Sgt Alfred D. Whitson (Obs. RAF VR), Rm. 54.
          F/S Charles E.A. Dunlop DFM (WOp/AG RAF), age 33, of Glasgow. Rm.
          36.

(147) 7/8.5.1941.   Blenheim IV P4860 XD-P of 139 Squadron

T/o 22.04 Horsham St. Faith for night shipping sweep in *Beats 8* and *9*,
crashed in Waddenzee off Wierum at 00.13 due to low flying. Wreckage
recovered by Dutch Air Force in June 1979. P4860 completed 41 sorties.

Crew: **Sgt Bill Middleton** (Pilot RAF VR), of Aberdeen, Scotland. Injured, PoW,
          in *Stalag 344* Lamsdorf.
          Sgt Bob 'Smudge' Coles (Obs. RAF VR), injured, PoW, in *Stalag 357*
          Kopernikus.
          Sgt Bob Hale (WOp/AG RAF VR), widower with a son, of Coventry.
          Injured, PoW, in *Stalag 357* Kopernikus.

(148) 15.5.1941.   Blenheim IV V6372 YH- of 21 Squadron

T/o 11.02 Watton for shipping sweep to Heligoland, shot down by Bf109 of *Uffz.* Strätling (2./JG 52, Eelde) at 13.45 off Vlieland on way back from convoy attack off Langeoog.

Crew: P/O James F.T. Ogilvie (Pilot RAF VR), Rm. 34.
        Sgt Reginald P. Mayers (Obs. RAF VR), of West Brigford, Nottinghamshire. Rm. 48.
        Sgt William V. Fillingham (WOp/AG RAF VR), age 21, of Wigan, Lancashire. Rm. 43.

(149) 24.5.1941.   Blenheim IV V5426 VE- of 110 Squadron

T/o 11.10 Wattisham for shipping sweep to Nordeney, shot down by Bf109 of *Lt.* Karl Rung (2./JG 52, Texel) at 14.30 120 km NW of Texel after attack on convoy off Borkum.

Crew: P/O Michael A. Scott (Pilot RAF VR, B.A., Hons. (Oxon), age 25, of Chester. Rm. 34.
        P/O Julian Gill (Obs. RAF VR), age 24, married, of Teddington, Middlesex. Rm. 32.
        Sgt Raymond A. Hewlett (WOp/AG RAF VR), of Taunton, Somerset. Rm. 45.

(150) 25.5.1941.   Blenheim IV R2791 XD-O of 139 Squadron

T/o 05.13 Horsham St. Faith for shipping sweep in *Beat 9*, hit by *Flak* and crashed into *Sperrbrecher Silvia* during attack on convoy W of Texel. *Silvia* burnt out and sunk. R2791 completed 48 sorties.

Crew: Sgt George A. Bye (Pilot RCAF), Rm. 61.
        Sgt William G. Thorneycroft (Obs. RAF VR), Rm. 53.
        Sgt Stanley B. Bransby (WOp/AG RAF VR), of Stockton, Co. Durham. Rm. 40.

(151) 25.5.1941.   Blenheim IV R3707 GB-U of 105 Squadron

T/o 14.05 Swanton Morley for shipping sweep in *Beat 8*, shot down by Bf109E of *Uffz.* Bodo Nette (1./JG 1, probably Bergen) after attack on convoy off Ameland.

Crew: P/O George E.J. Rushbrooke (Pilot RAF VR), Rm. 43.
        Sgt George E. Green (Obs. RAF VR), age 27, of Rolleston, Staffordshire. Rm. 43.
        Sgt Stanley Parr (WOp/AG RAF VR), age 25, of Macclesfield, Cheshire. Rm. 50.

(152) 25.5.1941.   Blenheim IV V6248 WV- of 18 Squadron

T/o 14.07 Oulton for Nordeney seaplane base, shot down by Bf109Fs of *Oblt.* Karl-Heinz Leesmann and *Ofw.* Karl Munz (both I./JG 52, Texel) at 17.00 N of Texel returning from aborted raid.

Crew: F/S David G. Keane (Pilot RAF VR), age 20, of Glasgow. Rm. 36.
        Sgt George M. Duffus (Obs. RAF VR), age 24, of Glasgow. Rm. 42.
        Sgt Ian F. Gow (WOp/AG RAF VR), age 20, of Netherlee, Renfrewshire. Rm. 44.

25.5.1941.   Blenheim IV R3666 WV- of 18 Squadron

T/o 14.07 Oulton for Nordeney seaplane base, claimed shot down by Bf109Fs of *Oblt.* Karl-Heinz Leesmann and *Ofw.* Karl Munz (both I./JG 52, Texel) N of Texel returning from aborted raid. A/c returned to base badly shot up. Repaired and eventually shot down off Den Helder on 23.7.1941.

Crew: P/O P.G.C. Wilson (Pilot), safe.
        P/O Ernest K. Aires (Obs. RAF VR), safe.
        Sgt Eric A. Lloyd (WOp/AG RAF), age 20, buried Llanelly, Wales.

(153) 28.5.1941.   Blenheim IV V6457 UX-T of 82 Squadron
T/o 12.58 Bodney for shipping sweep in *Beat 7*, shot down in flames by
Bf109E of *Oblt.* Paul Stolte (*St.Kpt. 3./JG 1*, De Kooy) at 15.45 30 km NW
of Texel.
Crew: **Sgt John H. McGowan** (Pilot RAF VR), age 22, of Shortlands, Kent.
Buried Terschelling.
Sgt Alan L. Walker (Obs. RAF VR), age 20, of Barnard Castle, Co.
Durham. Rm. 54.
Sgt Douglas N. Banks (WOp/AG RAF VR), age 23, of Treharris,
Glamorgan. Rm. 39.

(154) 28.5.1941.   Blenheim IV Z5968 QY-V of 235 Squadron
T/o 18.50 Bircham Newton for *Pirate* Patrol, shot down by Bf109Fs of Oblt.
Karl Heinz Leesmann and *Lt.* Karl Rung (both *I./JG 52*, Texel) between
20.55 and 21.03 off Texel or Terschelling.
Crew: **P/O John O. Fenton** (Pilot RAF VR), age 21, of Sevenoaks, Kent. Rm. 32.
Sgt Roland H. Johnson (Obs. RAF VR), age 23, of Newcastle-on-Tyne.
Buried Hamburg, Germany.
Sgt Orlando J. Dee (WOp/AG RAF VR), age 20, of Witnesham, Suffolk.
Buried Hamburg.

(155) 28.5.1941.   Blenheim IV V5453 QY-O of 235 Squadron
T/o 18.50 Bircham Newton for Pirate Patrol, shot down by Bf109Fs of *Oblt.*
Karl Heinz Leesmann and *Lt.* Karl Rung (both *I./JG 52*, Texel) between
20.55 and 21.03 off Texel or Terschelling.
Crew: **F/S Harold T. Naughtin** (Pilot RAF VR), age 21, of Rochester, Kent. Rm.
37.
Sgt Ronald Oldroyd (Obs. RAF VR), age 20, of Dalton, Huddersfield.
Rm. 49.
Sgt Stanley Gordon (WOp/AG RAF VR), age 20, of Heaton, Yorkshire.
Rm. 44.

(156) 2.6.1941.   Blenheim IV L9192 WV-Q of 18 Squadron
T/o 18.21 Oulton for shipping sweep off NW Germany, shot down by
Bf109F of *Ofw.* Karl Munz (*2./JG 52*, Texel) at 19.55 100 km W of Texel.
L9192 successfully completed 43 sorties.
Crew: **F/L Ian A. Mead** (Pilot RAF), age 24, married, of Bembridge, Isle of
Wight. Rm. 29.
Sgt Cyril C.G. Ashcroft (Obs. RAF VR), age 29, married, of Barnet,
Hertfordsshire. Rm. 38.
Sgt William F. Richards (WOp/AG RAF VR), age 33, married, of Bexley,
Kent. Rm. 51.

(157) 2.6.1941.   Blenheim IV V6239 XD- of 139 Squadron
T/o 18.07 Horsham St. Faith for shipping sweep off NW Germany, shot
down by 3 Bf109Fs of *Uffz.* Karl Hammerl (*1./JG 52*, Eelde), *Fw.* Walter
Jahnke and *Fw.* Oskar Wunder (both *2./JG 52*, Texel) 100 km W of Texel.
Crew: **Sgt Frank Boroski** (Pilot RCAF), Rm. 60.
Sgt Leonard A. Slade (Obs. RAF VR), age 25, of Greenford, Middlesex.
Rm. 52.
Sgt Alec Ball (WOp/AG RAF VR), age 21, of King's Norton, Birmingham.
Rm. 39.

(158) 4.6.1941. **Blenheim IV Z5744 XD-Z of 139 Squadron**
T/o 19.00 Horsham St. Faith for De Kooy A/F, shot down by Bf109E of *Uffz.*
Heinrich Nöcker *(3./JG 1*, De Kooy) W of Bergen aan Zee at 20.06 after
aborted raid.
Crew: P/O **Ian A. Lees** (Pilot RAF VR), age 26, of Edinburgh. Rm. 33.
        Sgt **Thomas C. Osborne** (Obs. RAF VR), age 22, of Newport,
        Monmouthshire. Rm. 49.
        Sgt **Charles Meredith** (WOp/AG RAF VR), age 21, of Bridgnorth. Rm. 48.

(159) 4.6.1941. **Blenheim IV R3903 XD-R of 139 Squadron**
T/o 19.00 Horsham St. Faith for De Kooy A/F, shot down by Bf109E of *Uffz.*
Heinrich Nöcker *(3./JG 1*, De Kooy) W of Bergen aan Zee at 20.08 after
aborted raid. R3903 completed 38 sorties.
Crew: P/O **Wylie Baser** (Pilot RAF VR), age 20, of South Shields, Co. Durham.
        Rm. 31.
        Sgt **Arthur W. Simpson** (Obs. RNZAF), age 32, married, of Wellington,
        New Zealand. Rm. 64.
        Sgt **Cyril E. Triggs** (WOp/AG RAF VR), age 23, of Cardiff. Rm. 53.

(160) 7.6.1941. **Blenheim IV T1921 OM- of 107 Squadron**
T/o 09.15 Great Massingham for shipping sweep in *Beat 9*, shot down by
Bf109 of *I./JG 52* or hit sea due to low flying during attack on convoy W of
IJmuiden. T1921 successfully completed 32 sorties.
Crew: Sgt **Harry F. Fordham** (Pilot RAF VR), Rm. 43.
        P/O **Theodore B. Grenon** (Obs. RAF VR), age 24, of Higher Town,
        Cornwall. Rm. 32.
        Sgt **Ronald G.L. Morley** (WOp/AG RAF VR), age 20, of Radford,
        Nottingham. Rm. 48.

(161) 7.6.1941. **Blenheim IV T2047 OM- of 107 Squadron**
T/o 09.15 Great Massingham for shipping sweep in *Beat 9*, shot down by
Bf109 of *I./JG 52* during attack on convoy W of IJmuiden.
Crew: Sgt **Francis S.B. Knox** (Pilot RAF VR), age 20, of Ballymoney, Co.
        Antrim, Northern Ireland. Rm. 46.
        Sgt **Gordon A. Kaye** (Obs. RAF VR), age 22, of Stamford Hill, London.
        Rm. 46.
        Sgt **Montague V. Berry** (WOp/AG RAF VR), age 20, of Willen Vicarage,
        Buckinghamshire. Rm. 39.

(162) 7.6.1941. **Blenheim IV V6316 GB- of 105 Squadron**
T/o 17.55 Swanton Morley for shipping sweep in *Beat 8*, shot down by
Bf109 of *I./JG 52* during attack on German vessel off Ameland.
Crew: P/O **Leslie S. Clayton** (Pilot RAF VR), age 28, married. Rm. 31.
        Sgt **Arthur J. Stiddard** (Obs. RAF VR), Rm. 53.
        P/O **Victor E.G. Phillips** (WOp/AG RAF VR), age 22, of Hove, Sussex.
        Rm. 43.
Note: On 7 June 1941, 3 Blenheims were claimed shot down in the Dutch coast area: Uffz.
Karl Hammerl (1./JG 52, Borkum), at 19.00 70 km NW of Borkum; Ofw. Oskar Wunder
(2./JG 52, Texel), at 20.15 hrs. 25 km NE of Ameland; Fw. Friedrich Karl Bachmann
(3./JG 52, Leeuwarden), at 20.35 120 km N of Texel.

(163) 9.6.1941. **Blenheim IV V6427 WV-B of 18 Squadron**
T/o 15.16 Oulton for shipping sweep in *Beat 8*, disappeared in fog bank W
of Texel around 16.00.
Crew: Sgt **Leslie B. Box** (Pilot RAF VR), age 28, married. Buried Bergen op
        Zoom.
        P/O **Paul Molloy** (Obs. RAF VR), age 23, of Romiley, Cheshire. Rm. 33.
        Sgt **George K. Bass** (WOp/AG RAF VR), age 22, of Barking, Essex.
        Rm. 39.

(164) 9.6.1941.   Blenheim IV V6428 WV-M of 18 Squadron

T/o 15.18 Oulton for shipping sweep in *Beat 8*, damaged by ship's *Flak* and shot down by Bf109F of *Fw.* Heinz Wilhelm Ahnert (*3./JG 52*, Leeuwarden) at 17.57 N of Schiermonnikoog during attack on convoy.

Crew: **F/S Ian A. 'Tubby' Bullivant** (Pilot RAF VR), age 24, of Hammersmith, London. Buried Anjum.

F/S Samuel D. 'Jock' Gallery (Obs. RAF), age 21, of Cambuslang, Lanarkshire. Rm. 36.

F/S Robert F. Hind (WOp/AG RAF), age 21, of Neasden, Middlesex. Rm. 36.

(165) 11.6.1941.   Blenheim IV V6367 OM- of 107 Squadron

T/o 09.31 Great Massingham for Special Targets in NW Germany, shot down by Bf109F of *Lt.* Otto Schlauch (*3./JG 52*, Leeuwarden) at 10.37 100 km NW of Texel.

Crew: **Sgt Peter J. Walker** (Pilot RAF VR), Rm. 54.

P/O Reginald G. Sammons (Obs. RAF VR), age 33, married, of Kingswood, Bristol. Rm. 34.

Sgt Victor A. Lewis (WOp/AG RAF VR), age 24, of Enstone, Oxfordshire. Rm. 47.

(166) 14.6.1941.   Blenheim IV V6334 VE- of 110 Squadron

T/o 06.19 Wattisham for *Circus 12* to St. Omer A/F, crashed in North Sea off France.

Crew: **F/L Peter Windram** (Pilot RAF), age 28. Buried Boulogne, France.

P/O Peter R.G. Howes (Obs. RAF VR), age24, of Kew Gardens, Surrey. Buried Bergen-op-Zoom.

F/S Robert L. Cox (WOp/AG RAF VR), age 32, of Eastbourne, Sussex. Rm. 36.

(167) 15.6.1941.   Blenheim IV V5887 RT- of 114 Squadron

T/o Leuchars (?) for North Sea shipping patrol, shot down by *Flak*-ship 10 km W of Hook of Holland. Crew probably on Coastal Command detachment.

Crew: **Sgt Dowsey** (Pilot), PoW.

P/O Charles F. Starkey (Obs. RAF VR), age 21, Rm. 34.

Sgt Duffield (WOp/AG), PoW.

(168) 15.6.1941.   Blenheim IV V6319 GB- of 105 Squadron

T/o 18.44 Swanton Morley for shipping sweep in *Beat 10*, shot down by *Flak* at 19.50 during attack on *E-boats* off Kijkduin.

Crew: **F/O Peter H. Watts** (Pilot RAF), Rm. 30.

F/S David D. Milroy (Obs. RAF VR), buried Hook of Holland.

Sgt Percy B. Murray (WOp/AG RAF VR), age 19, of Aberdeen. Buried Hook of Holland.

(169) 15.6.1941.   Blenheim IV V6375 VE- of 110 Squadron

T/o 18.27 Manston for shipping sweep in *Beat 9* or 10, shot down by Bf109F of *Uffz.* Barein (*I./JG 1*, probably Bergen) at 19.39 during attack on convoy 60 km W of Alkmaar.

Crew: **F/S Arthur E. Guesford** (Pilot RAF VR), age 23, married, of Bicknacre, Essex. Buried Romo Island, Denmark.

Sgt Clifford F. Shearn (Obs. RAF VR), Rm. 52.

Sgt Leslie P.C. Rolfe (WOp/AG RAF VR), age 21, of Swindon, Wiltshire. Buried Romo Island.

(170) 16.6.1941.   Blenheim IV V6512 WV-K of 18 Squadron

T/o 15.23 Oulton for shipping sweep in *Beat 10*, shot down by *Flak* from
German convoy off Hook of Holland.
Crew: P/O **Ian W. Watson** (Pilot RAF VR), age 24, of Edinburgh. Rm. 35.
         P/O **Ernest K. Aires** (Obs. RAF VR), Rm. 31.
         Sgt **Tom Dean** (WOp/AG RAF VR), Rm. 42.

(171) 16.6.1941.   Blenheim IV V6034 YH-D of 21 Squadron

T/o 13.19 Watton for shipping sweep in *Beat 7*, hit Squealer's mast during
attack off Borkum and crashed in North Sea.
Crew: Sgt **E.A. Rex Leavers DFM** (Pilot RAF VR), age 24, of Dunkirk,
         Nottingham. Buried Den Andel.
         Sgt **Ian Overheu DFM** (Obs. RNZAF), age 23, Rm. 64.
         Sgt **Joseph W.H. Phelps** (WOp/AG RAF VR), buried Sage.

(172) 16.6.1941.   Blenheim IV T1832 XD- of 139 Squadron

T/o 15.21 Horsham St. Faith for shipping sweep in *Beat 9*, shot down by
Bf109Fs of *Lt.* Karl Weber and *Fw.* Robert Portz (both 1./JG52, Eelde or
Borkum), at 17.00 in Texel area. T1832 completed 49 sorties.
Crew: F/O **Ralph R. Langley DFC** (Pilot RAF), Rm. 30.
         Sgt **Islwyn D. Scourfield** (Obs. RAF VR), Rm. 51.
         Sgt **Harry Gretton** (WOp/AG RAF), buried Esbjerg/Denmark.

(173) 16.6.1941.   Blenheim IV V6332 XD- of 139 Squadron

T/o 15.22 Horsham St. Faith for shipping sweep in *Beat 9*, claimed shot
down at 17.40 by Bf109Fs of *Lt.* Karl Weber and *Fw.* Robert Portz (both
1./JG 52, Eelde or Borkum) in Texel area, but a/c reached England and
crashed at Rackheath, Norfolk. A/c totally destroyed.
Crew: F/O **Kenneth M. Laird** (Pilot RAF), age 24, of Westmount, Quebec,
         Canada. Buried Norwich.
         Sgt **Leslie J.G. Wakefield** (Obs. RAF VR), age 27, married, of Birming-
         ham. Buried Norwich.
         Sgt **Robinson** (WOp/AG), injured.

(174) 30.6.1941.   Blenheim IV V5863 TR-X of 59 Squadron

T/o Thorney Island for shipping sweep off Dutch coast, hit balloon barrage
cables at Dover on return and crashed in sea.
Crew: P/O **John N. Whitmore** (Pilot RAF), age 20, of Ipswich, Suffolk. Buried
         Folkestone.
         Sgt **Dennis N. Dulley** (Obs. RAF VR), age 21, Rm. 42.
         Sgt **Patrick A. Truman** (WOp/AG RAF VR), age 25, married, Rm. 53.

(175) 1.7.1941.   Blenheim IV V6258 XD- of 139 Squadron

T/o 08.48 Horsham St. Faith for Oldenburg, shot down by Bf109F of *Fw.*
Friedrich Karl Bachmann (*3./JG 52*, Leeuwarden) at 12.48 and ditched 60
km NW of Vlieland.
Crew: Sgt **K. Fenton** (Pilot RAF VR), PoW, in *Stalag 357* Kopernikus.
         Sgt **A.A. Fuller** (Obs. RAF VR), PoW, in *Stalag 357* Kopernikus.
         Sgt **R.W. McDonald** (WOp/AG RAF VR), PoW, in *Stalag Luft III* Sagan.

(176) 2.7.1941.   Blenheim IVf Z6171 DM- of 248 Squadron

T/o Bircham Newton for Dutch coast shipping sweep, shot down in flames
by Bf109F of *Uffz.* Fritz Metzler *(2./JG 52*, Texel) at 10.58 90 km W of
Texel.
Crew: P/O **Ronald J. Powell** (Pilot RAF VR), age 28, of Church End, Finchley,
         Middlesex. Rm. 34.
         Sgt **Henry J. Robinson** (Obs. RAF VR), age 23, of South Hylton, Co.
         Durham. Rm. 51.
         F/S **William G. Sharratt** (Obs. RAF VR), age 26, of Blackpool, Lancashire.
         Rm. 37.

(177) 6.7.1941. **Blenheim IV T1824 OM- of 107 Squadron**
T/o 09.34 Great Massingham for shipping sweep in *Beat 10*, hit by *Flak*
from target *Flak*-ship in Scheldt estuary, presumed ditched.
Crew: Sgt L.G. Dicks (Pilot), PoW.
        Sgt D.W. Macalister (Obs.), PoW.
        Sgt David T. Brett (WOp/AG RAF), Rm. 40.

(178) 7.7.1941. **Blenheim IV V5502 GB-U of 105 Squadron**
T/o 11.27 Swanton Morley for shipping sweep between The Hague and
IJmuiden, shot down at 13.00 by *Flak*-ship during convoy attack off
Scheveningen.
Crew: S/L Anthony A.M. Scott (Pilot RAF), Rm. 28.
        Sgt Ronald G.J. Dewin (Obs. RAF VR), age 21, of Highbury, London.
        Rm. 42.
        F/S Patrick Conlon (WOp/AG RAF VR), buried The Hague.

(179) 7.7.1941. **Blenheim IV V6084 XD- of 139 Squadron**
T/o 11.42 Horsham St. Faith for shipping sweep between The Hague and
IJmuiden, shot down by ship's *Flak* during convoy attack off Scheveningen.
Crew: F/L Horace C. Hilton (Pilot RAF), age 22, Rm. 29.
        Sgt Jack Sykes (Obs. RAF VR), buried The Hague.
        Sgt John Clayton (WOp/AG RAF VR), age 24, of Baildon, Shipley,
        Yorkshire. Buried Bergen aan Zee.
Note: V5502 or V6084 may have been shot down by Maj. Dr. Erich Mix, Führer Jagd-
kräfte Holland (Bergen/Alkmaar), who claimed a Blenheim shot down 35 km W of The
Hague.

(180) 7.7.1941. **Blenheim IV Z7424 XD- of 139 Squadron**
T/o 11.42 Horsham St. Faith for shipping sweep between The Hague and
IJmuiden, shot down by Bf109 of *Uffz.* Fritz Metzler (2./*JG 52*, Texel) at
12.38 after convoy attack off Scheveningen and crashed in North Sea 100
km W of The Hague.
Crew: Sgt John A. Causon (Pilot RAF VR), age 21, of Cranham, Gloucester-
        shire. Rm. 41.
        Sgt Roy Spencer (Obs. RAF VR), age 24, of Laleston, Glamorgan. Buried
        Terschelling.
        Sgt William B. Cundill (WOp/AG RAF VR), age 23, married, of Ripon,
        Yorkshire. Buried Amsterdam.

(181) 12.7.1941. **Blenheim IV V6524 UX- of 82 Squadron**
T/o Bodney for low level practice formation flight, lost control after flying
into sea fog bank and crashed in North Sea, possibly off Walcheren.
Crew: Sgt John N. Hallam (Pilot RCAF), age 21, of Sarnia, Ontario, Canada.
        Buried Kiel.
        Sgt Herbert Hastings (Obs. RAF VR), age 26, married, of Radcliffe,
        Lancashire. Rm. 44.
        Sgt Wilfred L. Hiscock (WOp/AG RAF VR), age 21, of Melksham,
        Wiltshire. Rm. 45.

(182) 12.7.1941. **Blenheim IV Z7487 OM- of 107 Squadron**
T/o 11.20 Great Massingham for shipping sweep off Dutch coast, shot down
by ship's *Flak* at 12.35 during attack on convoy off IJmuiden.
Crew: W/C Arthur F.C. Booth (Pilot RAF & C.O. 107 Sqn.), age 32, married, of
        Cambridge. Buried Kiel.
        Sgt T. Scott (Obs. RAF VR), PoW.
        F/S Colin G. Goodfellow (WOp/AG RAF VR), Rm. 36.

(183) 16.7.1941.   Blenheim IV V6267 WV-M of 18 Squadron
T/o 15.17 Horsham St. Faith for Rotterdam docks, shot down by Rotterdam
Flak and crashed at 17.00 in Noordsingel at Rotterdam.
Crew: W/C **Thomas N. 'Tim' Partridge** DFC (Pilot RAF), age 26, buried
Rotterdam.
Sgt **George A. Dvorjetz** (Obs. RAF VR), age 25, of Claygate, Surrey.
Buried Rotterdam.
F/S **John O.N. Smith** DFM (WOp/AG RAF), age 21, of Lower Gornal,
Staffordshire. Buried Rotterdam.

(184) 16.7.1941.   Blenheim IV Z7496 WV-W of 18 Squadron
T/o 15.17 Horsham St. Faith for Rotterdam docks, shot down by Rotterdam
Flak and crashed at 17.06 near Ypenburg.
Crew: Sgt **Ronald J.B. Rost** (Pilot RAAF), age 20, of Manly, N.S.W., Australia.
Buried The Hague.
Sgt **John Hughes** (Obs. RAF VR), age 21, of Seacombe, Cheshire. Buried
The Hague.
Sgt **Stanley W. Winter** (WOp/AG RAF), age 25, of Millbrook, Southampton. Buried The Hague.

(185) 16.7.1941.   Blenheim IV V6240 YH-B of 21 Squadron
T/o 15.17 Watton for Rotterdam docks, shot down by *Vp1107* at 16.55 and
crashed in Waalhaven harbour.
Crew: Sgt **James E.S. Bevan** (Pilot RAF VR), age 19, buried Rotterdam.
P/O **Ralph M. Slade** (Obs. RAF VR), age 30, married, of Prestwick,
Ayrshire. Buried Rotterdam.
Sgt **Leonard R. Mynott** (WOp/AG RAF VR), age 24, of Clapham Park,
London. Rm. 49.

(186) 16.7.1941.   Blenheim IV Z7362 XD-V of 139 Squadron
T/o 15.17 Oulton for Rotterdam docks, shot down by *Flak*-ship of *13th
Vp.Fl.* at Waalhaven and crash-landed in Waalhaven district.
Crew: S/L **Eric Sidney-Smith** DFC (Pilot RAF), age 28, PoW in *Stalag Luft III*
Sagan.
P/O **R. Adrian White** (Obs. RAF), age 23, lightly injured, PoW in *Stalag
Luft III* Sagan.
F/S **Edmund G. Caban** DFM (WOp/AG RAF), age 21, injured, PoW in
Stalag Luft 357 Kopernikus.

(187) 19.7.1941.   Blenheim IV V6039 GB- of 105 Squadron
T/o 11.22 Swanton Morley for shipping sweep off The Hague, shot down by
ship's *Flak* during attack on convoy off The Hague.
Crew: Sgt **Ronald W. Taylor** (Pilot RNZAF), age 25, of Christchurch, Canterbury, New Zealand. Buried Noordwijk.
Sgt **Reginald F.G. Withrington** (Obs. RAF VR), age 26, of Shoreham-by-Sea, Sussex. Buried Bergen op Zoom.
Sgt **Selwyn Sparkes** (WOp/AG RAF VR), age 25, married, of South
Shields, Co. Durham. Buried Bergen-aan-Zee.

(188) 19.7.1941.   Blenheim IV Z7439 GB- of 105 Squadron
T/o 11.22 Swanton Morley for shipping sweep off The Hague, hit mast of
target ship off The Hague and crashed in flames in North Sea.
Crew: Sgt **Victor G. Farrow** (Pilot RAF VR), age 19, of Romford, Essex. Buried
The Hague.
F/O **Oswald H. Robinson** (Obs. RAF VR), age 21, of Canton, Cardiff.
Rm. 37.
Sgt **Edwin C. Saunders** (WOp/AG RAF VR), age 21, of Finsbury Park,
Middlesex. Buried The Hague.

(189) 23.7.1941.   Blenheim IV V6250 WV-E of 18 Squadron
T/o 11.45 Horsham St. Faith for shipping sweep IJmuiden to Den Helder,
shot down ca.12.53 by Bf110s of *Oblt.* Hotari Schmude, *Ofw.* Leschnik, and
Fw. Schmidt (*5./ZG 76*, De Kooy) and crashed off Kamperduin.
Crew: Sgt **Peter D. Baker** (Pilot RAF VR), Rm. 39.
        Sgt **William C.K. Bounds** (Obs. RAF VR), age 21, of Chepstow, Mon-
        mouthshire. Rm. 40.
        P/O **Leonard F. Evans** (WOp/AG RAF VR), age 29, of Hatch End,
        Middlesex. Rm. 32.

(190) 23.7.1941.   Blenheim IV R3666 WV-K of 18 Squadron
T/o 11.45 Horsham St. Faith for shipping sweep between IJmuiden and
Den Helder, shot down ca.12.53 by Bf110s of *Oblt.* Hotari Schmude, *Ofw.*
Leschnik, and *Fw.* Schmidt (*5./ZG 76*, De Kooy) off Kamperduin. R3666
completed 35 sorties.
Crew: Sgt **William M.G. Dunham** (Pilot RCAF), age 24, of Red Deer, Alberta,
        Canada. Rm. 61.
        Sgt **Ronald W. Adamson** (Obs. RAF VR), age 21, of Newcastle-on-Tyne.
        Buried Terschelling.
        Sgt **Norman L. Harding** (WOp/AG RAF VR), age 26, of Richmond,
        Surrey. Rm. 44.

23.7.1941.   Blenheim IV V6197 WV-D of 18 Squadron
T/o 11.45 Horsham St. Faith for shipping sweep between IJmuiden and
Den Helder, severely damaged by Bf110s of *5./ZG 76* (De Kooy) off
Kamperduin, crashed on landing at 13.45 at Horsham St. Faith, a/c
repaired.
Crew: Sgt **Wood** (Pilot), severely injured.
        Sgt **Johnson** (Obs.), severely injured.
        Sgt **Allan** (WOp/AG), safe.

(191) 23.7.1941.   Blenheim IV V6231 YH-Z of 21 Squadron
T/o 14.00 Manston for Channel Stop sweep off Zuydercoote, shot down by
Flak-ship during attack on escorted tanker in mouth of Scheldt.
Crew: Sgt **Henry P. Hartridge** (Pilot RCAF), age 21, of Balfour, B.C., Canada.
        Buried Flushing.
        Sgt **Charles D. Phillips** (Obs. RAF VR), buried Flushing.
        Sgt **Kenneth B. Minty** (WOp/AG RAF VR), age 22, of Three Bridges,
        Sussex. Buried Flushing.

(192) 23.7.1941.   Blenheim IV V6396 YH-W of 21 Squadron
T/o 14.00 Manston for Channel Stop sweep off Zuydercoote, shot down by
Flak-ship during attack on escorted tanker in mouth of Scheldt.
Crew: F/L **Howard Waples** DFC (Pilot RAF VR), age 23, of Southend-on-Sea,
        Essex. Rm. 29.
        Sgt **Norman J. Giblin** DFM (Obs. RAF VR), age 20, of Withington,
        Manchester. Buried Flushing.
        Sgt **Arthur W. Handley** (WOp/AG RAF VR), age 30, married, of Beeston,
        Nottinghamshire. Rm. 44.

(193) 23.7.1941.   Blenheim IV V6035 YH-O of 21 Squadron
T/o 14.00 Manston for *Channel Stop* sweep off Zuydercoote, shot down by
Flak-ship during attack on escorted tanker in mouth of Scheldt, crashed in
North Sea off Oostende/Belgium.
Crew: P/O **Philip B. Ashby** (Pilot RAF VR), age 20, buried Oostende.
        P/O **G.F. Lowes** (Obs. RAF), PoW in *Stalag Luft III* Sagan.
        P/O **Gerald H. Seeley** (WOp/AG RAF VR), buried Oostende.

(194) 23.7.1941.   Blenheim IV Z7438 YH-D of 21 Squadron
T/o 14.00 Manston for *Channel Stop* sweep off Zuydercoote, shot down by *Flak*-ship during attack on escorted tanker in mouth of Scheldt, crashed in North Sea off Oostende/Belgium.
Crew: F/L Campbell-Rogers (Pilot RAF), PoW, in *Stalag Luft III* Sagan.
Sgt John P. Sullivan (Obs. RAF), Rm. 53.
Sgt D.E. Bingham (WOp/AG RAF), PoW, in *Stalag 357* Kopernikus.

(195) 30.7.1941.   Blenheim IV V6266 XD- of 139 Squadron
T/o 14.00 Oulton for shipping sweep off NW Germany, shot down by Bf110 of *II./ZG 76* 180 km N of Texel.
Crew: Sgt George R. Menish (Pilot RCAF), age 24, of Salina, Kansas, U.S.A. Rm. 31.
P/O Peter Brown (Obs. RAF VR), age 28, married, of Gresty, Cheshire. Rm. 31.
Sgt Rowland Haley (WOp/AG RAF VR), age 20, of Wakefield, Yorkshire. Rm. 44.

(196) 30.7.1941.   Blenheim IV V6439 XD- of 139 Squadron
T/o 14.00 Oulton for shipping sweep off NW Germany, shot down by Bf110 of *II./ZG 76* 180 km N of Texel.
Crew: Sgt William S. Campbell (Pilot RAF VR), Rm. 40.
Sgt Robert G. McRobert (Obs. RAF VR), M.A. (Glasgow), age 22, of Dalmuir, Dunbartonshire. Rm. 48.
Sgt Stanley R.B. Severn (WOp/AG RAF VR), age 21, of Sunderland, Co. Durham. Rm. 51.

(197) 30.7.1941.   Blenheim IV V6176 XD- of 139 Squadron
T/o 14.00 Oulton for shipping sweep off NW Germany, shot down by Bf110 of *II./ZG 76* 180 km N of Texel.
Crew: Sgt Lawrence H. Gruer (Pilot RAF), age 20, Rm. 44.
Sgt John M. Blundell (Obs. RAF VR), age 28, of Eltham, London. Buried Esbjerg, Denmark.
Sgt Derek G. Dennis-Smither (WOp/AG RAF VR), Rm. 42.

(198) 30.7.1941.   Blenheim IV V6322 XD- of 139 Squadron
T/o 14.00 Oulton for shipping sweep off NW Germany, shot down by Bf110 of *II./ZG 76* 180 km N of Texel.
Crew: P/O Peter G. Shillitoe (Pilot RAF VR), Rm. 34.
Sgt Philip J. Walder (Obs. RAF VR), Rm. 54.
P/O Esmond C. Elder (WOp/AG RAF VR), age 33, married, of Castle Bromwich, Warwickshire. Buried Esbjerg, Denmark.
Note: On 30 July 1941, 4 Bf110 aircrew of II./ZG 76 claimed these 4 Blenheims shot down off Texel between 16.18 and 16.32: Oblt. Wilhelm Herget (Pilot 4./ZG76, Leeuwarden); Uffz. Arngrimm (Pilot 6./ZG76, Leeuwarden); Uffz. Werner Dobreck (Pilot 5./ZG76, De Kooy) and Uffz. Horst (WOp/AG 5./ZG76, De Kooy).

(199) 1.8.1941.   Blenheim IV N3568 OM- of 107 Squadron
T/o 11.15 Manston for *Channel Stop* sweep, shot down by ship's *Flak* after attack on vessel in mouth of Scheldt.
Crew: S/L Hugh F. Thomson (Pilot RAF), B.A. (Cantab.), age 28, married. Buried Flushing.
P/O Alasdair C. MacPherson (Obs. RAF VR), B.A., B.Th., Ph.D. (Cantab.) Trinity College, age 29, of Westminster, London. Buried Flushing.
F/S Leonard C. Williams (WOp/AG RAF VR), age 24, married. Buried Flushing.

(200) 1.8.1941. **Blenheim IV Z7498 OM- of 107 Squadron**
T/o 11.15 Manston for *Channel Stop* sweep, shot down by ship's *Flak* after
attack on vessel in mouth of Scheldt.
Crew: **Sgt Cullen E. Powell** (Pilot RAF VR), Rm. 50.
Sgt M. Roberts (Obs. RAF VR), PoW, in *Stalag 357* Kopernikus.
Sgt H.E. Hunt (WOp/AG RAF VR), PoW, in *Stalag 357* Kopernikus.

(201) 2.8.1941. **Blenheim IV V6026 UX-M of 82 Squadron**
T/o 13.15 Bodney for shipping sweep, shot down by *Flak*-ship during attack
on convoy 15 km. SW of Texel.
Crew: **W/C Kenyon O. Burt DFC** (Pilot RAF VR), Honours Degree in Modern
Languages Tripos, Cambridge, age 27, married, of Uplyme, Dorsetshire.
Buried Bergen op Zoom.
Sgt William T. Ellis DFM (Obs. RAF VR), age 30, of Nantwich, Cheshire.
Buried Kiel.
F/S Angus D.W. Curr DFM (WOp/AG RAF VR), age 21, of Edinburgh.
Buried Esbjerg, Denmark.

(202) 7/8.8.1941. **Blenheim IV L4899 MK- of 500 Squadron**
T/o 22.00 Bircham Newton for shipping sweep to Dutch Frisians, crashed
in North Sea.
Crew: **P/O Leslie Ward** (Pilot RAF), age 29, married, of Eastbourne, Sussex.
Rm. 35.
Sgt William S. Robinson (Obs. RAF VR), age 30, of Leigh, Lancashire.
Rm. 51.
F/S Ronald L. Burton (WOp/AG RAF Aux AF), age 26, of Snodland, Kent.
Rm. 35.

(203) 12.8.1941. **Blenheim IV T2437 UX-Y of 82 Squadron**
T/o 09.50 Bodney for Quadrath power station, shot down by *Flak* at
Strijensas near Moerdijkbridge at 12.10 on way in.
Crew: **P/O Graham C. Rolland** (Pilot RAF VR), age 18, of Bromley Cross,
Lancashire. Buried Strijen.
P/O Hugh M. Clark (Obs. RAF VR), age 24, of Ashford, Kent. Buried
Strijen.
Sgt Ernest Bainbridge (WOp/AG RAF VR), age 28, married, of
Barnoldswick, Lancashire. Buried Strijen.

(204) 12.8.1941. **Blenheim IV V6423 WV-P of 18 Squadron**
T/o 09.20 Horsham St. Faith for Knapsack power station, crashed at
Diest/Belgium on way in.
Crew: **F/O G.H. Hill** (Pilot RAF), PoW, in *Stalag Luft III* Sagan.
P/O R. Chadwick (Obs. RAF), PoW, in *Stalag Luft III* Sagan. Later
repatriated due to very severe leg injuries.
Sgt L.A.F. Parrish (WOp/AG RAF), PoW, in *Stalag 357* Kopernikus.

(205) 12.8.1941. **Blenheim IV V7451 YH-D of 21 Squadron**
T/o 09.30 Watton for Quadrath power station, shot down by *Flak* and
crashed at Potz near target, on way in.
Crew: **Sgt Jim Langston** (Pilot RAF VR), PoW, in *Stalag Luft 357* Kopernikus.
Sgt Dave Roberts (Obs. RAF VR), PoW, in *Stalag Luft VI* Heydekrug.
Sgt Kenneth V. Attew (WOp/AG RAF VR), age 21, of New Malden,
Surrey. Buried Rheinberg.

(206) 12.8.1941.   Blenheim IV V5725 XD- of 139 Squadron
T/o 09.49 Oulton for Knapsack power station, shot down by *Flak* over
target and crashed at Berrenrath.
Crew: **Sgt Harry Ingleby** (Pilot RCAF), age 25, of Ingleby, Canada. Buried
Rheinberg, Germany.
Sgt David F.J. Phillips (Obs. RAF VR), age 24, of Town Hill, Swansea.
Buried Rheinberg.
F/S George H. Appleyard (WOp/AG RAF), buried Rheinberg.

(207) 12.8.1941.   Blenheim IV Z7448 XD-Y of 139 Squadron
T/o 09.49 Oulton for Knapsack power station, probably hit by *Flak* over
target and crashed at Huecheln.
Crew: **Sgt G. Coast** (Pilot RAF), PoW, in *Stalag Luft 357* Kopernikus.
P/O K.J. Mackintosh (Obs. RAF), PoW, in *Stalag Luft III* Sagan.
Sgt Dennis A. Wilson (WOp/AG RAF VR), age 19, of Bromley, Kent.
Buried Rheinberg, Germany.

(208) 12.8.1941.   Blenheim IV V5859 MQ-Y of 226 Squadron
T/o 10.00 Martlesham Heath as Navigation Leader for withdrawal cover,
shot down at 12.53 by light *Flak* of *Battery 43/XI* and crashed near
Philippine.
Crew: **F/L Gwilym I. Lewis** (Pilot RAF), age 26, married, of Redditch, Worces-
tershire. Buried Flushing.
Sgt Nevill S. Cardell (Obs. RAF), buried Flushing.
Sgt Jack C. Woods (WOp/AG RAF VR), buried Flushing.

(209) 12.8.1941.   Blenheim IV Z7352 MQ- of 226 Squadron
T/o 10.00 Ipswich as Navigation Leader for British withdrawal cover, shot
down by Bf109E of *Uffz.* Zick (*I./JG 1*, Katwijk) at 13.00 in mouth of
Schelde off Zoutelande.
Crew: **F/L Hugh S. Young** (Pilot RAF), age 20, of Glasgow. Buried Noordwijk.
P/O Alexander C. Rossiter (Obs. RAF VR), age 25, married, of Cardiff.
Rm. 34.
Sgt John A. Anderson (WOp/AG RAF VR), age 21, of Reading, Berkshire.
Rm. 38.

(210) 12.8.1941.   Blenheim IV V6437 WV-C of 18 Squadron
T/o 09.20 Horsham St. Faith for Knapsack power station, hit high tension
cables over Dutch coast, tail sheared off and crashed in mouth of Scheldt,
on way back.
Crew: **P/O Malcolm T.K. Walkden** (Pilot RAF VR), age 24, of Knott End,
Lancashire. Rm. 35.
P/O Bernard F.W. Matthews (Obs. RAF VR), age 25, of Cambridge.
Rm. 33.
Sgt Albert C. Cutler (WOp/AG RAF VR), age 23, of Coventry. Buried
Flushing.

(211) 12.8.1941.   Blenheim IV V6261 XD-M of 139 Squadron
T/o 09.49 Oulton for Knapsack power station, damaged by light *Flak* and
finished off by Bf109E of *Obstlt.* Adolf Galland (*Stab./JG 26*, Wevelgem/
Belgium) at 13.18 on way back, crashed in mouth of River Scheldt off
Breskens.
Crew: **F/L George A. Herbert** (Pilot RNZAF), age 23, of Hamilton, Auckland,
New Zealand. Buried Bergen aan Zee.
P/O Courtney C.O. George (Obs. RAF VR), Rm. 32.
Sgt George Benton (WOp/AG RAF VR), age 21, of Eckington, Derbyshire.
Buried Bergen aan Zee.

(212) 12.8.1941.   Blenheim IV Z7281 RT-P of 114 Squadron
T/o 09.10 West Raynham for Knapsack power station, shot down by light
Flak and Bf109 of *Oblt.* Kurt Ruppert (*III./JG 26*, probably Woensdrecht)
at 13.20 and crashed in North Sea off Flushing on the way back.
Crew: **Sgt Douglas J. Wheatley** (Pilot RAF VR), age 20, of Whitwell, Yorkshire.
    Buried Sage, Germany.
    Sgt John L. West (Obs. RAF VR), buried Sage, Germany.
    Sgt John Stead (WOp/AG RAF VR), age 25, married, of Farnworth,
    Lancashire. Rm. 52.

(213) 12.8.1941.   Blenheim IV V6497 WV-U of 18 Squadron
T/o 09.25 Horsham St. Faith for Knapsack power station, shot down by
Bf109E of *Oblt.* Baron Freiherr Hubertus von Holtey (*Stab./JG 26*,
Wevelgem) at 13.28 and ditched in North Sea S of Flushing, on way back.
Crew: **S/L A.F.H. Mills** (Pilot RCAF), PoW, in *Stalag Luft III* Sagan.
    F/O W.A. Staniland (Obs. RAF), PoW, in *Stalag Luft III* Sagan.
    Sgt L.C. Mitchell (WOp/AG RAF), PoW, in *Stalag 357* Kopernikus.

(214) 12.8.1941.   Blenheim IV V5874 YH-P of 21 Squadron
T/o 09.28 Watton for Quadrath power station, hit high tension cables in
Dutch coast area on way back.
Crew: **P/O James W. Corfield** (Pilot RAF VR), age 25, of Bedford. Buried Den
    Burg/Texel.
    P/O Arthur L.A. Williams (Obs. RAF VR), buried Den Burg.
    P/O Maurice F. Williams (WOp/AG RAF VR), age 34, married, of
    Muswell Hill, Middlesex. Buried Den Burg.

(215) 15.8.1941.   Blenheim IV Z6036 MK- of 500 Squadron
T/o 10.30 Bircham Newton for ASR op., shot down by Bf110 of *Ofw.*
Kornacker (*6./ZG 76*, Leeuwarden) at 14.30 in North Sea.
Crew: **F/O Christopher M. Elgar** (Pilot RAF Aux. AF), age 32, of Bobbing,
    Sittingbourne, Kent. Rm. 30.
    Sgt Jack Halls (Obs. RAF VR), age 23, married, of Cambridge. Rm. 44.
    Sgt Douglas A. Butterfield (WOp/AG RAF VR), age 22, of Iver,
    Buckinghamshire. Rm. 40.

(216) 19.8.1941.   Blenheim IV V6236 RT-D of 114 Squadron
T/o 17.20 West Raynham for shipping sweep in *Beat 9*, shot down by Bf110
of *5./ZG 76* between 19.30 and 19.35 35 km NW of Vlieland during attack
on convoy.
Crew: **W/C James L. Nicol DSO** (Pilot RAF & C.O. 114 Sqn.), age 27, married, of
    Kingston-on-Thames. Rm. 28.
    F/S Edward T.W. Jones (Obs. RAF), age 22, of Bexleyheath, Kent. Buried
    Sage, Germany.
    F/O Herbert J. Madden DFC (WOp/AG RAF VR), age 32, married, of
    Bloomsbury, London. Rm. 30.

(217) 19.8.1941.   Blenheim IV Z7347 RT-U of 114 Squadron
T/o 17.20 West Raynham for shipping sweep in *Beat 9*, shot down by Bf110
of *5./ZG 76* between 1930 and 19.35 35 km NW of Vlieland during attack
on convoy.
Crew: **Sgt Reginald K. Clarke** (Pilot RAF VR), age 20, of Erdington, Birming-
    ham. Rm. 41.
    P/O Ronald A. Stratton (Obs. RAF VR), buried Sage, Germany.
    Sgt Peter A. Davies (WOp/AG RAF VR), age 19, of Plumstead, London.
    Buried Ameland.

(218) 19.8.1941.   Blenheim IV V6366 RT-N of 114 Squadron

T/o 17.15 West Raynham for shipping sweep in *Beat 9*, shot down by Bf110
of *5./ZG 76* between 19.30 and 19.35 35 km NW of Vlieland during attack
on convoy.

Crew: P/O Roderick U. McCracken (Pilot RNZAF), age 22, of Rangiora,
Canterbury, New Zealand. Rm. 63.

F/O Harry R. Bentley (Obs. RAF VR), age 22, of Irby, Cheshire. Rm. 31.

Sgt A. Clague (WOp/AG RAF VR), PoW, in *Stalag Luft VI* Heydekrug.

*Note: On 19 August 1941, two Pilots of II./ZG76 (De Kooy) shot down these three
Blenheims: Ofw. Siegfried Goebel (1 kill) and Uffz. Friedrich Pottharst (2 kills), both of
5./ZG76.*

(219) 21.8.1941.   Blenheim IV R3631 TR-B of 59 Squadron

T/o Thorney Island for shipping sweep, disappeared in North Sea.

Crew: P/O William F.W. Foster (Pilot RAF VR, from South Africa), Rm. 32.

Sgt James E. Mylchreest (Obs. RAF VR), age 23, of Liverpool. Rm. 49.

Sgt Gordon A. Crowther (WOp/AG RAF VR), age 22, of Cranford,
Middlesex. Rm. 42.

(220) 24.8.1941.   Blenheim IV Z6039 MK- of 500 Squadron

T/o 10.30 Bircham Newton for shipping sweep, shot down by *Flak* from two
harbour protection vessels at 13.05 15 km off Hook of Holland.

Crew: P/O Gordon C.M. Fletcher (Pilot RAF VR), age 23, of Golders Green,
Middlesex. Rm. 32.

Sgt John E. Mylrea (Obs. RCAF), of Los Angeles, California, U.S.A.
Rm. 61.

Sgt Hartley Walton (WOp/AG RAF), age 21, of Kellbrook, Yorkshire.
Rm. 54.

(221) 26.8.1941.   Blenheim IV Z7483 YH-N of 21 Squadron

T/o 11.55 Watton for shipping sweep in *Beat 9*, shot down by *Flak*-ship at
14.27 off Bergen aan Zee.

Crew: Sgt Alex S. Oman (Pilot RAF VR), Rm. 49.

Sgt Thomas Parkinson (Obs. RAF VR), age 24, of Anchorsholme,
Blackpool, Lancashire. Rm. 50.

Sgt Ronald Hamilton (WOp/AG RAF VR), age 24, married, of Jerbourg,
Guernsey, Channel Islands. Rm. 44.

(222) 26.8.1941.   Blenheim IV L8788 RH-N of 88 Squadron

T/o 10.30 Attlebridge for shipping sweep in *Beat 7*, shot down by ship's
Flak after attack on convoy N of Borkum. L8788 completed 35 sorties.

Crew: P/O George B. Dunn (Pilot RAF), age 25, of Skelmorlie, Ayrshire. Rm. 32.

P/O John R.A. Jones (Obs. RAF), age 25, married. Rm. 33.

F/S Basil D. Davies (WOp/AG RAF), Rm. 36.

(223) 26.8.1941.   Blenheim IV T7305 MQ-T of 226 Squadron

T/o 11.54 Wattisham for shipping sweep in *Beat 9*, shot down by ship's
Flak after attack on convoy 38 km North of IJmuiden, crashed in sea with
starboard engine on fire near convoy.

Crew: Sgt Gilbert V. Smith (Pilot RAF), age 19, of Townsville, Queensland,
Australia. Rm. 52.

Sgt Stanley Burdon (Obs. RAF VR), age 21, of Barnsley, Yorkshire.
Buried Bergen aan Zee.

Sgt Charles C. Topping (WOp/AG RCAF), age 22, of Marysville, Ontario,
Canada. Rm. 62.

26.8.1941.　　Blenheim IV Z7317 MQ- of 226 Squadron
T/o 11.54 Wattisham for shipping sweep in *Beat 9*, damaged by ship's *Flak*
during attack on convoy 38 km N of IJmuiden, belly-landed at base. A/c
repaired.
Crew:　　Sgt Bill O'Connell (Pilot RCAF), safe.
　　　　　Sgt Peter Saunders (Obs. RAF VR), safe.
　　　　　F/O Les Harrell (WOp/AG RAF), injured, invalided out of the RAF.

(224)　27/28.8.1941.　　Blenheim IV T1945 of No.2 OTU
T/o Catfoss for night training flight, got lost over North Sea and belly-
landed on Northern tip of beach at Texel at 05.40.
Crew:　　P/O N.H. Gifford (Pilot RCAF), PoW, in *Stalag Luft III* Sagan.

(225)　28.8.1941.　　Blenheim IV Z7299 MQ-F of 226 Squadron
Crashed on take-off for Rotterdam docks at Wattisham at 14.50 due to
engine failure, a/c written off.
Crew:　　Sgt Bill O'Connell (Pilot RCAF), safe.
　　　　　Sgt Peter Saunders (Obs. RAF VR), safe.
　　　　　P/O Robertson (WOp/AG RAF), safe.

(226)　28.8.1941.　　Blenheim IV Z7447 YH-A of 21 Squadron
T/o 17.41 Watton for Rotterdam docks, shot down by Rotterdam *Flak*
around 19.55 and crashed in Scheurpolder ('s Gravezande).
Crew:　　S/L Richard A. Shuttleworth (Pilot RAF), age 21, married. Died of
　　　　　wounds in Wilhelmina hospital, buried Amsterdam.
　　　　　F/S Dennis J. Mackan (Obs. RAF), age 22, of Fishponds, Bristol. Buried
　　　　　Hook of Holland.
　　　　　F/S George Brittain (WOp/AG RAF), age 20, of Carmichael, Lanarkshire.
　　　　　Buried Hook of Holland.

(227)　28.8.1941.　　Blenheim IV L9379 RH- of 88 Squadron
T/o 17.40 Attlebridge for Rotterdam docks, shot down by Rotterdam *Flak*
around 19.55 and crashed in Scheurpolder ('s Gravezande). L9379
completed 43 sorties.
Crew:　　P/O Tudor G. Edwards (Pilot RAF), B.Eng. (Liverpool), age 27, of
　　　　　Rhydymwyn, Flintshire. Buried Hook of Holland.
　　　　　P/O Frederick A. Letchford (Obs. RAF), age 29, married, of Swinton,
　　　　　Lancashire. Buried Hook of Holland.
　　　　　F/S Frank Tweedale (WOp/AG RAF), age 25, of Allerton, Liverpool.
　　　　　Buried Hook of Holland.

(228)　28.8.1941.　　Blenheim IV Z7445 RH-M of 88 Squadron
T/o 17.39 Attlebridge for Rotterdam docks, shot down by Rotterdam *Flak*
at 20.02 and crashed in slaughterhouse at Schiedam.
Crew:　　F/L James O. Alexander (Pilot RAF), age 23, married, of Victoria, B.C.
　　　　　Canada. Buried Rotterdam.
　　　　　Sgt Alexander J. Hardy (Obs. RAF), buried Rotterdam.
　　　　　F/S John L. Briggs (WOp/AG RAF), married. Buried Rotterdam.

(229)　28.8.1941.　　Blenheim IV V6436 YH-L of 21 Squadron
T/o 17.41 Watton for Rotterdam docks, shot down by Rotterdam *Flak*
between 19.55 and 20.24 and crashed at Maassluis.
Crew:　　F/O Frank K. Orme (Pilot RCAF), age 25, of Rockcliffe, Ontario, Canada.
　　　　　Buried Hook of Holland.
　　　　　F/O Stanley F.M. Gunnis (Obs. RAF VR), age 23, of Alloa, Clackmannash-
　　　　　ire. Buried Hook of Holland.
　　　　　F/O Albert H. Collins (AG RAF VR), age 34, married, of Shepherds' Bush,
　　　　　London. Buried Hook of Holland.

(230) 28.8.1941.   Blenheim IV Z7435 YH-S of 21 Squadron
T/o 17.41 Watton for Rotterdam docks, shot down by Bf109F of *Lt.* Hans
Müller (*6./JG 53*, Katwijk) at 20.15 and crashed at Rozenburg.
Crew: **Sgt Kenneth Hayes** (Pilot RAF VR), age 20, of South Norwood, Surrey.
    Buried Hook of Holland.
    Sgt Allan A.C. Shaddick (Obs. RAF VR), age 21, of East Dulwich,
    London. Buried Hook of Holland.
    Sgt Raymond F. Brian (WOp/AG RAF VR), age 20, of Birmingham.
    Buried Hook of Holland.

(231) 28.8.1941.   Blenheim IV Z7289 MQ-R of 226 Squadron
T/o 17.35 Wattisham for Rotterdam docks, shot down by Rotterdam *Flak* at
20.23 and belly-landed on flames at Kethel.
Crew: **P/O F.M.W. Johnstone** (Pilot RAF), PoW, in *Stalag Luft III* Sagan.
    Sgt R. Evans (Obs. RAF), PoW, in *Stalag Luft VI* Heydekrug.
    Sgt R.G. Drake (WOp/AG RAF), PoW, in *Stalag Luft VI* Heydekrug.

(232) 28.8.1941.   Blenheim IV V5825 YH-R of 21 Squadron
T/o 17.41 Watton for Rotterdam docks, shot down by Bf109F of *Lt.* Hans
Müller (*6./JG 53*, Katwijk) at 20.25 and crashed in North Sea SW of
Rotterdam.
Crew: **P/O W.L. MacDonald** (Pilot RAF), PoW, in *Stalag Luft III* Sagan.
    Sgt Raymond J. Somerfield (Obs. RAF VR), of Norton, Sheffield. Rm. 52.
    P/O W. Beckingham (WOp/AG RAF), PoW.

(233) 30/31.8.1941.   Blenheim IV V5525 MK-B of 500 Squadron
T/o Bircham Newton 21.21 for general recce, shot down by *Res. Flak
Abt./242* during attack on Schiphol AF and crashed at 23.37 at Amster-
damse Bos near Schiphol.
Crew: **Sgt David A. Crosbie** (Pilot RAF VR), age 23, of Glasgow. Buried
    Amsterdam.
    Sgt Douglas C. Hyslop (Pilot RAF VR), age 28, married, of Darnaway,
    Morayshire. Buried Amsterdam.
    Sgt Alan Harry Peek (WOp/AG RAF VR), age 20, of Lowestoft, Suffolk.
    Buried Amsterdam.

(234) 30/31.8.1941.   Blenheim IV Z6164 MK-V of 500 Squadron
T/o Bircham Newton 21.21 for Soesterberg airfield, crashed in North Sea
possibly off Noordwijk.
Crew: **F/O Ian H.N. Terry** (Pilot RAF VR), age 21, married, of Hampton,
    Middlesex. Rm. 30.
    Sgt Harry D. Poole (Obs. RAF VR), age 22, of Aylesford, Kent. Rm. 50.
    Sgt Alan C. Scrivens (WOp/AG RAF VR), age 20, of Hove, Sussex.
    Rm. 51.

(235) 2.9.1941.   Blenheim IV Z7274 XD- of 139 Squadron
T/o 10.23 Manston for shipping sweep off Belgian coast, shot down by
Flak-ship during attack on convoy off Zeebrugge/Belgium.
Crew: **S/L Kevin H. Walsh** (Pilot RAF), buried Wenduine/Belgium.
    F/S Alfred G. Hole (Obs. RAF), age 30, of Brislongton, Bristol. Buried
    Flushing.
    Sgt George H. Brook (WOp/AG RAF VR), age 29, of Huddersfield. Rm.
    40.

(236) 7.9.1941.   Blenheim IV Z7312 MQ-N of 226 Squadron

T/o 12.04 Wattisham for shipping Beat off Katwijk, shot down by Bf109F of *I./JG 52* at 14.00 during attack on convoy off The Hague.

Crew: F/L **Clarence E.C. Haggitt** (Pilot RAF), age 30, married, of Vancouver, B.C., Canada. Died in Wilhelmina Hospital, Amsterdam on 9-9-41. Buried Amsterdam.

P/O **Robert F. Bennett** (Obs. RAF VR), age 20, of Kensington, London. Rm. 31.

F/O **Charles D. Ramsay** (WOp/AG RAF VR), age 31, married, of Abergavenny, Monmouthshire. Rm. 30.

(237) 7.9.1941.   Blenheim IV Z7306 MQ-U of 226 Squadron

T/o 12.04 Wattisham for shipping *Beat* off Katwijk, shot down by Bf109F of *I./JG 52* at 14.00 during attack on convoy off The Hague.

Crew: Sgt **John D. Fieldman** (Pilot RAF VR), age 19, of Ipswich, Suffolk. Rm. 43.

Sgt **Frank K. Phillips** (Obs. RAF VR), age 24, of Twickenham, Middlesex. Buried Hook of Holland.

Sgt **John H. Carr** (WOp/AG RAF VR), age 21, of Erdington, Birmingham. Rm. 40.

7.9.1941.   Blenheim IV Z7304 MQ-S of 226 Squadron

T/o 12.04 Wattisham for shipping *Beat* off Katwijk, claimed destroyed by Bf109Fs of *I./JG 52* and *Flak*-ships during convoy attack off The Hague, but reached England badly shot up and belly-landed at base. A/c repaired.

Crew: P/O **William Gray** (Pilot RCAF), safe.

P/O **McCarthy** (Obs. RAF), safe.

P/O **Casey** (WOp/AG RCAF), injured.

Note: On 7 September 1941, 3 German Bf109 pilots claimed these 3 Blenheims shot down off The Hague: Uffz. Herbert Hohmeyer and Uffz. Otto Milbauer, both of 3./JG 52 (Katwijk), and Uffz. Walter Kühn of 1./JG 52 (Woensdrecht). Two Flak-ships also claimed to have contributed towards the destruction of these three Blenheims: Harbour protection vessels HS802 and HS812.

(238) 16.9.1941.   Blenheim IV V6339 WV-C of 18 Squadron

T/o 12.30 Horsham St. Faith for Squealer sweep in *Beat B*, hit sea off Texel with centre of under-fuselage, leaving wake in sea, then disappeared. Probably pilot error.

Crew: Sgt **Charles A. Tracey** (Pilot RAF VR), age 24, of Handsworth, Birmingham. Buried Den Burg/Texel.

P/O **Jack H. Rodgers** (Obs. RAF VR), age 25, of Sheffield, Yorkshire. Rm. 34.

Sgt **Albert H. Higgs** (WOp/AG RAF VR), age 25, married, of Smethwick, Staffordshire. Rm. 45.

(239) 18.9.1941.   Blenheim IV V6380 RH-G of 88 Squadron

T/o 09.40 Attlebridge for *Channel Stop* sweep in *Beat 9*, shot down by Bf110 of *Lt.* Hans-Heinrich Koenig (*5./ZG 76*, De Kooy) off Blankenberge/Belgium.

Crew: P/O **Robert M. Burlinson** (Pilot RCAF), age 23, of Tucson, Arizona, U.S.A. Buried Amsterdam.

P/O **Bruce E. Hislop** (Obs. RAAF), age 26, of St. Kilda, Victoria, Australia. Rm. 62.

Sgt **Maurice B. Stratton** (WOp/AG RAF VR), age 30, of Twickenham, Middlesex. Buried Bergen op Zoom.

(240) 20.9.1941.   Blenheim IV R3843 WV-F of 18 Squadron
T/o 12.37 Horsham St. Faith for shipping sweep in *Beat 9*, flew into bomb
bursts of another Blenheim during attack on convoy and crashed in flames
into sea off Zandvoort. R3843 successfully completed 34 sorties.
Crew: Sgt **John M. Nickleson** (Pilot RCAF), age 19, of Toronto, Ontario,
Canada. Rm. 60.
Sgt **Walter Meadows** (Obs. RAF), age 26, of Askrigg, Yorkshire. Buried
Bergen op Zoom.
Sgt **John E. Pearson** (WOp/AG RAF VR), age 25, of Erdington,
Birmingham. Buried Amsterdam.

(241) 20.9.1941.   Blenheim IV Z7310 MQ-V of 226 Squadron
T/o Wattisham for shipping sweep in *Beat 10*, shot down by *Flak*-ship
during attack on convoy off Hook of Holland.
Crew: F/L Mayer **H.R. Namias** (Pilot RAF VR), age 20, of Knightsbridge,
London. Rm. 29.
Sgt **Kenneth F. Hood** (Obs. RAF VR), age 19, of Brighton, Sussex. Buried
Rotterdam.
Sgt **John J. Robson** (WOp/AG RAF VR), of Crawcrook, Co. Durham.
Buried Rotterdam.

(242) 20.9.1941.   Blenheim IV V6422 MQ- of 226 Squadron
T/o Wattisham for shipping sweep in Beat 10, blew up by bursting bombs
during attack on convoy off Hook of Holland.
Crew: Sgt **James C.V. Colmer** (Pilot RAF VR), age 20, buried Amsterdam.
Sgt **Gordon K. Bartlett** (Obs. RAAF), age 21, of Hawthorn, South
Australia. Buried Amsterdam.
Sgt **Leslie Trevor** (WOp/AG RAF VR), age 31, Rm. 53.

(243) 23.9.1941.   Blenheim IV V5684 MK- of 500 Squadron
T/o Bircham Newton for shipping sweep, crashed in North Sea.
Crew: P/O **Sidney G. Nicoll** (Pilot RAF VR), Rm. 34.
F/O **Robert E.M. Hughes-Chamberlain** (Obs. RAF), age 22, of North-
wood, Middlesex. Rm. 30.
Sgt **Jack B. Crees** (WOp/AG RAF VR), age 25, of Mutley, Plymouth.
Rm. 41.

(244) 10/11.10.1941.   Blenheim IV V6171 MK-F of 500 Squadron
T/o Bircham Newton for Dutch coast shipping sweep, crashed in North
Sea.
Crew: F/O **E.A. Webb** (Pilot RAAF), PoW, in *Stalag 357* Kopernikus.
F/S **Robert C. Roberts** (Obs. RCAF), age 31, of St. Lambert, Quebec,
Canada. Rm. 60.
Sgt **Ronald H. Coomber** (WOp/AG RAF Aux.AF), age 20, of Harrietsham,
Kent. Rm. 41.

(245) 12.10.1941.   Blenheim IV V5824 UX-C of 82 Squadron
T/o 11.55 Bodney for shipping sweep between Scheveningen and IJmuiden,
shot down by *Flak*-ship *Vp1107* at 14.26 during attack on convoy off
IJmuiden.
Crew: Sgt **John J. Ashurst** (Pilot RAF VR), age 21, of Trethomas, Monmouth-
shire. Rm. 48.
Sgt **Thomas V. Steele** (Obs. RAF VR), Rm. 52.
Sgt **Reginald J. Banks** (WOp/AG RAF VR), age 21, of Farncombe,
Godalming, Surrey. Buried The Hague.

(246) 12.10.1941.   Blenheim IV L4880 UX-Z of 82 Squadron
T/o 11.55 Bodney for shipping sweep between Scheveningen and IJmuiden,
shot down by *Flak*-ship *Vp1107* at 14.26 during attack on convoy off
IJmuiden.
Crew: **Sgt Frederick E.V. Day** (Pilot RAF VR), age 21, of Blaengarw,
Glamorgan. Rm. 42.
Sgt Gregory A. Robbins (Obs. RAF VR), age 24, of Wateringbury, Kent.
Buried The Hague.
Sgt Frederick V.F. Lane (WOp/AG RAF VR), age 28, of Orpington, Kent.
Rm. 47.

(247) 15.10.1941.   Blenheim IV V6249 XD- of 139 Squadron
T/o 07.58 Oulton for shipping sweep in *Beat 7*, shot down by ship's *Flak* or
Bf109 of *3./JG 52* SW of Heligoland.
Crew: **S/L Richard T. Stubbs DFC** (Pilot RAF), age 25, married, of Chiswick,
Middlesex. Rm. 28.
P/O John W. Bradley (Obs. RAF VR), age 23, of Belfast. Rm. 31.
Sgt William P. Thom (WOp/AG RCAF), age 32, of Glasgow. Rm. 62.

(248) 15.10.1941.   Blenheim IV Z7320 XD- of 139 Squadron
T/o 07.58 Oulton for shipping sweep in *Beat 7*, shot down by ship's *Flak* or
Bf109 of *3./JG 52* SW of Heligoland.
Crew: **F/O Thomas R. Paxton** (Pilot RAF VR), age 21, of Chapel-en-le-Frith,
Derbyshire. Rm. 30.
P/O Herbert M. Clarke (Obs. RAF VR), age 27, married, of Nottingham.
Rm. 31.
F/O Royston C. Holloway (WOp/AG RAF VR), age 31, married, of
Worcester Park, Surrey. Rm. 30.

(249) 15.10.1941.   Blenheim IV Z7300 XD- of 139 Squadron
T/o 07.58 Oulton for shipping sweep in *Beat 7*, shot down by ship's *Flak* or
Bf109 of *3./JG 52* SW of Heligoland.
Crew: **Sgt Edward F.G. Gill** (Pilot RAF VR), Rm. 43.
Sgt Albert W. Humphries (Obs. RAF VR), age 21, of Cheltenham,
Gloucestershire. Rm. 45.
Sgt Duncan W. Marshall (WOp/AG RAF VR), age 23, Rm. 48.

(250) 15.10.1941.   Blenheim IV V5875 RT- of 114 Squadron
T/o 07.45 West Raynham for shipping sweep in *Beat 8*, shot down by Bf110
of *5./ZG 76* at 12.05 130 km WNW of Den Helder.
Crew: **Sgt Christian S. Balzer** (Pilot RAAF), age 22, of Lismore, N.S.W.,
Australia. Buried Harlingen.
Sgt Howard L. Elliott (Obs. RCAF), age 24, of Forgan, Saskatchewan,
Canada. Rm. 61.
Sgt Victor F.W. Slade (WOp/AG RAF), age 28, of East Ham, Essex.
Rm. 52.

(251) 15.10.1941.   Blenheim IV L9382 RT- of 114 Squadron
T/o 07.45 West Raynham for shipping sweep in *Beat 8*, shot down by Bf110
of *5./ZG 76* at 12.05 130 km WNW of Den Helder.
Crew: **P/O William H. Davidson** (Pilot RCAF), age 22, of Preston, Ontario,
Canada. Rm. 59.
Sgt Edwin K. Saul (Obs. RAF VR), Rm. 51.
Sgt David G. Peppler (WOp/AG RAF VR), Rm. 50.
Note: On 15 October 1941, these two 114 Squadron Blenheims were shot down by Ofw.
Siegfried Goebel and Lt. Hans Heinrich Koenig, both of 5./ZG 76 (De Kooy).

(252) 21.10.1941. Blenheim IV V5580 YH-X of 21 Squadron
T/o 12.15 Watton for shipping sweep in *Beat 8*, hit sea with propellers and ditched off Terschelling.
Crew: F/L Frederick C. Powles DFC (Pilot RAF), age 29, of Harrow, Middlesex.
Buried Sage, Germany.
Sgt John D. Life (Obs. RAF VR), age 21, of Ryde, Isle of Wight.
Buried Sage.
F/S Simon J. Williams (WOp/AG RAF), buried Sage.

(253) 21.10.1941. Blenheim IV V5634 UX-A of 82 Squadron
T/o 13.30 Bodney for shipping sweep in *Beat 9* (IJmuiden), shot down at 15.35 by Bf109F of *Fw.* Josef Ederer (*3./JG 53*, Katwijk) during attack on convoy off Katwijk.
Crew: P/O James H. Richardson (Pilot RAF), Rm. 34.
F/S Alec J. Park (Obs. RAF), age 21, of Barrow-in-Furness, Lancashire. Rm. 50.
F/S George C.P. Haines (WOp/AG RAF), Rm. 36.

(254) 21.10.1941. Blenheim IV V6146 UX-O of 82 Squadron
T/o 13.30 Bodney for shipping sweep in *Beat 9* (IJmuiden), shot down ca.14.30 by Bf109F of *Fw.* Josef Ederer (*3./JG 53*, Katwijk) during attack on convoy off Katwijk.
Crew: P/O Bruce B. Barber (Pilot RAAF), age 29, of Warsash, Hampshire. Rm. 62.
P/O Henry H. Pibus (Obs. RCAF), B.A. age 28, married, of Vancouver, B.C., Canada. Rm. 60.
Sgt Edward W. Paine (WOp/AG RAF), Rm. 49.

(255) 25.10.1941. Blenheim IV V5538 MK- of 500 Squadron
T/o 05.10 Bircham Newton for shipping sweep to The Hague area, crashed in North Sea.
Crew: P/O Logie W. Brown (Pilot RAF VR), age 21, of Allestree, Derbyshire. Rm. 31.
Sgt Paul A.V. Lyons (Obs. RAF VR), Rm. 47.
Sgt James K. Mitchell (WOp/AG RAF VR), age 20, of Gretna, Dumfriesshire. Rm. 48.

(256) 26.10.1941. Blenheim IV V6421 RH-Y of 88 Squadron
T/o 14.10 Attlebridge for shipping sweep off The Hague, hit by ship's *Flak* during attack on convoy and ditched 70 km WNW of The Hague.
Crew: P/O Jack Rollinson (Pilot RAF VR), age 19, of Huddersfield. Rm. 34.
P/O Arthur E. Day (Obs. RAF VR), age 23, of Banbury, Oxfordshire. Rm. 32.
Sgt Edward W. Andrews (WOp/AG RAF VR), age 29, married, of Beacon Hill. Rm. 38.

(257) 27.10.1941. Blenheim IV Z7309 RT-G of 114 Squadron
T/o 13.05 West Raynham for shipping sweep in *Beat 9*, shot down by Bf109F of *4./JG 53* at 15.06 after attack on convoy off Texel, exploded on impact.
Crew: P/O Walter G.C. Beatson (Pilot RAF VR), age 19, of Chardstock, Devon. Rm. 31.
P/O Haydn Jones (Obs. RAF VR), Rm. 33.
Sgt James Bradshaw (WOp/AG RCAF), age 33. Rm. 60.

(258) 27.10.1941.   Blenheim IV V5888 RT-A of 114 Squadron
T/o 13.05 West Raynham for shipping sweep in *Beat 9*, hit by ship's *Flak*
during attack on convoy off Texel and finished off by Bf109F of *4./JG 53* at
15.06, exploded on impact.
Crew: **Sgt James W. Bradley** (Pilot RAF), age 21, of Bromley, Kent. Rm. 40.
          P/O Raymond H. Batten (Obs. RAF), age 25, of Bristol. Rm. 31.
          Sgt Eric D. Kennedy (WOp/AG RAF VR), buried Terschelling.
*Note: On 27 October 1941, these two Blenheims of 114 Squadron were shot down by: Lt.
Fritz Dinger and Uffz. Fritz Muschter, both of 4./JG 53 (Leeuwarden).*

(259) 31/1.11.1941.   Blenheim IV V5537 MK-M of 500 Squadron
T/o Bircham Newton for shipping sweep off Dutch Frisians, crashed at
23.50 in IJsselmeer 6 km W of Lemmer.
Crew: **S/L Francis C. Phipps** (Pilot RAF), B.A. (Cantab.), age 27, married, of
          Sutton, Surrey. Rm. 28.
          Sgt Terence P. Mowan (Obs. RAF VR), age 21, of Peverell, Plymouth.
          Rm. 49.
          Sgt Allen A. Miles (WOp/AG RAF VR), Rm. 48.

(260) 4/5.11.1941.   Blenheim IV Z5959 MK-X of 500 Squadron
T/o 21.15 Bircham Newton for shipping sweep off Dutch Frisians, crashed
in North Sea off Terschelling.
Crew: **F/O William J. Sipprell** (Pilot RAF), age 20, of New Westminster, B.C.,
          Canada. Rm. 34.
          Sgt Amos T. Hall (Obs. RNZAF), age 28, of Dalmore, Dunedin, New
          Zealand. Rm. 64.
          Sgt Harry R. Davies (WOp/AG RAF VR), age 24, of Birmingham. Rm. 42.

(261) 10/11.1.1942.   Blenheim IV V6440 UX-X of 82 Squadron
T/o 17.38 Bodney for Soesterberg A/F, shot down by *Res. Flak Abt. 155* at
20.50 and crashed at Soesterberg village.
Crew: **F/L Kenneth H. Nash** (Pilot RAF), age 21, buried Amersfoort.
          Sgt Harry C. Downs (Obs. RNZAF), age 22, of Lowry Bay, Wellington,
          New Zealand. Buried Amersfoort.
          Sgt Edgar F.J. Cooper (WOp/AG RAF VR), age 26, married, of Bridgend,
          Glamorgan. Buried Amersfoort.

(262) 14/15.1.1942.   Blenheim IV V6391 RT-V of 114 Squadron
T/o 17.35 West Raynham for Schiphol A/F, shot down by ship's *Flak* at
20.42 off Schiermonnikoog.
Crew: **F/L Basil J. Adam** (Pilot RAAF), age 22, married, of St. Kilda, Victoria,
          Australia. Rm. 108.
          Sgt Joseph A. Willis (Obs. VR), age 25, of Gillingham, Kent. Rm. 96.
          P/O Frederick W.O. Street-Porter (WOp/AG RAF VR), of Canada.
          Rm. 67.

(263) 14/15.1.1942.   Blenheim IV V6378 UX-Z of 82 Squadron
T/o 18.12 Bodney for Schiphol A/F, crashed in North Sea.
Crew: **F/O Richard Harding-Browne** (Pilot RAAF), age 21, of Adelaide, South
          Australia. Rm. 110.
          P/O William G. Scarlett (Obs. RAF VR), age 28, married, of Palmer's
          Green. Rm. 71.
          P/O Edward W.M. Garstin (WOp/AG RAF VR), age 32, married, of
          Tunbridge Wells, Kent. Rm. 69.

(264) 28/29.1.1942.   Blenheim IV V5726 RT-R of 114 Squadron
T/o 18.00 West Raynham for Leeuwarden A/F, shot down by *Res. Flak Abt.*
242 at 22.30 and crashed near Schiphol.
Crew: **Sgt Thomas A. Peters** (Pilot RAF VR), age 21, of Isleworth, Middlesex.
Buried Amsterdam.
Sgt George N. Church (Obs. RAAF), age 22, married, of Banksia, NSW,
Australia. Buried Amsterdam.
Sgt Kenneth M. Bird (WOp/AG RAF VR), buried Amsterdam.

(265) 12.2.1942.   Blenheim IV Z7433 VE- of 110 Squadron
T/o 13.30 Wattisham for 'Channel Dash' sweep, shot down by Bf109F of
probably *Oblt.* Max Buchholz (*5./JG 1*, Haamstede) at 16.43, crashed in
flames 90 km W of Texel.
Crew: **Sgt Peter L. Reynolds** (Pilot RAF VR), age 20, of Hendon, Middlesex.
Rm. 92.
P/O Peter J. Hill (Obs. RAF VR), age 18, of Yardley, Birmingham. Rm. 70.
Sgt Hugh P.A. Guilfoyle (WOp/AG RAF VR), age 20, married, of Whalley,
Lancashire. Rm. 84.

(266) 12.2.1942.   Blenheim IV T1922 RT-K of 114 Squadron
T/o 14.10 West Raynham for 'Channel Dash' sweep, crashed in North Sea
off Dutch coast, possibly Pilot error.
Crew: **P/O Robert E. Drysdale** (Pilot RCAF), age 21, of Perth, Ontario, Canada.
Buried Flushing.
Sgt Arthur S. Maynard (Obs. RAF VR), buried Hook of Holland.
Sgt John S. Pullen (WOp/AG RAF VR), age 32, of Mount Barker, Western
Australia. Rm. 91.

(267) 26/27.3.1942.   Blenheim IV Z7307 RT-L of 114 Squadron
T/o 20.45 West Raynham for Soesterberg A/F, shot down by Bf110 of *Oblt.*
Paul Gildner (*II./NJG 2*, Leeuwarden) at 23.57 and crashed in Waddenzee
N of Wieringen.
Crew: **F/S William M. Popplestone** (Pilot RCAF), age 22, of Pilot Mound,
Manitoba, Canada. Buried Harlingen.
P/O William G.F. Hawkins (Obs. RAF VR), age 34, married, of Bromley,
Kent. Rm. 70.
P/O Cyril E. White (WOp/AG RAF VR), buried Harlingen.

(268) 26/27.3.1942.   Blenheim IV Z7700 RT-Q of 114 Squadron
T/o 21.40 West Raynham for Dutch A/F, crashed in North Sea.
Crew: **F/L E. Martin Bury** (Pilot RAF), age 30, married with a son, of Carlisle,
Western Australia. Rm. 65.
Sgt John S. Beauchamp (Obs. RAF VR), age 22, of Maida Vale, London.
Rm. 78.
Sgt Thomas Crilly (WOp/AG RAF VR), age 21, married, of Bellshill,
Lanarkshire. Rm. 80.

(269) 27/28.3.1942.   Blenheim IV Z7276 RT-N of 114 Squadron
T/o 19.20 West Raynham for Soesterberg A/F, shot down at 22.28 by *Flak*
of *2./Res.155, 5./Res.155, 2/le Flak Abt. 764* and crashed in flames near
Estate *'Djimat'* at Zeist.
Crew: **W/C J. Fraser G. Jenkins DSO, DFC** (Pilot & CO 114 Sqn. RAF VR),
B.A. (Cantab.), age 24, of Noctorum, Cheshire. Buried Amersfoort.
F/O H. Paul Brancker DFC & Bar MiD (Obs. RAF VR), age 30, of Four
Oaks, Sutton Coldfield, Warwickshire. Buried Amersfoort.
F/S Charles H. Gray DFM (WOp/AG RAF VR), age 21, of Prestwick,
Lancashire. Buried Amersfoort.

27/28.3.1942.   Blenheim IV R3620 RT-A of 114 Squadron
T/o 19.21 West Raynham for Schiphol A/F, damaged by *Flak* over target
and crashed on return at base. A/c repaired.
Crew: F/S Eric 'Tommy' Atkins (Pilot), injured.
Sgt Jock Sullivan (Obs.), safe.
Sgt Bill Harrison (WOp/AG), safe.

(270) 17/18.4.1942.   Blenheim IV Z7430 RT-Q of 114 Squadron
T/o 21.36 West Raynham for Schiphol A/F, damaged by light *Flak* over
target and crash-landed at 23.22 at Aalsmeer.
Crew: W/C George L.B 'Bok' Hull DFC (Pilot & C.O. 114 Sqn. RAF, of Southern
Rhodesia), PoW, in *Stalag Luft III* Sagan.
F/L Thomas H. Baker DFC DFM MiD (Obs. RAF), PoW, in
Stalag Luft III Sagan.
P/O Julian R. Morton (WOp/AG RAAF), PoW, in *Stalag Luft III* Sagan.

(271) 24/25.4.1942.   Blenheim IV V5458 RT-O of 114 Squadron
T/o 00.40 West Raynham for Leeuwarden A/F, crashed in North Sea off
Dutch coast.
Crew: Sgt Patrick McKenny (Pilot RAF VR), age 23, married, of Manchester.
Rm. 88.
Sgt James McIntyre (Obs. RAF VR), Rm. 88.
Sgt Joseph Lewis (WOp/AG RAF VR), age 26, of Lisburn, Co. Antrim.
Rm. 88.

(272) 26/27.4.1942.   Blenheim IV T2430 RT-Q of 114 Squadron
T/o 22.25 West Raynham for Eindhoven A/F, crashed and burnt out at
Pulham/Norfolk on return due to being damaged by Ju88 NF over Dutch
coast.
Crew: P/O J.R.N. (Bob) Molesworth (Pilot RAAF), injured, awarded DFC.
P/O E.F.K. (Tim) Denny (Obs.), injured, awarded DFC.
Sgt W.H. (Bill) Burberry (WOp/AG), injured.

(273) 6.5.1942.   Blenheim IV L8755 of 13 OTU.,
T/o Bicester for cross-country exercise including route over North Sea,
crashed in North Sea.
Crew: Sgt Thomas A. Crawford (Pilot RCAF), buried Ameland.
Sgt Donald J. McKenzie (Obs. RNZAF), age 27, of Awara Plains,
Southland, New Zealand. Rm. 117.
F/S Wesley N. Ward (WOp/AG RAF VR), Rm. 76.

(274) 6/7.5.1942.   Blenheim IV V6382 WV- of 18 Squadron
T/o 22.11 Wattisham for Eindhoven A/F, crashed in North Sea.
Crew: P/O Henry P. Palmer (Pilot RAF), age 20, of Portheawl, Glamorgan.
Rm. 71.
Sgt William E. Lindsell (Obs. RAF VR), age 21, of Finchley, Middlesex.
Rm. 88.
Sgt Ewart J. Andrews (WOp/AG RAF VR), Rm. 77.

(275) 1/2.6.1942.   Blenheim IV V6337 RT-D of 114 Squadron
T/o 22.41 West Raynham for Twente, Venlo or Bonn A/F, shot down by
Flak at 00.06 and crashed in English Channel.
Crew: Sgt John L. Mitchell (Pilot RAF), age 21, of Tottenham, Middlesex.
Buried Dunkirk, France.
Sgt Ronald M. McIntosh (Obs. RAF VR), age 32, married, of Newcastle-
on-Tyne. Buried Rockanje.
Sgt Leonard A. Fussey (WOp/AG RAF VR), buried Dunkirk.

(276) 1/2.6.1942.   Blenheim IV Z6186 OO-E of 13 Squadron
T/o 22.29 Wattisham for Venlo A/F, crashed in Germany.
Crew: F/L **Douglas G. Redman** (Pilot RAF), age 25, of Twyford, Hampshire.
Buried Reichswald, Germany.
F/S **Peter F.P. Enna** (Obs. RAF VR), age 22, of Sidcup, Kent. Buried
Reichswald, Germany
F/S **Thomas F. Trimmer** (WOp/AG RAF), age 22, of Brownsover,
Warwickshire. buried Reichswald, Germany

(277) 4/5.6.1942.   Blenheim IV L8800 RT-C of 114 Squadron
Hit tree and crashed on t/o West Raynham at 01.31 for Schiphol A/F and
burned out. L8800 successfully completed 32 sorties.
Crew: Sgt **Frank O. Cooke** (Pilot RAF), of Sandbach. Buried Sandbach/Cheshire.
Sgt **Jack M. Wallbridge** (Obs. RAF VR), age 24, married, of Birmingham.
Buried Birmingham.
F/S **Eric Kitcher** (WOp/AG RAF VR), age 21, married, of Wallington,
Surrey. Buried Clifton-on-Dunsmore, Warwickshire.

(278) 25/26.6.1942.   Blenheim IV T2254 OO-A of 13 Squadron
T/o 23.50 Wattisham for Venlo A/F, shot down by Bf110 of *Oblt*. Reinhold
Knacke (*I./NJG 1*, Venlo) and crashed at Aartselaar/Belgium.
Crew: F/O **Peter H. Looker** (Pilot RAF), age 22, of Surbiton, Surrey. Buried
Schoonselhof, Antwerp.
F/S **William G. O'Neill** (Obs. RNZAF), age 21, of Kaikone, Auckland, New
Zealand. Buried Antwerp.
Sgt **Gordon W. Cox** (WOp/AG RAF VR), age 22, of Odiham, Hampshire.
Buried Antwerp.

(279) 13/14.7.1942.   Blenheim IV V6071 WV- of 18 Squadron
T/o 00.10 Wattisham for Deelen A/F, shot down by *Res. Flak Abt. 242* at
01.19 and crashed at Amsterdamse Bos near Schiphol.
Crew: P/O **Peter C. Coulthard** (Pilot RAF VR), age 19, of Doncaster, Yorkshire.
Buried Amsterdam.
Sgt **Arthur D. Meech** (Obs. RAF VR), buried Amsterdam.
P/O **Lyn G.L. Ward** (WOp/AG RAF VR), buried Amsterdam.

(280) 25/26.7.1942.   Blenheim IV V6264 RT-X of 114 Squadron
T/o 23.55 West Raynham for Leeuwarden A/F, crashed in North Sea off
Dutch coast.
Crew: W/O I **Eugene E. Warnick** (Pilot RCAF), age 23, of Hamilton, Ontario,
Canada. Rm. 101.
F/S **Percy C. Leslie** (Obs. RCAF), Rm. 105.
F/S **Robert A. Smith** (WOp/AG RCAF), age 20, of Elgin, Albert Co., New
Brunswick, Canada. Rm. 106.

(281) 25/26.7.1942.   Blenheim IV R3837 RT-T of 114 Squadron
T/o 23.46 West Raynham for Venlo A/F, shot down by Bf110 of *Oblt*.
Reinhold Knacke (*I./NJG 1*, Venlo) and crashed at Schandeloo near Venlo
at 01.20.
Crew: Sgt **Leonard Causley** (Pilot RAF VR), age 28, married, of Plympton,
Devon. Buried Nijmegen.
Sgt **George R.S. Spencer** (Obs. RAF VR), age 30, married, of Ilford,
Essex. Buried Nijmegen.
Sgt **Lawrence A.L. Gray** (WOp/AG RAF VR), age 34, married, of Purley,
Surrey. Buried Nijmegen.

(282) 28/29.7.1942. Blenheim IV Z7351 WV- of 18 Squadron

T/o Wattisham 21.25 for Stade A/F, possibly shot down by ship's *Flak* at 22.35 and crashed in North Sea N of Terschelling.

Crew: P/O Swante O. Hill (Pilot RCAF), age 21, married, of Norwich. Buried Sage, Germany.

W/O II Donald R. McKinnon (Obs. RCAF), buried Sage.

Sgt Derek Williams (WOp/AG RAF VR), buried Sage.

(283) 31/1.8.1942. Blenheim IV V6432 WV- of 18 Squadron

T/o 23.06 Wattisham for Venlo A/F, shot down by Bf110 of *Hptm.* Werner Streib (*I./NJG 1*, Venlo) at 00.15, crashed at Kevelaer, Germany.

Crew: W/C Christopher H. Jones DFC (Pilot RAF & C.O. 18 Sqn.), buried Reichswald, Germany.

Sgt Kenneth M. Waylett (Obs. RAF VR), age 22, of Sholing, Southampton. Buried Reichswald.

Sgt Austen D. Evans (WOp/AG RAF VR), age 30, married, of Amblecote, Stourbridge, Worcestershire. Buried Reichswald.

Appendix II
German fighter pilots who gained Blenheim victories over Holland and their fates

Note: Ranks and units mentioned are those at the time of these pilots' Blenheim kills.

Oberleutnant Walter Adolph (*St.Kpt. 2./JG 26*)
KIA 18.9.41 NW of Ostend in combat with Blenheims and Spitfires. Ace with 27 victories, awarded *Ritterkreuz.*

Feldwebel Heinrich Wilhelm Ahnert (*3./JG 52*)
KIA 23.8.42 in Russia. Ace with 57 victories, awarded *Ritterkreuz.*

Unteroffizier Arngrimm (*6./ZG 76*)
Fate unknown.

Oberleutnant Roloff von Aspern (*St.Kpt. 2./JG 76*)
MIA 17.11.40 in air combat over mouth of River Thames. Ace with 18 victories.

Feldwebel Friedrich Karl Bachmann (*3./JG 52*)
KIA 4.9.42. Ace with 31 victories.

Unteroffizier Barein (*1./JG 1*)
Fate unknown.

Unteroffizier Karl-Heinz Bendert (*II./JG 27*)
Survived the war as ace with 55 victories, awarded *Ritterkreuz.*

Oberleutnant Helmut Bennemann (*Stab I./JG 52*)
Survived the war as ace with 93 victories, awarded *Ritterkreuz.*

Leutnant Hans Reinhard Bethke (*3./JG 52*)
KIA 2.9.43, 1 victory.

Feldwebel **Franz Blazytko** (*I./JG 1*)
POW 25.9.41 in Russia, ace with 29 victories. Survived the war.

Leutnant **Hans-Ekkehard Bob** (*9./JG 54*)
Survived the war as ace with 60 victories, awarded *Ritterkreuz*.

Leutnant **Borchert** (*I./JG 27*)
Fate unknown, 1 victory.

Oberleutnant **Erhard Braune** (*I./JG 1*)
Survived the war, ace with 14 victories.

Leutnant **Fritz Dinger** (*4./JG 53*)
KIA 27.7.43 at Scalea/Italy during Allied bombing raid. Ace with 67 victories, awarded Ritterkreuz.

Unteroffizier **Werner Dobreck** (*5./ZG 76*)
WIA 20.8.41 in combat with Blenheims and Spitfires/Hurricanes off Bergen-aan-Zee. Fate unknown.

Oberleutnant **Franz Eckerle** (*3./JG 76*)
MIA 14.2.42 over Welikije Luki/Russia. Ace with 59 number of victories, awarded *Ritterkreuz* with Oak Leaves.

Feldwebel **Josef Ederer** (*3./JG 53*)
Survived the war, ace with 7 victories.

Oberleutnant Christian Eichhoff (*2./JG 26*)
KIA 26.1.43, ace with 5 victories.

Hauptmann **Wolfgang Falck** (*St.Kpt. 2./ZG 76*)
Survived the war as ace with 7 victories. Founding Father of *Luftwaffe* Night Fighter Arm, awarded *Ritterkreuz*.

Leutnant **Emmerich Fluder** (*5./JG 27*)]
KIA 31.5.42, ace with 8 victories.

Oberleutnant **Gert Framm** (*I./JG 27*)
Survived the war as ace with 10 victories.

Oberstleutnant **Adolf Galland** (*Kommodore JG 26*)
Survived the war as ace with 103 victories. Awarded *Ritterkreuz* with Oak Leaves, Swords and Diamonds.

Oberfeldwebel/Oberleutnant **Paul Gildner** *(4./NJG 1* **and** *II./NJG 2)*
KIA 24/25.2.43 near Gilze Rijen A/F. Ace with 44 victories, 42 of these at night. Awarded *Ritterkreuz.*

Oberfeldwebel **Siegfried Göbel** *(5./ZG 76)*
At least 4 victories. Fate unknown.

Unteroffizier **Karl Hammerl** *(1./JG 52)*
WIA 2.3.43 in Russia, died in Russian captivity. Ace with 67 victories, awarded *Ritterkreuz.*

Oberleutnant **Wilhelm Herget** *(4./ZG 76*
Survived the war as ace with 73 victories, 53 of these at night. Awarded *Ritterkreuz* with Oak Leaves.

Unteroffizier **Herbert Hohmeyer** *(3./JG 52)*
KIA 5.1.44, ace with 14 victories.

Oberleutnant **Baron Freiherr Hubertus von Holtey** *(Stab./ JG 26)*
1 victory, survived the war.

Oberleutnant **Gerhard Homuth** *(I./JG 1)*
MIA 2.8.43 in combat with Russian fighters. Ace with 63 victories, awarded *Ritterkreuz.*

Unteroffizier **Horst** *(WOp/AG 5./ZG 76)*
Fate unknown.

Leutnant **Erbo Graf von Kageneck** *(I./JG 1)*
WIA 21.1.42 in combat with Hurricanes over Agedabia/Lybia, died 12.1.42. Ace with 67 victories, awarded *Ritterkreuz* with Oak Leaves.

Leutnant **Herbert Kargel** *(II./JG 27)]*
Survived the war with 1 victory.

Leutnant **Adolf Kinzinger** *(2./JG 54)*
Ace with at least 7 victories.

Oberleutnant **Reinhold Knacke** *(St.Kpt. I./NJG 1)*
KIA 3/4.2.43 in combat with RAF bomber at Achterveld/ Netherlands. Ace with 44 night victories, awarded *Ritterkreuz.*

Leutnant Hans-Heinrich König (5./ZG 76)
KIA 24.5.44 in combat with USAAF bombers over Kaltenkirchen/Germany. Ace with 28 victories, awarded *Ritterkreuz* posthumously.

Oberfeldwebel Kornacker (6./ZG 76)
Fate unknown.

Unteroffizier Krause (1./JG 1)
At least 2 victories. fate unknown.

Unteroffizier Walter Kuehn (1./JG 52)
KIA 31.12.41, ace with 5 victories.

Leutnant Hermann Kugeler (II./JG 27)
1 victory, survived the war.

Oberleutnant Karl-Heinz Leesmann (St.Kpt. 2./JG 52)
KIA 25.7.43 in combat with B-17s over Heligoland. Ace with 37 victories, awarded *Ritterkreuz*.

Oberfeldwebel Leschnik (5./ZG 76)
At least 2 victories, fate unknown.

Oberleutnant Arnold Lignitz (I./JG 20)
KIA 30.9.41, ace with 25 victories.

Unteroffizier Fritz Metzler (2./JG 52)
KIA 19.6.42 at Woltschansk/Russia, ace with 7 victories.

Feldwebel Rudolf Mickel (1./JG 1)
KIA 7.7.42 South of Baltrum/Germany, 3 victories.

Unteroffizier Otto Milbauer (3./JG 52)
KIA 30.11.41, 1 victory.

Leutnant Hans Müller (6./JG 53)
POW 25.3.43, ace with 15 victories.

Unteroffizier Fritz Muschter (4./JG 53
KIA 8.11.41, ace with 5 victories.

Oberfeldwebel Karl Munz (2./JG 52)
Survived the war as ace with 60 victories, awarded
Ritterkreuz.

Unteroffizier **Bodo Nette** *(1./JG 1)*
KIA 15.11.43 over Zwolle/Netherlands, 2 victories.

Unteroffizier **Heinrich Nöcker** *(3./JG 1)*
KIA 26.11.42 at Medjes-el-Rab/Tunesia.

Leutnant **Hans Ludwig Oertel** *(I./JG 1)*
KIA, 1 victory.

Feldwebel **Robert Portz** *(1./JG 52)*
KIA 18.1.42, ace with 10 victories.

Unteroffizier **Friedrich Pottharst** *(5./ZG 76)*
KIA 22.5.44.

Feldwebel **Herman Richter** *(I./JG 1)*
Fate unknown.

Feldwebel **Fritz Roeckel** *(II./JG 27)*
Fate unknown.

Leutnant **Karl Rung** *(2./JG 52)*
Survived the war with 4 victories.

Oberleutnant **Kurt Ruppert** *(III./JG 26)*
KIA 13.6.43, ace with 21 victories.

Unteroffizier **Arthur Schlacht** *(II./JG27)*
5 victories. Died.

Oberleutnant **Hans-Christian Schäfer** *(5./JG 27)*
2 victories, fate unknown.

Unteroffizier **Wilhelm Schilling** *(3./JG 21)*
Survived war as ace with 50 victories. Awarded *Ritterkreuz*.

Leutnant **Otto Schlauch** *(3./JG 52)*
Survived the war, ace with 12 victories.

Feldwebel **Schmidt** *(5./ZG 76)*
Fate unknown.

Oberleutnant **Hotari Schmude** *(I./JG 1)*
WIA 18.3.43 in combat with B-17s over North Sea.

Oberleutnant Georg Schneider (*St.Kpt. 9./JG54*)
KIA 27.6.40 at Soesterberg in combat with Blenheim of 82 Squadron. Ace with 7 victories.

Unteroffizier Hans Schubert (*3./JG 1*)
Survived the war.

Leutnant Joachim Schypek (*2./JG 76*)
POW 25.10.40 over England, 4 victories.

Oberleutnant Paul Stolte (*3./JG 1*)
KIA 10.10.43 over North Sea, ace with 43 victories.

Oberfeldwebel Max Stotz (*1./JG 76*)
MIA 19.8.43 over Witebsk/ Russia. Ace with 189 victories, awarded *Ritterkreuz* with Oak Leaves.

Unteroffizier Hans Strätling (*2./JG 52*)
KIA 27.1.42 at Rshew/Russia, 3 victories.

Leutnant/Major Werner Streib
(*I./ZG 1* and *Gr.Kom. I./NJG 1*)
Survived the war with 68 victories, 67 of these at night. First victory: Blenheim If of 600 Squadron on 10.5.40. Awarded *Ritterkreuz* with Swords and Oak Leaves.

Leutnant Otto Vinzent (*3./JG 54*)
Fate unknown.

Leutnant Karl Weber (*1./JG 52*)
KIA 29.5.42, 3 victories.

Leutnant Wilhelm Wiesinger (*II./JG 27*)
Ace with 10 victories. KIA.

Unteroffizier Richard Woick (*7./JG 54*)
Survived the war.

Leutnant Waldemar Wübke (*9./JG 54*)
Ace with at least 5 victories, survived the war but killed in plane crash in Bolivia/South America.

Oberfeldwebel Oskar Wunder (*2./JG 52*)
KIA 24.6.42, ace with 14 victories.

Unteroffizier Siegfried Zick (*2./JG 1*)
Survived the war with 76 victories over Western Front.

Unteroffizier Eugen-Ludwig Zweigart (*9./JG 54*)
KIA 8.6.44 in combat over invasion front at Le Cambaux/Normandy. Ace with 69 victories, awarded *Ritterkreuz*.

Appendix III

Main feats of arms by RAF Blenheims over the Netherlands, 1940-42.

Note: Single Blenheims of Coastal and Bomber Command carried out hundreds of individual attacks on targets along the Dutch coast, especially in 1941. On many occasions, slight damage was done to military installations and civilian properties, but these are not listed below, as no major damage was done by these attacks.

1940

11.3.40   *U-31*, a German Type VIIIA submarine, sunk by P4852 (S/Ldr. Miles 'Paddy' Delap) of 82 Squadron off Borkum. Salvaged and repaired, sunk by HMS 'Antelope' in Atlantic on 2.11.1940.

10.5.40   Dozens of Ju-52 transports destroyed at Waalhaven and Ypenburg A/Fs by Blenheims of XV and 40 Squadrons.

10.5.40   Seven Ju-52 transports destroyed by F/Lt. Davies, F/O Selway, F/O Joll, F/O Scott, Sgt. MacDonald and F/O Doulton (two Ju-52s) of 604 Squadron 'B' Flight fighter Blenheims at Scheveningen beach.

12.5.40   He111 possibly of *KG 27*, shot down off Hook of Holland by P4834 (F/Lt. Smith DFC & AC1 Newton) of Special Duty Flight.

13.5.40   Bf110 W.Nr. 10025 of *5./ZG 1*, shot down by Sgt. Tubbs of 235 Squadron over Flushing.

23.6.40   Bf109E-3 of *2./JG 54*, shot down by Sgt. Adams WOp/AG in R3593 (F/Lt. Stephens & crew) of 107 Squadron, crashed near Amsterdam. Pilot: *Lt.* Adolf Kinzinger, safe.

27.6.40   Bf109E-3 of *9./JG 54*, shot down by Sgt. Andrew Clark WOp/AG in R3731 (P/O Percy & crew) of 82 Squadron, crashed near Soesterberg A/F. Pilot: *Oblt.* Schneider, *St.Kpt. 9./JG 54*, killed.

28.7.40   Bf109E-3 of *Stab./II./JG 27*, shot down by Sgt. Beeby WOp/AG in R3865 (W/Cdr. Lart & crew, C.O. 82 Sqn.) after attack on Leeuwarden A/F, crashed at Franeker. Pilot: *Oblt.* Preisler, severely injured.

1.8.40   3 Bf109Es of *5./JG 27* destroyed by bombing & strafing
attack on Leeuwarden A/F, by N6181 (Sgt. Smythe &
crew) and P6908 (Sgt. Lorimer & crew) of 101 Squadron.

2.8.40   Bf109E-4 of *5./JG 27* shot down by Sgt. Reg Bassett
WOp/AG in T1862 (F/O Douch & crew) of 18 Squadron,
after attack on Leeuwarden A/F, crashed at Jelsum. Pilot:
Hptm. von Ankum-Frank, *St. Kap.* of *5./JG 27*, killed.

2.8.40   3 He111s of *I./KG 4* damaged and 4 German soldiers
injured by bombing attack on Soesterberg A/F by
Blenheim 'D' (F/Sgt. Broadhurst and crew) of 40
Squadron and/or L8780 (Sgt. Hards and crew) of 110
Squadron.

7.8.40.   2 Bf109Es of *4./JG 54* destroyed and 5 Bf109Es of *4./JG
54* severely damaged by bombing attack on Haamstede
A/F by R3821 (P/O Donald Wellings & crew) of 82
Squadron. 3 pilots and 3 airmen killed, 17 injured.

10.8.40   He111 of *K.Gr.126* heavily damaged and Ju88 of *III./KG
4* slightly damaged by bombing attack on Schiphol A/F by
L9339 (P/O Murray & crew) of 105 Squadron.

17/18.8.40   2 Bf109E-3s of *II./JG 54* damaged and German airman
killed by bombing attack on Flushing A/F probably by
N6182 (P/O Hill & crew) of 101 Squadron.

24.8.40   2 Arado Ar66s of *Stab./JG 54* destroyed, 1 Fieseler Storch
and 1 Bf108 *Taifun* of *Stab./KG 4* damaged by bombing
attack of T1890 (P/O Murray & crew) of 105 Squadron on
Schiphol A/F.

15/16.9.40   *M1206*, a German minesweeper, damaged in Flushing
harbour by bombing attack of a 218 Squadron Blenheim.
8 of crew killed and 11 injured.

23.9.40   German ASR vessel *No.11* of 20 tons damaged by a
Blenheim of 53 Squadron off Schouwen.

1941

17.1.41   Minesweeper *43* and unidentified vessel heavily damaged,
2 tugs slightly damaged off Hook of Holland and
Zandvoort by bombing and strafing attack by six
Blenheims of 59 Squadron (P/O Collier & crew in 'E'; P/O
Lishman & crew in 'J'; P/O McCurdy & crew in 'H'; F/Lt.
Guall & crew in 'T'; P/O Ullman & crew in 'M' and P/O
Womersley & crew in 'R').

22.1.41   *Flak* battery heavily damaged in Flushing harbour by
bombing attack of a Blenheim of 139 Squadron.

14/15.3.41 10,000 ton oil tank and 16 small oil tanks destroyed
- including the majority of the contents- in petrol harbour
of Pernis/Rotterdam by Blenheims of 18, 82 and 101
Squadrons and Whitleys of Bomber Command.

14.4.41 *Ceylon,* a merchant ship of 5235 tons damaged by a
Blenheim of 82 Squadron off Hook of Holland.

19.4.41 The merchant vessel *Solviken* of 2398 tons, damaged off
Scheveningen by a Blenheim of 101, 105 or 139
Squadrons.

23.4.41 The 5870-ton *Anhalt,* a German merchant ship, was
damaged by a Blenheim of 105 Squadron off Domburg.
Later repaired, it was finally sunk off Vaagso/Norway on
27.12.1941.

23.4.41 Minesweeper *M1404,* damaged by a Blenheim of 105
Squadron off Domburg. 8 of crew killed, 11 injured.

2.5.41 *Vp808 Reichspräsident von Hindenburg,* a German
Flak-ship of 321 tons, sunk by a Blenheim of 110
Squadron NW of Borkum.

6.5.41 The KW36 *Nederland V,* a Katwijk-based Dutch fishing
vessel sunk by a Blenheim of 21 Squadron off Texel. Crew
of 6 killed.

22.5.41 The *Finse,* a 1618-ton merchant shipdamaged by a
Blenheim of 105 Squadron off Borkum.

24.5.41 The *A.H. Hansen,* a Danish merchant ship of 1578 tons,
sunk by four Blenheims of 21 Squadron led by S/L Cooper
15 miles W of Borkum.

25.5.41 *Sperrbrecher 33 Silvia,* a German Flak-ship of 1049 tons
burnt out and sunk off Texel after Blenheim R2791 of 139
Squadron (Sgt. Bye and crew) crashed into the ship.

4.6.41 Bf109E-4 WNr. 1524 of *3./JG 1,* damaged by WOp/AG of
139 Squadron, ditched in North Sea. Pilot: *Uffz.* Franz
Rademacher, rescued by German ASR.

4.6.41 9 railway waggons at The Hague destroyed by a
Blenheim of 105 Squadron.

20.6.41 *IJM209 Sursum Corda,* an IJmuiden-based Dutch fishing
vessel sunk by 2 Blenheims of 18 Squadron near Den
Helder. Crew of 4 rescued by German ASR.

14.7.41 The *Aspen,* a Swedish merchent ship of 1305 tons, sunk
by an 18 Squadron Blenheim 13 kms. North of IJmuiden.

16.7.41 The *Hermod* of 5193 tons and the *Knute Nelson* of 5749
tons, both Norwegian merchant ships, heavily damaged

in Rotterdam harbour. Lightly damaged:2653-ton *Cimbria* and the 2,031-ton *Hafnia*, both Danishmerchant ships; 5,334-ton *Gotha* and 10,547-ton *Oranjefontein*, both Dutch ships; 8,456-ton German *Treuenfels* and a gunboat. Docks, buildings and harbour installations in Rotterdam harbour were also damaged in raid by Blenheims of 18, 21, 105 and 226 Squadrons.

19.7.41   The *Hermann Fritzen*, a German merchant ship of 3845 tons damaged off Scheveningen by a Blenheim of 105 Squadron.

23.7.41   *KW135*, a Katwijk-based Dutch fishing vessel sunk by a Blenheim of 139 Squadron off Kamperduin. 1 of crew killed, 5 rescued by German ASR.

2.8.41   *H855*, a 492-ton German coastal guard ship of 492 tons sunk by 3 Blenheims of 82 Squadron 15 kms SW of Texel. Before the ship was sunk, it shot down W/C Burt and crew, CO of 82 Squadron.

18.8.41   *IJM418*, an IJmuiden-based Dutch fishing ship, sunk by 6 Blenheims of 139 Squadron 52 km NW of IJmuiden. 2 of crew killed, 9 rescued by German ASR.

18.8.41   *IJM253* and *IJM432*, 2 IJmuiden-based fishing ships sunk by 12 Blenheims of 21 and 82 Squadrons, led by S/L Edrich of 21 Squadron, 30 km SW of De Kooy. All crew members, 22 fishermen, missing.

26.8.41   The *Stadt Emden*, a German merchant ship of 5180 tons, damaged by a Blenheim of 139 or 226 Squadrons 6 km NW of IJmuiden. 1 crew member severely injured. Ship repaired and sunk off Den Helder by Beaufighters of the North Coates Strike Wing on 13.6.1943.

28.8.41   The *Zuiderdam*, a Dutch merchant ship of 12,150 tons, capsized and severely damaged by fire in Wilton-Feyenoord docks in Schiedam/Rotterdam harbour after attack by a Blenheim of 21, 88 or 226 Squadrons. Repaired in 1942/43. Sunk by Germans on 22.9.1944 as harbour blockade ship in Rotterdam harbour. Scrapped after 1945. *Westerdam*, a Dutch merchant ship of 12,000 tons, sunk in Wilton-Feyenoord docks in Schiedam by a Blenheim of 21, 88 or 226 Squadron. Repaired 1942/43. Sunk by the Dutch resistance on 16.1.1945 in Merwede harbour/Rotterdam. Repaired 1945/46 and in use in Holland-America Line from 24.6.1946. *Oranjefontein*, a German merchant ship of 10,574tons, damaged and partially sunk probably by Blenheim of F/L Namias of 226 Squadron in Rotterdam harbour. Repaired in second half of 1941, in use as troop ship throughout the war and as liner after the war. Widespread but no severe damage to military installations and some civilian property in Rotterdam harbour area during raid by Blenheims of 21, 88 and 226 Squadrons.

7.9.41   *H811*, a German coastal guard ship of 221 tons, sunk off The Hague by 2 Blenheims of 226 Squadron.

15.9.41   *Arna*, a merchant ship of 4390 tons, sunk off Borkum by a Blenheim of 114 Squadron.

20.9.41   *Metz*, a German merchant ship of 728 tons, sunk off Vlaardingen by a Blenheim of 226 Squadron.

21.10.41   *Hilda*, a Norwegian merchant ship of 1676 tons, sunk off IJmuiden by a Blenheim of 82 Squadron.

27.10.41   *Gunlog*, a Danish merchant ship of 1396 tons, sunk off Texel by a Blenheim of 114 Squadron.

1942

25/26.4.42 Blenheim of 114 Squadron bombed Leeuwarden A/F, hit the cross-section of the runways which caused the closing down of the A/F.

29/30.4.42 5 hangars and 2 Bf110s W.Nrs. 3167 and 3319 of *II./NJG 2* destroyed and widespread damage to installations at Leeuwarden A/F by bombing of Blenheims of 114 Squadron.

2/3.7.42   1 Bf110F4 W.Nr. 2694 of *I./NJG 1* 10% damaged at Venlo A/F by Blenheim of 18 Squadron, 2 Bf109s severely damaged on Venlo, Leeuwarden and/or Twente A/Fs, repair workshop and main building destroyed and barracks damaged on unidentified Dutch A/Fs by Blenheims of 18 and 114 Squadron.

Luftwaffe ranks, units and their RAF equivalents.

Luftwaffe	Royal Air Force
Flieger(Flg)	Aircraftman 2 (AC2)
Gefreiter(Gfr)	Aircraftman 1 (AC1)
Obergefreiter(Ogfr)	Leading Aircraftman (LAC)
Hauptgefreiter	
Unteroffizier(Uffz)	Corporal (Cpl)
Unterfeldwebel(Fw)	
Feldwebel(Fw)	Sergeant (Sgt)
Oberfeldwebel(Ofw)	Flight Sergeant (F/S)
Stabsfeldwebel (StFw)	Warrant Officer (W/O)
Leutnant(Lt)	Pilot Officer (P/O)
Oberleutnant(Oblt)	Flying Officer (F/O)
Hauptmann(Hptm)	Flight Lieutenant (F/L)
Major(Maj)	Squadron Leader (S/L)
Oberstleutnant(Obstlt)	Wing Commander (W/C)
Oberst (Obst)	Group Captain (G/C)

Organisation and abbreviations of operational Luftwaffe units.

Operational units were sub-divided as follows:

Geschwader	(Wing)
Gruppe	(Squadron)
Staffel	(Flight)
Schwarm	(four-aircraft unit)
Rotte	(two-aircraft unit)

Each *Geschwader* consisted of between 100 and 120 aircraft. These aircraft were divided over a *Geschwader Stab* (Wing Staff) and three *Gruppen,* each of which consisted of between 30 and 35 aircraft. Each *Gruppe* was sub-divided into a *Gruppen Stab* (Squadron Staff) and three *Staffeln* of some ten aircraft each. A *Staffel* consisted of between two to three *Schwärme* of four aircraft. The smallest fighting unit was the *Rotte* of 2 aircraft, a leader and his wingman. Bomber units operated in sections of three aircraft, each section known as a *Kette*.

The operational task of a *Geschwader* is recognised by its prefix.

Thus, a Night Fighter Wing (*Nachtjagdgeschwader*) was abbreviated to NJG. Day Fighter Wings were merely abbreviated to JG (*Jagdgeschwader*). *Gruppen* were indicated with Roman characters; thus, the third *Gruppe* of the 53rd Fighter Wing was abbreviated to *III./JG 53*. As already stated; each *Gruppe* was sub-divided into three Staffeln, which were indicated with Arabic numerals. Thus, the eighth Flight of the 53rd Fighter Wing was technically designated *8.III./JG 53*, but was usually abbreviated to *8./JG53* showing it to be the second *Staffel* within *III./JG 53*.

The following unit abbreviations are of interest in the context of this book:

Day Fighter Wing or *Jagdgeschwader*, abbreviated to *JG*; Night Fighter Wing or *Nachtjagdgeschwader*, abbreviated to *NJG*; 'Destroyer' Long Range Fighter Wing or *Zerstörergeschwader*, abbreviated to *ZG*; Bomber Wing or *Kampfgeschwader*, abbreviated to *KG*.

Glossary of terms and abbreviations.

AASF	Advanced Air Striking Force.
AC	Air Component of the B.E.F.
ACC	Army Cooperation Command.
A/F	Airfield.
AM	Air-Marshal.
ASR.	Air Sea Rescue.
Aux AF	Auxiliary Air Force.
AVM	Air Vice-Marshal.
BEF	British Expeditionary Force.
Circus	RAF operation strongly escorted by fighters intended to lure German fighters into combat.
CC	Coastal Command.
C-in-C	Commander in Chief.
EFTS	Elementary Flying Training School.
ETA	Estimated Time of Arrival.
FC	Fighter Command.
Flak	*Flieger Abwehr Kanone,* Anti-Aircraft gun.
Fliegerhorst	*Luftwaffe* airfield.
Fringe target	Target on enemy coastline.
FTR	Failed To Return.
GP	bomb General Purpose bomb.
GR	General Reconnaissance.
Gruppen Kommandeur	Squadron Leader.
HOOKOS	Hook of Holland-Ostend patrol.
KG z.b.V. 9	*Kampf Geschwader zur besonderen Verwendung 9;* Bomber Wing with special task.
KIA	Killed In Action.
MIA	Missing In Action.
MiD	Mentioned in Dispatches.

Operation Fuller	Operation to prevent the passage of German capital ships through the Straits of Dover.
OTU	Operational Training Unit.
PoW	Prisoner Of War.
PRU	Photo Reconnaissance Unit.
RDF	Radio Direction Finding.
Ritterkreuz	Knight's Cross.
SAP. bomb	Semi Armour Piercing bomb.
SASO	Senior Air Staff Officer.
Schwarmführer	Leader of a four-aircraft formation.
Squealer	Small German ship, often fishing vessel, equipped with radio equipment to report movement of RAF aircraft.
St.Kap	*Staffel Kapitän*, i.e. Flight Commander.
Zerstörer	'Destroyer', i.e. Messerschmitt Bf110.

Bibliography

Published and Unpublished Works

Abbott, J.K.   :*Gathering of Demons* (Ontario 1987).

Aders G. & Held W.   :*Jagdgeschwader 51 'Mölders'* (Stuttgart 1985).

Air Ministry.   :Notes on fighting and defensive tactics for bomber aircraft (Blenheim) London 1940).

Ashworth, C.   :*RAF Coastal Command 1936-1969* (Sparkford 1992).

Barker, R.   :*The ship-busters. The story of the R.A.F. torpedo-bombers* (London 1957).

     :*Strike Hard, Strike Sure* (London 1965).

     :*The Thousand Plan* (Chatham 1966).

Bell, E.D.   :*Hyderabad Squadron. The story of No.110 (Hyderabad) Squadron Royal Air Force* (Air Britain).

Boiten, T.   :*Night Fighting in the German Reich's Aerial Defence, 1933-1945. History of a Strategic Failure* (unpublished manuscript,Groningen 1992).

de Booy, H.Th.   :*Tusschen Mijnen en Grondzeeen* (Amsterdam 1946).

Bowyer, C.   :*Coastal Command at War* (London 1979).

Brookes, A.   :*Bomber Squadron at War* (London 1983).

de Bruin R. e.a.   :*Illusies en incidenten. De Militaire Luchtvaart en de Neutraliteitshandhaving tot 10 Mei 1940.*

Butterworth, A.   :*With Courage and Faith. The Story of No.18 Squadron Royal Air Force* (Tonbridge 1989).

Chorley, W.R.   :*Royal Air Force Bomber Command Losses of the Second World War. Vol.I & II 1939-1940*(Earl Shilton 1992/93).

Deighton, L.   :*Blitzkrieg* (1981).

Derix, J.	:*Vliegveld Venlo, Vol. I & II* (Horst 1990).
Dixon, W.M.	:*A history of 107 Squadron* (Feltwell 1963).
Embry, B.	:*Mission Completed* (London 1958).
Fairhead H. & Collis, B.	:*Airfield Focus, Vol. 4: Horsham St. Faith* (Bretton 1992).
Fast, N.	*:Das Jagdgeschwader 52, I. Band* (Bergisch Gladbach 1988).
Fearnley, L.	:*Blenheim Odyssey* (Farnham 1990).
Fernhout, J.N.	:*Het verband tussen de Luftwaffe-verliezen in mei '40 en de Duitse invasieplannen voor Engeland,* in'*Militaire Spectator*' 8 (1992).
Fischer, W.	:*Eine Deutsche Vorpostenflottille im Zweiten Weltkrieg,* in '*Marine Rundschau*' 5 (1963).
Fleming, P.	:*Invasie 1940* (Leiden 1957).
Galland, A.	:*Die Ersten und die Letzten. Jagdflieger im Zweiten Weltkrieg* (München 1970).
Goulding J. & Moyes, P.	:*RAF Bomber Command and its aircraft 1936-1940* (London 1975).
Gibbs, P.	:*Not Peace But A Sword* (London 1993).
Gillman, R.E.	:*The Shiphunters* (London 1976).
Gunn, P.B.	:*RAF Great Massingham. A Norfolk airfield at war 1940-1945* (King's Lynn 1990).
	:*Airfield Focus Vol.5: Bircham Newton* (Bretton 1992).
Halliday, H.A.	:*The Royal Canadian Air Force at War 1939-1945* (Toronto 1990).
Harris, A.	:*Bomber Offensive* (London 1947).
Hastings, M.	:*Bomber Command* (London 1987).
van den Hout a.o. J.P.	:*Vijf jaar luchtfront. Het vliegveld Gilze-Rijen in de Tweede Wereldoorlog, Vol. II, III and IV* (Baarle-Nassau 1985).
Jansen, A.A.	:*Gevleugeld Verleden* (Baarn 1982).
	:*Wespennest Leeuwarden, Vol. I & III.*
Jackson, J.	:*Air War over France May-June 1940* (London 1974).
de Jong, L.	:*Het Koninkrijk der Nederlanden in de Tweede Wereldoorlog, Vol.3. Mei '40* ('s-Gravenhage 1970).

Knoke, H.   :*Die Grosse Jagd. Bordbuch eines deutschen Jagdfliegers* (Rinteln 1952).

Korthals Altes,
Luchtgevaar A.   :*Luchtaanvallen op Nederland 1940-1945* (Amsterdam 1984).

Kristensen a.o. H.K.,   :*Vestallierede luftangreb i Danmark under 2. verdenskrig* (Aarhus 1988).

Kurowski, F.   :*Der Luftkrieg über Deutschland* (Düsseldorf 1977).

Mason, F.K.   :*Battle over Britain* (London 1969).

Messenger, C.   :*Cologne, the First 1000-bomber Raid* (London 1982).

Middlebrook M.
& Everitt, C.   :*The Bomber Command war diaries. An Operational Reference Book, 1939-1945* (Harmondsworth 1985).

Ministerie van
Voorlichting,   :Coastal Command speurt, beschermt, valt aan (London 1943).

Mombeek, E.   :*Reichsverteidigung. Die Geschichte des Jagdgeschwaders 1 'Oesau'* (Brussels 1993).

Nesbit, R.C.   :*The Strike Wings. Special Anti-Shipping Squadrons 1942-1945* (London 1984).

Obermaier, E.   :*Die Ritterkreuzträger der Luftwaffe 1939-1945. Band I Jagdflieger* (Mainz 1989).

Onderwater, H.   :*En toen was het stil. De luchtoorlog boven Rotterdam en IJsselmonde 1940-1945* (Baarn 1981).

Oughton, J.D.   :*Bristol, an Aircraft Album* (London 1973).

Parry, S.W.   :*Intruders over Britain. The Luftwaffe night fighter offensive 1940-45* (Surbiton 1987).

Passmore, R.   :*Blenheim Boy* (London 1981).

Priller, J.   :*J.G.26. Geschichte eines Jagd-Geschwaders* (Stuttgart 1980).

Ramsey, W.G., (ed.)   :*The Battle of Britain, Then and Now* (London 1985).

Ransom, D.   :*Battle Axe. A History of 105 Squadron Royal Air Force* (1967).

Rawlings, J.D.R.   :*Fighter Squadrons of the R.A.F. and Their Aircraft* (London 1978).

Rickson P.A.
& Holliday, A.M.   :*Mission Accomplished* (London 1974).

F. Runge, F.   :*Der Seekrieg 1939-1945* (Stuttgart 1962).

P. Schenk, P.   :*Invasion of England 1940. The planning of Operation Sealion* (London 1990).

Sherring, C.C.   :*For Your Own Eye* (privately published autobiography 1945).

Shipley, E.   :*139 (Jamaica) Squadron* (Pontefract 1990).

Taylor, E.   :*Operation Millennium. 'Bomber' Harris's Raid on Cologne, May 1942* (London 1987).

Taylor, W.J.   :*Raynham Reflections. A short history of RAF West Raynham* (Corby 1989).

Terraine, J.   :*The Right of the Line. The RAF in the European War 1939-1945.*

Thomas, H.A.W.   :*Englische Flieger aus Seenot Gerettet*, in '*Das Jägerblatt*' 5 (1986).

Toussaint, H., (ed.).   :*Wir von der Vlissinger Flak: Traditionsbuch der Marine Flak Abteilung 703* (Vlissingen 1941).

Wagner, G.   :*Lagevortraege des Oberbefehlshabers der Kriegsmarine vor Hitler. 1939-1945* (München 1972).

Warner, G.   :*The Forgotten Bomber* (Sparkford 1991).

Whittle, K.   :*An Electrician goes to War* (Swindon 1994).

Wood D.
& Dempster, D.   :The Narrow Margin (London 1969).

Zwanenburg, G.J.   :*En nooit was het stil... Kroniek van een luchtoorlog. Vol.I.*

Archives

Abschussliste (victory rolls)

I./JG 1 (1941 - 1942)

1./JG 1 (1941)

3./JG 1 (1941)

II./JG 1 (1942)

2./JG 52 (18th May - 7th July 1941)

II./ZG 76 (Oct. 1940 - Oct. 1941).

(Above from Ab A. Jansen Collection.)

Ely Cathedral

Public Record Office:

2 Group RAF Roll of Honour, in

AIR 14/746-747.	Directives to No.2 Group, June 1940 - March 1942.
AIR 14/776.	Air Ministry Directives, Vol.II July 1940 - July 1941.
AIR 14/801.	March - October 1941. Daylight attacks on enemy shipping at sea.
AIR 14/1936/1937.	AOC 2 Group correspondence with C-in C Bomber Command, Nov. 1940 - Jan. 1942, including Report on damage assessment of enemy shipping attacked by 2 Group Blenheims, dated 27th May 1941.
AIR 20/4057.	No.2 Group Operations, 1941-1943, including: Paper on the ideal day bomber force - Spring 1941; Daily reports on enemy shipping and fringe targets attacked by 2 Group Blenheims, March 17 - 30 July 1941; Resumé of attack on shipping in Rotterdam harbour by Blenheim aircraft of Bomber Command on the day of 16th July, 1941; Note on Station Commanders Conference Number 2 Group Headquarters 3rd. November 1941.
AIR 24/229.	Bomber Command Operations Record Book March 1941.
AIR 25/22.	2 Group Operations Book, 1936-1940.
AIR 25/23.	2 Group Operations Record Book, 1941-43.
AIR 25/29.	2 Group Operations Record Book, May-July 1940. Appendixes.
AIR 27 Various	XV, 18, 21, 40, 53, 57, 59, 82, 88, 101, 105, 107, 110, 114, 139, 226, 235, 248, 500, 600, 604 Squadron Record Books.
AIR 35/328.	The destruction of the Meuse bridges at Maastricht on the eve of the German Invasion of Holland.

RAF Museum:

B1723.	Private diary of G/Cpt. Hugh P. Lloyd, Bomber Command H.Q. G/Cpt. Operations & Plans, 1940.
B3086.	'*Worm's Eye View*'. The diary of a Pilot Officer in 18 Squadron during the Phoney War and the Battle of Britain.
B3109.	History of the RAF's Photographic Reconnaissance Unit in diary form. Vol.I.
B3260.	Retrospective Diary of Special Duty Flight.
L118.	Photo Album S/Ldr. Charles Bardswell, Intell. RAF Watton 1940/41.

Index

Personnel - Royal Air Force

Personnel - Luftwaffe

Personnel - Miscellaneous:

Units - Royal Air Force

Units - Luftwaffe

Places